AFTERBURNER

Southeast Asia. (Courtesy of Chris Robinson)

JOHN DARRELL SHERWOOD

AFTERBURNER

Naval Aviators and the Vietnam War

New York University Press • *New York and London*

NEW YORK UNIVERSITY PRESS
New York and London
www.nyupress.org

Editing, design, and composition © 2004 by New York University

Library of Congress Cataloging-in-Print Data
Sherwood, John Darrell, 1966–
Afterburner : naval aviators and the Vietnam War / John Darrell Sherwood.
p. cm.
Includes bibliographical references and index.
ISBN 0–8147–9842–X (cloth : alk. paper)
1. Vietnamese Conflict, 1961–1975—Aerial operations, American.   2. Vietnamese Conflict, 1961–1975—Naval operations, American.   3. United States Navy—History—Vietnamese Conflict, 1961–1975.   I. Title.
DS558.8.S539   2004
959.704'345—dc22   2003027760

New York University Press books are printed on acid-free paper,
and their binding materials are chosen for strength and durability.

Manufactured in the United States of America

10 9 8 7 6 5 4 3 2 1

Contents

Acknowledgments

I AM TRULY FORTUNATE to work for the U.S. Navy's official history office: the Naval Historical Center (NHC) in Washington, DC. NHC has the greatest concentration of expertise in the world on the history of the U.S. Navy, and I am humbled to be able to tap into this knowledge on a daily basis. I am also humbled by the amount of time and effort many NHC staff members put into *Afterburner* to make it a better book. No project gets commissioned and executed at the center without the blessings of our director, Dr. William Dudley, and I am grateful for his leadership. I also wish to thank all the deputy directors who served during the course of this project: Captains Todd Creekman, Andy Hall, and Duane Heughan.

In one way or another, every staff person at NHC contributed to this project, but the following individuals deserve special mention: Bernard Cavalcante, Ken Johnson, Mike Walker, Regina Akers, Wade Wyckoff, Kathy Lloyd, and John Hodges of the Operational Archives; John Reilly, Tim Francis, and Kevin Hurst of the Ships History Branch; Davis Elliot, Shirley Martin, Angela Williams, Jean Hort, Tonya Simpson, Barbara Auman, Glenn Helm, Young Park, and David Brown of the Navy Department Library; Terry Hedgepeth, Tod Baker, Roy Grossnick, and Mark Evans of the Aviation History Branch; Ella Nargele, Randy Potter, and Rashad Wali Shakir of the Information Management Branch; Mark Werthheimer, Chuck Haberlein, Ed Finney, and Robert Hanshew of the Curator Branch; Ricardo Vigil and Jack Green of the Support Staff Branch; Wanda Pomey of the Senior Historian's Office; and Sabreena Edwards, the Contemporary History Branch administrative assistant.

One could not ask for a better group of colleagues than I have at NHC's Contemporary Branch. Randy Papadopoulos, Jeff Barlow, Bob Schneller, Bob Cressman, and Gary Weir, our branch head, provided advice and thoughtful criticism for this book from the onset. Everyone in the branch read and critiqued excerpts of the book, but Bob Schneller and Bob Cressman formally reviewed and critiqued the book, as did Ed Marolda, the Senior Historian. The author of several excellent histories of the Navy in Vietnam, Ed also allowed me to access his files and made himself available on a daily basis to answer questions and discuss research problems. *Afterburner* is certainly a better book as a result of his efforts and those of all the others within NHC who reviewed it.

Outside of NHC, I wish to thank the following scholars for their critical reviews of the manuscript: John Morrow of the University of Georgia, Wayne Thompson of the Air Force History Support Office, Dan Mortensen of the Air University, and Charles "Joe" Gross of the Air National Guard History Office. Other non-NHC archivists, historians, government officials, and librarians who assisted me are as follows: Virginia Washington of the National Archives; Ivonne Kinkaid of the Air Force History Support Office; Fred Graboske, Gary Solis, and Fred Allison of the Marine Corps Historical Center; Paul Stillwell of the U.S. Naval Institute; Paul Jacobsmeyer of the Joint Chiefs of Staff History Office; and Ron Marshal of the Naval Criminal and Investigative Service.

Oral history interviews have always been a fundamental source in my writing. They not only offer unique insights into combat operations but allow me to tell the story of naval aviation partly in the words of the aviators themselves. I am therefore indebted to the following aviators for taking time out from their busy lives to be interviewed: William Angus, Harold "Skip" Bennett, Ralph Brubaker, Charlie Carr, Kevin Cheney, Randy Cunnningham, Brian Dempsey, Gus Eggert, Jack Ensch, Lou Ferrecane, Jack Finley, Jim Fox, Paul Galanti, Daniel Gibson, Brian Grant, William Harris, Jerry Houston, Roger Lerseth, John Markle, Jim McBride, Ron McKeown, Kevin Moore, Robert Murphy, Peter Optekar, Ron Polfer, Phil Schuyler, Roger Sheets, Theodore Sienicki, Clyde Smith, Leighton Smith, Tom Sprouse, Foster Teague, Marland Townsend, and Darrell Whitcomb. One aviator, James B. "J. B." Souder, not only participated in one of my longest interviews (about twenty hours) but also gave me an abbreviated version of the air-intercept course he used to teach at the Naval Air Technical Training Center, Glynco, Georgia. Larry Nowell, a former air-intercept controller on *Chicago* (CG-11) and a man who helped direct twelve MiG kills in 1972, also helped answer numerous questions about the intricacies of radar intercept missions. As both of these "teachers" will freely admit, I was not their best student, but in the end, I hope they will be pleased with my descriptions of air-to-air engagements in this book. Much of my ability to put these complex battles in layperson's terms is a result of my long conversations with these men.

Institutions as well as individuals were crucial to the success of this project. Without the help of the following institutions, I would never have been able to track down aviators from the Vietnam War era for oral history interviews: the Association of Naval Aviation, the Tailhook Association, the Red River Valley Fighter Pilot's Association, the Marine Corps Aviation Association, the Marine All Weather Attack Association, the Reserve Officers Association, the Military Officers Association, the Air Force Association, the Naval League of the United States, and the U.S. Naval Institute. The Naval Historical Foundation (NHF) was founded in 1926 out of concern for the preservation of naval history and traditions. Among other duties, it supports NHC's publications program in a variety of ways. The foundation facilitated my research by transcribing many of the *Afterburner* oral histories. It also hired and paid cartographer Chris Robinson to draw the book's excellent maps. Three NHF personnel deserve a special Bravo Zulu for all their work on *Afterburner*: Todd Creekman, Dave Winkler, and Frank Arre.

On the editing front, this manuscript benefited from the careful attention of not one but two great editors. Sandy Doyle of NHC and Debbie Gershenowitz of New York University Press worked tirelessly to help me streamline the manuscript and make it more palatable for a popular, non-Navy audience. Sandy also helped copyedit the book and ironed out any inconsistencies she discovered.

A few people who do not fall into any categories listed here but who were nevertheless integral to the success of this project are Keith Barkema of the Navy–Marine Corps Intranet, for help with computer issues; Don Gastwirth, for his critique of my book proposal and advice on the publishing world; Michelle Smith, for indexing the text; István Toperczer, author of an excellent book on the Vietnamese People's Air Force, for answering questions about the VPAF and providing me with several unique photos of MiGs; and my wife, Darina, for her unwavering support.

The Pentagon attack and the two subsequent wars that occurred during the writing of this book placed unprecedented demands on the NHC and its staff. Many of the center historians, including myself, had to put their long-term projects aside from time to time to perform such duties as interviewing Pentagon survivors, documenting current operations, or writing historical information papers to support decision makers in the Pentagon and in the fleet, but while these "collateral duties" often absorbed a great amount of time and energy, they did not rob the Navy of its pre-2001 history. The Vietnam War, in particular, offers many helpful insights for Navy war fighters currently engaged in the global war on terrorism. I hope this book will be of use to them. Therefore, I dedicate it to all who serve in the U.S. Navy—past, present, and future.

Prologue

THE VIETNAM WAR ended nearly thirty years ago, yet the image of the war looms large in American memory. New films on the subject continually grace the silver screen, politicians often invoke its memory when debating foreign policy, and the American reading public continues to devour new books on Vietnam in large numbers. Even a monthly magazine is devoted exclusively to the war. Like the Civil War or World War II before it, the subject of Vietnam continues to capture the imagination of the reading public. Readers are always eager for fresh approaches and interpretations of America's longest war.

Afterburner examines the most expensive and controversial part of America's long involvement in Southeast Asia: the air war from 1968 to 1972. More than half of the $200 billion the United States spent in Vietnam went to air operations. The United States dropped over 7.6 million tons of bombs on Vietnam, Laos, and Cambodia between 1964 and 1973 and lost more than 8,500 aircraft in the process. This tonnage far exceeded that expended in World War II and Korea. Yet, for all this investment, air power, while occasionally influential, was never decisive. America failed to prevent South Vietnam from being overthrown by North Vietnam.

Whereas several significant books have been published in recent years on Air Force operations during the Vietnam War, naval aviators have not received the same amount of attention. Many Navy records from the Vietnam War era have only recently been declassified, making access to this history difficult for researchers who do not possess security clearances.

The U.S. Navy, however, contributed a total of seventeen carriers to the air war. Those carriers made seventy-three cruises lasting a total of 8,248 days. The *Coral Sea* alone conducted a record of seven cruises for a total of 873 days at sea. Of the 1,626 Navy personnel killed in action during the war, 317 were aviators. The Navy lost 531 fixed-wing aircraft in combat and suffered another 299 losses through accidents. Task Force

77, the carrier task force based off the coast of North Vietnam in the Gulf of Tonkin, often included five carriers, 400 aircraft, twenty-five supporting ships, and 30,000 sailors and naval air crewmen. This task force, along with Marine aviators, dropped 1.5 million tons of bombs during the course of the war—approximately 24 percent of the total tonnage dropped by America in the air war.

What little has been written on the subject of naval aviation in Southeast Asia tends to focus mainly on the earlier 1965–68 period. No book has examined the 1968–72 period in detail, especially the most intense year of the air war, 1972. During that year, North Vietnam launched the first large-scale conventional attack on South Vietnam of the war, hoping to crush the South Vietnamese armed forces and bring the war to a sudden, violent conclusion. Only a small number of Air Force aircraft, a handful of Army advisers, and the Navy carriers in the Gulf of Tonkin were on hand to aid the South Vietnamese in stemming the tide of the Communist onslaught. In the end, naval air power proved vital during that epic struggle because of its ability to surge rapidly to confront a developing threat. In a matter of a few short weeks, the Navy's carrier presence in the Gulf of Tonkin jumped from two to six ships, and Navy aircraft flew the majority of strikes during the critical early days of the offensive.

Once the invasion was effectively halted, carrier aircraft proved instrumental during President Nixon's campaigns to punish North Vietnam for this aggression: Operations Linebacker I (April–October 1972) and Pocket Money (May 1972–January 1973). During these campaigns, naval aviators mined Haiphong harbor, fought the most intense air-to-air duels with enemy MiGs, and struck several formerly off-limit targets for the first time in the war.

The final large-scale air operation of the war was the December 1972 Linebacker II attack—Nixon's famous B-52 raids against Hanoi and Haiphong. This operation ultimately convinced the North Vietnamese to agree to a peace settlement acceptable to American negotiators. As in nearly every earlier air campaign of the war, naval aviators took to the skies during Linebacker II, bombing targets in Hanoi and Haiphong, as well as paving the way for Air Force B-52s by attacking surface-to-air missile sites and other air defense positions in North Vietnam.

As the title of this book suggests, the final stages of the air war in Vietnam may have begun as a slow burn, but by 1972 they reached the intensity of an "afterburner": a device that injects fuel into the hot exhaust of a tactical jet fighter for extra thrust. Although air power did not win the war for the United States in 1972, it helped prevent North Vietnam from successfully invading South Vietnam, punished the North for its aggression, secured the release of the American POWs, and, most important, successfully extricated America from its longest war.

This book explores the monumental post-1968 air battles by looking closely at the backgrounds and experiences of twenty-one fliers who fought in the naval air war. Some performed exemplary service and stand out as role models; others made grave errors. Together, these aviators represent a broad cross section of the personnel who fought in the Navy's air war over Vietnam. Collectively, they shed light not only on the Navy's operations during the period but also on the institutional culture of naval aviation during America's longest war. Naval aviation was the most critical component of the Navy's military power during the Vietnam War. After the war, it continued to be the dominant force projection arm of the Navy—not to mention an increasingly crucial component of overall U.S. military power—from Desert Storm through Operation Iraqi Freedom. Therefore, understanding its institutional culture is critical for appreciating the overall capabilities as well as shortcomings of naval aviation in modern war.

Afterburner begins at a point when the intensity of air operations over Southeast Asia diminished markedly. From President Lyndon Johnson's halt of bombing operations against North Vietnam in October 1968 until early 1972, neither the Navy nor the Air Force participated in any large-scale bombing operations against the North. For the most part, the entire air effort of the carrier task force shifted to bombing the Communist supply lines in Laos—a loose collection of roads and trails known as the Ho Chi Minh Trail. Part I begins this story by focusing heavily on the Laotian campaign. It also provides a general introduction to the lives and experiences of naval aviators in Southeast Asia.

Part II shifts the focus away from operations to particular issues that affected the daily lives of naval aviators in the latter years of the Vietnam War. The first theme is technological change and the rise of the nonpilot aviator—the naval flight officer (NFO). In naval tactical aviation, NFOs perform a variety of critical missions, ranging from navigation to controlling the radar and electronic warfare equipment. An F-4 fighter, for example, cannot effectively employ its sophisticated air-intercept radar and the guided missiles associated with that system without the assistance of an NFO. Despite the crucial role played by the NFOs, most accounts of the air war over Vietnam downplay their contributions by focusing mainly on pilots. These histories often fail to recognize that by the end of the Vietnam War most Navy combat aircraft required the services of an NFO because these planes were too complex for one person to operate alone. In essence, the NFO "came of age" during the Vietnam War, and tensions arose as this new class of aviators began to demand more parity with pilots. In no Navy community was this tension more apparent than among fighters. Part II explores these tensions and the social challenges posed by the new role of NFOs, following one naval flight officer's odyssey in a squadron undergoing the transition from single-seat F-8 fighters to dual-seat F-4s in 1972.

Part III addresses prisoners of war. During the Vietnam War, the vast majority of POWs were American aviators. This special status made them prime targets for propaganda exploitation by the North Vietnamese, who took great pride in humiliating "Yankee air pirates" by parading them in front of civilians and compelling them to make antiwar statements. POWs were also used to great effect as bargaining chips in peace talks with the U.S. government. In short, the POWs fought a war within a war: their resistance or cooperation with the enemy often had political ramifications that extended far beyond the confines of the notorious POW prison, the Hanoi Hilton. Part III examines this special group of naval aviators, paying particular attention to the plight of POWs shot down during the latter part of the war.

Afterburner then returns to operations, concentrating first on the Navy's mining of Haiphong harbor, one of the most successful naval operations of the war. Part IV examines this critical operation in its historical, political, strategic, and tactical contexts. It also looks at the men behind the mission and at how their success was shaped not only by the technology of the A-6 Intruder and the mines they carried but also by their skill as pilots and bombardier-navigators.

Part V explores the nature of air-to-air combat in 1972 and the impact of Top Gun, the Navy Fighter Weapons School, on the air war. It focuses heavily on the story of Ronald "Mugs" McKeown, one of the Navy's leading MiG killers and a founding father of Top Gun. Part V explains why the Navy achieved a much higher kill ratio than the Air Force did with similar aircraft and weapons systems.

Part VI assesses naval aviation's role in the Easter Offensive, Linebacker I, and Linebacker II—the final, climactic chapters in the air war over North Vietnam. While the Air Force, with its laser-guided bombs and large B-52 heavy bombers, stole most of the show during the latter two campaigns, the Navy nevertheless performed vital missions by knocking down numerous bridges during Linebacker I and suppressing enemy surface-to-air missiles for the B-52s in Linebacker II. During the Easter Offensive, naval air proved even more significant by providing the majority of U.S. close air support sorties (air action against hostile targets that are in close proximity to friendly forces) over South Vietnam during the initial months of the invasion. Without naval air, the South Vietnamese Army might not have stopped the Easter Offensive, and South Vietnam might have fallen in 1972 rather than 1975. Part VI not only offers an overview of naval aviation's role in this campaign and in the Linebacker offensives that followed but also closely examines the lives of several aviators who fought in these operations.

A NOTE ON SOURCES AND METHODS

Those expecting a traditional official history might be disappointed with this book. It is not a strict chronology of the air war in Vietnam, detailing every air action fought. In its most literal form, the air war over Vietnam consisted of thousands of small engagements unsuited to a strictly chronological approach. To describe every air action would serve no purpose except to produce lethargy for the reader.

Instead, this book combines traditional naval history based on documents (command histories, intelligence reports, Center for Naval Analyses studies, fleet message traffic, etc.) and "new" military history based on oral history. The descriptions of major naval air operations are based on archival research, but the heart of the book lies in its twenty-one biographical portraits, which examine the air war through the eyes of the men themselves.

A biographical approach allows readers to connect with real people instead of relying on dry descriptions of air campaigns filled with facts and figures about sorties launched, bombs dropped, and enemy killed to tell the story of the air war. Admiral Leighton Warren Smith, the man who led America's air war against Serbia in 1994, once remarked that he learned more about leadership from reading Patrick O'Brian's historical novels about a fictitious British officer who served with the Royal Navy during the Napoleonic Wars than he did from any historical tome. Why couldn't the Navy's official historians produce a book as engaging as an O'Brian novel but based on the lives of actual aviators rather than fictitious characters?

Furthermore, Secretary of the Navy John Lehman established a contemporary history branch within the Navy Staff in 1987 explicitly "to support its doctrinal development and training and professional education of its personnel." What could be more informative for the officer flying in the modern age than a book detailing the experiences of the men who fought America's first modern air war? Some of the technology has changed, but the fundamental act of strapping on a jet and flying off the deck of a carrier remains constant.

Introduction

The Navy's Air War in Southeast Asia prior to 1968

AS IS SO OFTEN THE CASE in America's overseas wars, Navy airmen were among the first U.S. servicemen to see combat in Vietnam's second war of independence, and they fought in nearly every major engagement from the Gulf of Tonkin in 1964 to the evacuation of Saigon in 1975.

The Navy's aerial involvement in Vietnam dates back to the late 1950s, when America began to make regular patrols of the South China Sea. In 1959, the North Vietnamese began constructing the Ho Chi Minh Trail through southern Laos and into the mountains of South Vietnam. They transported arms and other supplies via this land route and by sea to the Communist Viet Cong guerrillas in South Vietnam, initiating an armed struggle to overthrow the government of the Republic of Vietnam. During the early 1960s, the Navy countered this aggression by initiating unarmed reconnaissance missions into Laos. On 6 June 1964, enemy ground fire downed an RF-8 photo reconnaissance plane flown by Lieutenant Charles Klusmann, making him the first Navy pilot to be shot down during the war and prompting American policy makers to begin authorizing armed escorts for reconnaissance flights into Laos.[1]

In the summer of 1964 naval air power's role in Southeast Asia again escalated with the Gulf of Tonkin episode. Since early 1964, South Vietnamese Navy patrol boats had engaged in a series of hit-and-run attacks against installations along the North Vietnamese coast. As part of a response to these raids, the North Vietnamese sent out three motor torpedo boats to attack *Maddox*, a U.S. destroyer engaged in an intelligence-gathering mission along the coast of North Vietnam. The torpedoes they fired missed their target, but one round from a Communist deck gun hit the American destroyer. Planes from the aircraft carrier *Ticonderoga* reacted quickly, shooting up the trio of attackers, leaving

7

one boat dead in the water. The destroyer emerged from the scuffle unscathed.

Not wanting to back down in the face of aggression, President Lyndon Johnson ordered *Maddox* to resume her mission on 4 August, this time reinforced by *Turner Joy,* another destroyer. That night, the ships reported making contact and then being attacked by several fast craft far out to sea. Special intelligence and other information convinced officers in the naval chain of command and U.S. leaders in Washington that North Vietnamese naval forces had fired torpedoes at the destroyers, although most analysts now believe that an attack never occurred. Planes from carriers *Ticonderoga* and *Constellation* hit an oil storage site in the coastal North Vietnamese city of Vinh and damaged or destroyed about thirty enemy naval vessels in port or along the coast. More significantly, on 7 August the U.S. Congress overwhelmingly passed the Tonkin Gulf Resolution, which gave the president broad powers to use military force as he saw fit against the Vietnamese Communist forces.

The air war quieted down for the Navy until February 1965. That month, Viet Cong guerrillas hit a U.S. compound in Pleiku, killing nine Americans and wounding another hundred. The United States retaliated shortly thereafter in a series of air raids against North Vietnam called Flaming Dart I. Aircraft from *Coral Sea* and *Hancock* launched large strikes against the barracks at Dong Hoi, a town just north of the demilitarized zone (DMZ) between North and South Vietnam, and *Ranger*'s carrier air wing attacked the barracks at Vit Thu Lu in North Vietnam. The Vietnamese Communists, in turn, retaliated by hitting a hotel in Qui Nhon, South Vietnam, killing twenty-nine American soldiers. Outraged, Admiral U. S. Grant Sharp, Commander in Chief, Pacific (CINCPAC), called for immediate action. The resulting operation, Flaming Dart II, commenced the following day with massive Navy strikes against the Chanh Hoa barracks, thirty-five miles north of the DMZ. These were the first Alpha strikes of the war—an air strike of thirty aircraft of various types: sixteen attack aircraft (A-4s initially and later on in the war, A-6s and A-7s), ten fighter escorts (F-8s or F-4s), two special antiradar bombers known as "Iron Hands" (usually A-4s), and a variety of support aircraft (tankers, electronic warfare planes, and helicopters for search and rescue).

The results of Flaming Dart proved inconclusive. Vietnamese Communists in the South continued to launch terrorist attacks against U.S. installations despite the threat of continued reprisal raids. In an attempt to convince Hanoi to abandon its support of the southern insurgency, President Johnson launched a new campaign in March 1965 called Rolling Thunder. This campaign sought to use an incremental application of force to persuade the North Vietnamese to come to the negotiating table and end the war. Hence, the first strikes of the campaign were against relatively low-value targets in the southern sections of North Vietnam. On 2 March, Air Force planes struck the Xom Bang ammunition depot 35 miles north of the DMZ. Twelve days later Air Force and Navy planes struck an ammunition dump 100 miles south of Hanoi. On 29 March, six A-3Bs from *Ranger* dropped bombs on Bach Long Vi Island. North Vietnam failed to blink. Instead, it began to increase its air defenses in the Hanoi and Haiphong region. On 5 April, an RF-8 from *Coral Sea* brought back pictures of the first surface-to-air missile (SAM) site to be positively identified. By July, several more sites were photographed, but it was not until several American planes were lost, including A-4s from *Midway*, that President Johnson authorized anti-SAM missions.[2] The Navy launched its first counter-SAM mission in August. On these missions, known as by the code name "Iron Hand," A-4s equipped with Shrike missiles hunted SAM sites by searching for their radar emissions. When a radar signal was picked up, the Shrike would home in on the beam to destroy the site. The Navy also employed electronic warfare planes (EF-10B Skynights and EA-3B Skywarriors) to locate SAM radars for Iron Hand aircraft or jam them during Alpha strikes.

When it became clear that North Vietnam was in no hurry to negotiate in the summer of 1965, President Johnson began to employ air power more for interdicting supplies than for strategic persuasion. For the next three years and five months, Rolling Thunder sought to reduce the flow of troops and supplies flowing south by bombing roads, railroads, bridges, and supply depots.

Almost from its onset, the campaign was marked by a basic dispute between senior American military leaders, who argued for brief, intense strikes designed to isolate North Vietnam from external supply sources and destroy its production and transportation systems, and President Johnson and Secretary of Defense Robert McNamara, who chose to alternate escalation with bombing halts in the hope of persuading the North Vietnamese to settle on a peace agreement acceptable to the United States and South Vietnam. During the three years of Rolling Thunder, Johnson and McNamara instituted a total of seven pauses. They also insisted on unprecedented tactical control, dictating the numbers and types of aircraft, kinds of ordnance, and even flight paths. Johnson and his close advisers chose targets during Tuesday lunch meetings.

The administration divided North Vietnam into six zones called route packages and formulated complex rules of engagement for each zone. Navy planes could attack targets only in Route Packages 2 through 4 and 6b. Targets in the other zones were reserved for the Air Force. Until 1966, no Navy plane could attack a target in Route Package 2 without an airborne forward air controller (FAC) to carefully direct strike fighters to their targets. Additionally, all targets in Route Package 6 required White House permission to be attacked. Many of the most valuable targets, including most in downtown Hanoi and Haiphong, were declared off-limits for much of the campaign.

North Vietnam exploited the U.S. bombing restrictions at every turn. For example, it used the prohibited areas in Hanoi and Haiphong as sanctuaries to base SAMs and Soviet-manufactured MiG fighters. During Rolling Thunder, 54 U.S. aircraft fell victim to SAMs, and 430 to antiaircraft guns of various calibers. The North, employing an air denial strategy, used high-altitude SAMs to compel American aircraft to fly low, thereby bringing them in range of antiaircraft guns. Over 200,000 North Vietnamese worked in air defense, either manning guns, managing air raid shelters, or firing at planes with rifles. Another 500,000 worked on repairing roads, railways, and bridges.

Because of their value and scarcity, MiGs were used sparingly. Generally, they made only one pass at a strike package before retreating home. During the entire war, enemy aircraft shot down just 16 Navy aircraft, or 3.3 percent of the 473 naval aircraft lost in the war. As one former Navy fighter pilot put it, "No Navy strike was ever turned back because of the MiG threat."[3] But the threat posed by the North Vietnamese Air Force could have been greatly reduced had the Navy been allowed to bomb the airfields in Hanoi and Haiphong early on in the war.

The first thirty MiG-17s and MiG-15s arrived in Hanoi in August 1964, the same month as the Gulf of Tonkin incidents. By June the North Vietnamese Air Force possessed over seventy aircraft, including the modern, supersonic MiG-21. Yet, most of the airfields in Route Package 6 lay immune from attack until 1967. All told, Navy and Marine fighters downed only thirty-three (plus two AN-2s utility biplanes) of these elusive foes from 1965 to 1968.

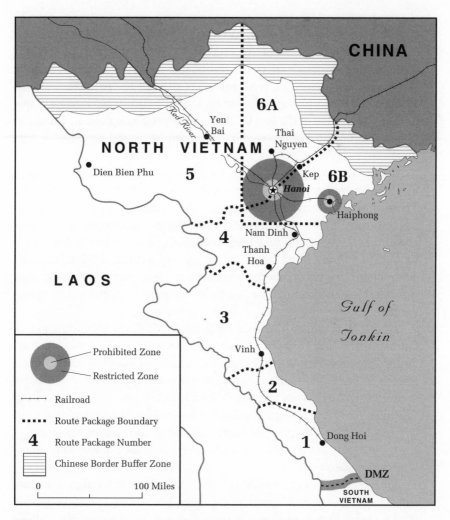

U.S. Bombing Zones in North Vietnam. (Courtesy of Chris Robinson)

A major problem with Rolling Thunder was that it did not follow traditional air power strategies. It did not first destroy the North Vietnamese air defense system to achieve air superiority and then move on to other high-value targets. Instead, the campaign targeted the North Vietnamese air defenses in an ad hoc fashion, generally to protect a specific strike or in direct retaliation for losses incurred. This planning shortcoming made it one of the most costly air campaigns in history. In the first twenty months alone, America lost more than 300 aircraft.

Rolling Thunder went through five distinct phases. In Phase I (March–June 1965), a variety of targets, including ammunition depots, radar sites, and barracks, were hit in an attempt to "persuade" North Vietnam to come to the negotiating table. It did little, however, but harden the resolve of the North Vietnamese people to fight and spurred the creation of one of the world's most sophisticated air defense networks.

Phase II (July 1965–January 1966) was an interdiction campaign that concentrated primarily on roads, bridges, boats, and railroads. These attacks destroyed an estimated 4,600 trucks, 4,700 boats, and 800 railroad cars. At the urging of Admiral Sharp, the talented and iconoclastic CINCPAC, the Joint Chiefs of Staff (JCS) shifted its focus in January 1966 to petroleum products. Sharp argued that by focusing the campaign narrowly on energy resources, the JCS might be able to break the deadlock and compel the North Vietnamese to sign a peace agreement.

Phase III (January–October 1966) targeted North Vietnam's petroleum, oil, and lubricant (POL) resources. Although it destroyed an estimated 70 percent of North Vietnam's petroleum supplies, the ever-resourceful North Vietnamese did not require much in the way of fuel resources to carry on their war in the South. Thirty percent of pre–Rolling Thunder petroleum resources, distributed in fifty-five-gallon drums all over the countryside, proved more than adequate to continue supplying their lightly armed infantry and guerrillas in the South and even intensify the action.

Phase IV (October 1966–May 1967) shifted the campaign to industrial targets and power-generating plants. For the first time, U.S. warplanes struck targets in Hanoi, but similar to the petroleum raids, these more aggressive tactics failed to have much impact on a fundamentally nonindustrialized nation fighting a guerrilla war beyond its borders. Moreover, targeting more heavily defended targets such as the Thai Nguyen Steel Works meant more U.S. losses. By mid-May 1967, over 600 Air Force, Navy, and Marine aircraft had been lost.

The one bright spot of Phase IV for the Navy was that in February 1967, the JCS for the first time authorized mining operations along the panhandle region of North Vietnam. Navy aircraft seeded inland roads and waterways with 500-pound magnetic mines and several river mouths with more potent 1,000-pound mines. The Navy laid five fields of mines during 1967, primarily with A-6A Intruder attack planes. However, North Vietnam's largest ports, including Haiphong, Hon Gai, and Cam Pha, remained off-limits. As a result, this campaign had little impact on North Vietnam's ability to send and receive war supplies destined for the National Liberation Front (Viet Cong) in the South.

Phase V (May 1967–October 1968) focused on what remained of North Vietnam's industrial infrastructure as well as "fleeting targets" of opportunity. In January 1968, however, the Tet Offensive interrupted the campaign. Tet consisted of a series of surprise Communist attacks against major cities and military installations throughout South Vietnam, beginning during the Vietnamese New Year celebrations. In most areas, the fighting lasted only a couple of days, but in Saigon the struggle lasted for over a week, and in Hue, until early March.

Militarily, the Tet Offensive was a failure for the North Vietnamese and their Communist allies in the South. The revolts did not spur a general uprising of the masses as General Vo Nguyen Giap, the North Vietnamese commander, had hoped. Instead, they ended up being suicidal attacks against superior U.S. and South Vietnamese firepower. More than 58,000 North Vietnamese and Viet Cong troops died in the offensive; the United States lost only 3,895, and South Vietnam, 4,954.

Nevertheless, Tet was a turning point of the war. The American media portrayed the offensive as a military disaster for the United States by transmitting dramatic images of urban warfare in Saigon and Hue to an American public increasingly frustrated by the war and its costs in American lives. Proponents of the war declined to 41 percent by March 1968, and the offensive contributed to President Johnson's poor performance in the New Hampshire primary against Eugene McCarthy, an obscure antiwar candidate, and his subsequent decision to withdraw from the presidential race. Even though U.S. forces decimated their opponents on the ground, the political elites back home lost confidence in the American war effort after Tet.

Not surprisingly, Rolling Thunder also fell victim to the negative publicity generated by Tet. In April 1968, President Johnson, bruised from his recent defeat in New Hampshire and facing an antiwar movement galvanized by the violence of the Tet Offensive, opted to halt bombing above the nineteenth parallel and pursue peace negotiations with the North Vietnamese. During the eleven months of Phase V, immediately preceding the bombing pause, U.S. sorties averaged over

13,000 a month and destroyed over 5,600 trucks, 2,500 rail cars, and 11,500 boats. As in Phase IV, however, North Vietnamese air defenses continued to stiffen. By 1967, U.S. pilots confronted one of the most comprehensive air defense systems in the world. On any given month of that year, the Vietnamese fired over 25,000 tons of flak from 10,000 antiaircraft guns and hundreds of missiles from more than twenty-five SAM battalions.

Symbolizing the mounting frustration of pilots over their increasing losses was the 1967 bridge campaign. The Navy and Air Force struck the vital Paul Doumer Bridge (the main north-south rail bridge over the Red River in Hanoi) three times, but each time the resilient North Vietnamese repaired it. Another railroad bridge at Thanh Hoa proved even tougher to topple. During three and a half years, the Navy and Air Force flew over 700 sorties against the structure at a cost of numerous aircraft destroyed and damaged. The Navy even scored a direct hit against the bridge with a 1,100-pound TV-guided smart bomb but still did not drop a span.

By the end of Phase V of Rolling Thunder, the United States had dropped a total of 643,000 tons of bombs on North Vietnam—more than was expended during the entire Korean War. This tonnage destroyed 65 percent of North Vietnam's petroleum storage capacity and 60 percent of its power-generating resources. Over 10,000 trucks were destroyed in the interdiction part of the campaign alone. Yet for all this damage, Rolling Thunder failed to achieve any of its strategic goals. No peace agreement resulted from the bombing, and the interdiction campaign had no measurable impact on the ground situation in the South. The North Vietnamese actually increased their ability to move supplies southward during Rolling Thunder and launched a general offensive against the South in 1968.

Up until 1968, the North Vietnamese conducted the war in the South primarily with the guerrillas of the National Liberation Front, forces that required little in the way of heavy supplies. All these troops needed to inflict increasingly serious casualties on American troops was rice, bullets, hand grenades, and maybe the occasional mortar round. Destroying 65 percent of North Vietnam's oil supplies meant little to a nation whose primary mode of transportation was the bicycle and whose main source of energy for farming was the water buffalo. Throughout Rolling Thunder, American planners never quite came to grips with this basic fact and continued to waste precious air power resources on a campaign that was having only a modest impact on the ability of North Vietnam to wage guerrilla war in the South. Overall, Rolling Thunder cost America more than 919 aircraft and more than $2 billion.

American policy makers also had difficulty understanding Vietnamese politics and culture, as well as the leaders' long time horizons and their high tolerance for losses. Ho Chi Minh was willing to carry on his revolutionary struggle in 1968 even after losing 58,000 troops in Tet operations plus another 52,000 civilians as a result of Rolling Thunder. President Johnson, by contrast, was answerable to an American public that demanded rapid results and possessed a very low tolerance for losses, especially those involving manpower. The deaths of a little fewer than 4,000 American troops during Tet forced Johnson not only to give up his presidential aspirations in 1968 but also to end Rolling Thunder.

At the conclusion of this campaign, the United States, for the most part, ceased bombing operations altogether against North Vietnam. From 1968 to 1972, the primary focus of American air power shifted to interdiction in Laos—a campaign designed to cover the American withdrawal from South Vietnam. Air operations against the North resumed in 1972 only after a bold conventional attack by the North Vietnamese Army (NVA) against South Vietnam. But the Linebacker attacks ultimately were not designed to win the war, but merely to beat back the invasion and secure the release of 801 American prisoners of war, most of whom were pilots shot down during Rolling Thunder. In essence, America lost the air war against North Vietnam when President Johnson halted Rolling Thunder.[4]

PART I

NAVY OPERATIONS AGAINST LAOS

The Story of Shangri-La's Last Cruise, 1970

ON 5 MARCH 1970, the venerable *Shangri-La* departed Mayport, Florida, for what would be its last cruise. *Shangri-La* would operate on Yankee Station during one of the calmest periods of the war. Bombing restrictions imposed by Washington meant that the brunt of the carrier's sorties would be directed not against North Vietnam but against targets in Laos and along South Vietnam's western border. Interdicting road traffic flowing down the Ho Chi Minh Trail became the *Shang's* main contribution to the war effort—an often frustrating and fruitless task for the men on board the carrier. By the end of the conflict, Air Force, Navy, and Marine aircraft would drop over 3 million tons of bombs on Laos, three times the tonnage directed at North Vietnam. Laos would emerge from the Vietnam War as the second most bombed country in the annals of warfare.

Yet despite all the tonnage dropped, American air power failed to stem the tide of North Vietnamese aggression against the South. In fact, the North Vietnamese Army managed to defeat a major invasion by the South Vietnamese Army into Laos in 1971 and then go on to launch its own offensive during the spring of 1972.

Faithfully recording the *Shang's* contribution to Laotian interdiction campaign was Lieutenant Commander James J. McBride, an A-4 pilot with the VA-12 "Clinchers" squadron. In his 450-page, single-spaced diary of the cruise, McBride provided a day-by-day account of the Navy's air war in Laos during 1970 and one of the most detailed accounts of carrier life written during the Vietnam War. McBride described everything from living conditions to flight deck operations, and he revealed much about the life and times of Vietnam-era carrier pilots and their unique floating bases.

I

Anchors Aweigh

James McBride, the Shangri-La,
and the Long Cruise to Yankee Station

JAMES MCBRIDE CAME FROM a large midwestern family with strong working-class values. Born in 1935 in Chicago, Jim spent most of his youth in Wisconsin, where his father worked as a steamfitter for the burgeoning World War II defense industry. An Irish Catholic altar boy with strong religious convictions, the younger McBride became interested in the priesthood early on in his life, and with encouragement from local priests and a scholarship from the parish, ended up attending St. Lawrence Seminary on the foggy shores of Lake Winnebago, Wisconsin. Upon graduation, Jim decided he needed to see the world before committing himself to God. He moved back to his family's home in Baraboo, Wisconsin, a small town northwest of Madison, and began working as a day laborer and drilling weekends with the local National Guard unit while he plotted his next move in life.

A writer by inclination, McBride decided in 1957 to become a journalist. He enrolled in Rockford College in Rockford, Illinois, for a year before transferring to Marquette University in Milwaukee. The draft spoiled these plans, compelling him upon graduation in 1960 to either sign up for an officer candidate program or face an uncertain future as a foot soldier in Vietnam. Because his two younger brothers were both serving with the Navy as enlisted sailors at the time, McBride opted to enter that service's Officer Candidate School (OCS) program in Newport, Rhode Island.

Before traveling to Newport, McBride had never been east of Gary, Indiana. Despite the culture shock of the East Coast, McBride adapted quickly to the rigors of OCS, something for which the Catholic priests at St. Lawrence had prepared him well. As McBride recalled, "I learned a lot about the 'black shoe' [surface] Navy which I never would have learned had I attended Aviation Officer Candidate School in Pensacola." After graduating from Newport in 1962, McBride traveled to Pensacola for flight training and eventually ended up in a multiengine, transport squadron based out of Norfolk. With this unit, Air Transport Squadron 22, McBride flew transport planes all over the world, including missions into Guantanamo Bay during the height of the Cuban missile crisis to evacuate American dependents. He even took a trip to Vietnam in 1963 to drop off military advisers in Saigon.

The glamour of this foreign travel, as well as the potential to land a lucrative airlines job, made transport duty attractive for many pilots, but not McBride. McBride yearned to fly off the deck of a carrier: "I had this crazy idea that if I was going to serve as a naval aviator, I had to fly off carriers." With his skipper's help, McBride successfully petitioned the commander of an E-1B, "Willy Fudd," squadron to agree to a transfer. The E-1, an airborne early warning plane, carried a large radar (enclosed in a dome) on its back and typically directed fighters toward enemy aircraft approaching a carrier task force. The ungainly E-1B hardly represented the pinnacle of carrier aviation; in fact, such an assignment might have been greeted by laughter from a group of fighter pilots, but for McBride it represented a vital stepping-stone into the more glamorous world of jets, or "fast movers," as they were often called.[1]

In May 1965, McBride deployed with Detachment 62 of Carrier Airborne Early Warning Squadron 12 to Vietnam and experienced his first taste of the air war over Southeast Asia. Although the primary job of the E-1 was to fly ten miles off the coast of Vietnam to scan the skies for MiGs with its over-the-horizon radar, McBride on occasion flew "ash and trash missions" over the beach to pick up mail in Saigon or perform other errands. He even participated in an experimental night flare-dropping mission with the E-1. On that mission, McBride flew over the designated target and ordered one of his radar men to kick four flares out the hatch of the E-1. Initially, only two of the flares ignited, but another one did so as it hit the ground, touching off a secondary explosion. Using this secondary explosion as a beacon, attack planes pulverized the target. McBride received a letter of commendation from his carrier air wing commander (CAG) for the mission; however, given the difficulty of ejecting flares from the E-1, the CAG opted to cancel the experiment and return the E-1s to their original surveillance and fighter direction duties.

McBride returned to the United States in 1966 and ended up being assigned to Attack Squadron 12 (VA-12), an A-4 squadron destined to deploy in 1970 with *Shangri-La*. Now married and the father of three small children, McBride did not yearn for another combat tour, but once ordered to deploy, in the time-honored tradition of Navy officers everywhere, he complied with his orders and resolutely made the best of his plight by purchasing a new mattress for his bunk and bringing two shelves of books on board. During the next nine and a half months, those books, along with his personal diary, "The *Shang* Log," would relieve him from the stresses of war and the long separation from his family.

THE *SHANG*: A BRIEF HISTORY

Named after a fictitious Himalayan kingdom popularized by James Hilton in his novel *Lost Horizon*, the original *Shangri-La* was an *Essex*-class carrier. During World War II, the Navy decided it needed a carrier slightly smaller than the prewar *Saratoga* (CV-3) but with enough aircraft capacity to defeat any Japanese carrier in a one-to-one engagement. A total of twenty-four of these ships were built, all in less time than it took to construct a single modern carrier in the 1990s.

The *Shang* was commissioned as CV-38 on 15 September 1944, and by April its planes were in action over Okino Daito Jima, a group of islands several hundred miles southeast of Okinawa. The planes successfully bombed radar and radio installations there. The *Shang* then cruised to Okinawa, where its air wing provided close air support for the Tenth Army until the middle of May 1945. In June, the carrier launched air strikes on the Japanese home island of Kyushu, and in July it began hitting other home islands, culminating in attacks against Tokyo and its nearby shipping lanes. In addition to bombing numerous ground targets, the *Shang*'s planes hit the battleships *Nagato* and *Haruna* and the cruiser *Oyoda*.[2]

After World War II, the *Shang* served with the Navy's Pacific Fleet until she was placed in the reserve fleet in 1947. In 1952, the *Shang* traveled to Puget Sound to receive modifications at a total cost of $7 million (over $33 million in 2004 dollars), resulting in the transformation of its straight deck into a more modern angled deck carrier with steam catapults and a mirror landing system.

Between 1955 and 1960, the *Shang* participated in a series of cruises in the western Pacific and then moved to a new home in Mayport, Florida. During the next two years, she participated in cruises in the Caribbean, the Atlantic, and the Mediterranean and then again endured a major overhaul, this time in New York. Four of her five-inch mounts were removed, and she received new search and height-finding radars and a new arrester system. Workmen also renovated much of her electrical and engineering equipment. More Mediterranean cruises followed, and finally another overhaul in 1965. On 30 June 1969, she was redesignated an antisubmarine warfare carrier (CVS-38)—a role she would never serve. Instead, to augment the Laotian interdiction operations, the *Shang* was ordered to join the Seventh Fleet for strike operations off the coast of Vietnam. She continued to perform the role of an attack carrier until her final decommissioning on 30 July 1971. Attack Carrier Air Wing 8 formally joined the carrier on 1 January 1970 and stayed with her until December 1970. Air Wing 8 consisted of three squadrons of A-4s, two of F-8s, one of RF-8s, and an airborne early warning detachment of E-1Bs.[3]

THE CRUISE BEGINS: 5 MARCH 1970

Even though the *Shang* had received numerous overhauls and renovations during her long career, she was still an old ship by 1970, with a garden variety of ailments and other idiosyncrasies. In fact, when VA-12 learned that it would be deploying to the western Pacific on the *Shang*, many members of the unit laughed. "That old hulk will never make it," exclaimed one of the unit's most vocal pessimists, and true to his predictions, such problems as broken shafts, inoperative elevators, fractured launch valves, and a sickly evaporator would plague the ship throughout her last cruise. Some of the more cynical crew members would refer to their ship as the "Shitty *Shang*" or the "Chancre."

Nevertheless, the demands of America's longest war prevailed, and rumors that *Shang* would not sail proved untrue. The ship left Mayport on the morning of 5 March 1970. "In keeping with the ways of the *Shang*," wrote McBride, "we were required to be aboard at 0545 and mustered on station. It made for a very early and sleepy drive from home, twenty miles inland. Gabrielle [his wife] did not wait around to see the ship depart from the carrier pier at Mayport. The parting had been going on for several days of silent resignation to the fact that we would be living apart again. No doubt Gabrielle was anxious to get home to our three small children, who were being watched after by our neighbor."[4]

After McBride's departure, the thirty-five-year-old pilot retired to his stateroom to begin unpacking. Jim had to share the four-man room with only two other officers for the cruise, Lieutenant Commander Ray Lodge, the squadron maintenance officer, and Lieutenant Junior Grade (jg) Joe Uhrig, a new pilot with the unit. Nicknamed the SOB, for "senior officers' bunkroom," the small room had four bunks, four gray steel chairs, and four small desks built into the bulkheads of the chamber. Ray and Jim transformed this small gray prisonlike cell into something more akin to a college dorm room. They covered the floor with one-foot squares of rug remnants all in different colors and held together with duct tape. They used colored adhesive paper to hide the dull gray bulkheads and an Indian tapestry to obscure the ceiling. The men even purchased a forbidden refrigerator and hid it next to the washbasin underneath a beach blanket.

Pilots could gain some respite from the stifling heat of Southeast Asia by popping open a cool soft drink or even an occasional beer. The *Shang*'s air-conditioning system rarely kept the room under 90 degrees, but some of the junior officers in staterooms under the flight deck in the forward part of the ship experienced temperatures over 100 degrees, forcing the VA-12 skipper to allow them to sleep in the ready room. During the overhaul by the Philadelphia Naval Shipyard in 1965, the Navy approved improvements to the ship's air-conditioning system, but the alteration was poorly executed and only partially completed.[5]

Another problem identified but not fully solved in the 1965 overhaul involved fresh-water evaporation. In 1966, the Navy authorized upgraded individual water usage standards from twenty-five to thirty gallons of fresh water per man, per day. The *Shang*, however, could produce only about twenty-two gallons per day for each of its 3,063 officers and men and still have enough water left over to run its boilers and steam catapults. In 1967, the Navy substituted a 100,000-gallon evaporator for one of the carrier's 20,000-gallon units.[6] Still, even after the replacement, fresh-water shortages existed, especially in the tropical environment of Southeast Asia. "The way to get a warm fresh water shower is to know when the engineering spaces change their watches," wrote McBride. "It is natural that they would delay shutting down water lines until after their own men had the opportunity to take a shower. This might mean you have to get up at 0400 to take your shower but after a few days without a fresh water washdown it is worth the sacrifice." Even drinking water could be affected by the poor performance of the evaporators. To test the saline content of the water, McBride generally took a small sip from a water fountain (the scuttlebutt) before filling a water bottle. Occasionally, JP-5 aviation fuel (kerosene) would leak into the fresh-water system. As the safety officer, McBride jokingly warned the squadron not to smoke near a fountain "as it could be a fire hazard." During the *Shang*'s Gulf of Tonkin line period in May, the fresh-water situation deteriorated to such a degree that the ship's plan of the day issued a warning that the laundry rooms might soon be compelled to wash clothes with salt water just like in the days of sail. Five days later, on 23 May, the *Shang* actually began taking on board fresh water during two at-sea replenishments.[7]

What the ship lacked in the way of water, it often made up for with its quality food. During the 1965 overhaul, the Navy invested over $280,000 in galley improvements, including the repair and overhaul of mess equipment and the enlargement of both officer and enlisted galleys.[8] But in the end it was the cooks and not their equipment that really made the *Shang*'s food services shine. These men worked extremely hard to avoid serving the same food day after day and occasionally prepared thematic meals such as a Bostonian boiled dinner, New Orleans–style Creole shrimp and rice, Texas barbecued chicken and black-eyed peas, or Georgia fried ham and hominy grits. Cooks attempted to honor religious practices on Friday by serving fish or a meat substitute such as macaroni and cheese. Finally, the Navy's Bureau of Supplies and Accounts encouraged every cook to "become an inseparable companion" with the Navy Recipe Service's file of 700 recipes printed on five-by-eight note cards.[9] According to McBride, "If all else fails to interest one's appetite, there is always a good supply of bread and peanut butter."[10]

Aviators on the *Shang* could dine either in the "dirty shirt mess," a cafeteria-style affair where one could wear a flight suit, or in the officers' wardroom, a more formal dining room complete with table linens, china, and waiters. Because most aviators flew at odd hours and rarely lived by a normal schedule, most of the men in the squadron dined in the dirty shirt mess and only on rare occasions dressed up in the uniform of the day (usually khaki) and ate in the formal wardroom. No matter where they chose to dine, officers had to pay for their meals via a monthly mess bill tabulated by the treasurer of the officers' mess (usually only a few dollars per month).[11] The squadron also used the mess purse to buy items for the benefit of the unit, such as uniform patches and coffee mugs, and to pay for party expenses and flowers for births and deaths in the squadron family.[12]

Other diversions for the pilots of VA-12 were nightly movies. "These flicks are often the highlight of the day," wrote McBride, "and in many ways movies keep us in contact with another world that we are familiar and comfortable with." Beginning at 1900, officers not flying would convene in the ready room to watch the movie picked by the duty officer. The selection of the evening would be judged by the following criteria: "how much ordnance is expended (violence and people killed), skin exposed (sex), and some comprehension (screenplay)." A least a half dozen members of the unit tracked these three elements—especially "the body count." Not surprisingly, *You Only Live Twice*, a James Bond film replete with ordnance and sex, achieved the highest scores during the 1970 cruise. Other recreational activities included card games, basketball and volleyball in the hangar deck, and, when flight operations were not in effect, jogging on the flight deck.[13]

CROSSING THE LINE: 11 MARCH 1970

When the *Shang* crossed the equator off the coast of South America, all operations ceased for a "crossing the line," or "shellback," ceremony. These ceremonies, performed by navy ships of nearly every nationality when they cross the equator, date back to the Vikings; they used to serve as a means to pay homage to Neptune or some other potentate of the sea and to initiate new sailors into the rigors of life at sea. During early ceremonies, a live ox or a goat might be sacrificed to ensure a safe journey. Early rituals also subjected new seamen to incredible abuses such as being dropped from a yardarm into the sea.

By the onset of the Vietnam War, shellback was far tamer than it had been during the age of sail. Nevertheless, many of the basic traditions of the ritual endured. Those who wished to work and live in the realm of Neptune were required to pay their respects upon crossing the equator, and this homage was always paid by the newcomer (or pollywog). Those who successfully "crossed the line" became the sons of Neptune, or shellbacks. Shellbacks treasure and safeguard their certificate, addressed "to all Sailors wherever ye may be: and to all Mermaids, Whales, Sea Serpents, Porpoises, Sharks, Dolphins, Eels, Skates, Suckers, Crabs, Lobsters and all other living things of the sea," because it documents their completion of the initiation and saves them from having to repeat the ugly process. McBride, who had crossed the line during his cruise with *Independence,* kept his card in a very safe place and always took it on deployments, "for one never knows when one could be crossing the equator again."[14]

The events on the *Shang* began with Neptunus Rex and his royal court (usually a group of highly experienced petty officers) coming on board and summoning all 4,000 pollywogs on the ship to appear before the king's court and face charges. With subpoenas in their mouths, the wogs mustered in Hangar Bay 1, where they met the shellbacks, who then prodded them to Elevator 1 with pieces of fire hose. On their hands and knees, the wogs assembled on the flight deck along the starboard catapult. All had to kiss the stomach of the royal baby, a fat sailor whose belly was covered with "mustard, ketchup, and other tasty ingredients." The royal doctors then fed "some weird mixture of spicy sauces to selected pollywogs," and then all wogs went to the royal jail for a saltwater washdown. They then crawled through garbage, swam across a water tank, and finally ran through a gauntlet of fire hose–prodding shellbacks on the fantail. Only then did they finally receive the coveted shellback certificate.

According to McBride, "The whole shellback ceremony seemed relatively well-run." He did not think "as many skinned knees or sore asses were received as there were on the *Independence* in 1965."

SUBIC BAY: 5–7 APRIL

After a brief stop in Rio De Janeiro, the *Shang* continued its trip around South America and then proceeded to its next port of call, Subic Bay, Philippines. When weather permitted, the squadron flew practice missions. It also attended numerous intelligence briefings in preparation for combat, but time still passed slowly for McBride and the others. Although he did his best to pass the time by writing in his journal, attending Holy Week and Easter services, and participating in an occasional flight deck volleyball game, he still felt a great sense of relief when the carrier finally pulled into Subic Bay.

In contrast to Rio de Janeiro, a large civilian metropolis, Subic Bay was a dedicated naval facility complete with officers' clubs, a golf course, and Navy-owned beaches. Neighboring Olongapo functioned as a classic garrison town with the usual seedy hotels, bars, and prostitutes. During the Vietnam War, Olongapo would play host to nearly every sailor who fought in the conflict and ultimately form a fundamental backdrop to the sea war in Vietnam—a place to unwind and escape the pressures of war and the maritime life. The availability of cheap liquor, drugs, and prostitutes combined with the stress of war encouraged many (including some married men) to take up with a local prostitute. In some squadrons, including VA-12, the skipper would escort all officers new to Olongapo on their first visit to its famous bars and strip clubs. This tradition, appropriately called an "alpha strike," often set the tone for the entire liberty period. A spirit of "eat, drink, and be merry for tomorrow we may die" prevailed during these liberty calls, and the garishness of Olongapo only heightened these emotions.

Before VA-12 reached the shore, the flight surgeon gave the crew a lecture on venereal disease. He also cautioned the men about homosexuals posing as females because these prostitutes spread disease more easily than their female counterparts. After his lecture, he handed out condoms but again warned the men that they were only 60 to 70 percent effective against the spread of disease. While talks about VD often took on a grave tone, in practice, flight surgeons generally handled cases among pilots and naval flight officers quietly. Given the Navy's often-critical shortages of aircrews, a wing could ill afford to send one of its pilots to quarantine for a common case of gonorrhea.

Like many officers in the squadron, Jim began his liberty with a nice meal in the officers' club. Fortified and relaxed, McBride then took a shuttle bus to the main gate and proceeded across the river that formed a boundary between the Subic Bay naval base and the town of Olongapo. "Crossing the bridge," wrote McBride, "is like going into a whole different and strange world. Olongapo is very bright with lights from the rows of clubs and noisy from the music blasting from the numerous bars." Jim and his shipmates spent a couple of hours on a second-floor veranda at a bar called Willows, drinking beer and watching the throngs of sailors moving up and down the main street. After a couple of beers, he decided to join the crowd on the dance floor and do "some wild, rock and roll dancing" with one of the local bar girls. In Olongapo, prostitutes technically could not walk the street (although many did anyway); instead, they plied their trade in bars. In addition to the usual services, these girls encouraged men to buy them tea and other drinks at inflated prices, and they would dance and chat with any lonely sailor who found himself in the bar. "What is your name? What ship are you from? Do you have a girlfriend?" they would inquire. McBride suspected that they knew the ship schedules better than many in the Navy.[15]

The next day, McBride and other members of VA-12 attended the nine-hour Jungle Environment Survival Training (JEST) course. Philippine natives took groups of aviators into a jungle area about thirty minutes from Subic Bay and taught the men basic survival skills: what plants can be eaten, how to build a quick shelter, how to camouflage one's self in the jungle, and so on. The men then went to the commissary to pick up items for their stateroom pantry—pretzels, cookies, dried fruit, and soft drinks. The following day they returned to pick up booze. The Navy authorized the men to buy up to five fifths of hard liquor a month and an unlimited amount of beer. "Naturally we seemed to forget that Navy regulations state that no liquor at all will be kept on board U.S. Navy ships. It is not like we are going to drink all this booze while aboard the ship. How nice it is sometimes to rationalize that his violation of Navy rules could be considered as just another benefit of the combat cruise." During the cruise, McBride usually kept two cans of beer hidden in his refrigerator. "On stand down day [the day when the carrier leaves Tonkin Gulf and halts combat operations] we might have a brew. The beer is long gone before our return to Subic. The empty beer cans go over the side at night filled with water to rest on the bottom of the Gulf of Tonkin."

One of the final things Jim did before leaving Subic was call his wife and children. It took eight minutes for him to get a weak connection to Florida. Gabrielle, his wife, answered the phone with a surprised tone in her voice, but she quickly recovered from the shock of hearing her husband's voice and began filling Jim in on details of home life. After a few minutes of talk, she handed the phone to his children. "Maybe talking to my boys was not such a good idea as Dominic told me to come home and his little voice really broke me up. I wish that there was some way that I could explain to this three year old son of mine why I can not come home right now." Jim spent the remainder of the evening writing letters to his family rather than heading into town with the boys.[16]

TRANSIT TO YANKEE STATION: 8–10 APRIL 1970

The *Shang* took its time in cruising to Yankee Station (the area off the coast of North Vietnam where U.S. Navy aircraft carriers conducted offensive air operations against North Vietnam) to allow the air wing to freshen up its skills after its long transit from the States. The pilots of VA-12 made practice bombing runs at Scarborough Shoals, a large rock formation off the west coast of Luzon that from the air looks like a giant pork chop.

The A-4 Skyhawk, which the attack squadron flew, was a revolutionary jet bomber on its first sorties of the war in 1964, but by 1970 it was almost antiquated. The Skyhawk, or "scooter," as its pilots often called it, was designed in the early 1950s by the Douglas Aircraft Company with three goals in mind: it had to fly over 500 mph, carry a 2,000-pound bomb load to any target in a 460-mile radius, and cost less than $1 million ($6.9 million in 2004 dollars) apiece. Ed Heinemann, the man who designed the A-4, went against the prevailing trends in military aircraft design at the time by building a plane that was small, light, and simple rather than large and complex. The delta-shaped wing of the plane was so small that it did not need to be folded for storage—a characteristic that eliminated wing hinges, thereby reducing weight and maintenance requirements. Nor did the plane have a backup hydraulics system for its landing gear. In the event of an emergency, a pilot could force his landing gear down mechanically using the power of the airstream and G-forces. The engine had 7,000 pounds of thrust but no afterburner—another maintenance- and weight-saving feature. Finally, the skin of the aircraft was just .064 inches thick, a remarkable innovation for the time. Taken together, these engineering improvements allowed the small plane to carry up to 5,975 pounds of ordnance, nearly three times more than the Navy specified.[17]

But there were other aspects of the plane that pilots particularly appreciated. Its small size gave them a feeling of invincibility. "How could enemy gunners hit such a small plane?" these men reasoned.[18] Pilots

A shot of one of VA-212's A-4Cs. The A-4 flew one-third of all Navy sorties during the war and suffered 38 percent of its air losses. (Courtesy of James McBride)

also enjoyed the plane's roll rate of 720 degrees per second, which gave the pilot a good sweep of everything in site, but the most beloved aspect of the plane was its ergonomic cockpit. Rear Admiral Robert Kirksey, a decorated veteran of numerous A-4 operations during the war, described it this way: "The A-4 cockpit was arranged so that you could devote a lot of time to the outside environment." After having developed a basic familiarity with the airplane, a pilot could drop his left hand in the cockpit and be right at the throttle and speed brakes. The handle to the control stick, with all ordnance-dropping systems and guns, was convenient. The armament panel was also easy to set up. "All you had to do," claimed Kirksey, "was hit one switch and you were ready to do your mission."[19]

The A-4, though, was not without problems. Its inherently unstable nature made it impossible to trim and lock up (i.e., keep steady in level flight). A pilot had to constantly tinker with the flight controls to keep the A-4 on course, much as a helmsman plays with the tiller of a sailboat to maintain a steady heading. According to Kirksey, this instability could make it difficult to land on a carrier. "It is a little wobbly and the long landing gear seems to be reaching down to grasp the flight deck."[20]

The A-4 also suffered the highest loss rate of any Navy plane: a total of 195 went down over the skies of Vietnam, compared with 75 F-4s, 51 A-6s, and 58 F-8s.[21] The first Navy POW, Everett Alvarez, flew the Skyhawk, as did many other famous POWs, including James Stockdale and John McCain. Part of the reason the Navy lost so many A-4s is that these planes generally flew the most dangerous missions early in the war when the Navy was just beginning to learn how to manage the various antiaircraft threats over North Vietnam. During the war's later stages, A-4s continued to fly the more dangerous day missions because they did not possess the sophisticated night and all-weather navigation systems contained on the more modern A-6 and A-7. Finally, the Skyhawk's high loss rates can be attributed to the fact that these planes flew more sorties than any other Navy aircraft during the war. A-4 sorties represented one-third of all Navy sorties flown in the war and 38 percent of its carrier air losses.[22]

McBride and other members of the squadron were well aware of the A-4's record and yearned to fly the more modern A-7E Corsair, a plane flown by its sister wing on *America*.

The A-7E Corsair II could fly faster (a maximum speed of 645 knots versus 577); carry four times more bombs than the A-4 Skyhawk (twenty Mk-82 500-pound bombs versus five for the A-4); and deliver them more than twice as accurately.[23] The Navy, however, could not afford to equip all its carriers with the A-7, and so VA-12 had to manage with the older A-4.

Because of the bombing halt against North Vietnam, VA-12 would not have to confront the full magnitude of the North's air defense systems; nevertheless, pilots in the unit continually complained about the advanced age of their planes. In particular, they were dismayed that the Navy compelled them to take the older C model on the cruise rather than equipping them with the more modern A-4Es or Fs. "Our West Coast squadron pilots of VA-152 are flying the A-4F models and their maintenance problems are only half as bad as the two A-4C squadrons," complained McBride.

The day before arriving at Yankee Station, Jim spent the day attending intelligence briefings, reviewing charts, and checking his emergency gear. All pilots customize their survival kits according to their own tastes and whims. Some carry extra ammunition or even an extra pistol, thinking these items might improve their survival over hostile territory. The more pragmatic generally stock up on water and radio batteries. McBride took a standard issue .38-caliber revolver and loaded it with tracer rounds, "preferring to signal a rescue helicopter to fighting off Viet Cong, who I am sure are much better armed than I am." He also added more plastic water containers, some LifeSavers candy, and a red bandanna. With nearly forty pounds of equipment, he felt ready for his 0630 launch the next day.[24]

2

The War Nobody Was
Supposed to Know About

Laos and McBride's First Line Tour

THE NAVY'S AIR WAR IN LAOS:
STEEL TIGER AND COMMANDO HUNT

Jim's first mission of the tour would be a bombing run against an area of Laos known as Steel Tiger, which refers to the Laotian panhandle, a rugged area dominated by jungles and steep mountains, ranging from 1,800 to more than 5,000 feet in height. The Annamite Mountains consist of eroded limestone and form a natural boundary between Laos and Vietnam. Vehicles can cross this natural barrier only via a limited number of passes: Ban Karai, in lower North Vietnam; Mu Gia, in the northern panhandle of North Vietnam; and Ban Raving, just east and slightly north of the DMZ. Travel is further restricted by weather. The rainy season lasts from mid-May to mid-September, and the dry season begins in November following a six-week transitional period between the two seasons. Precipitation ranges from 50 to more than 200 inches a year, feeding a variety of vegetation: layered jungles of bamboo, air plants, banana palms, and tropical hardwoods at lower altitudes; and scrub oak, pine, and rhododendron at higher altitudes.

In 1959, the North Vietnamese started constructing a series of trails through this area to provide logistical support for their war against the South. This system, which Americans ultimately called the Ho Chi Minh Trail, began as a series of linked trails for porters, pack animals, and bicycle riders. Porters carried loads averaging 100 pounds, and bikers regularly hauled 330-pound loads.[1] Walkers and riders moved between way stations located roughly a day's travel apart. At these stations, supplies could be temporarily stored in bunkers, and laborers could receive food and medical attention.

In 1964, the North Vietnamese Army began improving some trails to accommodate trucks, which by the end of the year were transporting over 400 tons south per week. By 1966, the trail consisted of 820 miles of fair-weather roads, and by 1968, up to 10,000 trucks could shuttle down the system at any given time. The Vietnamese used a variety of trucks in Laos, including the Soviet-made, four-ton-capacity MAZ-502 and Ural ZIS-355M, but the most common early in the war was the Soviet two-ton-capacity GAZ-63. The GAZ-63, with its small, seventy-horsepower, six-cylinder engine, could achieve only about 41 mph on the highway, but on the rough, underdeveloped roads in Laos, speed was not an issue. The Vietnamese found the truck's narrow, 130-inch wheelbase and, more important, its four-wheel drive ideal for traversing the narrow dirt roads in Laos.[2] As the war progressed, the North Vietnamese had replaced most of the GAZ-63s with larger, four-ton-capacity ZIL-157s. The ZIL could not travel any faster than the GAZ, but it could haul more material, and with its six-wheel drive and self-inflating and deflating tires, it was ideal for the varying road conditions in Laos.[3]

Trucks may have allowed the Vietnamese to begin to move more goods down the trail, but they did not simplify the process. An item that traveled from Hanoi to South Vietnam would be subjected to numerous transfers in and out of different types of vehicles and wayside storage areas. Almost all movement was by a series of short shuttles rather than long-distance hauling. Drivers maneuvered their trucks over the same routes night after night, becoming thoroughly familiar with the terrain. They needed this expert knowledge of local terrain to cope with the near-constant harassment of American air power. "We were hit frequently by American airplanes," recalled Than Minh Son, a driver. "If ten out of a hundred trucks arrived safely, that was a great victory. If a bomb hit in front of us, we drove through the forest and made a new road."[4] To operate, maintain, and defend this flow of traffic moving down the trail, North Vietnam ultimately stationed over 100,000 truck drivers, bike riders, porters, engineers, laborers, antiaircraft gunners, and medical technicians along the trails.[5]

For American air planners, the Ho Chi Minh network emerged as a target as early as 1964, when Seventh Fleet aircraft began conducting Yankee Team spy missions into this area with RF-8 photo reconnaissance jets. With the Gulf of Tonkin Resolution and the escalation of the war in 1965, the Air Force and Navy initiated Operation Steel Tiger, a limited interdiction campaign aimed at halting enemy troop and supply movements in the Laotian panhandle. By mid-1965, Navy and Air Force pilots were flying over 1,000 Steel Tiger sorties a month, mainly against trucks, bridges, and troop concentrations but also against "choke points"—principal entry points from Vietnam to Laos such as the Mu Gia Pass.[6]

Despite America's increasing commitment to air interdiction in Laos, the North Vietnamese continued their infiltration, exceeding intelligence estimates that they would send 4,500 men and 300 tons of supplies a month into South Vietnam. To thwart the effort, the United States launched a new campaign called Tiger Hound in 1965, designed to concentrate more air power on a section of the Ho Chi Minh Trail contiguous to South Vietnam. The Air Force established an airborne command and control system to manage air strikes in the area, and by the end of December, Navy and Marine aircraft had flown 425 strikes (over half of the logged sorties), chiefly against trucks, storage areas, bridges, buildings, and enemy antiaircraft sites. On 11 December, the Air Force introduced B-52s for the first time in the campaign to strike the Mu Gia Pass choke point.

By May, Tiger Hound strikes had destroyed an estimated 3,000 buildings, 1,400 trucks, numerous bridges, and more than 200 antiaircraft sites. Still, supplies continued to flow south. Recognizing the need for a plane that could loiter for long periods of time over the jungle, the Air Force began deploying propeller-driven AC-47 gunships to remain over strategic areas and lay massive amounts of firepower on any targets of opportunity encountered. These converted cargo planes, armed with three 7.62-mm Gatling guns (each capable of firing 6,000 rounds per minute), proved highly effective against trucks but also very vulnerable to antiaircraft guns, since their weapons were ineffective beyond 1,500 yards. By mid-May 1966, the Vietnamese had shot down four of these aircraft and eighteen other planes in the Steel Tiger and Tiger Hound zones, forcing the Air Force to withdraw the AC-47 from operations and rely more heavily on Navy and Air Force fast movers such as the F-4, A-4, and F-105. In February 1967, a new gunship, the AC-130, entered service for the first time. Armed with longer range 20-mm Gatling guns and 40-mm cannon equipped with low-light-level television, laser range finders, and infrared detection systems, the AC-130 dramatically improved the statistical results of the campaign. In 1968, planners claimed 7,332 trucks destroyed, compared with 3,291 the previous year.[7]

As was often the case during the Vietnam War, as American technology became more sophisticated, so, too, did North Vietnamese countermeasures. Although no road on the Ho Chi Minh Trail network was paved or wider than one lane, road construction mushroomed from 80 kilometers during the 1966–67 dry season to more than 306 kilometers by August 1968. Conscripted Laotian villagers did most of this construction, using hand implements and working at night to avoid bomb attacks. These peasant laborers focused most of their attention on converting preexisting trails to roads rather than creating completely new thoroughfares. Bulldozers, earth graders, and engineering troops did get employed on longer roads and those that required extensive earthmoving, but for the most part, construction of the trail was done in a decentralized manner with local help. Wherever possible, the Vietnamese constructed roads under tree canopies, making good use of natural camouflage. They also planted bushes and constructed trellisworks of bamboo saplings to cover exposed portions of roads. Finally, in a climate plagued by monsoon weather from May to October, these laborers became masters in solving drainage problems via corduroying, graveling short sections, installing culverts, and creating drainage ditches.[8]

To counter these and other innovations and locate the Vietnamese roads and the traffic they carried, the Air Force began developing a system unique in the history of warfare, the Igloo White sensor system. The idea of a sensor system for Laos dates back to a 1966 memo written by Roger Fisher, a professor at the Harvard Law School, to John McNoughton, assistant secretary of defense (international affairs) and Fisher's former boss in the Pentagon. In it, Fisher suggested a barrier of mines and barbed wire in Laos as an alternative to a sustained bombing offensive against North Vietnam. The memo made the rounds of the Pentagon, and ultimately Secretary of Defense Robert McNamara commissioned a panel of distinguished scientists to produce a study of "technical possibilities" relating to military operations in Vietnam. The study (actually a series of four reports known collectively as the Jason Report) concluded that the Rolling Thunder bombing campaign against North Vietnam was having no real effect on the fighting in the South. It recommended that air assets be concentrated on interdicting supplies flowing through Laos, especially through the limited number of passes between Laos and South Vietnam, and that a barrier of barbed wire, mines, and sensors be placed between the borders of the two countries to augment the effort. This barrier, the scientists explained, would consist of acoustic sensors (modified versions of the type used in antisubmarine warfare), spread out over a carefully plotted area that would listen for targets for planes to attack. Thousands of aspirin-sized gravel mines would enhance the effort by emitting loud noises when detonated by tires or boots (they also could disable vehicles and blow off the feet of unlucky porters). The Jason Report did point out that the Vietnamese might thwart the effectiveness of the barrier by such means as tricking sensors, developing new routes, and employing more antiaircraft weapons. Nevertheless, it recommended that the administration implement the concept with the hope that as enemy countermeasures improved, so, too, would American technology and ingenuity.

The Jason Report's critique of the Rolling Thunder campaign struck a chord with McNamara, who believed that increasing the bombing against North Vietnam would only lead to more losses without inflicting an appropriate amount of damage on the enemy or persuading him to abandon the air war in the North. The barrier concept, on the other hand, offered McNamara a limited and carefully controlled operation designed to change the policy of the North rather than obliterate the country (that the system might destroy large areas of a neutral country did not occur to McNamara or his planners).[9]

The Joint Chiefs of Staff supported the barrier concept as long as it did not divert money from other programs, but Admiral U. S. Grant Sharp, CINCPAC, vehemently objected. In a memorandum to General Earl Wheeler, chairman of the JCS, Sharp criticized the barrier as essentially defensive. "Although it could most certainly slow down North Vietnamese infiltration into the south by making their lines of communication longer, it could not stop the flow altogether," he argued. "There were too many other lines of communication available." Sharp instead recommended intensive mining of Haiphong and other minor ports along the coast of South Vietnam.[10] Policy makers rejected the mining concept in 1966 over fears that it might serve to widen the war by damaging Chinese or Soviet ships.

The barrier concept would endure. In December 1967, work began on the conventional portion of the barrier—a 600- to 1,000-meter-wide expanse of cleared ground along the border between North and South

Vietnam containing mines, sensors, barbed wire, watchtowers, and manned strongpoints. Almost from its inception, the "McNamara line," code-named "Project Dye Marker," ran into problems. Enemy attacks against Marine positions along the DMZ, the siege of Khe Sanh (one of the line's major strongpoints), and ultimately the Tet Offensive thoroughly disrupted the project and caused it to finally grind to a halt in 1968. It was simply too dangerous for Seabees and Marine construction troops to build the ground barrier in the midst of increased hostilities along the border.

The DMZ barrier died after Tet, but the Laotian barrier endured because this sensor system was planted from the relative safety of the skies and did not require ground construction teams to work in hostile territory. Navy OP-2E patrol planes, Navy helicopters, and Air Force helicopters (later F-4s) planted three types of sensors along suspected areas of the Ho Chi Minh Trail: seismic detectors, acoustic detectors, and engine detectors. These devices sensed either ground vibrations (seismic), air-transmitted sound (acoustic), or electromagnetic emanations from transmissions.[11] All the sensors came in cylindrical housings and contained low-powered radios for transmitting information. The parachute-dropped acoustic sensors entangled themselves in the branches of trees, and the seismic sensors buried their snouts in the ground. All sensors contained antitamper devices and could self-destruct if necessary. Based on Navy antisubmarine warfare technology developed during the Cold War, the devices dropped in 1968 could either transmit information in real time to a relay aircraft or remain silent until commanded by the plane to transmit stored information on noises or earth tremors that had occurred in the past. The average sensor lasted about forty-five days and cost approximately $619, with more expensive models costing as much as $2,997.[12]

Once in place, the devices reported their data to a relay aircraft, which then transmitted the information to the Infiltration Surveillance Center at Nakhon Phanom Air Base in northern Thailand. A computer stored the information, and analysts queried the database continually. When they found a worthwhile target, they called an airborne battlefield command and control center, a modified C-130 transport plane, which in turn directed jet fighters guided by on-site forward air controllers to strike the targets. By May 1970, seventy-two sensor strings monitored the roads and trails of Laos.[13]

The first major test of the sensor system occurred not in Laos but at Khe Sanh, South Vietnam. During the 1968 siege of that Marine base, the Air Force dropped sensors to monitor enemy troop movements around the area and used the Nakhon Phanom surveillance center to analyze the data. The system worked better than expected. On the night of 3–4 February, sensors indicated the presence of more than 2,000 troops near Marine hill outposts outside of the base. On the basis of this information, artillery and air power pounded the area, breaking up an intended attack on the Marines. Overall, sensors helped direct the employment of more than 100,000 tons of munitions at Khe Sanh and kill an estimated 1,288 North Vietnamese troops. This success prompted planners to make the Laos sensor system the centerpiece of the air war after President Johnson ordered an end to all bombing of North Vietnam in March 1968.

The resulting campaign, Commando Hunt, lasted through April 1972. It was longest air interdiction campaign in the history of warfare. The most intensive portions of the campaign fell during the November–April dry season (Commando Hunts I, III, V, VII) because it was then that the North Vietnamese moved the most trucks along the narrow dirt roads of the Ho Chi Minh Trail. Lesser campaigns (Commando Hunts II, IV, and VI) were mounted during the May–October wet season.

The first phase of the program, Commando Hunt I, officially began during the November 1968 to April 1969 dry season and sought to close major choke points such as the roads leading to the Mu Gia or Ban Karai passes. On 20 July 1968, the Air Force and Navy launched a series of major strikes against a portion of Route 137, the main access road to the Ban Karai Pass. The segment abutted a vertical wall of karst on one side and a stream on the other—an ideal choke point. More than 100 Navy and Air Force strikes expended some 224 tons of bombs against the karst, effectively blocking the road with debris. During August, Air Force and Navy jets launched another 257 strikes to sustain the effort. Overall, the earlier strikes reduced truck traffic from twenty-six per day in June to thirteen per day in July to only four per day in August and provided a model for Commando Hunt I.[14]

During that first campaign, sortie rates jumped from 4,700 in October to more than 15,000 by December 1968, and the North Vietnamese began relying more on rivers instead of roads to transport goods. Navy aircraft flew more than 3,700 missions into Laos during December 1968, approximately 24 percent of all sorties flown. These Navy planes operated primarily under direction of Air Force forward air control aircraft and entered and departed Laos via a special Navy flight corridor established just below the DMZ in South Vietnam. By January, one-half of the monthly total of 118 Navy sorties in Laos were being flown at night. The Navy also began seeding waterways with Mk-36 pressure magnetic mines for the first time during this month.[15]

Commando Hunt II, which began in May 1969 and coincided with the onset of the southwest monsoon, sought to hamper North Vietnamese efforts to repair bombed and washed-out roads. For the first time, fighter-bombers began conducting armed reconnaissance attacks along designated free-fire zones. Navy aircraft continued to seed rivers and land routes with Mk-36 and Mk-40 pressure magnetic mines, and by August, the Navy was flying over 32 percent of all tactical air strikes for Commando Hunt. The Navy also introduced so-called pouncer tactics whereby an A-6 Intruder, equipped with an airborne moving target indicator (AMTI), tracked enemy vehicles and then dropped flares so that Navy F-4s and A-7s could pounce on the convoy. AMTI deliveries constituted 166 out of the Navy's total of 202 sorties flown in Laos during June 1969, but the program was discontinued in July as a result of an almost complete lack of identifiable moving targets in the Laotian road system.[16]

As the dry season in Laos commenced in late 1969, planners began to scale down Commando Hunt operations. The November 1969 to April 1970 Commando Hunt III campaign emphasized daytime strikes against roads and night attacks against antiaircraft sites. In November, Navy aircrews flew a total of 2,747 strike sorties into Laos, 34 percent of the combined services effort.[17] In December, Navy aircraft destroyed 425 out of the 1,200 trucks destroyed by U.S. aircraft in the Steel Tiger region of Laos.

Navy A-6 aircraft, in particular, proved vital to a subordinate operation of Commando Hunt III called Commando Bolt. An array of four sensor strings, each with three to six sensors spaced 660 feet apart, represented the heart of Commando Bolt. Officers at the surveillance center ordered aircraft to place the strings along heavily used roads in very precise strings. As traffic traveled along the roads, the surveillance center estimated the speed and size of the convoy and used a computer to determine when the trucks would pass by the next sensor. The strike controller radioed this information to A-6s, and a Navy bombardier-navigator then fed it into the A-6's computer, which in turn told him the course, altitude, and speed necessary to detonate the bombs precisely on the point of impact just as the trucks went over it.[18]

Despite the best efforts of the A-6s and Air Force F-4s, the success of Commando Bolt remains unclear due to difficulties in obtaining good, poststrike intelligence for night operations. The 500-pound bombs used by the A-6s and F-4s also were not the best weapons for interdiction because their compact bursting radius required almost a direct hit to destroy a truck.

Throughout Commando Hunt, the best interdiction weapon was the Air Force AC-130 gunship. The sensor array and massive firepower of the plane simply dwarfed that of the Navy and Air Force fast movers. During Commando Hunt III, for instance, AC-130s demolished 822 out of the 2,562 vehicles destroyed during the campaign, or 32 percent—almost the same number of vehicles destroyed by all Navy A-4s, A-6s, and A-7 combined. As historian Earl Tilford writes, the AC-130 was "the centerpiece" of Commando Hunt.[19]

The production-line bombing of Laos slowly transformed the country from a jungle backwater into a wasteland. During Commando Hunt III alone, B-52s deposited 380,000 bombs on the Laotian landscape, causing tremendous landslides, altering the courses of rivers, flattening mountains, and transforming rugged jungles into moonscapes. Chemical defoliants stripped bare huge swaths of rain forest. Yet despite this destruction and technological wizardry, enemy defenses actually increased during the campaign from 445 antiaircraft sites in November 1969 to 607 sites in April 1970, the month McBride and VA-12 joined the effort.[20] Certainly, the campaign contributed to North Vietnam's unwillingness to launch a major offensive against the South until 1972, but it did not prevent the People's Army of North Vietnam from fighting a stubborn and bloody war of attrition during the intervening years. Most notably, in March 1971, the North Vietnamese Army amassed 40,000 troops, including two tank regiments, to beat back an Army of the Republic of Vietnam (ARVN) invasion of Laos, code-named "Lam Son 719."[21] Expressing some of the same concerns over the effort that Admiral Sharp had voiced many years earlier, Air Force Chief of Staff Michael Ryan lamented that "however great the toll in vehicles on the trail, trucks parked on docks at Haiphong or some other North Vietnamese port presented an easier target than those skittering underneath a jungle canopy."[22]

THE FIRST LINE TOUR: 11 APRIL TO 1 MAY

At long last, the *Shang* arrived on station, and McBride could begin the job he set sail to accomplish: flying strike missions in support of America's air war in Southeast Asia.[23] During April, Task Force 77, the Navy's carrier battle group off the coast of North Vietnam, devoted almost its entire strike effort to Laos: 3,312 out of a total of 3,528 strike sorties. Twenty-three percent of these runs targeted truck parks; 35 percent, vehicles; 12 percent, defenses; 21 percent, roads; and 9 percent, "other." A-6s continued to support Commando Bolt, flying 322 full systems runs and 28 airborne moving target indicator strikes.

The situation did not change much late in the month with the onset of President Nixon's invasion of Cambodia. Beginning on 29 April, 50,000 ARVN and 30,000 U.S. troops initiated a series of operations designed to dislodge NVA and Viet Cong troops operating out of base areas just over the border in Cambodia. Air Force B-52s and tactical fighters provided most of the support for this operation, while Navy planes concentrated most of their efforts in Laos. By May, the Navy was flying over half of all U.S. strike sorties flown in the Steel Tiger area, with most of this effort concentrated on the Ban Raving Pass and the tri-border area of Laos, Cambodia, and South Vietnam.[24]

Jim's first mission was a four-plane strike into the Steel Tiger on 11 April. Before he launched, UH-2B Sea Sprite helicopters from Combat Helicopter Squadron 2 took to the air and hovered at low altitude near the ship in case Jim's plane failed and he had to bail out. Next came the E-1B Willy Fudds, which would fly fifty miles ahead of the carrier, scanning the skies for hostile MiG activity, ready to vector fighters to any potentially hostile contact. During flight operations, two F-8 fighters flew on combat air patrol (CAP) to protect the carrier from MiGs while another two flew farther out on barrier combat air patrol (BARCAP) to protect the entire surface group. Last but certainly not least came the A-4 strike aircraft from the *Shang*'s three attack squadrons, VA-12, VA-152, and VA-172. In essence, the carrier and all its accompanying ships and aircraft existed to support this small offensive arm.

The *Shang* possessed two steam catapults for launching aircraft, both forward on the bow. Sailors referred to as "green shirts" ran these catapults. "Yellow shirts" controlled all movement on the flight deck and the hanger deck below it. "Brown shirts," the plane captains, conducted the final maintenance checks of aircraft. "Red shirts" armed the planes with bombs and handled all ordnance on the deck, and "purple shirts" fueled aircraft. "Many of these guys on the flight deck were real pros with years of experience," wrote McBride. They had to be. The whole process of preparing a plane for battle and launching it from the carrier is often compared to a carefully choreographed ballet. Everyone involved must know their job intimately and understand where it fits into the general process or disaster can result. Just prior to McBride's launch, the jet blast from an F-8 blew a plane captain overboard. Immediately, a helicopter swooped over and plucked the stunned but uninjured man from the water. After examining him for injuries, a flight surgeon told him to take the day off. The man protested, and the surgeon allowed him to continue his critical work on the flight deck.

Because the *Shang*'s old boilers could barely produce the twenty knots of wind required for a successful takeoff of a fully armed A-4, each plane in Jim's flight carried only three rather than the usual four 500-pound bombs that day. Red shirts removed the bomb safety pins, which prevent an explosion in the event of an accidental drop, just before McBride's plane eased into the catapult track. "The three cat officers on the *Shang* are our best friends, especially at this point. All are experienced aviators, serving a tour of duty in the ship's company. We like to think they have a special love and concern for us," McBride often reminded himself during this anxious period. The cat officer checked the catapult gauges to make sure the *Shang*'s boiler was producing enough steam to get McBride's bomb-laden A-4 into the air. He then signaled McBride to power up the engine by waving two fingers in the air. McBride responded by easing his throttle forward to full power with his left hand. On this day, the plane came to life normally. McBride snapped a salute to the officer to signal his readiness to be launched. Almost before he could regain control of the stick with his right hand, the cat officer faced forward, kneeled to the flight deck, and brought his right arm forward in imitation of a fencer's jab. In the catwalk, a sailor then mashed the firing button, propelling McBride and his aircraft down the 150-foot track and into the air. "Geronimo," McBride yelled halfheartedly as his plane careened forward. "My Geronimo yell, which

I always shout as my body is propelled down the cat, was a little restrained that morning because my plane did not spring into the air but had a slow, steady climb out."

The flight used the Navy corridor just below the DMZ to enter into Laos. McBride looked down and savored the view briefly before pulling his attention back to the war: 18,000 feet below him were the rich green jungles of Vietnam set in sharp relief by the blue water of the Gulf of Tonkin. By the time the flight crossed the beach, the planes were spread out in a combat formation, with each aircraft 200 feet away from the others, scanning the skies for hostile MiGs. Once over Laos, the lead plane, flown by Jim's roommate Ray Lodge, made contact with an Air Force forward air controller in an O-1E Bird Dog, a small, propeller-driven, high-wing plane with a maximum speed of 150 miles per hour.[25]

The FAC informed the flight that there was a suspected truck storage area below him and that he would mark it with a white phosphorus "Willy Pete" rocket. A white or yellow waxy solid, white phosphorus, when it reacts with oxygen, produces large amounts of smoke and toxic garliclike fumes.[26] Air Force FACs used white phosphorus throughout the war to mark targets during daylight hours. Because visibility was good on that day, Ray spotted the smoke immediately and then led the flight along a ridgeline coming in toward the target from the north. Lodge pickled his bombs off first. McBride then made a run 40 degrees from his flight path so as not to present a good target for any antiaircraft gunner below.

> I rolled the plane over on its left wing 90 degrees, pointed the nose to a 45-degree angle of dive, and aimed the green circle of the bombing sight slightly down from below where Ray's bombs had hit. With a 45-degree dive angle set, 450 knots of airspeed building, and my altimeter unwinding like crazy, my scan went rapidly between the bombsight and flight instruments. At approximately the desired 7,000 feet of altitude, I pressed the bomb release button on the control stick and felt my load of destruction come off the aircraft. Instantaneously, I pulled back on the stick to get the desired 4g's of forced effort to climb quickly out of danger. When I looked over my shoulder at the target, I could see where the bombs had hit and exploded. My head went quickly back into the cockpit to check my instruments and then outside again to scan for Ray's aircraft.

As squadron policy dictated, Ray dropped all his ordnance on the first pass to minimize his exposure over hostile terrain.

Once all the A-4s had made their runs, the FAC orbited the target and inspected the results. Much to their pleasure, he reported seeing secondary fires, a good indication that the team had indeed hit some trucks. "It felt good coming back to the *Shang*," Jim wrote in his diary that evening. "We reached our target, scored good hits, and found our way back to the ship with plenty of time to spare." The entire mission from start to finish lasted only 1.6 hours. McBride remained in his flight suit after the mission because the squadron had scheduled him to fly another hop that day. Fortunately, the squadron canceled the mission because it had only one flight-ready plane available that evening; the rest of the squadron's old aircraft were down for maintenance.

Maintenance problems often proved as relentless as enemy antiaircraft gunners along the trail for the men of VA-12. "Our aircraft are old," McBride wrote on 18 April, "parts often are hard to come by, and our maintenance crews are working long, hard hours under tough conditions. We were hoping to make a 60-mission day but have come up short each time. The other day, for example, we only completed 39 of the 60 scheduled missions."

Given the age of the A-4Cs, the situation failed to change much during the duration of the cruise. One day during his second line tour, McBride again expressed exasperation over maintenance issues. "It was a frustrating day for me with no flying. I got started twice but never launched because maintenance problems required me to down both aircraft. On the first launch I lost my radio while taxiing forward. On the second go my tail hook would not come down during the pre-launch checks. So it was one of those days and we all have them."

Maintenance-related problems were not limited to aircraft but occasionally manifested themselves in the machinery of the carrier itself. On 30 April, an F-8 Crusader made a "cold cat shot" on the port catapult. A terrifying experience for the pilot, a cold cat occurs when the catapult fails to produce enough power to successfully launch an aircraft. In the case of the F-8, when the pilot realized he was not accelerating properly down the deck, he pulled the ejection handle, and an explosive charge literally blew his seat out of the aircraft just as the plane hit the water. The seat then separated from him, his parachute inflated, and he swung a couple of times and then landed on the flight deck—a lucky man to say the least. "That is the fourth aircraft loss for the *Shang* just two months into the deployment," McBride ruminated. "At this rate, we could be out of aircraft by October."

In addition to causing maintenance problems, old technology also could affect mission performance. While some of their Air Force colleagues began scoring spectacular successes in the 1970s against hard-to-hit targets such as antiaircraft artillery (AAA) sites with new laser-guided bombs, A-4C pilots continued to be frustrated with the poor accuracy of their dumb bombs (in contrast to laser-guided munitions, dumb bombs cannot be directed after they are released by the pilot). McBride's personal experiences confirmed these findings. On 23 April, he dropped his bombs 50 meters (164 feet) short of the intended target. The next day his bombs again fell short. As he observed, "Perhaps the FAC pilot better tell me to aim at a spot about 50 meters ahead of where he wants." On 28 April, due to a "misunderstanding" between him and a ground controller, he dropped his bombs sixty seconds early during a radar-directed bombing run. The controller "said it was OK, even if we did not get near the target since it was all enemy territory. Strange way to fight a war, but then again, we have been over here in 'Nam dropping bombs for the last seven years. Somebody must know what we are doing."[27] Clearly, the A-4 did not represent the best platform with which to attack small targets such as trucks and bicycles in the dense jungles of Laos.

Still, the little plane could perform wonders when flown by a skilled pilot. On 23 May, McBride managed to place his bombs within five meters of a rail junction—good hits but still not accurate enough to completely cut the track. Four days later, his wingman, Dick Tolotti, got a medium secondary explosion "which the FAC said looked like a truck." In short, the supreme skill of Navy pilots often compensated for the antiquated nature of their technology. Frederick Nyc, an Air Force forward air controller during Commando Hunt in 1969, claims that Navy A-4 pilots were "always welcome. It seemed to us that they tried just a little bit harder. A-4s were among the very few aircraft that used the winds that our navigator figured by using the Doppler radar. For whatever reason, the A-4s dropped bombs more accurately than other fast movers did."[28]

Although bombing accuracy problems inherent in old technology frequently could be overcome by a skillful pilot, poor weather often proved to be a tougher foe for a plane not equipped with special all-weather navigation equipment. The southwest monsoon brings heavy cloud cover and ample rainfall over the Gulf of Tonkin during April and then shifts west of the mountains to Laos in May. This transition period between northeast and southwest monsoons brings the warmest temperatures of the year to Southeast Asia. High temperature and high relative humidity produce a sweltering environment, especially in the jungles of Vietnam. Small streams dry up, plants lose their leaves, and unpaved roads become dust bowls. A smoky haze, from mountain tribes burning off new farm plots, covers the mountainous areas of Vietnam, while lower areas become enshrouded with fog called "crachin," caused by the clash of cold water from the South China Sea and warm westerly winds. This layer of fog, light rain, and drizzle can be 5,000 feet thick and extend 100 miles into the Gulf of Tonkin.[29]

For McBride's squadron, the crachin forced the operations officer to cancel most flights on 21 April and divert those launched to Danang for recovery. For those on duty, days like that grated on the nerves. "I spent most of the night and morning in the ready room waiting to fly and listening to all the stories of those who did fly," wrote McBride. "Dick Tolotti, the landing signal officer [LSO], confirmed that the weather around the ship was miserable. 'It was not fit for man nor beast,' he declared from under his foul weather gear." Navy sortie rates actually declined in April by 476 from the previous month, primarily due to weather.[30] McBride flew only 14 strike missions during that month, and many other pilots in the squadron flew even fewer.

McBride felt bitter and cranky as the *Shang* left the Gulf of Tonkin after its first line tour. "If the *Shang* were truly a trim fighting carrier one might take pride in the thought of returning again and really being a contributing force to the war effort," he ruminated on 2 May. "This line period rather shows the carrier to be an old ship barely managing to meet her combat commitments."

3

Life on and off the Line

LIBERTY AND A SECOND LINE TOUR

McBride's second liberty at Subic was quieter and less boisterous than the first. As he recalled:

> Most of the officers from the air wing wound up at the Cubi O Club this evening. I thought that the returning combat aviators were rather subdued and peaceful. The base officers would have felt comfortable bringing their wives to the club this evening. It is hard to say why the group of aviators was so quiet. Maybe most were silently reflecting on their last stay in these friendly spaces of good food and drink following our transit. At the time we were a bit nervous and a little apprehensive about going into combat. Now combat does not seem to be scary or threatening. Our first line period was more an effort to meet our scheduled missions, adjust to the daily routine of operational combat flying and live with the many problems of the old *Shang*.[1]

Liberty ended on 11 May, and the *Shang* got under way at 0855. The temperature in McBride's quarters hit 94 degrees that day, and water shortages compelled the engineering department to cut off all water for VA-12's showers and toilets until more could be taken in during an underway replenishment. In his diary entry of 12 May, McBride pondered the stark contrast between the relative luxuries of liberty and the austerity of shipboard life:

> The one day transit from the Philippines to Yankee Station might be considered a time of adjustment to a different world. One day it is shore leave in a civilized environment and then the next day back to preparing for carrier combat operations: no more sandy beaches, green jungles, or endless activities ashore. It now boils down to our aircraft carrier and the sea everywhere one looks.

McBride did not have to wait long. The next day he flew a day mission over eastern Laos: "We dropped our bombs on a suspected truck stop and storage area. We were told our bombs successfully cut a road. I did not see the road as I released my ordnance on the FAC's smoke." On 14 May, maintenance problems with McBride's aircraft kept him out of the air, but on the fifteenth he again bombed another truck staging area, this time under the direction of Nail 56, another Nakhon Phanom–based Air Force FAC. Weather, a bad cold, and aircraft availability problems kept McBride on the ground until 19 May. "As seen so far during this deployment, our aircraft availability, weather conditions and problems on the *Shang* have changed these ideal launch and recovery operations considerably. The last launch is often cancelled for these reasons. Bad weather conditions can screw up the whole evolution of flight operations."

McBride finally got a training hop with a Willy Fudd E-1B on 19 May. He suspected that bomb shortages or poor weather over the target area compelled the CAG to begin scheduling training missions rather than combat runs. By May, the crachin had all but disappeared from the Gulf of Tonkin with the commencement of the southwest monsoon, but weather in the highlands and in Laos began to deteriorate with the onset of the rainy season. As a result, the members of VA-12 began to rely more and more on radar-directed bombing, code-named "Combat Skyspot," through clouds as opposed to visual dive bombing.[2]

McBride flew a Skyspot mission on 20 May and then another on 21 May. Although these missions exposed him to much less ground fire than standard FAC-directed runs, they often proved less satisfying and more frustrating. On 21 May, Jim's Skyspot controller failed to pick up McBride's Identification Friend or Foe (IFF) beacon, making it virtually impossible to plot his plane on the scope. The controller finally directed McBride and his wingman, Lieutenant (jg) Denny Flynn, to drop their loads over a suspected enemy position in South Vietnam. As McBride recalled, "Down our string of Mark 82s fell through the clouds to explode somewhere below." On 25 May, the weather improved enough for McBride to hit a target in Laos under the direction of a FAC. As he came off his run, he noticed "red tracer rounds left to right ahead of his aircraft." McBride felt they could have been 23-mm, but he had no idea where they came from. Along the trail, 23- and 37-mm guns were the most common antiaircraft artillery, although higher caliber weapons ranging from 57- to 100-mm occasionally made an appearance—especially after 1970.[3] Because the more prevalent 23-mm gun depended on a gunner visually spotting fast-flying American aircraft and was effective only at ranges under 6,600 feet, American jet losses in Laos did not tend to be great. From November 1969 to April 1970, the Navy lost only four A-4s, four A-6s, and three A-7s in the Steel Tiger area of Laos, mostly to 37-mm guns. With respect to vulnerability, the A-4 ranked higher than the A-6 and the A-7 in terms of sorties versus hits, but interestingly enough, the tough little scooter ranked higher in survivability: the number of hits divided by the number of aircraft lost.[4]

After flying two combat hops in a row, McBride was surprised to see his name listed for tanker duty on 26 May. The A-4 refueled other aircraft via a D-704 "Buddy Store," a 300-gallon external fuel tank with a fifty-foot refueling hose reeled up inside it. A small propeller on the front of the tank powers a small hydraulic pump, which in turn powers the reel. Specialized plumbing connects the store with the A-4's internal fuel cells, allowing the fuel to be transferred from a tanker's main fuel supplies to the store and then into the receiver aircraft. Not surprisingly for the *Shang*, age ended up being a factor with its Buddy Stores, some of which were as old as the A-4Cs carrying them. Because of the abuse they sustained during carrier launches and recoveries, the tanks were usually in poor shape, and a pilot never knew whether his store was functional until he got airborne. On McBride's 26 May flight, he spent two hours circling over the *Shang* before he realized his Buddy Store had problems. Two pilots came up for practice plugs prior to recovery and reported that the Buddy Store was streaming hydraulic fluid—not a good thing because it could indicate a complete system failure. Luckily, McBride successfully retracted the hose. If he had been unable to retract it, he could have guillotined the hose, a dangerous maneuver that often leads to fires, or landed the plane with hose extended, the preferred maneuver but one that causes heavy damage to the Buddy Store. After dumping a thousand pounds of fuel to get down to proper landing weight, McBride successfully arrested and scored an "OK" on his landing.

Jim flew one more combat mission before the end of the second line tour, a truck-bombing run on Laos. His bombs fell five meters short, but his wingman, Dick Tolotti, scored a direct hit. The next evening, 28 May, the squadron assigned him to the Carrier Air Traffic Control Center to observe the controllers. On that day, the newly promoted air wing commander, Captain William Stollenwerck, struck the ramp section of the carrier while attempting a landing. The tail section of his F-8 smashed hard into the ramp, but his hook caught an arresting wire, causing the plane to come to a screeching halt. Few pilots survive such a serious accident, but Stollenwerck walked away from this one. Shaken by the event, he ultimately gave up his command. "I feel sorry for the man and am a little disappointed he is departing," McBride ruminated. "Rumor has it Captain Poorman pressured him into flying the night of the ramp strike because Stoly had limited his flying to daylight hops. Maybe Captain Stollenwerck simply had enough of the *Shang*, Captain Poorman, and the Vietnam War."

In the end, VA-12 dropped more than 900,000 pounds of ordnance on the enemy (primarily in Laos) during its first two line tours. April proved to be the busiest month, with 730 hours logged for the unit. April also marked the conclusion of Commando Hunt III. Overall, Navy planes flew more than 50 percent of all sorties for this campaign with A-4s, representing 20 percent of this Navy effort.[5] Together, Navy and Air Force pilots, with the help of the Igloo White sensor system, destroyed more than 32,000 tons of cargo and 11,000 trucks during the 1969–70 dry season in Laos. Based on these numbers, the Seventh Air Force argued that this effort greatly contributed to the North Vietnamese decision not to launch a major offensive during this period.

Still, the campaign failed to completely choke off the supply flow south. In fact, the flow actually increased during the January and February time frame, from 65 tons per day in December 1969 to 148 in February 1970. Furthermore, the cost of maintaining the sophisticated Igloo White system and attacking the targets it identified far exceeded what North Vietnam and its allies paid to replace vehicles. During Commando Hunt III, enemy gunners scored more than 310 hits on American aircraft and downed 60. A substantial enemy defense force was already in Laos at the onset of Commando Hunt III, but more were added so that by December there were twice as many gun positions along the trails than the year before. During the first phase of the campaign, the North Vietnamese even added surface-to-air missile sites along the Laotian border in North Vietnam. Despite all the increased defenses and new roads in Laos, the entire Ho Chi Minh Trail did not appear to be diverting a significant amount of North Vietnamese manpower away from the battlefield. American intelligence experts estimated that by April 1970, operating, servicing, and defending the trail required no more than 10 percent of North Vietnam's armed forces or 3 percent of the able-bodied men between fifteen and thirty-four years of age.[6]

THE THIRD LINE TOUR

A combination of poor weather over Laos and more mechanical problems on the *Shang* served to curtail the number of combat hops flown by VA-12 on the squadron's third line tour (14 June to 2 July). On night missions, in particular, the southwest monsoon often wound up being a tougher enemy than the Vietnamese.

Typical of these missions was one flown on 25 June, by McBride, who took off that dark, stormy night for a target in southern Laos. Immediately, he tried to lock on to a radio beacon to guide him and his wingman, Jack Kennerly, to the target, but he could not get a clear signal. He then switched to dead reckoning and finally found a Covey FAC circling over the target area, which even managed to find a target through the dense cloud cover. As he recorded later, "We bombed where his rockets presented a nice yellow glow. All ordnance on target but no secondary explosions. We dodged thunderstorms back for a rough radar controlled approach. The guys on the radarscopes must have been tired. I logged 2.0 hours of nighttime and 1.5 hours under instrument conditions. I was glad to be back on board."

The next evening the situation deteriorated even further. During the briefing, McBride leaned over to his wingman, Jim Wickes, and told him that given the weather, "they could not possibly launch us." Rain and clouds obscured both the target area and the Gulf of Tonkin, but the command group still felt obligated to make a small contribution to the war effort. That contribution ended up being McBride and Wickes.

After starting his engine, McBride listened to the radio, hoping and praying for an abort. Lightning filled the sky from all angles as two men removed McBride's tie-down chains in preparation for launch. As McBride recalled:

> I could barely make out the yellow night wands as a yellow shirt directed me forward past the darkened line of planes. The red blur of the island superstructure washed by my starboard wing tip. It didn't look good for a cancellation of our mission. I was wondering what the cat officer was thinking as he touched the deck with his wand and my

plane shot down the bow. The world outside my cockpit was very dark as I concentrated on maintaining the proper nose altitude for the slow climb above the invisible Gulf. The flight deck must have been anxious to get us off so they could run for some shelter from the rain. We were in the clouds and rain the entire flight. We accepted a Combat Skyspot from the surprised Quang Tri controller. Quang Tri lost track of us on two runs due to his radar gear malfunctioning so we had to abort the effort. We jettisoned our bombs through the clouds into the Gulf water. Perhaps we were able to kill a few Communist fish with our unarmed bombs in the process. We started our approach almost as soon as we got behind the carrier and close to the recovery course simply because we were the only *Shang* aircraft for the last recovery. My flying was rough coming aboard so I was not surprised to receive a fair (OK) grade. It was a safe pass and getting on deck counted tonight.

Considering all the other problems suffered by the *Shang* during her last cruise, it came as no surprise to Jim and the other "Clinchers" of VA-12 that the old ship continued to experience maintenance problems during the third line period. On 20 June, her number three evaporator went down. Milling shops at Subic manufactured new parts for the evaporator, and on 22 June John Filose of VA-12 flew to Subic Bay to pick up the parts. Just as the evaporator problem was being solved, the ship's liquid oxygen plant broke down, forcing the ship to borrow liquid oxygen from "any available source" until the machine could be repaired. The *Shang* finally gave out for good on 2 July, when a coupling on the number one shaft sheared off. Divers sent down to investigate reported that the number one screw was not turning, compelling the ship to cease operations in the Gulf of Tonkin and head for Japan for repairs.[7]

LEAVE

For the men of VA-12, repairs for the *Shang* meant they would now have some time off from the war. Based on available R&R flights, Jim decided to spend his leave with his family in San Diego. McBride, his wife, Gabrielle, and his three children aged four, six, and ten stayed in a rented a two-bedroom apartment for twelve days in the seashore village of La Jolla just north of San Diego—a community in which McBride felt comfortable. "We noticed many beautiful homes as we walked around the village," he noted later. "There must be an unwritten but understood code which says, 'no hippies allowed.'" The McBride family spent most of their time lounging on the beach, visiting local sites, and enjoying such mundane activities as shopping for groceries at the base exchange and eating breakfast at a local pancake house. "We do not talk about Vietnam, the ship, the squadron or my return. Our time is too precious to spoil with talk of the real world. We wanted to enjoy our time together and not allow anything to get in the way of being a family again. Returning to our La Jolla lodgings we must have looked like a typical, suntanned California family enjoying paradise."

But the reality of McBride's situation eventually revealed itself in the mood and feelings of his wife. On the last night of the vacation, she rested in his arms on the couch for a long time before they went to bed. "She said she sensed I was anxious to get back to my squadron. I told her I would rather be going back home with them. Her remark expressed her sadness towards our separation. She would be alone for another five months." The next day, the family headed for Lindbergh Airport to go their separate ways. "We had time before my loved ones departed on a National Airline flight at 0800. Tears were held in check as we exchanged hugs and kisses. We had a fabulous time of togetherness in San Diego. Now it is a matter of surviving until my return. I helped my family board the aircraft and watched it climb into the clear blue sky. It was my turn to prepare for my flight in the opposite direction."

FOURTH LINE TOUR

Returning to the squadron and his daily flying routine helped Jim to quickly get over any homesickness experienced upon leaving his family. On his first mission of the tour, he scored a 100 percent hit on an interdiction point in Laos. In general, McBride's accuracy began to show strong signs of improvement during this line period. As an experienced veteran now, he was less nervous in combat zones, enabling him to be more effective on bombing runs. On 12 August, Ray Lodge and McBride hit a suspected truck park a few miles south of Tchepone and received a rare compliment from Nail 41. "You guys are really uncanny," Nail 41 radioed as he gave a bomb damage assessment of 100 percent on target. A short time later, McBride and Lodge received letters of commendation from the 23d Tactical Air Support Squadron. Based on that letter, the two men later received Navy Commendation Medals with Combat V devices for that mission. "I often wonder if this medal for our great bombing," McBride bashfully thought during the awards ceremony, "made up for all the bombs I tossed all around the target area on a number of less noteworthy missions."

Three days after the Nail 41 episode, McBride celebrated the tenth anniversary of his enlistment in the Navy. "Ten years ago today I entered the Navy's Officer Candidate School at Newport, Rhode Island, to fulfill my military obligation. Little did I know I would go to flight training, receive my wings and wind up making the Navy a career. Although I have many doubts about the Vietnam War, I would do it all over again. We have been in this conflict for over six years without an end in sight."

Although McBride loved to fly and loved being a member of VA-12, the daily routine of flying combat missions in a seemingly endless war often grated on him. He especially found the *Shang*'s perpetual state of disrepair to be discouraging. Even with all the repairs completed to the ship during its recent in-port stay in Japan, water shortages still existed on board. Nothing dampened his spirits more than returning from a hot and sweaty mission, getting undressed, and stepping into the shower room only to discover that the water had been shut down. Near the end of tour, Jim's annoyance over the pathetic state of affairs on the once mighty *Shangri-La* finally began to get this ordinarily optimistic officer down: "It could be the lack of sleep, decent drinking water or the need for a hot shower. We were late for chow, the meal was served on paper plates and there wasn't any ice. Back in the senior officer's bunkroom, feeling sorry for myself, I finished the last can of beer. A wretched day should qualify as a special occasion for a beer. Nothing like pure rationalization to avoid the truth of a blue mood. I will toss the can over the catwalk after dark. The beer solved some of my depression as I felt better." So, too, did a patch made up by one of his squadron mates to poke fun at the situation. The patch, called CASREP 70, featured a lightning bolt striking the *Shangri-La* with a list of many of the ship's major ailments in bold type around its edges. The fourth line period ended on 17 August, and McBride once again found himself on a brief liberty in the Philippines.

4

The War over Laos Continues

McBride's Final Line Tours

For the men of VA-12, their last two line periods very much resembled their earlier sojourns. Jim McBride and company flew more missions into Laos in support of Commando Hunt, and after each they wondered to what extent their small efforts were helping America win the Vietnam War. After one mission on 11 September, McBride lamented:

> Each pilot was more concerned about running into another aircraft than making a smooth ordnance run. The result was bombs tossed all over the place with a few landing near the target. I could sense the feeling of frustration in the voice of Nail 31 as he called our hits. The generous guy gave BDA [bomb damage assessment] as 50 percent on target. Maybe the guy was satisfied to have 25 bombs explode near the target. I hope our flying circus and terrible bombing exhibition did not cause the FAC to lose faith in Navy attack pilots.

After a strafing run during the next line tour, Jim again pondered his accomplishments. "The FAC gave us damage assessment for all bombs 100 percent within 30 meters of the target. He followed this with a body count of five. How he came up with this figure I have no idea. Since we had two aircraft on the mission the air intelligence officer marked down a two and a half body count for each pilot. I am too far along in this war to argue the point, as silly as it sounds."

Maintenance problems, as usual, also continued to plague the unit. On 22 September, Lieutenant Jack Hartman successfully ejected during the second cold catapult shot of the cruise. In reaction to the episode,

Fleet Air, Western Pacific grounded all A-4Cs on the *Shang* from 24 to 28 September, sharply reducing the combat effectiveness of the ship. Several aircraft immediately flew to Japan to be inspected for problems. Given that the mishap occurred so near the end of the cruise, Ray Lodge and several others in the unit questioned the efficacy of a major repair effort for the A-4Cs. "Wouldn't it be economically wiser," these men reasoned, "to send the *Shang* home and the A-4Cs to the scrap yard?" NBC's *Today Show* suggested that the ship might come home early, causing spirits to rise among the wives in Jacksonville.

The Navy, however, had other plans and pressed ahead with the repair effort, compelling the unit to embark on one last fifteen-day line tour. Jim flew his seventieth and final mission of the Vietnam War on 5 November. As McBride recorded, "There were a number of parties in the air wing officers' staterooms this evening. We had champagne in the senior officer's bunkroom, the first time for the bubbly." The men were excited to finally be heading home after a long, often frustrating cruise. As soon as the ship reached Subic Bay, Jim informed his wife of the situation. "Gabrielle sounds as happy as I remember at any time during the long cruise. I felt a glow myself as I wandered over to the club for dinner."[1]

THE *SHANG* LEAVES THE LINE, BUT COMMANDO HUNT CONTINUES

As happy as the men were to be heading home, few believed their bombing efforts actually amounted to much in the grand scheme of things. The final operational briefing, given by Lieutenant (jg) Trux Simmons, was appropriately entitled "How We Won the War (Almost)." The title was meant to be humorous, but there was a surprising amount of truth in it, not just with respect to the mission flown by VA-12 but for the entire Commando Hunt series of campaigns.

During much of VA-12's period on the line, naval activity over Laos actually declined while the enemy logistics system just got better and better. By the end of Commando Hunt IV (May through September 1970), U.S. tactical air activity had diminished to an average of 417 sorties per day for the third quarter of 1970; the corresponding figure for the previous wet season had been 780. Poor weather and a lack of targets contributed to this decline, but it was caused primarily by cutbacks ordered by the Joint Chiefs of Staff. During fiscal year 1971 (July 1970–June 1971), the JCS authorized only 14,000 fighter-attack sorties per month in Southeast Asia: 10,000 Air Force, 2,700 Navy, and 1,300 Marine.[2] These reductions caused carrier activity to decline to its lowest levels of the war up to this point. In November, the Seventh Fleet reduced its carrier presence in the gulf from four to three.[3]

The sharp decline in U.S. air activity spurred the Vietnamese into a massive road construction effort. Bypasses were built around areas hit hard during Commando Hunt III. The Vietnamese also built new roads, bridges, and transshipment points in North Vietnam proper. One truck park in Haiphong held over 1,200 vehicles, and eight others in the Hanoi-Haiphong area held 5,000 more.[4] Battalion-sized convoys of 40 to 60 trucks would move from these areas down the system of roads in Laos. Area bosses, relying on the latest information on which routes were open, directed these convoys through numerous bypasses and subsegments, switching routes at the last possible moment. From an airplane, all an observer could see of this complex system were the main roads, but by standing on a road, one could see many small bypass roads leading into the jungle and back to the main road.

With this new road network in place, Seventh Air Force planners concluded that the North Vietnamese would launch a major resupply effort for their forces in the Republic of Vietnam during the next dry season, thus setting the stage for Commando Hunt V. While VA-12 flew only a few missions between 10 October 1970 and 30 April 1971, the Navy as a whole would continue to provide massive support for air interdiction in Laos until the end of the war.

Commando Hunt V focused on similar types of targets as had earlier campaigns—trucks, roads, transshipment points, supply dumps, and repair facilities. The plan allocated 70 percent of the 14,000 authorized tactical air sorties per month to the Steel Tiger area, and the majority of AC-130 and AC-119 gunship sorties.[5] This massive investment of air power caused traffic in the Steel Tiger area to come to a virtual standstill during the day. At night, the gunships came out to hammer the convoys on the move, claiming over 12,000 vehicles destroyed—60 percent of the 20,000 vehicles bombed during the campaign. All told, Seventh Air Force planners claimed that Commando Hunt V forces prevented 89 percent of all material entering Laos from arriving in South Vietnam, and reduced the enemy's throughput of supplies to about one third of the previous dry season.[6]

But impressive statistics alone fail to tell the whole story of the campaign. As some of McBride's experiences with FAC pilots confirm, these men often fudged details to give pilots better kill scores than they deserved. "It was very difficult," recalled General William Momyer, the Seventh Air Force commanding officer, "to reach a good basis for assessment of damage to the enemy truck inventory, especially when claims were exceeding the total truck inventory by a factor of two at times."[7] During the course of four dry season Commando Hunt campaigns, Air Force planners claimed that U.S. forces destroyed 46,000 North Vietnamese trucks. However, the Vietnamese imported only 24,000 trucks during this same period. Tests conducted in the United States showed that trucks hit by munitions are rarely destroyed unless they burn. Conceivably, the Vietnamese were repairing many of the trucks in their trailside repair facilities—a factor that could explain this disparity between U.S. kill claims and the total number of North Vietnamese truck imports.[8]

In addition to containing questionable kill statistics, in its final conclusions the Seventh Air Force's report on Commando Hunt V glosses over the Lam Son 719 disaster. If interdiction was so successful, how were the Vietnamese able to defeat a major South Vietnamese invasion into Laos in 1971? As the ground component of Commando Hunt V, Lam Som 719 was designed to reduce supplies flowing through Laos by capturing the primary transshipment hub, Tchepone, and severing the country in two. Fifteen thousand South Vietnamese troops invaded Laos on 8 February 1971, building fire support bases along their invasion corridor to provide security for the sustained offensive. The North Vietnamese Army quickly reacted to the invasion, bringing five divisions into the area along with heavy 122- and 130-mm artillery and tanks. The North Vietnamese Army reaction force ultimately stopped the invasion dead in its tracks about twelve miles into Laos during the third week of the operation. American advisers urged the South Vietnamese commander, General Hoang Xuan Lam, to commit more troops to the operation and attempt to draw the North Vietnamese into a major battle; never again, they argued, would South Vietnam have so much air power at its disposal. Lam, fearing excessive casualties, opted instead for a token helicopter assault against Tchepone, followed by a general ARVN withdrawal from Laos. In the end, only about half of the original invading force made it out of Laos during a chaotic retreat. NVA troops ultimately killed 45 percent of the 15,000-man invading force in one of the worst disasters ever to befall upon ARVN. What is more, the entire campaign had almost no effect on the logistics flow southward. After the ARVN withdrawal, sensors actually detected more southbound traffic on the trail than before the campaign.

Despite mounting evidence that Commando Hunt was not dramatically reducing the military capability of Communist forces in South Vietnam, planners in Washington continued to be more impressed by the statistics of the campaign than by its actual results. Late in the Commando Hunt V campaign, President Nixon met with his top military advisers in San Clemente, California, to discuss interdiction in Laos. The group, whose membership included representatives from the services, the State and Defense Departments, the National Security Council (NSC), and the CIA, concluded in April 1971 that Commando Hunt was indeed successfully stemming the flow of supplies to South Vietnam and, in so doing, helping to protect Vietnamization (his program to turn over the defense of South Vietnam to the Vietnamese) and the ongoing withdrawal of U.S. forces from South Vietnam. The group, therefore, recommended that the effort continue.[9]

The last dry season interdiction effort in southern Laos was Commando Hunt VII, a slightly smaller campaign than Commando Hunt V in terms of sorties flown but more sophisticated than any of its predecessors in terms of tactics and technology. For this campaign, the Defense Department allotted the Seventh Air Force just 10,000 fighter and attack sorties per month and 700 gunship sorties—a decrease of 4,300 from Commando Hunt V. Phase I of the plan called for B-52s to bomb the three main mountain passes into Laos (Mu Gia, Ban Raving, and Ban Karai). Sensors would then be placed in those passes to detect repair efforts, which would be bombed immediately by fighters. Phase II called for blocking belts of mines to be sown across crucial supply routes. Presumably the mining would result in more lucrative targets as traffic was backed up and forced to travel over longer routes. Finally, Phase III would destroy with more B-52 and fighter raids what few supplies managed to get through Laos at the major entrance gates to South Vietnam.

During Phase I, B-52s and tactical fighters dropped 14,000 five-hundred-pound bombs and 17,100 seven-hundred-fifty-pound bombs primarily on the Mu Gia and Ban Karai passes. This bombing did little to affect the flow of traffic into Laos. After so many years of bombing, these passes no longer contained any vegetation. Bypasses could easily be constructed in this treeless environment, and craters in roads could be quickly filled with soil from other craters. Lack of vegetation also meant that these roads dried more quickly after a rain than those covered with tropical flora.

Phase II involved the creation of three blocking belts: one each near Tchepone, Ban Bak, and Chavane. To thwart trucking, Navy A-7s seeded the belts with Mk-36 magnetic-influence mines. F-4s, in turn, deposited wide-area antipersonnel mines and gravel mines to protect the Mk-36s. The minefields closed some blocking points for as long as forty-one days, but failed to have much of an effect on others. The North Vietnamese could clear belts of antipersonnel mines by using rocks attached to strings, and Mk-36s could be defused by hand.

For Phases I and II, enemy air defenses proved much more potent a threat than in earlier campaigns. During Commando Hunt VII, antiaircraft fire actually increased from 345 guns to 545. The North Vietnamese also brought eight SAM battalions into Steel Tiger, which effectively put an end to B-52 attacks against the Mu Gia and Ban Karai passes in December 1971. Antiaircraft fire did the same for the AC-119s, and by the end of the campaign, even the more capable AC-130s could not be flown in much of the Steel Tiger area. The Seventh Air Force flew a total of 4,066 sorties against antiaircraft sites, a figure nearly equal to the 4,209 sorties flown against trucks.[10]

The Vietnamese also began interfering with the sensor strings. They eventually discovered that aircraft dropping sensors dived differently than those on bombing missions. With this information, they began plotting and neutralizing various strings. They also learned to thwart airborne sensors such as Black Crow by shielding ignition systems with aluminum foil and covering engines with mats of banana and bamboo leaves to insulate hot spots from infrared sensors.

The third phase of the campaign never fully got off the ground. On 31 March 1972 the North Vietnamese Army launched a massive spring offensive into South Vietnam—a move that caused the Seventh Air Force to abruptly terminate Commando Hunt and divert all available air assets to thwarting this offensive.

In pure numerical terms, Commando Hunt VII, like most of its predecessors, appeared to be a stunning success. The Seventh Air Force claimed 4,727 trucks destroyed—not nearly as many as the 11,009 claimed to have been destroyed in Commando Hunt V, but still enough to prevent 84 percent of the 30,947 tons of supplies entering Laos from reaching the Communist forces in South Vietnam. However, with the mere 5,024 tons of supplies that did make it south, along with supplies stockpiled during the earlier Commando Hunt campaigns, the North Vietnamese were still able to launch their Easter Offensive, a campaign that nearly brought the Republic of Vietnam to its knees.

NET ASSESSMENT

At almost every point in each Commando Hunt campaign, the North Vietnamese managed to thwart even the most sophisticated American technology. New roads were created to bypass choke points and blocking points, sappers defused mines as well as sensors, and strategically important mountain passes were protected with antiaircraft guns and SAMs. Once over the mountains, the North Vietnamese moved supplies along a 12,000-mile maze of roads only barely understood by American intelligence officers. Blocking belts only served to slow down traffic, not stop it, because so many bypasses existed in the jungles and forests of the Laotian panhandle. By the end of Commando Hunt VII, the Vietnamese could also move supplies at night with near impunity because enemy air defenses had driven the American gunships from most vital areas of the Steel Tiger network.

Although ultimate responsibility for the failure of Commando Hunt rests primarily with the Seventh Air Force, the organization that planned and ran the effort, the Navy cannot be completely exonerated from responsibility for this tremendous waste of American resources. Navy aircraft flew more than 10,000 sorties for Commando Hunt VII alone and many more sorties during earlier campaigns. Navy mining and acoustic technology was widely employed in Commando Hunt, and Navy aircraft deployed much of this technology.

Despite the Navy's heavy involvement in the campaign, Admiral Sharp and others in the Navy hierarchy very much opposed interdiction in Laos in favor of a more concentrated mining effort designed to close all of North Vietnam's major ports. Once mining was rejected, however, the Navy agreed to bear its share of the Laotian burden: Laos, after all, was the only game in town between 1968 and 1972, and the

Navy needed to participate to justify the massive investment of resources deployed in the Gulf of Tonkin.

For the men of *Shangri La* and other carriers involved, operations in Laos proved to be some of the most frustrating of the war. Unlike close air support missions in South Vietnam or some of the more massive raids of Rolling Thunder, Laotian missions generally offered pilots little in the way of tangible rewards such as a simple thank-you from a beleaguered ground commander or the satisfaction of seeing a bridge destroyed or a petroleum tank burning. At best, a pilot flying into Laos could hope to get a positive report from a forward air controller, but more often than not, pilots like McBride flew back to their ships wondering if their bombs actually destroyed more than a few trees or some innocent jungle fauna.

On the positive side, Commando Hunt proved much less dangerous than Rolling Thunder for A-4 pilots. The *Shangri-La* lost only one aircraft to enemy action during its entire 1970 cruise: an A-4C from Attack Squadron 172. During the Commando Hunt VII campaign, Air Force, Navy, and Marine pilots flew 43,860 sorties in Steel Tiger and lost only thirteen aircraft to antiaircraft fire and another ten to SAMs.[11] In short, what Commando Hunt lacked in the way of exciting targets, it more than made up for in the ease and safety of its missions.

No attack pilot with any self-respect, however, could take pride in flying easy missions. What Ray Lodge and some of the other more aggressive types wanted was to bomb forbidden targets in North Vietnam. When it became clear during the cruise that Nixon did not intend to lift the bombing restrictions, some were only too anxious to end their futile attacks into Laos and return home to their families. The Navy, as is often the case, had other ideas for these men, and the *Shang* ended up serving out its entire tour.

In addition to the Laotian missions, the men of VA-12 often expressed outrage over the deplorable mechanical condition of the *Shang*. Broken shafts, inoperative elevators, fractured launch valves, a broken oxygen plant, and a sickly evaporator reduced the operational effectiveness of the ship during 1970 and made life uncomfortable at times for crew members. "Why didn't the Navy," these men asked, "send these warriors out in a more modern deck with newer aircraft?" True, a wing composed of A-7s and A-6s rather than A-4s could have delivered two-thirds more ordnance in the same number of days on line. But would their substitution for the *Shang* have significantly improved the results of the Commando Hunt campaign? The ability of A-6s and A-7s to deliver ordnance with a high degree of accuracy at night and in bad weather certainly may have bolstered the statistical results of the campaign, but it is doubtful that these aircraft would have reduced the combat effectiveness of North Vietnamese Army and Viet Cong forces enough to prevent the Lam Som 719 fiasco or the Easter Offensive. In 1970, the Navy could ill afford to depreciate its most valuable assets on a campaign that many of its leaders believed would ultimately end in failure. On the other hand, the service was under orders to provide sorties for the campaign. By sending the *Shang* to Southeast Asia, the Navy leadership managed to meet its obligations with one of its least capable platforms.

Sending an East Coast carrier also provided some measure of relief for Navy fliers in the Western Pacific, a community that bore the brunt of combat for most of the Vietnam War, and a rare opportunity for men stationed in the East to fly combat in Southeast Asia. Sure, many grumbled about the *Shang* and its A-4Cs, but like McBride, most privately took great pride in the seventy or so missions they flew during the war.

THE *SHANG* RETURNS HOME

The long period of separation for most *Shang* families finally came to an end on 17 December 1970, but many members of the air wing flew home as part of an advance party returning to Cecil Field, Florida, on 9 November, just days after the final line tour ended. McBride and some others did not receive this "magic carpet" treatment and would not see their families for another month. McBride spent much of the long cruise home doing paperwork and preparing for the squadron to move out of its temporary floating home. The time provided him with an opportunity, increasingly rare in modern war, to transition slowly from war to peace.

After brief stops in Australia, New Zealand, and Brazil, the *Shang* finally steamed into Mayport on 17 December 1970. McBride and other members of the air wing still on the carrier flew home one day early. As McBride recorded, "A Navy band was playing when we came down from our cockpits and walked across the ramp to the awaiting families. My full attention was directed towards my wife and children racing across the ramp towards me. I received four hugs simultaneously. 'Welcome home, sweetheart,' Gabrielle said, with tears in her eyes."

The next day, the Jacksonville paper ran a front-page story announcing the return of the carrier. McBride arrived at the pier a couple hours after the big welcome home ceremony to unpack his gear from his stateroom. It took him less than an hour to clear out of what had been his home away from home for the past nine and a half months. According to his account, "We had the opportunity to say good-bye to many of the ship's company officers whom we have known for the last year. We made one final check of the stateroom to assure we had everything removed. Joe managed to sell our infamous refrigerator to someone on the ship so we were not obliged to carry it off the carrier. We left the three keys to the stateroom on my desk and said our farewells. With this the 1970 WESTPAC deployment of the *Shang* and VA-12 was over."[12]

PART II

DOUBLE ANCHORS

The Naval Flight Officer Experience, 1968–72

IN MOST ACCOUNTS of the naval air war in Vietnam, pilots command center stage. Rarely do we get a glimpse at the naval flight officers who shared the cockpit with these men: the radar intercept officers (RIOs) who flew F-4s, the bombardier-navigators (BNs) in the A-6, or the reconnaissance attack navigators (RANs) in the A-5. However, every fleet aircraft except the F-8, A-4, and A-7 required a second man in the cockpit to accomplish its mission, and by 1970 the Navy required 4,500 NFOs to fulfill its operational goals. This number constituted 20 percent of the officers in the Navy aeronautical organization.[1]

Despite the high demand for NFOs during the war, the Navy did not provide these men with an equal opportunity to obtain command positions until very late in the conflict. Since World War II, the status of officers who served in aircraft but did not actually fly them had been ambiguous. A 1924 statute prohibited NFOs, known as observers up until 1965, from commanding a squadron, wing, carrier, or air station. As a result, many either switched career fields or left the Navy after a couple of flying assignments. To rectify the situation, the Navy eventually pushed through legislation in 1970 that enabled NFOs to command aviation units, but this bill did not eliminate all the inequalities suffered by this group.[2]

The training of NFOs, for example, remained deplorable and substandard throughout the 1960s and early 1970s. Up until 1965, the Naval Aviation Observer School at Pensacola taught "back-seaters" only academic courses in navigation; no airborne training was provided. In 1965, naval aviation observers were redesignated as naval flight officers and provided limited air navigation training in UC-45J Beechcraft and two jet familiarization flights in the T-1A Seastar, but "airmanship and other skills associated with tactical aviation received little attention."[3] Not until 1972 did the Navy offer all NFO basic trainees exposure to high-altitude, high-speed route navigation and communication in a jet aircraft specifically outfitted to train navigators in their role—the T-39 Sabreliner.

But giving NFOs better training and the opportunity to command did not erase the discrimination and scorn that these men often confronted in a squadron once they completed their undergraduate training and fleet-replacement training. The relationship between pilots and NFOs has been described as comparable to a guide dog and an ungrateful blind man. To a pilot, not controlling an aircraft was comparable to impotence, and many simply could not treat NFOs with equality no matter how professional or competent the NFOs appeared to be.

In no area of naval aviation did this situation prove more true than in the F-4 community. Accustomed to flying single-seat aircraft such as the F-8, many older fighter pilots perceived the F-4 as simply a "double-barreled F-8" and resented the very presence of a guy in the backseat. Often, they loudly proclaimed that 600 pounds of extra fuel would be more useful than having a guy in the trunk. Naturally, these same men sought to run the F-4 weapons system with as little assistance from the NFO as humanly possible. This proclivity meant favoring the AIM-9 Sidewinder, heat-seeking missile over the longer-range, radar-guided AIM-7 Sparrow for MiG engagements. In an AIM-9 attack, a pilot had to get behind his adversary, listen for a Sidewinder tone (the audible signal that indicated the missile seeker head was sensing the infrared signature of an enemy aircraft), and let the missile go. By contrast, a Sparrow attack required the pilot to wait patiently until his NFO had acquired a target with his radar and achieved a radar lock before he could fire a missile. The missile would then travel along the beam to the target, which the radar had locked on to, until it struck a target and exploded.

A radar-guided missile kill, in short, required teamwork; particularly at night, it required complex teamwork—something single-seat fighter pilots often lacked even with each other. They rarely sympathized with the NFO, hunched over his radar, trying desperately to separate a target from various forms of screen clutter, perform rapid mathematical calculations, and communicate in a high-speed, high-threat environment. In some respects, good RIO skills required more situational awareness than piloting: a pilot merely needs to be able to think ahead in time and space, whereas a good RIO not only needs to think ahead but also must translate two-dimensional data to a three-dimensional combat environment. RIOs also must be able to conquer extreme nausea and claustrophobia that one experiences in the cramped back-seat of the F-4.

Part of the reason F-4 pilots often discounted the contribution of NFOs during much of the war was the poor performance of the AIM-7 D and E model Sparrows. Overall, only eight of the Navy's fifty-four kills during the Vietnam War were made with radar-guided missiles. During the entire Rolling Thunder period, out of 330 Sparrows fired by Air Force and Navy planes, only 27 scored hits. The rest either missed or suffered some form of mechanical failure.

Because of these problems, the Navy's aviation bureaucracy praised the fighter community's single-seat mentality because it was producing better statistics than those of the Navy's rival, the Air Force. During the Rolling Thunder period, Navy single-seat F-8s scored eighteen kills during the 1967–68 period with no losses, whereas the more sophisticated F-4 had only fourteen. The Navy's reaction to the poor F-4 performance during Rolling Thunder was to create the Top Gun school at Naval Air Station (NAS) Miramar in California to teach these pilots and NFOs better dogfighting skills. Top Gun, in the end, did improve the Navy F-4 kill ratio: during Linebacker, Navy F-4s shot down twenty-four aircraft and lost only four aircraft, for a 6:1 kill ratio. However, it did so by focusing mainly on close-in engagements with the Sidewinder. Arguably, the Navy could have achieved even higher scores had it employed the new AIM-7E2 "Dogfight" Sparrow rather than the AIM-7E late in the war. The AIM-7E2 had a minimum range of 1,500 feet instead of 3,000 feet, better fusing, and better maneuvering capability than the AIM-7E. With it, the Air Force shot down thirty aircraft during Linebacker. The Navy, by comparison, downed only one plane during the same period with the older AIM-7Es.[4]

Few officers experienced the frustration of working in the F-4 community as a radar intercept officer to the extent that Lieutenant Commander James B. Souder did. A spirited man from an impoverished family, Souder spent much of his youth working to rise above his social background, graduate from college, and become a naval officer. Once in the Navy, he absolutely refused to play the part of the bottom rail. Rather than complacently accepting his fate as a "second-rate citizen" back-seater and simply "going along for the ride," Souder mastered the F-4 radar system and then struggled to convince pilots to take seriously both him and the radar missiles he controlled. Although he did not always succeed in this endeavor, his story stands out as an example of the hardships many F-4 NFOs confronted during the Vietnam War and the various ways certain individuals struggled to overcome them.

Souder triumphed over institutionally ingrained prejudice through his personality and will. Rather than accept second-class status, he continually fought for first-class treatment for NFOs, whether through subtle acts such as refusing to carry a pilot's helmet bag or through outright confrontations with recalcitrant pilot leaders over tactical matters. Some pilots, in turn, began to treat him with begrudging respect, but respect alone did not help Souder in his various MiG encounters. In his two battles with MiGs, pilot incompetence denied him an aerial victory in one instance and got him shot down in another. These engagements represent textbook examples of how many members of the Navy fighter community squandered and misused their NFOs and paid severe penalties as a consequence. The overall lesson of the NFO experience in Vietnam is not simply that two sets of eyes are better than one but that complex weapons systems often require well-developed teamwork to function successfully.

5

The Guy in the Backseat

The Odyssey of James B. Souder, NFO

JAMES B. "J. B." SOUDER came from a hardscrabble background. His father served as an enlisted man on the heavy cruiser *Salt Lake City* during World War II and then sold, engraved, and erected gravestones for a living after the war. J. B. hardly knew the man. As he recalled, "My dad was just essentially a no-count bum. He had five wives and six children and just abandoned all of them."[1]

Souder was born on 10 September 1940 in Elizabethton, a small Appalachian village in northeastern Tennessee. When J. B. was four, his father and mother divorced, and the boy went to live with his mother, who worked at the uranium processing facility in Oak Ridge, Tennessee. She subsequently moved to Florida to take a job as a sales clerk for Sears, Roebuck. During much of his childhood, Souder bounced back and forth between his grandparents' home in Tennessee and his mother's in Florida. Although his mom worked hard to support J. B. and his older sister, she did not earn enough money to raise the family on her own, so J. B.'s grandmother, Levica Anderson, cared for him during most of his childhood. Outspoken and assertive, Levica preached the virtues of listening to people with more experience and knowledge, and telling the truth. In the end, much of Souder's own outspokenness and brutal honesty harkens back to his days listening to his grandmother's lectures.

Because money was always tight, J. B. labored from the age of nine until he joined the Navy. He first worked as a newspaper delivery boy in Saint Petersburg, then, when he turned thirteen, began stocking fruit at a local market. During high school, he bagged groceries for a supermarket and mowed lawns. He also started competitive swimming at the age of twelve. Despite his hard labor and thrift, J. B. knew early on that he would never save enough money to attend college, so he became determined to earn a swimming scholarship. During the winter months he spent every morning before school practicing with the Fort Lauderdale High School swim team in an unheated outdoor saltwater pool. His perseverance earned him two 1958 Florida state high school championship titles, selection to the High School All-American Swim Team, and a swimming scholarship at the University of Florida, Gainesville.

At Gainesville, Souder went on to set a Florida pool record in his event in 1959, and again in 1960 by becoming a Southeastern Conference champion in the 200-yard breaststroke and the 400-yard medley. But swimming took its toll on him. The chlorine hurt his eyes and made it difficult for him to study late at night. He also needed to work part-time doing odd jobs in fraternities and sororities (cutting hair, delivering laundry, and serving food) to pay for food and incidental expenses. As a result, his academic marks suffered, and by his junior year, he knew he would not graduate unless drastic actions were taken. "I just kissed off the swimming and said that part of my life was over."

J. B. gave up his scholarship and transferred to Florida State University in Tallahassee to get a fresh start in academic endeavors and finish his degree. Unlike at Gainesville, where professors often devoted more energy to their individual research than to teaching, Florida State instructors "really taught." "You could go to class and listen and take notes and never open a book and make a C, so if you opened your books in addition to attending class, you could make As and Bs, and that's what I did." Souder's academic performance improved to such an extent that he managed to impress several Navy aviation recruiters with his high grades. Although he had no intention of joining the Navy, the recruiters managed to entice Souder into taking a pilot physical. They promised to pay for a trip to NAS Jacksonville, put him up in the bachelor officers' quarters (BOQ) for the weekend, give him meal tickets for the chief petty officers' mess, and pay for a free physical exam worth about $1,000. If he passed the physical, they also guaranteed him a ride in the T-34 mentor, a propeller-driven trainer with a maximum speed of 188 mph. "Yahoo," Souder enthusiastically proclaimed to them. "That's all for me."

At the physical, Souder barely passed the color vision test and admitted that he might be color-blind, but the doctors said he was only color-deficient and passed him. After his indoctrination flight in the T-34, Souder became so infected with a desire to fly Navy airplanes that he decided to go to the first preflight class he could get into after college.

The twenty-three-year-old Souder reported to Pensacola on 3 January 1963, just twelve days after his college graduation. On 17 May, he graduated from preflight and received a commission as ensign, United States Naval Reserve. That summer, he attended basic jet training at Naval Auxiliary Air Station Meridian, Mississippi. About 90 percent of the way through the jet syllabus, though, Souder began having difficulty with his vision. "I honestly didn't realize that my vision had deteriorated clinically," he recalled. "I just noticed that things looked a little blurry at night, and after all the horror stories I'd heard about night carrier landings I needed a little advice on what to do. My mistake was that I took a Marine Corps captain into my confidence, told him about the blurry night vision, and asked him what I should do. He marched me straight to the flight surgeon, and my pilot training was over."

Heartbroken and discouraged, Souder initially refused an offer to become a naval flight officer. By this point in his career he had soloed more than six times in a jet and felt he was "not dumb enough to get in the backseat and fly around behind some other idiot who didn't know that much more about flying than I did." Instead, J. B. ended up as the supervisor of classified materials shipping and receiving for the Defense Intelligence Agency in Washington, DC. At night, he would sit with his friends on the front stoop of his apartment building in Arlington, Virginia, drinking beer and watching the planes land at National Airport: "God," he mused, "I've just got this yearning to go fly, to see the world." Salvation came in the form of a second offer to become a naval flight officer. A detailer at the Bureau of Personnel, desperate for NFOs, confronted Souder one day and persuaded him to give navigator school a shot. Souder reported for NFO training in Pensacola on 3 January 1965, exactly two years from the day he first reported for preflight school.

In 1965, the sixteen-week Basic Naval Aviation Officers School (BNAO), referred to by its students as the "Banana School," had two phases: academics and flight indoctrination. The academic phase consisted of 523 hours of classroom study in basic aviation subjects such as navigation and aircraft communications. The flight phase, designed primarily to acclimate students to working conditions in the air, lasted for 20 hours and merely allowed students to practice basic navigation and radio communication skills, learn the visual and instrument flight rules, and do basic cross-country flight planning.[2] "I had a good sixteen weeks of review of aviation courses I'd had in pilot training, but I enjoyed the course, the instructors, and being back in the saddle flying." Souder also enjoyed living in a "snake ranch" on Pensacola Beach with four other guys, "having lots of weekend parties, and chasing every girl in sight."

After Pensacola, Souder traveled north to Glynco, Georgia, for advanced training in radar intercept techniques. At Glynco, officers destined to be RIOs received an additional 60 hours of flight training plus 260 hours of academic training on equipment, local flight rules, survival, jet flight planning and navigation, communications, and airborne intercept procedures.[3] Souder enjoyed Glynco but felt that the radar intercept portion of the course might have been better if students had had the opportunity to train on modern F-4 radars. Instead, the program relied on T-39s equipped with older F-8E radars. Souder finished third in his class and received his NFO wings on 8 July 1965.

He spent the next seven weeks in a legal course at Newport, Rhode Island. The course, designed to give an officer enough legal training to perform as a unit legal officer, turned out to be enjoyable for J. B. "I beat all ninety-seven of the other guys in class, including all twenty brand-new Marine Corps lawyers, in the moot-court part of the training—I still can't get over it! Those instructors told me, 'You should go to law school.' I said, 'Thank you very much, I've got too much self-respect.'"

Souder's career as an NFO commenced on his twenty-fifth birthday (10 September 1965), when he checked into Fighter Squadron 121 (VF-121) at NAS Miramar for aircrew replacement training. "Thus began the most challenging, most rewarding, most confusing, most fulfilling, most depressing, most fun . . . and the very strangest years of my life, as a radar-intercept-officer, flying in United States Navy F-4s."

During the Vietnam War, the Navy had two types of squadrons: replacement air groups, known as RAGs, and operational squadrons. RAGs, like VF-21, trained pilots for operational carrier units. It was in a RAG where pilots learned to fly new aircraft models and requalified for carrier landings after extended shore assignments in a headquarters staff or at a school. Souder flew his first F-4 familiarization flight with the RAG on 27 October 1965 and fell in love with the machine at first sight: "I thought it was a neat airplane. It had a tremendous climb capability and it was a very, very sturdy airplane and I felt good in it. You could beat the hell out of it and survive. I loved the airplane." Throughout the Vietnam War, the F-4 served as a workhorse fighter for both the Navy and the Air Force. The two-engine turbojet could achieve a max-

An overhead view of a Navy F-4B. Throughout the Vietnam War, the F-4 served as the workhorse fighter for both the Navy and the Air Force. This VF-114 Phantom is flying a combat mission over North Vietnam in March 1968. (Courtesy of Naval Historical Center)

imum level speed of 1,500 mph and a maximum cruising speed of 816 mph. Its armament consisted of four AIM-7 Sparrow semiactive radar homing air-to-air missiles in semirecessed slots in the fuselage belly, plus two to four AIM-9 Sidewinder infrared homing air-to-air missiles carried under the wings on the inboard pylons. A total offensive load of up to 16,000 pounds could be carried on the centerline and four under-wing hard points. But it was the plane's radar, not its speed or load-bearing capability, that proved the supreme technological break-through at the time. The F-4's radar could guide radar-homing Sparrow missiles to MiGs up to twelve miles away. The Soviet and Chinese arse-nals did not have anything comparable. Yet the Navy failed to employ this system effectively during the Vietnam War period because the sys-tem required the skills of a radar operator to use, which many fighter pilots, accustomed to operating alone in a single-seat fighter, found dif-ficult to accept.

While Souder was going through the replacement aircrew training, several pilots from VF-154 were in the process of transitioning from the F-8 to the F-4. "Those single-seat pilots were something to behold," re-called Souder. "Many had just returned from Vietnam—where the ac-tion had barely started—but they perceived themselves as 'seasoned war veterans' and they were impossible to deal with. They were the most arrogant, most abrasive, most overbearing, hardest-headed bunch of bastards I had ever encountered both inside and outside the Navy." To these former F-8 pilots, the RIOs were simply "a bunch of 'yes sir big boss man, let-me-carry-your-helmet-bag-for-you boys.' They didn't understand us, they didn't know why we existed, and they didn't care to learn. To them, any pilot who needed someone to 'help' him in the airplane was only half a pilot, and therefore a wuss." However, at this stage in his training, Souder possessed neither the authority nor the experience to challenge the arrogance he often confronted in the midst of the front-seaters. Fortunately, the pilot Souder was assigned to fly with during his initial F-4 training, Commander Ken Wallace, turned out to be one of the most modest, self-effacing men Souder ever met in his Navy career.[4]

So impressed was Souder with Wallace during their training together in the replacement air group (RAG) that he hoped to follow the commander to his next assignment, executive officer (second-in-command) of VF-154. Instead, he received orders to VF-154, but only five days after he arrived at the squadron in March 1966, VF-143 lost an NFO in a fatal accident, and Navy detailers quickly scrambled to find the most competent NFO in the RAG to take his place. Since Souder had received high marks in aircrew replacement training, his name soon headed the list, and he found himself on a plane bound for Yokosuka, Japan.

Once on *Ranger* with VF-143, the "Pukin' Dogs," Souder was reunited with an old friend, Terry Born, from his hometown of Fort Lauderdale, a man with whom he had swum at the University of Florida and with whom he had lived in the Phi Delta Theta fraternity house. Born was without a RIO when J. B. arrived at the squadron, so Souder was a natural candidate. The squadron operations officer, not knowing of Souder and Born's prior history, asked Born to take Souder under his wing and fly with him.

Terry Born had been one of Souder's closest friends in college. He also had a reputation for being an extremely rigid, self-disciplined pilot and a general "hard ass" when it came to operating off a carrier and flying combat missions: his Pukin' Dog squadron mates had jokingly labeled him with the call sign of "Jonas," after the ruthless Jonas Cord from the movie *The Carpetbaggers*.[5] Born was known to demand the same type of performance from his RIO that he demanded from himself, and he was an impatient instructor.

After about ten easy missions in the South, J. B.'s first mission in North Vietnam occurred early in May. The target that day was a truck refueling station on a little side road near Vinh—a city notorious for its antiaircraft artillery. As the NFO, Souder needed to monitor airspeed, altitude, and dive angle and prompt the pilot on when to drop his bombs. "I remember we were making our roll-in. The AAA was going off all over the place and I caught myself reflexively ducking my head as these big explosions went off all around me. Hell, I completely messed up the bomb run." After that mission, Born told Souder that he had to do his job no matter what was going on around him, and Souder vowed to keep his eyes on the instruments during bombing runs from then onward. Souder, however, continued to make mistakes, and Born began to "slowly boil" inside.

A few nights later, Born and Souder launched from *Ranger* to intercept two unidentified surface contacts. While Born flew the F-4 500 feet off the Gulf of Tonkin at 300 knots, Souder searched for the targets and tracked his leader's position (Souder and Born were flying as the wingman that night) on the F-4's radar. Souder also stayed in contact with a controller whose calls seemed inconsistent with their known position. At one point, he told Born, "something doesn't make sense . . . one of those guys is totally fucked-up." Souder then began questioning the controller about the calls and navigation plots. Born, thinking that his RIO was "fucking up again," got impatient and started scolding Souder. Ignoring the barrage of criticism being hurled in his direction, Souder continued to concentrate on the problem at hand and soon figured out that the lead plane in the element was using an incorrect tactical air navigation (TACAN) station for navigation.[6] Souder tried to inform Born of the situation, but Born immediately dismissed the notion and told Souder to "get your head out of your ass and get it right back there."[7] Souder then informed the lead RIO and the controller of his theory, and they confirmed that he was right. The returns, though, ended up being false radar signals (gremlins)—a factor that only increased the resentment building in Born toward Souder. When the two men returned to the carrier, they did not speak with each other except for essential communications. After three days, the two sat down and rehashed the flight so they could both understand exactly what had happened, and then apologized to each other. They next formulated a plan to eliminate future disagreements or mistakes from the time their "feet hit the plane's boarding ladder until we got back out of it." The plan called for the person who made a mistake, no matter how small, to buy a beer for the other party. "Eighty-three beers later," Souder recalled, "I finally figured out what I was doing in the backseat of an F-4."

One of the high points of that first tour was a fighter patrol in June 1966 in support of an A-4 strike against the massive petroleum storage tank farm in Haiphong. This was the first U.S. attack of the war against this major facility.[8] "We were watching the A-4s go in there and drop their bombs and fire their rockets when all of a sudden, kaboom, there goes a big tank. I remember saying, 'Terry, we were there. We were there! 29 June 1966. We stopped the war,' and I remember looking in my rearview mirrors 125 miles from the target on the way back to the ship and still seeing smoke coming up from those tanks." At this point in his career, the young Souder naively believed that one well-placed air strike was the beginning of a major air campaign that would end the war. By the time his second tour concluded in 1967, he had begun to lose his optimism and take a more jaundiced view of the struggle. By his last tour in 1972, his only goal was to help America win the release of his friends and comrades—the POWs held by the North Vietnamese.

J. B.'s first combat cruise ended on 25 August 1966, and some of the crews immediately began rotating back to the East Coast or to other squadrons in the West. Terry Born cross decked to VF-96 in what would ultimately end up being a fruitless attempt to get a MiG kill. As for J. B., he had several months remaining on his tour with VF-143, so he stayed with the Pukin' Dogs, got promoted to lieutenant, and lived the typical life of a Miramar-based bachelor: he rented a place on Mission Beach, bought a Honda 250-cc motorcycle, played volleyball on the weekends during his days off, and patronized local bars nearly every night. He also trained rigorously for his next cruise.

Now somewhat seasoned, with 96 missions in his logbook, Souder began to consider the realistic possibility of getting a MiG, but he knew his chances would be remote unless he got crewed with the right pilot. During 1967, Navy fighters flew 3,356 sorties, but only 20 of those flights actually engaged MiGs.[9] Naturally, everyone wanted to fly when the MiGs were in the air, but generally only the most senior officers in a squadron managed to get on the flight schedule during these periods. Senior officers also tended to act as the shooters in the two-plane Navy fighting formations. Souder therefore knew he needed to crew with a pilot of rank to have even a remote shot at getting a MiG, but he had one advantage working in his favor. First, Terry Born had turned him into one of the squadron's finest RIOs. Second, the new skipper of the squadron, Commander William Lawrence, knew of Souder's skills.

Lawrence and Souder had gotten to know each other during *Ranger's* long return voyage from the 1966 cruise. While most of VF-143 got "magic carpeted" to San Diego on a chartered airline, Lawrence, then the squadron's executive officer (XO), and Souder sailed back with the ship to finish paperwork and clean out the squadron areas for the next incoming unit. During their time together, Lawrence had a "profound" impact on Souder. Another native of Tennessee, Lawrence attended the Naval Academy and rose to command the midshipmen brigade during his senior year, 1951. He then went on to become a test pilot at Patuxent River naval air station and in 1958 became the first naval aviator to fly twice the speed of sound in a Navy aircraft, the F-8U Crusader III. Described by James Michener in his book *Space* as the "ablest flier that Pax River was to produce," Lawrence awed Souder with his work ethic, high morals, and intellect. Souder, in turn, impressed Lawrence with his knowledge of the F-4B system—so much, in fact, that when Lawrence took command of the unit on 15 June 1967, he assigned J. B. to fly with his XO, Commander Dave Grosshuesch. Lawrence knew that Grosshuesch was inexperienced and needed a combat-experienced NFO to be a "backseat driver."

After a few missions, Souder started thinking of Dave as his "voice-actuated autopilot; at times I had to literally tell him where to fly, and what buttons to push." Sadly, only thirteen days after assigning Souder to fly with Grosshuesch, Lawrence ended up being shot down while prosecuting an attack on one of the AAA sites near Nam Dinh.[10] Lawrence would spend the next six years of his life in Hanoi and become a key factor behind Souder's decision to volunteer for a third combat cruise in 1972.

In the meantime, Souder focused all his energies on the challenge of flying with Grosshuesch. During 1967, U.S. air attacks on North Vietnam reached their peak, with 14,500 armed reconnaissance sorties per month authorized. This accelerated air strike tempo was accompanied by an increase in MiG sightings. Between 9 April and 5 June, American aircraft downed thirty-four MiG-17s in air-to-air combat. MiG activity then decreased late in the summer of 1967 but began to pick up again in October, the month J. B. and Grosshuesch finally tangled with a MiG.[11]

6

The Anatomy of a MiG Kill

BY 26 OCTOBER, Souder had flown about 190 missions, 80 of them with Grosshuesch. The mission that day was a MiG patrol in support of a coordinated strike against Hanoi. Grosshuesch and Souder would fly lead in an F-4 code-named "Taproom 3" with Lieutenants (jg) Robert Hickey and Jeremy Morris backing him up in another F-4 code-named "Taproom 4."

It appeared as if 26 October would be the day when all of Souder's training and hard work would pay off—a day when he could leverage his knowledge of the F-4 weapons system to finally make a kill. If J. B., with the help of his sea-based controllers, could simply find a MiG and get a missile lock with the F-4's radar, he stood a better-than-even chance of killing a MiG before the MiG could kill him, but as often happens in war, human error combined with equipment malfunctions would shatter Souder's dreams.

During the preflight briefing with the mission crews, Souder expounded upon several points related to the AIM-7 Sparrow missile. He stressed that the Sparrow would work fine in a tail-on situation if the proper launch parameters were met. Souder wanted the pilots to save the heat-seeking Sidewinders for close-in engagements and utilize the radar-guided Sparrows for long-range shots. Part of his motivation was selfish: the Sparrow "kept the RO in the scheme." Souder also had some good technical arguments for pushing the Sparrow. First, firing two made the aircraft 870 pounds lighter and more maneuverable in case of a dogfight. Second, the new AIM-7E Sparrows carried by Navy F-4s in 1967 had much more capability than the earlier AIM-7Ds. The AIM-7D worked extremely well against large, nonmaneuvering bombers flying head-on at 40,000 feet but could rarely down a high-speed fighter in a rear-quadrant shot. By contrast, the E functioned much better in rear-aspect firings and could be fired head-on at a longer range from a target (13.5 versus 8.3 miles). The secret behind the E's improved performance lay in its ability to acquire a target closing at a minimum rate of 50 knots versus 180 knots for the D model.

Two other F-4s would be flying that day in a second MiG patrol at a specific location. As a result, Souder still did not have enough confidence in the ground-controlled intercept (GCI) radar controllers (in this case based in a ship) to risk taking a long-range shot and possibly hitting one of his shipmates. "Considering all the screw-ups with the various controllers' radars, procedures, individual competence, etc., throughout the war so far, it was my opinion that absolutely, positively, no-way-in-hell should we fire on a target without a positive visual identification (VID) that it was an enemy aircraft."

Grosshuesch and the other pilot in the element, Robert Hickey, argued vociferously against J. B. on this point and several others. They claimed that the Sparrow "was no damn good when fired from behind a target," and that it would work only in a head-on situation. Each one swore that the only missile he would fire in a rear-quarter engagement was the Sidewinder. They also "sloughed off" Souder's caution to be vigilant about target selection in the area of the other section's patrol. Worse yet, "They shouted me down about visually identifying a target before they shot a missile. Hickey asked Grosshuesch to make a ruling on my admonition to not fire without visually identifying the enemy plane, and Grosshuesch did, saying that if the controlling agency cleared us to fire, that we would fire without a visual identification (VID). I ended my brief by saying that I knew what I was talking about, and that they were all three 'fuckin' crazy.'"

The mission was timed to get Taprooms 3 and 4 on station twenty minutes after the strike force got to the target so that they could pick off any MiGs attempting to hit the strike force on its return home. Souder and Grosshuesch sat on the flight deck for about fifteen minutes with a hose pumping fuel on board their aircraft as fast as it used it. Once launched and at a cruising altitude of 17,000 feet, Souder contacted a radar controller on the cruiser *Long Beach*, code-named "Harbormaster." Souder was starting to give Harbormaster his flight's fuel status, radar status, weapons load, and other specifications when the air controller suddenly interrupted the conversation to alert them to a possible MiG contact.

The controller quickly lost contact with the MiGs, and the two U.S. planes continued on toward the North Vietnamese mainland. Souder and Grosshuesch at this point were on a bearing of 303 degrees on the radar control ship Red Crown's compass and 87 miles away from that vessel ("Red Crown 303, 87," in naval aviation jargon). Red Crown maintained a positive identification radar advisory zone (PIRAZ) for Navy ships operating in the Gulf of Tonkin and served to warn the fleet of incoming hostile aircraft and coordinate a SAM or fighter response to these threats. By 1967, the Navy operated three radar ships—Red Crown, situated twenty-five miles from the mouth of the Red River; Harbormaster, located south of Red Crown; and a third ship to the north—and began to employ the PIRAZ in an air battle command and control as well as an air traffic control role. With the new SPS-48 radars, PIRAZ ships could cover not only the Gulf of Tonkin but also much of the overland area of North Vietnam and could vector U.S. fighters from all services to hostile aircraft practically from the moment of a MiG's takeoff.

PIRAZ was augmented by an Air Force EC-121 airborne radar aircraft, known as "Big Eye," which covered inland areas beyond the range of PIRAZ. Big Eye had a long-range radar that could provide decent inland coverage, but it could not pick out MiGs in the Hanoi metropolitan area. Unlike a modern airborne warning and control system (AWACS) plane, the EC-121 also did not have a look-down capability—the ability to distinguish aircraft flying below the EC-121. As a result, low-flying MiGs often got lost in ground clutter.[1]

The Harbormaster controller had been looking at the other flight of F-4s (Taprooms 1 and 2) when suddenly a bandit call came up on an emergency frequency, known as "Guard," monitored by all aircraft. The controller indicated that a MiG had been spotted fifteen miles from Hanoi, code-named "Bull's-eye." In this instance, the controller transmitting on the Guard frequency was in an Air Force Big Eye aircraft. The Harbormaster controller then attempted to track this bogey on his scope and directed Taprooms 3 and 4 to intercept the plane, now fifty-six miles away from Souder's element and on the 348-degree bearing.

At this point, Souder had an azimuth and a range on the MiG but still needed the MiG's heading (the direction that the MiG was flying) and altitude to compute the intercept geometry. Harbormaster soon calculated that the MiG's altitude was 13,000 feet and transmitted that information to Souder.

Taproom 3 (Souder and Grosshuesch) was then headed 270 degrees on the aircraft's compass toward the North Vietnamese coast. Souder prompted Grosshuesch to arm the missiles and select Sparrows. In a matter of a few seconds, just as Taproom 3 zoomed within five miles of the coast, Harbormaster came back on the air, much more deliberately now, and ordered Souder and Grossshuech to come north toward the bandit, which Harbormaster believed was now thirty-two miles away from them.

Taprooms 3 and 4 turned to the north and crossed the coast near the outlets of the Day Giang and Song Nin rivers, an area called the "hour-glass" after the curvy shape of the two rivers. Souder told Grosshuesch to start a slow descent because he wanted to get below any potential target. The F-4 acquisition radar worked best when aimed up and away from the ground "clutter," but Souder could not go too low because of a layer of clouds at 5,000 feet. Getting below that layer would make it hard to pick out a target through all the noise the clouds would generate on the scopes. Souder also could not hang right on top of the clouds because that would make his aircraft more vulnerable to a midair collision with a SAM. To avoid these missiles, a pilot needed to acquire them visually as soon as possible and then take appropriate evasive maneuvers—flying too close to or within clouds tended to greatly undermine this imperative.

Harbormaster then called out that the bandit was now at 311, 22, which meant that the MiG had gone from 8 degrees at 32 miles to 311 degrees at 22 miles in a matter of seconds. "What in the hell is he flying? The guy must be going 3,000 miles an hour!" Souder thought to himself as his frustration intensified with the now frazzled Harbormaster controller. Trying to get a contact on the MiG, Souder thumbed the antenna control wheel as fast as he could, and just as his F-4 passed 12,000 feet, his radar scope went dead. Morris, in the other aircraft, then called out a tallyho, indicating that he had spotted the MiG about twelve miles from its current position.

Morris: Tap 3 from 4, contact.
Souder: Rog, my weapon's bent [broken]!

Souder then told Grosshuesch to come left 20 degrees to a heading of 340.

Souder (to Harbormaster): Say again the call.
Harbormaster: 293 at 14. You're cleared to shoot; but he is in a fade at this time.

Souder asked himself, "What in the hell is goin' on?" A few seconds earlier the controller had told him that the bandit was at his 341-degree magnetic at fifteen miles away, 23,000 feet high, going Mach 1 (600 knots), and on a heading 288, which was directly away from Souder and Grosshuesch. Now, almost instantaneously, the bandit was on a bearing of 287-degree magnetic from Taproom 3, and only nine miles away.

> I computed that the only target known to man which could be leaving that track on a radar would be the Starship *Enterprise* at its normal operating speed of Warp-8. Those calls were all over the sky, so it was obvious to even a brand-new ensign right out of intercept training that it was more than one target or the controller's tracking computer was going nuts. On top of all that, the bandit was in a fade, disappearing off his scope, and the controller had cleared us to fire! We'd gotten a series of unreliable calls, and I didn't trust this controller, so the situation called for at least "calculated skepticism" on our parts.

While still on the 340 heading, Morris in Taproom 4 got a radar contact, and Grosshuesch authorized them to take the lead.

Taproom 4 came left, crossing behind Taproom 3 to a heading of 270, and Taproom 3 did an in-place turn, which positioned it just behind Taproom 4's abeam position on the right-hand side. By then, the two planes had dropped to 8,000 feet and accelerated to 500 knots. Souder checked his position on his TACAN and noticed that the two bandits had just entered the area being flown by squadron mates, Lieutenant Commander Bill Marr and Lieutenant (jg) Phil Taylor (NFO) in Taproom 1 and Lieutenant Eddie Davidson with Lieutenant (jg) Dan Van Norem (NFO) in Taproom 2.

Hickey: Tap 3, Tap 4. Are we cleared to fire without a visual I.D.?
Grosshuesch: Cleared to fire.

Grosshuesch continued to descend, and as Souder watched in terror, a missile ripped off the rail on the underside of Taproom 4's wing, streaked straight out for a mile, and then nose-dived and disappeared. A split second later, two Phantoms with big "Pukin' Dogs" painted on their sides appeared exactly where the missile had nose-dived. As they approached Souder and Grosshuesch's abeam position, they began a right turn toward the south, and Souder thought, "Good God, that was close. I told that fuckin' idiot not to fire without a VID!"

Meanwhile, Grosshuesch, in the highly charged moment, still believed the planes, now due south of him, were MiGs. Pilots often refer to this behavior as "buck fever."

Souder: Tallyho. Tallyho. It's an F-4. It's an F-4.

As Souder told Grosshuesch to level off, to his profound horror, Hickey started a hard left turn and ripped off a second missile at Marr and Davidson.

Grosshuesch: Break it off 3, that looks like an F-4.

Souder (screaming over the intercom): He's gone nuts X.O., Goddamn it! He's out of control! He's gonna kill somebody!

Hickey and Morris fired a third missile.

Souder (now screaming over the Mike): IT'S AN F-4!

Grosshuesch, now a little in-trail behind Hickey and in a hard left turn, flew right over a crack in the clouds. Well aware that he needed to know where he was at all times, Souder peered through this opening, saw a sharply defined "W" in the river below and knew immediately his location. That part of the river, or "the boobs," as the aviators called it, curled right around the city of Phu Ly. Hickey then reversed his turn to the south and fired a fourth missile as Souder continued to exhort him to cease fire.

Souder and Grosshuesch, now about 2,000 feet higher than the other three Phantoms and turning south behind them, overtook all of them from above and to their left. Hickey finally heard the transmissions because he stopped firing missiles and asked Taproom 3 where they were.

As Souder explained his position to Taproom 4, he looked down at his radar and to his utmost surprise, it sparkled on. Occasionally, high-G turns would reseat the cannon plugs on failed radars and make them operational again. Souder and Grosshuesch retook the lead from Tap 4. Still seething with anger, Souder ruminated on what had just happened:

"How in the hell could they have done such a thing?" Souder recalled that during training at Yuma, Commander Marland Townsend, the former squadron CO, had confined Hickey and Morris to quarters for three days for bombing the wrong target. Harbormaster then called out a second bandit call. This time the MiGs were seventeen miles away from the PIRAZ ship on a 226 bearing and at an altitude of 23,000 feet.

Souder started searching at level and kept thumb-wheeling the radar antenna upward until it passed 10 degrees. "Damn it," he thought. "Where in the hell is he? I'm already looking 20,000 feet above us." Souder kept looking high. "By now it was anybody's guess at what altitude the MiG really was, and I could just as logically have been looking low, but since I was already up this high with the antenna, I'd just take it to its limits. Sweep left, sweep right, go up 2 degrees. Sweep left, sweep right, go up 2 degrees. There he was! I was looking 30 degrees above us. He had to be above 30,000 feet!" Souder finally locked up the target at 20 degrees left and began getting steering information. The controller's calls had been off by 40 degrees.

The steering dot on Souder's radar then started to wiggle out to the left. He told Grosshuesch to come port. The steering dot started accelerating out to the left, so Souder again told Grosshuesch to come port hard and climb. The F-4 radar had look angles limited to 60 degrees on either side of the nose, so Souder walked the dot as close to the right edge of the scope as he dared. As the range decreased from twelve to five miles, Grosshuesch finally saw the MiG. Dave transmitted a bandit call, but the aircraft was still five miles away and just a silver speck in the sky. "How in hell could he say it was a bandit?" J. B. again reflected.

Souder (intercom): Alright now, Dave, be sure it's a MiG and not an F-8. Let's be sure to positively I.D. it.

Souder could hear Grosshuesch's breathing getting heavier and faster. With just under four miles between Taproom 3 and the target, the target started to drift toward Souder's nose, which meant he had more speed than Taproom 3. Taproom 3 was in maximum afterburner going as fast as it could, so Souder needed to act quickly or the plane would escape. The bandit continued drifting to Souder and Hickey's nose as they kept climbing, trying to catch it. As the target came to the nose of Taproom 3, Grosshuesch confirmed it and made a second "bandit" call.

Souder again reminded Grosshuesch over the intercom to get a positive VID on the bandit before firing. (Souder's training instructors had emphasized the visual similarities between the F-8 and MiG-21 and implored their students not to confuse the two aircraft in the heat of battle.) Just then the MiG passed through the freezing altitude and discharged a thin contrail, and J. B. saw him. "He was sleek, silver and sharp-edged; very distinct against the clear, azure blue sky. I had time to think what a beautiful airplane it was, too. It seemed almost a shame to blow it up. Instantly I was proud of what we'd done. We'd taken our time and done the VID correctly like we'd been trained and encouraged to do, and no doubt about it, it wasn't an F-8."

Although he had been calling out the position of the MiG throughout the engagement, Souder still had not received any confirmation from Morris in Tap 4 that he had seen the MiG. Souder called out, "He's on the nose at a mile." But Morris still did not reply. "Jesus!" Souder thought. "Where in the hell was Morris looking?" Throughout the climb, Taproom 3 had made some small, gradual turns to the left, and by now it was heading due east. It took a full 90-degree turn to the left for it to fall in behind the MiG, but the turn cost Taproom 3 some energy, and Souder worried about the possibility of a trailing MiG lurking somewhere behind them. Rear-quarter, high-speed attacks occurred often in late 1967, so the likelihood of a trap could not be ruled out. The Vietnamese People's Air Force (VPAF) would gladly sacrifice a MiG to down a Phantom. Souder reminded Morris to check 6 (his rear).

Grosshuesch unloaded the G-forces and pushed over a little to accelerate and regain airspeed and build up some overtake speed. Within seconds, he was exactly where he wanted to be, all according to the textbook, with the target right on his nose at a mile and a half, about 200 to 300 feet above him. "I relished the moment for just an instant," recalled Souder. "The picture couldn't have been prettier. We had ended up right here in the middle of the missile launch envelope; and were loaded for bear with two Sparrows and four Sidewinders. I was looking up a MiG-21's tailpipe, which looked as big as a gun barrel poked right between my eyes. We were at his slightly low 6 o'clock position, just where all those months of training and hundreds of intercepts had taught me to get us, and now we had a little surprise in store for an unwitting MiG pilot." Souder ordered Grosshuesch to shoot.

Ordinarily it takes 1.5 seconds for a Sparrow to fire off its rails after a pilot pulls the trigger. During that brief delay, more than ninety electronic and pneumatic steps take place before the missile fires. After a long pause, Souder waited a second more and then again ordered Grosshuesch to fire. "I'm trying to, nothing's coming off," Grosshuesch explained over the intercom.

Souder then made a quick visual check on a cluster of ten circuit breakers under his armpit, to the left and rear of his ejection seat. Those switches governed the firing circuits for the Sparrows, and they were all "in." The missile was active, but for some reason not coming off the rail. With no time to pull and reset circuit breakers because Taproom 3 was now getting closer and closer to Hanoi on its present bearing, Souder decided to switch from Sparrows to heat-seeking Sidewinder missiles. The Sidewinder emitted a good growl in Souder and Grosshuesch's headset, indicating that the missile's heat-seeking heads detected the hot exhaust emanating from the MiG's tailpipe. Again, Souder ordered him to shoot, but nothing happened.

Souder began to wonder if Dave was pulling the trigger, but he hesitated to ask the question, afraid of insulting the commander. Instead, he told Taproom 4 to step up to take the shot.

Hickey: Roger, where is he?

Souder's frustration intensified. "Why can't he keep the MiG in sight?" Souder thought to himself. "He's had it in his sight twice, why does he keep losing it?" Souder again reminded Morris that the MiG was dead ahead and still high.

Grosshuesch: Four, hold your fire until you get a better look.

Once again Souder realized that he still had not heard a "contact" call from Morris, so once more he attempted to guide Hickey to the MiG with his calls.

Hickey: OK. I've got him!
Morris (sounding effervescent): I've got him!
Souder: Shoot him, Tap 4!

Taproom 4 finally moved up to 200 feet ahead and 200 feet below Taproom 3 and ejected a Sparrow. It steered just a little bit to the MiG's right, started a shallow little climb, and in "a brilliant silver-white, silent explosion," detonated directly under the MiG's left wing tip. The MiG-21 immediately did a left roll of 90 degrees, creating a thin white trail that looked like vapor coming off his left wing, and J. B. thought, "Dammit! The missile missed him!" The MiG then reversed back through wings level to about a 70-degree bank to the right. J. B. thought that the MiG pilot, having heard the explosion, was rocking his wings so he could get a good look behind him, but just then he reversed his roll again and went end over end.

The pilot of the MiG was Major Mai Van Cuong, a top ace who ultimately ended the war with eight kills. Cuong's wingman that day was Nguyen Van Coc, the highest scorer in the Vietnamese People's Air Force with nine kills to his name. Cuong successfully bailed out on 26 October and currently serves in the VPAF as a colonel. Coc went on to become chief of staff of the VPAF until 1998.

The MiG then turned around and appeared to be heading straight toward Taprooms 3 and 4. "Jesus!" Souder cringed. "We'd been told those things could turn, but Goddamn, he turned around right in place! That quick turn made me again think the missile hadn't gotten him after all; and it looked like he was now reversing course to get in a shot at us. What'n the hell is going on? I wanted confirmation from Bob that his missile had actually hit the MiG, but just then Harbormaster broke in and requested a status check on the MiG."

Hickey now indicated that he had once again lost sight of the MiG. "I was really getting impatient with Hickey and Morris!" Souder recalled. "How could they see the MiG, shoot a missile, and then lose sight again? Twice, Hickey had lost sight of the MiG and the whole time the MiG was right in front of me!" Souder, starting to become unglued, yelled into the mike: "He's still on my nose. He's right in front of us, for God's sake!"

The MiG's nose had just fallen through the horizon and now pointed downward. Soon the MiG began to roll into a flat spin. During this time, Grosshuesch got on the radio, confirmed the kill, and told Souder to settle down and stop yelling. He then throttled back, started descending, and pulled out to the right to circle around the spinning MiG. With the MiG at his nine o'clock, about 500 feet away, 70 to 80 degrees nose-down, Souder saw a little explosion over the cockpit, and the pilot came streaking out of the plane, but he could not make out a parachute.

The two planes then headed back to the carrier, did a victory roll, and landed. On their way to the debriefing, the aviators paused to

From left to right: Lieutenant (jg) Jeremy Morris, Lieutenant (jg) Robert Hickey, Commander David Grosshuesch, and Lieutenant James Souder discuss the events leading up to Morris and Hickey's MiG kill on 26 October 1967. As the sweat stains imply, this picture was taken just minutes after the pilots landed that day on *Constellation* (CVA-64). (Courtesy of U.S. Navy, James B. Souder)

concoct a story to explain why the wingman and not the lead plane got the kill. Since Navy fighting formations tend to be fluid and flexible, Grosshuesch, Souder, Hickey, and Morris agreed to say that Hickey simply fired first and leave it at that. The group also agreed not to mention any part of the mission other than the intercept that culminated in the kill. Souder wanted to tell the truth, but "it would only have hurt Grosshuesch's career. I knew it would cost me a Silver Star, but even telling the truth would not guarantee that I'd get one either."

Souder and Grosshuesch talked briefly with their ordnance officer and told him about not being able to get a missile off. He said he would do a "piss-check" on the plane—a check of the continuity of the electrical circuits in the missile system—and report back to them with his findings. All four aviators then went to the ready room, which rapidly filled up with squadron members intent on hearing the story of the kill. Morris and Hickey proceeded to tell their version of events but failed to mention the near fratricide that occurred early on in the mission. They did discuss with incredulity the success of the Sparrow in the engagement. As it turned out, Hickey fired a Sparrow because he knew he had expended his Sidewinders when he accidentally fired on Marr and Davidson.[2]

While Hickey and Morris were telling their story, Grosshuesch began telling the operations and strike operations officers his version of events: "J. B. was sittin' back there yelling 'shoot him, shoot him,' and I was trying to, and nothing was coming off." As Grosshuesch told the tale, he began gesturing with his hands, and when he got to the part about J. B. yelling to shoot, he extended his right hand and made an up-and-down gesture with his thumb over his clenched fist, mimicking the motion it would take to push the bomb release button on the Phantom's control stick. The two listeners' eyes fell on the gesture in resigned acknowledgment of what had happened. In an F-4, one shoots missiles with the trigger, not the thumb button. Grosshuesch, a former F-3 Demon pilot accustomed to launching missiles with the thumb button, probably got so flustered he failed to remember which type of aircraft he was flying. In the excitement of the moment, he pushed the bomb release button rather than the missile trigger. Later, the ordnance officer told Souder and Grosshuesch that he had done the "piss-check" on the plane and could find nothing wrong with the missile launch system.

That night Hickey telephoned Souder and asked him to come up to a stateroom where he, Morris, and Grosshuesch were trying to reconstruct the action for a message to the Task Force 77 commander. Whiskey flowed freely in celebratory anticipation of the Silver Stars this message would garner for Hickey and Morris. Souder gave them the true facts as he knew them and then went back to his stateroom.

The next day the Navy flew the four men to Saigon for a press conference on the Navy's twenty-fourth MiG kill of the war. During the interview, Souder "just sat back and sarcastically giggled to myself while my pilot, who led the intercept, and the other two brave, gallant MiG-killers fumble-fucked their way through the story of their courageous airborne combat. It was disgusting, but the press wasn't smart enough to figure out the truth, so they got away with it. Screw it. I got a chance to see a little bit of Saigon, and we all had a steak and a few bottles of Vietnamese beer at a rooftop restaurant that night, and we flew back to the *Connie* the next day."

A few more days passed, and then one night, Grosshuesch stopped by Souder's stateroom to talk. In a halting, uncharacteristically quiet voice, he confessed that he felt bad about trying to "bomb" the MiG and "screwing" J. B. out of a Silver Star. "We talked for a while," Souder explained, "and I found myself consoling him, telling him not to worry about it, to forget it, that it was just one of the crazy things that happened in a war." Grosshuesch then said, "Jaybee, you deserve a Silver Star, and I deserve nothing." Grosshuesch, however, did not go to any of his commanding officers and tell the truth about what had transpired.

In addition to revealing the shortcomings of VF-143's executive officer, this MiG engagement revealed a number of lessons that the Navy never learned during the course of the Vietnam War. First, the pilot often did not play the central role in an F-4 MiG kill—especially one made beyond visual ranges. The PIRAZ operator and the RIO often shared this role. The PIRAZ or Big Eye radar operators needed first to find the MiG, and then direct the F-4 to within range of the F-4's radar. In theory, this interception process appeared simple, but as the Souder episode illustrates, the devil lay in the details. It required tremendous talent to pick out a MiG from myriad returns, determine the bogey's exact heading, altitude, and airspeed, and then direct a friendly interceptor to a point where it could shoot that MiG down. Clouds, friendly aircraft, and electrical interference all functioned to obscure the MiG and complicate the tracking problem. Even if a controller managed to ferret out enough information on a target from his scope to successfully plot its position, he still needed to convey that information to the F-4 in a timely manner—no easy task, as the engagement aptly illustrates. Considering all the confusion that day, if Souder had not been a highly competent RIO, he probably would have not made the intercept at all, and no MiG would have been shot-down by his squadron mates.

Even after the PIRAZ controller directed an F-4 to within radar range of a MiG, the battle was only half over. The NFO still needed to get his radar pointed at the same target and get a missile lock. If contradictory, confusing, or garbled information was emanating from PIRAZ, this seemingly minor task could demand all the skill, intuition, and experience an NFO could muster. The NFO virtually needed to put himself in the cockpit of the MiG and begin to think and react like the MiG pilot to get a firm fix on these tiny dots in the sky. He rarely had time to consult charts but had to repeatedly check the compass. In a jet age air-to-air engagement, the outcome of a battle can be determined in a second, and this outcome often boiled down to the NFO being able to acquire a target on his radar screen before the elusive MiG "dived for the weeds" or received a warning from his ground controller and escaped.

Once radar lock was achieved, the last step before a missile could be fired was to obtain a visual identification of the enemy plane. While Grosshuesch, Hickey, and Morris questioned the need for a VID, arguing that PIRAZ could be trusted to vector them to the correct aircraft, more experienced aviators such as Souder knew that in an airspace crowded with friendly aircraft, a VID often proved imperative—a lesson Hickey and Morris almost learned the hard way. The VID required more maneuvering, gas, and time, but the story did not necessarily end there. The 1960s-era air-to-air missiles often proved unreliable even under perfect conditions. Occasionally, more than one needed to be fired to hit the mark. Hickey and Morris were correct in arguing that the AIM-9 was more reliable than the AIM-7, but it was not always the correct missile to fire in all circumstances. For long-range shots, even in the rear quarter, an AIM-7 was more effective. Furthermore, by firing an AIM-7, a pilot lightened his aircraft and held his Sidewinders in reserve in case a close-in dogfight developed. Why no one listened to J. B. as he tried to argue these points with his squadron mates before the mission is puzzling, but the longer Souder remained in the Navy, the more he realized that the core of his problems related to the wings on his flight suit, not his experience, knowledge, integrity, and skill as an aviator. Most pilots still considered NFOs to be glorified navigators and not integral members of a combat team.[3]

Pilots like Hickey often failed to understand, until too late, how important NFOs were in aerial combat. As the Hickey-Morris MiG kill demonstrated, the difficult work of acquiring a long-range target on a radar, and then tracking that target until a VID could be made and a missile launched, was primarily the job of the NFO. Pilots, in many instances, were simply "voice-actuated autopilots," as Souder suggests, and not nearly as crucial to the overall outcome as the guy in the backseat.

7

"The Navy Needs You, J. B."

Glynco, VF-121, and VF-51

GLYNCO

Souder's final fitness report from VF-143 read, "Lt. Souder's capabilities as a RIO are considered outstanding. His excellent knowledge of the F-4 weapons system and his ability to get the most out of any weapons system has won him the reputation of the finest RIO in the squadron . . . his calm and resourceful performance during extensive combat . . . resulted in his being recommended for three Distinguished Flying Crosses." This excellent report and a new assignment as a radar intercept instructor at the Naval Air Technical Training Center, Glynco, partly helped to dissipate some of his anger over the MiG and the generally poor treatment he received from some of the pilots during F-4 training. Still, Souder started to question the efficacy of a naval career as an NFO and began contemplating a switch to civilian aviation. In fact, one of the main reasons he chose a Glynco, Georgia, assignment was to gain more experience in the T-39D "Sabreliner," a military derivative of a civilian jet. "A lot of the pilots were flying as much as possible on weekends so they could build flight time and fatten their logbooks for airline interviews, and they'd bribe the NFOs (who had the students) to pick them as their weekend drivers. The bribe was that the NFOs could do the takeoffs, instrument departures and approaches, and the landings. That kind of flight time could come in very handy when trying to get a good flying job as a civilian."[1]

Over the course of one year, the RIO course officer placed Souder in charge of sixteen future radar intercept officers. Souder taught these men that the air-to-air intercept was a fundamental part of being a back-seater in an F-4. Souder soon discovered a hidden talent for teaching and took pride in his accomplishments as an instructor. Being able to take the lessons he learned in Vietnam and apply them to help a future generation of NFOs gave new purpose to his career. "I really enjoyed all aspects of instructing. I thoroughly enjoyed helping other people learn new and unusual concepts. I wouldn't settle for less than total under-standing. I believed it was my job to teach them, and if they failed, I failed—after all, their lives and the lives of their squadron mates may some day depend on what I was teaching them."

Despite his satisfaction with life as an instructor, Souder still did not perceive himself as a Navy careerist. He instead chose to separate from the service and begin a civilian career as soon as his tour ended in Jan-uary 1969. In the hopes of getting a civilian flying job and moving back to Fort Lauderdale, Souder had worked on earning his civilian private pilot license and commercial pilot license during his one-year tour at Glynco. In January 1969, he moved back to Fort Lauderdale, and by June 1969 he finished getting the ratings he needed, including an in-structor's rating and a multiengine rating. On 2 July, he loaded up his stereo and motorcycle and drove up to New York City to share an apart-ment with his old friend and mentor, Terry Born.

CIVILIAN LIFE AND A BRIEF STINT IN THE NAVAL RESERVES

Born, now a civilian pilot with the airlines, lived in an apartment one block from La Guardia Airport. The first day he arrived, Souder imme-diately secured himself a position as an instructor pilot for the La Guardia Flying Service. Souder intended to use the job as a logical step-ping-stone to the airlines, since it allowed him to log many pilot hours in Cessna-150 and Piper Cherokee-140 aircraft. However, instructing civilians ended up being more demanding than Souder expected. "I had no idea how depressing and frustrating and scary teaching inept civilians with absolutely no aptitude for flying could be, but boy, did I find out . . . and BIG time!"

One day, Souder took a Polish national who could barely speak English out for a flight. As the two men taxied toward the runway, the tower ordered them to hold short of one of La Guardia's main runways. The Pole apparently did not understand because he continued to taxi toward the active runway just as an American Airlines 727 began its takeoff roll. "I had to tell him three times not to taxi onto the active run-way but to stop short of it, and the third time I told him, since he was getting perilously close to getting us killed, I yelled it at him! He got the idea that time and he stomped the brakes so violently that the metal actually failed, ripped apart, and tore the disc right off of the wheel."

During August 1969, Souder received a call from the program manager for the Navy's only reserve F-4 squadron, VF-22L1, stationed at NAS Los Alamitos, California—just south of Los Angeles. Apparently, the squadron needed NFOs for a summer cruise, and three VF-143 veterans in the unit had recommended Souder. Happy to earn some extra cash, especially since bad fog was forcing him to cancel many of his classes, Souder agreed to join the unit and soon found himself in a T-33 flying across the country to join the squadron for the two-week "summer cruise."

When Souder returned to New York, he discovered that continued poor weather had virtually shut down his flight school, and so he began searching for more work. Initially, he opted to fly Lear-25 jets as a charter pilot, but he soon found corporate flying to be incompatible with his personality: "You're just Mr. Step and Fetch It for a bunch of rich bastards." Souder thought more and more that maybe a Navy career was the right choice for him after all. In March 1970, he contacted the Bureau of Personnel (BuPers) to inquire about the possibility of reenlisting. BuPers, suffering from a serious shortage of NFOs at the time, was anxious to get inactive reservists to "come back home": for fiscal year 1970, the Navy possessed only 2,700 trained NFOs on active duty, but it required 4,700. For J. B., reenlisting served a couple of ends. First, it allowed him to avoid a potentially dull job with the airlines as a flight engineer, or "airborne boy," as he called them; second, J. B.'s sense of honor demanded that he return to Vietnam. "I came back in with promised orders to VF-92 at Miramar, via VF-121, for a refresher syllabus in the Phantom. I could have gone to an East Coast squadron that would have gone to the Med, but I wanted to go to the West Coast and go back to Vietnam to help get that damned war over and get our POWs home. That seemed like the most important thing I could do at the time, to make the most important contribution I could make for the good of the U.S. Navy."[2]

VF-121

In September 1970, Souder's second Navy career began in VF-121, the West Coast replacement air group squadron based at Miramar. Given his two-week reserve tour thirteen months earlier, not to mention his combat experience, Souder did not need much refresher training in the F-4. After two hops with a new instructor, the teacher turned to him and asked, "Hell, you've been out how long? Yesterday?" The man then went to the squadron executive officer and lobbied to make Souder an instructor, and J. B. wound up flying all the training flights as an instructor as opposed to a student.

Souder spent most of his time at 121 transitioning former F-8 pilots from VF-51 and VF-111 into the F-4. Although J. B. had experienced more than his fair share of fighter pilot arrogance, he found the veteran pilots of VF-51 an unusually incorrigible group. Almost as soon as they began flying F-4s, the VF-51 pilots started wearing a new patch sporting the slogan "World's Last Great F-8 Squadron . . . World's First Great F-4 Squadron." This outraged Souder. "Just who in the hell did these guys think they were? . . . They hadn't even flown the goddamn airplane yet."

TOOTER

At the very center of all the VF-51 hype was a legendary pilot named Foster Schuler Teague, or "Tooter," as his pilots affectionately called him.[3] Tooter, the squadron executive officer at that time, grew up in Bosier City, Louisiana, and spoke with an often exaggerated southern drawl. The son of a wealthy real estate developer, Teague attended Texas A&M University, played freshman football, and earned a varsity letter as a sophomore under coach Ray George. In spring training of 1954 under a new coach, Paul "Bear" Bryant, Tooter's football career ended with a severe neck injury.[4]

He entered the Navy upon graduation in 1956. Teague, who had first learned to fly at the young age of thirteen and owned his own aircraft throughout college, breezed through pilot training in 1957 and won a coveted fighter pilot slot, first flying the F11F-1 Tiger and later transitioning to the F-8 Crusader.

In 1966, Teague flew his first combat missions in Vietnam as an F-8 pilot with VF-111 on *Oriskany*. While on that cruise, he earned his first Navy Commendation Medal during a rescue mission for Rick Adams, who had been shot down by a surface-to-air missile near Hanoi in July 1966. He later earned a Silver Star on 31 August for a similar rescue mission involving his roommate Lieutenant Commander Tom Tucker. On that mission, Teague was escorting Tucker on a photo reconnaissance flight over Haiphong harbor when Tucker, flying an RF-8, took some fire from a 37-mm antiaircraft gun, lost control of the aircraft, and ejected. Several motorized junks immediately sped toward Tucker. Teague blew up one with a bomb and strafed two others. The area around Tucker appeared so dangerous that PIRAZ advised the rescue helicopter to abort the pickup, but the helicopter, urged on by Teague, continued in and picked him up anyway. After he became commander of VF-51, Tucker would reward Teague for his part in the rescue by choosing him to be his executive officer.[5]

The rescue of Tom Tucker could very well have been the crowning achievement of Teague's first combat cruise, but tragedy would strike *Oriskany* on 26 October 1966, and Foster Teague was near the center of the action. On that day at 0718, Airmen Apprentices James Sider and George James were stowing flares in a compartment near Hangar Bay 1, tossing the six-foot-long Mk-24 parachute flares casually to one another. During one of the tosses, the lanyard of a flare caught on something and started a fire. James panicked and ran; Sider then compounded his errors by kicking the smoldering flare into the flare locker and shutting the door. He then yelled "Fire!" and began to run toward the hangar bay. As fire-fighting teams attempted to find the source of the smoke wafting through the hangar, the flare locker exploded, knocking down firefighters and spraying the bay with smoke, flames, and burning pieces of magnesium. The resulting fire and smoke would ultimately kill thirty-six officers and eight enlisted men before it could be contained four and a half hours later at 1158.[6]

Teague and many other members of the air wing lay sound asleep in their staterooms when the alarm sounded. Wondering if this was just another drill, the men stumbled into the passageway only to find all escapes blocked by heavy smoke or flames. The men, shaken and groggy, elected instead to descend an unventilated storage shaft. Ultimately, eleven officers and two enlisted men joined them in the trunk and distributed themselves on platforms connected by a long ladder. After forty minutes, the senior man in the trunk, Commander Charles A. Lindbergh Swanson, the XO of VF-163, decided to act. He asked for a volunteer to probe outside the trunk for a possible escape route with an oxygen breathing apparatus (OBA), a mask with approximately twenty minutes of liquid oxygen in an attached cylinder. Teague, who remembered his OBA training, agreed to take on the mission and climbed up the scuttle into the smoke and darkness of the second deck. Teague felt heat emanating from the watertight door leading aft and reasoned that an aircraft must have blown up on the main deck. He then went forward and again up the ladder to the main deck. All routes were blocked, and so he climbed back down to the second deck, looking for any survivors. On his hands and knees, he felt his way over a dead body to get to his stateroom, where he recovered some water and returned to the trunk. "I told them that there was no way out. I then lay down next to my roommate and lit a cigarette." It would be three long hours before a rescue team reached the trunk and saved the men.[7]

Teague remained with VF-111 after the *Oriskany* cruise and ended up being appointed as officer-in-charge of Detachment 11, a group of F-8 pilots who were assigned to a combat cruise with *Intrepid* between May and December 1967 to provide Air Wing 11 with additional assets for target combat air patrol and photographic reconnaissance. For his command of that unit, nicknamed "Omar's Orphans," he received another Silver Star to add to his growing collection of decorations, but the highlight of that tour was not the command but a mission that occurred on 12 August 1967. On that day, Teague flew a photo escort mission against the Ke Sat Highway Bridge between Hanoi and Haiphong just south of Route 5. As he pulled up from the target, he took some ground fire (probably 37-mm). Teague, confident that his F-8 would not blow up, nursed the heavily damaged plane thirty-six miles until he was over the beach. He then ejected and landed in chest-deep water. A rescue helicopter swooped in, and a parajumper (PJ) dropped into the water and hooked Teague to a cable. Given the volume of ground fire in the rescue zone, the pilot then decided to drag Teague and the PJ three miles away from the beach before finally hoisting the two men to the helicopter.[8]

The Orphans arrived back in the United States on 5 December 1967 after flying more than 250 combat missions with Air Wing 111. Relieved to have survived two back-to-back combat cruises, the *Oriskany* fire, and a bailout over North Vietnam, Teague looked forward to a short stateside stint with VF-111 followed by an easy tour at the Naval War College. As he and his wife began to help the movers pack his belongings during the summer of 1968 for the move to Newport, Rhode Island, Teague received a call from the aviation command detailer, Richard Miller, telling him that his orders had been changed and he was now to report to VX-4. "Dick," Teague pleaded, "as we speak, the people are carrying boxes to the truck. . . . I got my orders in hand. . . . I sold my house!"

"Look," Miller responded, "this is the way it comes down. You can have your choice of living anywhere on the West Coast. But you're going to VX-4. These are special orders. That's all I can tell you . . . it's out of my hands."[9]

Air Test and Evaluation Squadron 4 (VX-4) originated as a test unit for Airborne Early Warning (AEW) aircraft from 1950 until it was decommissioned a year later in 1951. In 1952, the Navy recommissioned the unit to evaluate air-launched guided missiles. The mission of VX-4 gradually expanded to include aircraft tests and the publication of tactical manuals. By the time Teague entered the squadron, VX-4 could lay claim to having tested such major weapons systems as the Sparrow, Sidewinder, and Bullpup missiles, as well as such aircraft as the F-8 Crusader and F-4 Phantom II.

The VX-4 commander, Captain Jim Foster, wanted Teague on his team because a unique opportunity had recently presented itself to the Navy. The United States had just acquired two MiG-17s and two MiG-21s, and Foster wanted VX-4 to be the unit designated to test the aircraft. "Normally it would be an Air Force thing to exploit the MiG," explained Foster, "but Tooter and his guys had a written test plan. They said, 'If I had it, this is what I'd do with it.' It was typed, drawn and bound. . . . At the first meeting, we laid down the plan. Hell the Air Force was just getting started."[10]

Teague arrived at Point Mugu unaware that his plan, written recently at Miramar, had secured Navy access to some of the crown jewels of the U.S. intelligence community. Foster told him only that they were going to send him to the desert for 200 days. Teague, Foster, and VX-4's resident test pilot, Ronald "Mugs" McKeown, were spirited away to a secret location for tests involving the MiGs. Although Teague ultimately flew both aircraft, he was placed in charge of the MiG-17 tests, code-named "Have Drill." The MiG-17 Fresco, first developed in 1953 by the Soviet Union, was an improved version of the MiG-15 of Korean War fame. The agile little fighter could not fly above the speed of sound, nor did it generally carry air-to-air missiles or advanced radar. Instead, it relied on the same armament that the Korean War MiG-15 carried: two 23-mm and one 37-mm cannon. Nevertheless, as a dogfighter, the agile MiG-17 proved to be an impressive adversary. An Air Force study of the MiG-17 in 1965 stated that "the light weight of the

MiG-17 gave it a significant turn advantage over modern U.S. fighters in a slow, close fight—commonly known as a 'Knife Fight'—and the MiG's cannon armament was much more effective in a close engagement."[11]

Teague's experience correlated with the findings of that earlier study. He wrote in his Have Drill report that the MiG-17 was "capable of defeating any USN tactical airplane in a turning fight at speeds of 475 knots indicated air speed and below." The basic physics of a turning dogfight made this slow-speed turning advantage significant. As an aircraft turns, gravitational forces make the plane heavier and slow it down. As a result, a MiG-17 could gradually gain a maneuverability advantage over the F-4 if it could lure the big American jet into a traditional dogfight encounter as opposed to a long-range missile engagement.[12]

Teague also learned that the plane "was simple and reliable enough to operate from remote sites with a minimum of support equipment." As he put it in a later interview, "The airplane armament never failed. It was a palletized system. You took the whole gun out of the aircraft, loaded it, and cranked it back in. You could be back in the aircraft and flying again in twenty minutes."[13]

Teague stayed with the drill program for a year and then briefed every Navy and Marine squadron on the major findings of his Have Drill report. He then headed out to sea once again on 17 May 1970—this time as the executive officer of VF-51 on board the *Bon Homme Richard*. The *Bonny Dick* cruise turned out to be an uneventful series of MiG patrols and bombing runs into Laos. However, it did allow Teague to begin thinking about how he would go about changing the squadron once he assumed command after the tour ended. Whom would he choose to be his replacement pilots? Who would hold positions of command? Teague knew almost every pilot personally on the West Coast, and he handpicked some of the best to be VF-51 senior leaders. Near the top of his list was Jerry "Devil" Houston.

DEVIL

Jerry Houston had recently served with Teague on the *Bon Homme Richard* and during Have Drill, but the two men's relationship stretched all the way back to their college years. They met on their first day at

Texas A&M in the autumn of 1952. It happened in the parking lot behind Hart Hall, the athletic dorm. Jerry helped Tooter carry his footlocker up the stairs to a third-floor room; Tooter, in turn, reciprocated. They lived across the passageway from each other and soon became friends. Tooter played tackle; Jerry was a halfback. Both lettered as freshmen. Then Tooter earned a varsity letter as a sophomore while Jerry redshirted.

Jerry dropped out of college in 1955 to earn big wages working in the oilfields in Farmington, New Mexico. As a twenty-one-year-old, he had two cars, two motorcycles, and a half interest in an airplane: "a PT-19 which I paid $375 for." After two rides in the backseat, he took off by himself and tried to solo. "Luckily, I didn't get airborne, or I would have been dead." He ground looped it on the takeoff roll. So he taxied back in and sold his half interest the next day.

With the draft bearing down, Houston enlisted in the Naval Aviation Cadet program. As a former college football player, Jerry was allowed to study on his own and did not have to attend ground school. All he had to do was meet his flight schedule and play football. This arrangement encouraged Houston to take a casual approach toward the academic portions of flight school. As a consequence, he did not get assigned to fighters upon graduation. He asked his instructor why. "Jesus, Jerry," the instructor replied, "you've got the second highest flight grade of anyone who has ever gone through the program, but what the hell happened to your ground school grades? They count for half, you know."

Houston wound up instead in Fleet Air Support Squadron 9, a supply plane unit. Two days after arriving at the unit's base at Cecil Field in Jacksonville, Florida, one of his squadron mates, Roger Box, asked if he could borrow Houston's car. When Jerry asked why, Box told him he had heard a rumor that a nearby FJ-3 Fury squadron, VF-173, needed a fighter pilot. To make a long story short, both men ended up in the fighter squadron, flying nearly fifty hours a month in the Fury and having the time of their lives.

Jerry spent five months in VF-173. He then transitioned to the F-8 and deployed to the Mediterranean in *Forrestal*. In July 1960, when the ship returned from deployment, Jerry got out of the Navy and spent the next two years finishing up his college degree at Texas A&M and supervising a secondary recovery water flood project near Breckenridge, Texas. In 1964, the Breckenridge project dried up. Missing life in the

Navy, Houston decided to reenlist. He ended up securing a position as a T-2 jet trainer instructor at NAS Meridian in Mississippi.

Returning to the Navy proved easier than expected for Houston. "I showed up in March and was never a happier person in my life," he said. In an attempt to catch up with his peers, Houston flew every hop he could, including cross-country flights on weekends. The air war in Vietnam then erupted in the summer of 1964 with the Gulf of Tonkin incident, and Houston made it his number one goal to get out to Vietnam and fight before the war ended. He secured an early release from Meridian, attended RAG training, and joined VF-194 in mid-November 1966, on Yankee Station. He recalled, "We had two of the best fighter squadrons in the Navy (VF-194 and VF-191), but we never saw a MiG."

In December 1967, Houston did a second tour on the *Ticonderoga* with VF-194 and again experienced heavy SAM and AAA flying missions over North Vietnam. Overall, the carrier's two fighter squadrons lost three aircraft and saw numerous others damaged in combat. *Ticonderoga*, however, did experience one spectacular success during the cruise. One of Houston's friends, John "Pirate" Nichols, made a dramatic MiG-17 kill on 9 July 1968—one of few F-8 gun kills of the war. "We had a $100 bet [later reduced to $50] over who would get the first MiG, and John won that day, but as I gave Pirate his money, I became more determined than ever to get one of those MiGs myself." Devil's dream would not materialize for four years, but serving with the Screaming Eagles of VF-51 made the wait worthwhile.[14]

LOOKING GOOD VERSUS BEING GOOD

Although Teague knew quite a bit about the West Coast fighter pilot community and could handpick fighter pilots like Houston to be part of his VF-51 team, the NFO community was in many respects a mystery to this single-seat pilot in 1971. As a result, he relied on the detailers in BuPers to recruit the best back-seaters possible for his unit. In particular, Teague needed a senior-ranking NFO, a "Big Daddy NFO," to serve as his administrative officer—fifth in the squadron hierarchy after the XO, the operations officer, and the maintenance officer. The RAG instructors at VF-121 thought Lieutenant Commander Souder was "one of the best NFOs they had ever seen," and Teague made a special effort to have BuPers recruit Souder for the unit.

Souder, still smarting from his VF-154 experience with F-8 drivers, initially dug in his heels and refused the assignment. The detailer persisted: "The Navy really needs you, and it won't be like VF-154, we promise." As Souder explained the situation, "That damned detailer went through every sad story in the book, and every 'the Navy needs you' line ever written, and every personal appeal anyone could ever think of, and he wore at me and wore on me until I just finally gave in and told him: 'Yes, I'll do it.'"

Souder initially was amused by VF-51 and its antics. In reference to the squadron's red-and-white striped logo, everything in the squadron was "shit-hot, shit-hot, three white stripes or shit-hot, shit-hot, three red stripes." The unit had a full-time steward who maintained an artificial wood-paneled ready room. "It was shit-hot to have him there; and the ready room itself was shit-hot; we had sandwiches in the ready room at lunch time, which was shit-hot; we had a beer keg in a refrigerator in our ready room for consumption after flights, and that was shit-hot; and we had shiny decks and red and white stripes everywhere throughout our spaces, which was shit-hot; and we all had shiny boots and squadron patches and Phantom patches and rank insignia on our flight suits and that was *really* shit-hot." But the epitome of shit-hot was the squadron's gaggle of F-4Bs. An artistically inclined enlisted member of the unit painted large, ungainly eagles on each of the Phantoms. The modernistic birds ran the entire length of the planes and featured large flared tails with four red stripes and three white stripes! As a finishing touch, the man painted eagle talons on the doors of the landing gear and hands flashing the middle finger on the insides of the chaff doors.

Souder appreciated the high spirits of VF-51, but the unit's military academy mentality sometimes grated on him. Souder, accustomed to a more relaxed, operational atmosphere, expected to be treated more as a junior colleague than a "Cheerie Aye-Aye, Sir," midshipman. However, if this spit-and-polish attitude improved morale of the unit overall, he was willing to put up with it. Besides, he looked forward to honing his air combat maneuvering (ACM) skills again with pros such as Devil Houston and Tooter Teague.

Souder's initial impressions of Devil's flying confirmed his reputation. The night before VF-51's initial round of training at Yuma, Arizona, the squadron dined at a local Mexican restaurant. The dinner was accompanied by giant margaritas and tequila shots. Afterward, most of the unit proceeded directly to bed, but Devil, Tooter, and several other pilots went to the BOQ lounge, played cards, and drank whiskey until the wee hours of the evening. At the 0500 briefing, Souder noticed that Houston "looked like hell; his hair was a mess, he had bloodshot red eyes, and he appeared like he hadn't had any sleep the night before." The mission that day was bombing, and Houston flew eight passes and dropped eight bombs just like the rest of the unit. However, after each run, he removed his oxygen mask and vomited into the helmet bag. According to Souder, "He had a few multiple heaves on the downwind legs, too, but he always finished them or stifled them long enough to do his next run, then he'd pull off the target and throw up again . . . and he was getting the best hits of anybody! He even got one or two bull's-eyes! When his radar officer (RO) would call 'off' after each run, we could hear Devil in the background heaving his guts out."

Souder's respect for Houston jumped several notches that day. "It would be stupid to stay up and gamble all night, and it would be stupid to drink whiskey all night, and it would be stupid to drink so much that it'd make you sick when flying the next day; but it would be 'shit-hot' if you did all that and got away with it. On the other hand, it would be *unforgivable* to do all that and *not* be able to fly the next day."

BLACKJACK

Teague eventually took command of VF-51 in June 1971 and recruited Commander Jack "Blackjack" Finley to be his executive officer. Finley, born in Tennessee in 1935, attended Culver Military Academy in Culver, Indiana, where he excelled as an equestrian and a polo player. From Culver, he matriculated to the United States Naval Academy, earned high marks, and won a coveted slot in aviation training at Pensacola in 1957.

Upon completion of aviation training, Finley joined VF-124, an F-8 training squadron. While there, he met Foster Teague, a man who would eventually become a lifelong friend and fierce competitor. Finley's first cruise was with VF-51 in 1960. He later took another WEST-PAC cruise with VF-51 in 1963, where he saw limited action in the skies over Laos and North Vietnam as an escort for photoreconnaissance missions.

After that latter cruise, Finley attended test pilot school at Edwards Air Force Base and then entered the highly prestigious astronaut program. The Vietnam War, however, quickly changed his mind about being an astronaut. "My buddies were getting shot at, and I was sitting around playing astronaut," Finley explained. "So I said I gotta go over there again and see if I can do it."

After a Mediterranean cruise with VF-13, Finley deployed to Vietnam with VF-111 on board the *Shangri-La* in 1970. Given the bombing halt in 1970, Finley did not see much action during that tour; he decided to volunteer to go back, this time with his old squadron, VF-51.[15]

THE BIG DADDY RO

With Finley and Houston on board, Teague now had two officers on whom he could absolutely depend to enforce his will in the squadron. The extreme loyalty to Teague displayed by Houston and Finley made some officers uncomfortable, however, especially those who flew in the backseats. "That unbending, uncompromising loyalty to Tooter bothered me," Souder complained. "Both Blackjack and Devil practiced it, and it became painfully obvious to the rest of us that when Tooter spoke, he expected us to jump . . . even to our deaths, because that's the practical response Blackjack and Devil displayed. No matter what the subject, and no matter how stupid the premise, their response was always 'YES, SIR.'"

Souder's first major run-ins with this troika came in his capacity as the ranking radar intercept officer in the squadron, or the "Big Daddy RO." Most of Souder's disagreements with Teague revolved around personnel matters and tactics. With respect to crewing the F-4, for example, Souder argued that in a combat situation, flight leaders should have the most capable ROs in their backseats. Flight leaders would be leading fifteen- to thirty-five-plane Alpha strikes and would need the most capable assistance possible with navigating, communicating, coordinating electronic countermeasures, targeting, and so forth. The squadron policy ultimately adopted by Teague, by contrast, teamed up the most capable pilots with the least capable ROs and vice versa, thereby averaging out the capabilities of each airplane with no regard for the extra responsibilities of the Alpha strike leaders. For whatever reason, Teague simply did not recognize the fact that a skilled RO in the lead plane could be a true force multiplier in a combat situation. As he himself often put it, "I've been flying single-seat fighters for fourteen years, and I ain't never had to have anybody tell me how to fight my air-plane and especially not the guy in the trunk."

In accordance with squadron policy, Houston assigned Souder to fly with the least experienced pilot in the unit, Rick Hoffing. Hoffing had a bad reputation as a pilot even before entering the squadron, and Teague had done his best to convince BuPers not to assign him to the unit, but to no avail. "Hoffing was too nice and too easygoing, too baby-faced, too soft to be a fighter pilot," recalled Souder. "He didn't have the right disposition to be a fighter pilot, and once those guys in VF-51 got down on you, they wouldn't kick you; they'd stomp you." To punish Hoffing for his poor piloting and Souder for his seditious behavior, Teague requested that Houston assign these men to ferry a plane with damaged landing gear back to Miramar and not to return to the squadron until the bombing training ended. "We flew the plane back uneventfully," explained Souder, "but as we left, I couldn't help but feel like I'd been banished from Fallon." Souder and Hoffing did not stay to-gether as a team for long. To appease Souder, who complained inces-santly about Hoffing's piloting skills, Houston reassigned him to fly with "Blackjack" Finley. Houston also eventually stripped Hoffing of his wings and transferred him out of the squadron.[16]

DEBATES WITH LEADERSHIP

If the crewing assignments and other disagreements epitomized pilot contempt for the NFOs as fellow aviators, various debates between Souder and the command group over how best to use two radar warn-ing systems, the AN/APR-25 and AN/APR-27, revealed the ignorance of many F-8 pilots with respect to much of the exotic technology of the F-4. The AN/APR-25 alerted a Phantom crew to enemy radar signals. It sounded an audio signal and displayed an electronic strobe in the di-rection of any or all radars that were illuminating the F-4. The strobe originated in the center of a little round scope about three inches in di-ameter, and both the strobe and the audio signal were coded differently for AAA, SAMs, or MiGs. The closer an F-4 was to an enemy radar, the longer the strobe reached out to the edge of the scope, and the louder the audio got. If a SAM was launched at you, the various strobes on the scope disappeared except for the one main strobe, which pointed in the direction of the SAM.

The AN/APR-27 received and processed SA-2 surface-to-air missile guidance signals and indicated the level of threat posed. Two levels of threat are detected: missile alert and missile launch. When the APR-27 recognized the presence of missile guidance signals in the normal (or rest) position, it put out a missile alert tone. When a missile actually launched and began receiving steering commands, a red light flashed rapidly, and the audio tone of the system changed from a low-frequency warble to a much higher-frequency warble.

Houston, unfamiliar with the capabilities of these systems, issued a squadron policy that if anyone encountered an AN/APR-27 missile launch warning, he should "go right for the deck." To the NFOs, this dictate made no sense because it was the AN/APR-25, not the AN/APR-27, that indicated a SAM's direction. The AN/APR-27 only told an F-4 crew that the SAM battery had activated its tracking and guidance radar. The proper action to take upon receiving a warning from the AN/APR-27 was to check the AN/APR-25 for the strobe's direction, then look out in that direction for the SAM, being sure to look at all altitudes. Both systems working in conjunction gave a pilot plenty of time to react in the event of a SAM launch. To go "right for the deck," as Houston had told the squadron to do, was an overreaction. As Souder explained, "It may have sent us down there with a SAM coming right up our butts, or may have caused us to have midair collisions with other planes in the strike group in the mad scramble to get down, or may have put us in an extremely limited altitude envelope for further maneuvering to evade the SAM, and it definitely would have driven us down into the small-arms envelope."

In defense of Houston, he did listen to Souder's suggestions when it came to air combat maneuvers, a subject Houston knew much more about than F-4 avionics. Souder petitioned Houston to allow the ROs to direct one ACM engagement from start to finish from the backseat. That meant the pilot would simply become a "voice-actuated autopilot" for the RO. "By doing exactly what the RO directed him to do," explained Souder, "the ROs would have to study the principles of ACM in order to be able to direct the pilots through the engagements, and of course, with the pilots doing what the ROs told them to do, the ROs would be able to learn from their own mistakes."

Controversy, however, continued to plague Souder when it came to crewing assignments. During the unit's air-to-ground training at NAS Fallon, Nevada, Teague ordered everyone in the squadron to submit a list of people with whom they wished to fly. The operations department would then use these lists to determine actual combat crews. Houston ended up with one of the least competent ROs in the squadron, and Souder, with one of the least competent pilots. Worse yet, Teague, who would often lead wing-level Alpha strikes, wound up with Ralph Howell—one of Souder's former students three years prior at Glynco, Georgia.

A new ensign and a graduate of the Navy Enlisted Scientific Program (NESEP), Howell appeared to have promise back at Glynco. NESEP took the most promising enlisted personnel, the cream of the crop, ran them through a battery of tests and interviews, and then sent them to college on a Navy scholarship to get a scientific or engineering degree. When they graduated, the Navy commissioned them as officers and allowed them to apply for any officer career field they desired. Howell chose aviation. A quiet, unassuming, serious-minded older student, Howell learned the RIO concepts easily, but something about his personality worried Souder: "I distinctly remember wondering if he'd have the force of personality to do well directing a pilot if he ever really needed to." Ironically, Souder's concerns back in 1968 would return to haunt him in VF-51. As Souder recalled,

> Three years after I had first realized my concern for that particular aspect of Ralph's basic personality, I was to have my own personal welfare, and that of the whole squadron, either directly profit from it or suffer from it, because Ralph's personality would directly influence and contribute to the development of Tooter's image of an RO. That image, of course, would determine Tooter's opinions about how valuable we were to a pilot, and therefore how much in-flight authority to give us. Ultimately, I thought a lot of what would happen to us in combat would probably be influenced by the positive or negative effect Ralph had on Tooter. Ralph was a good guy; quiet, easygoing, acquiescing, accommodating, always very subordinating. But maybe, just maybe, Ralph was a little *too* good a guy. . . . I was *really* worried.

One of the few forums where Souder believed he could influence the squadron as a whole was the all-officers meetings, during which he would often speak up on such issues as crewing, tactics, and technology. Although his opinions occasionally conflicted with those of the command group, Souder did not hesitate to voice them if the matter appeared compelling enough. With the possible exception of Teague, he had seen more combat than anyone else in the unit. Therefore, he believed he had the moral authority to speak out on operational issues. The life-and-death urgency of war demanded boldness, even at the risk of impetuosity.

Matters started coming to a head one day during a discussion on MiG tactics. After listening to the pilots boast and argue over who would get the first MiG, Souder, the only man in the room who had actually gone head-to-head with a MiG in combat, stood up and interrupted the cabal:

> Don't you guys be so anxious to get a MiG that you do something stupid. Don't go running off on some wild vector if you don't know where that vector will take you. The Vietnamese have set traps a lot of times by baiting fighters with MiGs, either by hanging right over flak traps or laying in the weeds waiting to jump them from behind. Some of our guys took the vectors and flew right into traps, and today they're either dead or still in Hanoi. You'll get your chance to get a MiG, but do it on your terms. We want to play ball, but we want to play ball when it's our ball, and our bat, and hopefully, our ballpark.

He then sat down, and Teague immediately got up, pointed at Souder with his lit cigarette, and emphatically stated: "If any pilot in this squadron doesn't take a vector for a MiG he'll never fly again . . . not in this squadron; and that's squadron policy."

A few days later, Souder again incurred Teague's anger during a briefing about MiG tactics. Souder, citing lessons learned at Top Gun, and Have Drill, declared that "if you're in a 2 v 1, one guy string him out and the other guy shoot him." This line of reasoning appeared to be consistent with Teague's very own Have Drill report, which stated, "Engage [MiG-17s] only as a section with strict mutual support." After Souder sat down, Teague leapt up and said, "As long as I'm C.O. of this squadron, no guy is going to set up the other guy so the other guy can get a shot at the MiG. You fight your own fight! . . . Now, that's squadron policy!"

Clearly, Teague was beginning to tire of Souder's lectures, but in fairness to Teague, he did make an effort to warn Souder privately that any future insubordination at meetings would not be tolerated and would be expounded upon in Souder's next fitness report. Teague, as was characteristic of his leadership style, also decided to give Souder a barroom lecture on the subject at a squadron happy hour. One Wednesday night at the O Club, he told Souder, "You know, J. B., it's here in the club that you make your reputation, not in the airplane." After several rounds of scotch, Souder and Teague went out to the parking lot, ostensibly to fetch a pack of cigarettes from Teague's car. Once out there, he started yelling at Souder, telling him, "You'd better stop defying me, and you'd better stop crossing me, and if you don't, I'll make sure you never get promoted." To add emphasis to this message,

> he sneered and actually foamed at the mouth, and blazed his eyes down at me. He then reared his knee up almost to his chest and like a riled-up mule, back-whacked and totally kicked in the side of the car parked next to his, a car parked in a special parking space reserved for squadron commanders. He went back and forth between the fender openings, kicking backward so he could use his heel, which would let him whack the hardest. He was drunk, and I thought that he shouldn't be doing that to the car, but he often made his points in unusual ways which seemed perfectly ordinary to him, and this was just one of them. We went back into the O club and resumed drinking and partying like nothing had happened, until it closed.

For the next few days, Souder contemplated his predicament: "I considered taking the easy way out and just giving up and just shutting my mouth and just falling into line and enduring his stupid edicts and taking my chances when we got back to Vietnam." Souder then began to think about how he had gotten himself into the predicament. Yes, he wanted to fly again, and his chances of doing so as a civilian were slim. But he also reenlisted because he truly perceived himself as a naval officer and yearned to make the service his career:

> I had returned to the Navy because I knew that I could do some good there. I had returned to the Navy and chosen a West Coast squadron because I thought maybe I could go back to Vietnam and help get that mess over and help bring our POWs home. I had finally relented and given in to BuPers and taken the orders to VF-51 because I thought I could do some good there, and possibly keep some other guys from getting killed or going to Hanoi. I thought about all that, then I thought about just shutting up and going along with the "shit-hot,

shit-hot, three white stripes" and not trying to do a damn thing about helping transition this goddamn squadron to F-4s, . . . but I just couldn't do it. I had been sent to VF-51 to serve the best interests of the squadron. I had been sent to VF-51 to serve the best interests of the United States Navy, . . . to serve the best interests of the United States of America; and to help keep some damn good naval officers alive. I had not been sent to VF-51 to serve the personal interests of Foster Schuler Teague. . . . A little voice kept whispering to me from the far recesses of my mind . . . moral courage.

Souder would continue to fight for his beliefs despite the consequences.

8

War and Ejection from the Squadron

ON 12 NOVEMBER 1971, *Coral Sea* departed NAS Alameda and steamed west to Hawaii and eventually to Southeast Asia. As the ship passed under the Golden Gate Bridge, Souder got a knot in his stomach and a lump in his throat. "Somehow I knew that I wasn't coming home on that ship," he recalled. "I didn't know if I'd get killed, captured, lost in Olongapo and eaten alive by the pigs or what, but I just knew intuitively that I wasn't coming home on that ship."

Souder began his sea tour flying with Blackjack Finley, and almost from the beginning, the two personalities clashed. Souder complained that Finley was too hyperactive and careless, and Finley criticized Souder for talking too much during the flight.[1] Nevertheless, they worked hard to get along because each saw distinct benefits in the relationship. For J. B., flying with Blackjack, the squadron executive officer, often put him in the lead position, thereby increasing his chances of getting a MiG; for Finley, Souder's combat experience might improve his own chances of getting a MiG should a contact arise.

Unfortunately for both men, the initial missions flown in December ended up being routine missions into low-threat areas of Laos with no MiG activity whatsoever. Bored and seeking to learn something from the forward air controllers with whom he worked, Souder volunteered on 7 January 1972 to do an exchange tour with the Air Force "Nail" forward air controllers based in Nakhon Phanom, Thailand.

Souder spent four days at Nakhon Phanom and flew two missions with the Nails, forward air controllers who flew OV-10 Broncos, a two-seat, propeller-driven observation plane. He learned that these men possessed not only ample amounts of courage but brains as well. "They gave me several tips about things we Navy guys could do to help them do their jobs." Souder learned how to recognize the landmarks these men used for navigation and how to estimate how much time it took to move an F-4 from a rendezvous point to a target. Timing, he learned, was critical to these pilots because they often controlled multiple flights simultaneously on different radio frequencies and tight schedules.

With the Nails, Souder also got a taste of how pilots and navigators worked with one another in the Air Force OV-10 community. One of his pilots, Captain Ron Helsel, allowed him to take off and fly the plane extensively during the mission. Ron even allowed Souder to fire some target-marking smoke rockets. He pointed out a screw in the canopy for Souder to use as a sight and let J. B. roll in and mark a target with a rocket from 8,000 feet. Helsel, in short, treated Souder as a true colleague—something he had rarely experienced with the three senior pilots in VF-51.

With some regret, Souder departed Thailand four days after his arrival to return to VF-51. The Nails told him he was the only exchange aviator who had flown more than one mission with them. Back on board the ship, Souder intended to disseminate the information he had gained to the NFO community. He went ahead and taped a large navigation chart with all the visual checkpoints he had learned from the Nails on the squadron blackboard and chalked a note beside it: "ROs, learn to recognize these visual checkpoints and their positions from Danang TACAN!" Several hours later, J. B. returned to the ready room and noticed that his chart had been removed. The next day, in the back of the ready room, Houston told him, "Don't put out things telling the ROs what to learn. Ops will put out what we want the ROs to learn." Souder protested, arguing that the Nails had made it very clear to him that they wanted all the aircrews with whom they worked to learn those checkpoints. Houston held his ground, and Souder seethed.

About a week later, as operations against North Vietnam started to pick up, Houston and Souder again locked horns—this time over a navigational matter. In an all-officers meeting, Devil stood up and announced, "In this squadron, we don't want the ROs carrying charts." Souder immediately objected, but Houston defended the policy, claiming that he wanted ROs to focus on what was going on outside the cockpit, and not on charts.

Incredulous, Souder cornered Jack Finley at the end of the meeting and asked him how ROs were supposed to find targets if they could not carry charts. Finley replied, "We follow the lead fighter! We just follow the man!" Souder then asked him how the lead was supposed to find the target. Jack then told Souder to come with him to his stateroom.

Once the two men were behind closed doors, Jack half apologized and said that Souder was right but that the squadron policy was final.

A week later, Air Wing 15 received a tasking to bomb five SAM sites along the coast in Route Package 4, just north of Vinh. Two F-4 squadrons, two A-7 squadrons, and an A-6 squadron would participate in the strike, with each squadron assigned to a single SAM site. The SAM sites were lined up almost in a straight line. The plan was for the entire strike force to fly to the offshore island of Hon Me, and then for each squadron to break off in a different direction and head toward its own particular target.

VF-51 launched and joined the other squadrons as planned. Teague and Howell led one of the sections, and Finley and Souder, the other. As soon as Souder and Finley got close to Hon Me, they started to get AAA and SAM radar warnings on their AN/APR-25. Teague began to descend and increase airspeed to ensure that the flight had enough energy to evade any SAMs fired. The squadron crossed over Hon Me at 3,000 feet and 500 knots, and then Teague began jinking and heading away from VF-51's assigned heading. Souder checked his chart and immediately got on the intercom with Finley: "Tooter's going to the wrong target!"

Finley did not acknowledge the transmission and started pulling hard banks of 80 to 90 degrees. These maneuvers brought the aircraft within 1,000 feet of the sea. Souder became more emphatic: "He's headed for VA-22's target. Our target is about 30 degrees to the left!" Souder knew the flight was going toward the wrong target because he was carrying a chart, in direct violation of squadron policy.

"There ain't nothing I can do about it now," replied Jack as he continued to jink the plane. The AN/APR-27 then sounded, and Souder went to work tracking SAMs. Three sites fired missiles, apparently at the flights north of VF-51. VF-51 then leveled off at 800 feet and streaked over the target at 500 knots. The two sections bombed the SAM site's launchers and the support vehicles, destroying the target completely but leaving the assigned site untouched.

All the way back to the ship, Souder burned with anger. After he and Jack landed, they proceeded to the Integrated Operational Intelligence Center to debrief the mission and provide bomb damage assessment to the intelligence officers. As the two men entered, they noticed that Admiral Howard Greer's chief of staff was there asking questions about the mission—an indication of its high priority. Aviators filtered in, and finally Commander Mink Ermine, the designated Alpha strike leader and commanding officer of VA-22, came into the room. He appeared agitated, but when he noticed Teague in the room, his anger turned to impishness. He began his debriefing just like many of the other officers, but when he got to talking about his bomb run, he glanced toward Teague and then bellowed out so everyone in the room could hear, "There I was, we came around the corner and rolled in on the target at about 8,000 feet, and just as I was about to mash the pickle, all of a sudden I had a bomb-sight full of F-4s! Big, ugly, red F-4s! And I said 'Well goddamn, there's Tooter, he got my target for me,' so I pulled off without dropping." Souder felt vindicated, but he still fumed over the fact that Finley had not alerted Teague when Souder informed him that the flight was off course.

Relations between the two men continued to worsen until they broke down completely during a routine morning preflight check. Finley tended to rush through preflight, hoping that any serious problems would be picked up by the maintenance crews. Souder, on the other hand, was methodical and thorough. Their contrasting flight styles caused routine clashes, but none was serious enough to break up the team until one day Finley's casual approach nearly caused a serious accident.

As the ordnance men armed the missiles on the F-4, standard procedure called for the aviators to put their hands out of the cockpit to ensure that no buttons got pushed accidentally. The two men then needed to get their hands back into the cockpit before the fuel probe check began. Otherwise, the probe could slam out and rip off the RO's right arm. Finley routinely failed to warn his RO before the check despite the fact that the naval aviation flight manual (NATOPS) specifically required it. After one such incident several days earlier, Souder told him, "Jack, you know what? I am going to take a little piece of fishing line or nylon cord and tie one end around the end of that fuel probe and then run it back through my cockpit and up there and tie the other end around your balls so that when you want to put the fuel probe out, you have to tell me and I'll untie the knot. And then if you don't tell me, that will be the last time you'll put that fuel probe out without telling me."

"Ha, ha, funny joke, shipmate," Finley replied, but he still did not change his ways. During the morning preflight two days later, Souder noticed that the intercom link between the two men was broken. J. B.

hopped out of the aircraft on the left side and signaled one of the aviation electronics mates (AEs) to help him with the problem. The AE
stood on the left engine intake with Souder, removed the rear seat pan,
and put it on the right engine intake. He then began working on the
wiring for the intercom. All of a sudden, out came the fuel probe, slamming it into the seat pan and propelling it twenty feet down the deck.
"It scared the shit out of me and everybody on deck and so forth, and it
was simply because Finley refused to go by NATOPS and tell me the
probe was coming out." The maintenance people retrieved the pan and
bent it back into shape, and Souder got back into the aircraft. After a
communications check, Souder let Finley know how he felt: "OK, Jack,
this is the last fucking time I fly with you. That's it. We're done." The
two men flew the hop as planned, and when they both got out of the
plane, Finley attempted to smooth things over.

"Now, look, babe." Finley called everyone Babe.

"What about it?" Souder said. "No, that's it, Jack. I'm fucking finished with you." That was the final time these two men flew together.[2]

Souder flew with several different pilots for almost two months until he
was finally crewed with a young, first cruise lieutenant, Al Molinare.
Flying with a junior officer relegated Souder to the role of follower
rather than leader during MiG patrols, but by this point, he did not care.
He opted to put aside his ambition to kill a MiG and instead focus on
giving Al any help he needed and just staying alive. "Al was a quiet,
unassuming young guy, a good stick, and very responsive to me. While
a student in the replacement air group, he'd been given an award for
being an exceptional pilot in the air-to-air phase of training, so that
made me feel good."

What did not make Souder feel good was his own physical condition. By April 27, he was "fucking tired." Already during the month of
April he had flown forty-nine missions with ten different pilots. In the
last five days, he had flown twelve missions, three of them on 26 April
and two the following day, the day of his shoot-down. That is a lot of
flying, even for a seasoned veteran. But the North Vietnamese were
now in the midst of a major offensive against South Vietnam, and air
power represented one of the few means available to policy makers this
late in the war to exercise American military might.

Souder sipped a cup of black coffee in the VF-51 ready room before
his scheduled afternoon mission. That day he and Molinare flew wing

for Teague and Ralph Howell. The two F-4Bs took off from *Coral Sea* and headed toward the Hanoi area but soon got diverted to Vinh because of bad weather near the objective. J. B. spotted a lone truck on Route 1A outside of Vinh, and the two F-4s swept in and bombed the truck to oblivion. "The poor bastard never knew what happened," recalled Souder. "A thousand cluster bombs hit him at one time." The two planes rejoined each other about eighty to ninety miles south of Hanoi and established a MiG patrol by the strike group's secondary target. Teague immediately called Red Crown to inquire about MiG activity. "We're drilling holes in the sky at low altitude forty miles from the closest MiG base, and eighty miles from Hanoi, and Tooter starts bugging and bugging the controller for bogey dope." Finally, Red Crown gave them a vector on a MiG-21 that had just taken off from Phuc Yen airfield eighty miles away.

"Al, fuel check."

"7,100."

"Goddamn it," he thought to himself. The flight had briefed a 7,200-pound "bingo" fuel state—the minimum fuel the F-4 needed to make it back to the carrier safely. J. B. knew that the flight did not have enough fuel to chase a MiG eighty miles away, and he knew that trying to find a MiG over that rough terrain would be difficult, especially with undercast conditions. "It would be too easy for the bogey to hide under the clouds and surprise us from the rear." Souder consulted his charts.

"OK, Al. We're going to meet the MiG off the end of finger lake, and this is a trap, and we're going to be shot down."

"360 at 75," announced Red Crown. The MiG was five miles closer, heading directly toward them.

"360 at 70."

This was just the type of scenario that J. B. had discussed with his roommate Robbie Griesser a few months earlier. He knew intuitively that one of the planes in his flight would not return that day, and it was "going to be us, and not Teague with that golden horseshoe up his ass." Souder struggled to contain his increasing anger; he concentrated on planning an egress route to take after the engagement and the best route to fly inland to a safe area should their plane be "fatally hit." He told Al, "If we take a bad hit and are going to go down, try to go west toward the mountains . . . that's our best chance for a pick-up."[3] They were still too far away to start searching for the MiG with his old APQ-72 radar.

He remembered telling Teague at a squadron meeting that the Vietnamese would take advantage of the F-4B's radar by flying under clouds and hiding in the ground clutter. Back at Miramar, during training, Souder had repeatedly implored Teague to fly low if he got a MiG call over land, but today, Teague continued to fly toward the MiG at 8,000 feet. "I could really use an F-4J right now with its new pulse Doppler radar," Souder lamented to himself. With standard radar, one needed to be at co-altitude or, better yet, below the bogey's altitude, to spot a MiG, but with a Doppler, one could pick out a moving target even through ground clutter.

"Take it down, Al."

"Uh, how far? We gotta stay in position."

"We can go down 1,000 feet. Go ahead and push it down a thousand."

Molinare settled the plane down to 7,000 feet. The two F-4s were still in a combat spread, with Teague and Howell to the left about a mile and a half to two miles abeam of Molinare and Souder. At about twenty-five miles Souder started looking for him on the radar. "I'm looking, looking, and I don't see a damn thing. And Teague is the leader, so I'm not saying anything on the radio. But I'm just yearning to tell him to take it down, damn it. Get underneath. Let's get down there, but I had to stay with him. So he stays at 8,000 feet at 420 knots, smoking like a son of a bitch." At Top Gun, Souder had learned that one should always go into minimum afterburner about fifteen miles from a target. Otherwise, the MiG pilot might spot the mile-long black plume of smoke that trailed the F-4. The two planes were now passing within three miles east of Bai Thuong airfield.

"Bearcat 1. Check your eleven o'clock low."

"Roger that," Teague responded.

Souder wanted to say, "Hey, dumbshit, what the hell are we doing over an enemy airfield low on gas and forty to fifty miles between us and the coast," but he kept his mouth shut. Several days earlier, he had been chastised by Finley for talking too much on the radio, so he remained silent. Instead, he continued looking at the radar and out of the cockpit around and behind them, searching desperately for the wily MiG.

At a controller's call of "360 at 4," he abandoned the radar and took a long look at the section's rear area to the left, between the two aircraft.

He then looked behind him to the right, outside the section. As he was looking at his five o'clock position, Red Crown announced, "Whoops, he might have slipped behind you. Check 220 at 4."

Souder swung back around and darted his eyes at the heading indicator to confirm 220 was at his seven o'clock position, preparatory to looking at that position, and then, *bam*, an Atoll missile slammed below the airplane, disabling both engines. "It was like you're sitting in a limousine and somebody slammed your trunk back there. We were thrust forward in our straps, and it felt like you're coming out of afterburner when you're supersonic."

The MiG-21 that shot down Souder and Molinare was flown by Hoang Quoc Dung, a MiG-21 pilot of the 921st Fighter Regiment based at Noi Bai. He and another pilot, Cao Son Khao, were vectored to Bearcats 1 and 2 by ground controllers. When Dung closed on the Phantoms at low altitude, he executed an Immelman turn, achieved missile lock, and fired at Bearcat 2. It was a textbook ground-controlled intercept at long range. This was Dung's only kill of the war. He still serves with the Vietnamese People's Air Force as a war college professor.[4]

As soon as the missile impacted, J. B. keyed his mike: "This is Bearcat 2. We've taken a hit and we're going down." Souder then looked left in the 240 direction to see if the MiG was threatening Teague. He didn't see the MiG. He then looked right and saw the hydraulic plume of a second missile that had just gone underneath Souder's right wing.

"Turn left," Souder told Al in an attempt to get him to head for the relative safety of the mountains, which were a much safer spot for a helicopter extraction than the open land beneath them and between them and the coast.

"What's going on with the engines?"

"The left one's at zero, and the throttle is loose—no reaction to the throttle. The right one is at 70 percent [close to idle at that altitude], and the throttle is frozen."

Teague then transmitted to a tanker plane, which had been calling out its position relative to Bearcat flight during the missile impact.

"I'm going to need 3,000 pounds."

Al then transmitted, "Yeah, I'm gonna need 3,000 pounds, too."

"Al, we don't need any fuel, goddamn it. We're going down. Don't you understand? We've been shot down. Turn left!" Al turned right instead.

"Al, what are you doing?"

"Uh, I'm trying to make for the water."

"Goddamn it. We're going down. Turn left." The plane was now in a 30-degree banking turn. "Wait a minute, wait a minute. Don't touch the stick. What do the hydraulic gauges say?"

"They're all zero."

"OK. Don't touch the stick. Complete a right 270 and head for the mountains." Souder switched his radar to standby and stowed it forward in preparation for the ejection.

"Hey, Bearcat 2," Tooter then called out, "can you tighten up the turn to set up the MiG for me?"

"Don't touch the stick, Al," Souder said, and he instantly recalled the meeting at which Teague flatly stated, contrary to Souder's teaching, that no pilot in VF-51 would ever set up the MiG for the other guy to shoot. He fought the nearly overpowering temptation to say, "Sorry, Bearcat, that's against squadron policy," and remained silent.

As they passed a heading of 180, Al said, "There he is. There's the MiG."

"Where?" Souder demanded as he pulled out his radar and switched it back on.

"The son of a bitch got us, but we can still get him. Where is he?" Souder looked at the scope, but to no avail.

"Ah, he's off the scope. He's out there at three o'clock."

Souder then looked out the canopy, hoping to spot the MiG with the naked eye, but he spotted no MiG. The F-4 continued to descend, by now passing 4,000 feet. Souder again stowed the radar.

"Where do we go?" Al asked.

"Just pick the highest mountain you can find, and put your nose on it."

"OK."

Molinare steadied up heading 270 and maintained the 250-knot best-glide airspeed. Teague then broke in: "Bearcat 2, there's stuff coming off your airplane."

"There's nothing I can do about it now," responded Souder. "I'm kind of busy." The altimeter now read 3,000 feet.

"OK, I'm going to lose it," Al said. "We're going to do a roll to the right; get it on the upside."

"OK, I've got you selected." Souder would eject both aviators when the proper angle was reached. As the aircraft rolled and came

45 degrees short of the wings-level position, Souder jerked the handle. *Bang, thwoosh, thut, thut, thut, thump,* and Souder was in his parachute, about 1,500 feet above the ground. "I looked around as fast as I could, and there's the damn airplane directly below me. It's in the ground in a massive fireball, and I looked off to my left, and I see Al hanging there. It looked like he was about 100 yards away." Souder called Teague on his radio: "This is Bearcat 2 Bravo. I'm out of the airplane and I'm OK. Ask Robbie [Griesser] what I'm going to do." Souder had concocted a plan months before to make for a river and swim to a safe extraction area at night in the event of a shoot-down. He did not want to broadcast this plan over the radio and hoped Teague would consult his roommate Griesser for information about the plan.

"Say again over?"

"Ask Robbie Griesser what I'm going to do."

"Roger that. Well, about all I can say is to try to make for the mountains."

"Roger, I understand. I gotta go."

Ironically, as Souder drifted down toward an uncertain fate in North Vietnam, feelings of relief competed with those of fear and dread. No longer would he need to fight with the VF-51 command group over policies detrimental to the ROs and often to the squadron at large. In fact, his stay in the Hanoi Hilton, despite interrogations, hardships, and deprivations, would be generally less stressful to him than his time spent in VF-51.

Clearly, some of the stress Souder endured was of his own making. Challenging senior leadership at all-officers meetings generally caused more heat than light. No matter how much he wanted to get his points across to the squadron, his interests might have been better served if he had refrained from arguing directly with the leadership in front of the squadron. Finley and Houston, in particular, often proved quite reasonable when confronted on an issue privately. Houston even sided with Souder's reasoning on crewing late in the tour, when he suddenly realized that his own chances of getting a MiG were slim unless he could get a high-caliber RO like Kevin Moore in his backseat (ultimately, those two would kill a MiG over the very same location where Souder and Molinare got shot down). However, while Houston and Finley were at times sympathetic with some of Souder's ideas in private, they nearly always refused to press the issues with each other or

Teague. As a result, Souder felt the only way to get his points across, even if the leadership refused to adopt them, was in the forum of the all-officers meeting. For him, organizational politics and good behavior took a backseat to survival. "This wasn't a corporate board meeting where at most a company might lose money if no one challenged the boss's ideas directly," he reasoned. "This was *war*, and people could die or become imprisoned based on the policies being debated in the meetings."[5]

If the style by which Souder attacked the command group may have turned off some members of the unit, most agreed with the substance of what he was saying. Souder clearly understood the F-4's radar and avionics systems better than the command group, and those officers might have benefited from his reasoning on these issues.

With respect to the Sparrow missile, Teague and Houston were correct in viewing it with skepticism. Overall, 612 AIM-7s were fired during the war for 56 kills, and a kill rate of less than 9 percent. The AIM-9's kill rate at the end of the war, by comparison, stood at 18 percent. However, if the AIM-9Gs used in Linebacker are removed from the statistics, the rate drops to 14 percent. Furthermore, the failure rate of both missiles remained much more even throughout the conflict: 66 percent in the case of the AIM-7 and 47 percent for the AIM-9.[6] Souder, though, was not arguing that the AIM-7 was a better missile; rather, he argued that if doctrine called for the missiles to be hung on the airplanes, then there were times when the missiles should be fired, such as at long ranges and in front-aspect engagements. As Hickey's engagement demonstrated, the Sparrow could achieve a kill when used properly, or even improperly with a little luck.

Ironically, Teague ordered the squadron to stop carrying the AIM-7 after Souder's shoot-down, arguing that the shoot-down may have resulted from Souder paying too much attention to radar and not checking his six o'clock often enough—a viewpoint that directly contradicts the facts as Souder stated them. On the controller's call of four miles, Souder abandoned the radar and started checking his six constantly, inside and outside.

Souder got shot down because Teague was keeping the flight at a dangerously high altitude. If the two planes had been down at 1,000 feet, Souder and Molinare might have survived the attack. First, being low would have maximized their chance of spotting a MiG with the F-4's radar—a system that functioned much better in a "look-up" aspect over land. Second, Souder's chances of eyeballing the MiG would have improved at a lower altitude: a six o'clock high aircraft is much easier to spot than one at six o'clock low. From his experience in Have Drill, Teague should have understood these basic concepts. That he did not may have resulted from his excitement over the prospect of getting a MiG or from his tendency to outright ignore suggestions from Souder. What remains clear is that he did not hold NFOs in high regard, and perhaps this bigotry prevented him from taking them and their ideas seriously.

Not every RO in VF-51 and certainly not every F-4 RO in the Navy confronted the type of discrimination Souder faced in his career, but Souder's experiences do reveal that some pilots viewed NFOs as second-class citizens, or "non-flying officers," even into the 1970s. Unfortunately for Souder, he would have to serve some hard time in Hanoi before he could return to flying and feel some degree of vindication.

PART III

THE POW EXPERIENCE FROM 1969 TO 1973

Unity over Self

THE HISTORY OF POWS in Vietnam remains one of the war's most painful and bitter chapters. The conflict claimed only 800 U.S. POWs, but the captivity period for many of the prisoners proved the longest in U.S. history.[1] This alone made them unique. But other issues make this story critical to the overall history of the Vietnam War. First, all but 71 of the POWs were aviators with officer rank and unique credentials. Their special status made them prime targets for propaganda exploitation. The Communist leadership in Hanoi coerced the POWs into making antiwar statements, paraded them in front of Vietnamese civilians to arouse anti-American sentiment, released them on occasion to prominent American antiwar activists, and used them as negotiating chips in peace talks with the U.S. government. In short, American POWs fought a war within a war, and their resistance or cooperation with the enemy often had political ramifications that extended far beyond the confines of the Hanoi Hilton. Similarly, the armed services' policies toward POWs and their families took on equally high stakes and absorbed more and more of the attention of senior military officials as the hostilities continued. Not surprisingly, the release of American POWs emerged as President Nixon's chief demand in the 1972 peace talks and the raison d'être behind Operations Linebacker I and II.[2]

The POW experience in Southeast Asia fell into two distinct periods. From 1965 through 1969, the North Vietnamese tortured American prisoners regularly, kept them in stocks, and failed to provide them with adequate nutrition. They also used solitary confinement to undermine morale and compel POWs to make propaganda statements condemning the U.S. government and the war. After the death of Ho Chi Minh in September 1969, the North Vietnamese leadership began to take a softer stance toward POWs: torture subsided, and general conditions in the camps improved somewhat, although camp authorities occasionally reduced food rations and often employed isolation to weaken the POW leadership. This change resulted partly because of the top leadership change in Hanoi, partly because of strong criticism received from the international community, and partly because Hanoi began to realize after 1968 that the war might end in the near future and they had to clean up their act.

For the 236 men shot down after 1968, the net result of this policy shift was that their POW experience was markedly different from that of the more senior group of men downed prior to 1969. These newer shoot-downs became known as the FNGs, for "fucking new guys," and the FNGs affectionately referred to their more senior comrades as FOGs, for "fucking old guys."

The FOGs fought the most arduous war of resistance with the North Vietnamese. Forty percent of these men languished in solitary confinement for periods in excess of six months. Of these, one-half existed alone for over a year; 10 percent for over two years; and four men for over four years.[3] Lieutenant Colonel Robinson Risner, the senior Air Force officer for most of the war, lived in solitary confinement during most of 1965 to 1969 and damaged his voice by gargling lye soap before a taped confession. The Vietnamese had intended to compel Risner to confess that the U.S. Air Force had committed war crimes against the Vietnamese people. Commander James Stockdale, his Navy counterpart and a future vice presidential candidate, pounded his face black and blue with a heavy mahogany stool to disfigure it for a similar confessional. Both men willingly risked permanent physical damage to thwart North Vietnamese efforts to extract propaganda from them.

Other FOGs risked their lives in heroic escape attempts. Major George "Bud" Day, USAF, despite a broken arm and twisted knee, managed to escape from his captors near the DMZ. During his two-week flight, he suffered injury from American bombs and Viet Cong bullets. He eventually made it to South Vietnam before being recaptured and severely tortured. Air Force captains John A. Dramesi and Edwin L. Atterberry escaped on 10 May 1969 by climbing a prison wall. They made food bags and filled them with high-energy items such as raw sugar; covered their faces in skin cream that matched the complexion of Vietnamese skin; and wore black clothes, surgical masks of the sort peasants wore on the street to prevent the spread of disease, and conical hats (made from the straw mats that covered the beds in the prison) to blend in with the local population in Hanoi. They even carried baskets on bamboo poles to further enhance their disguise. Atterberry, an experienced telephone lineman before the war, shorted the electric wires running along the top of the wall, and the two men vanished over it before the guards restored power and got the searchlights back on. Their extraordinary preparations proved tragically futile in the end. The Vietnamese quickly captured the men the next day and punished both (as well as their cellmates) severely: they beat Atterberry to death and nearly killed Dramesi as well.[4]

During these early years, the most common form of torture involved the use of ropes. This treatment is described in gruesome detail by Lieutenant Commander Hugh A. "Al" Stafford, a Navy A-4 pilot:

> Several guards arrived, carrying ropes and straps, some of them stained with blood. Beginning at the shoulder, they wrapped my arms, carefully and patiently, tightening each loop until the rope would not take any more tension, then throwing another loop, lower, and then repeating the process, until my arms were circled with loops of rope like ceremonial bracelets. When I thought that the pain was as bad as it could be, the guards forced my arms together, behind me, until the elbows were touching, then tied them together. Then my arms were raised toward my head and pulled by a long rope down toward my ankles, which were lashed together. I was being bent into a tight circle. I was passing out, now, then coming to and blacking out again. Without actually deciding to, I started answering their questions.[5]

Stockdale, who endured rope torture with a broken left shoulder, described the process in terms similar to rape. "The guard put a bare foot on my right (thank God) shoulder and mounted my back as my head slumped toward my knees." The guard, nicknamed Pigeye, then placed his foot directly on the POW's bowed head and pressed it against the bricks in the floor between the calves of his legs. Everything then began closing in on Stockdale: "the tremendous pain of lower arms and shoulders—the claustrophobia—the hopelessness of it all." After Stockdale finally relented, Pigeye "dismounted and I raised my head as he methodically started loosening the arm bindings. I'd never felt such relief in my life, even as the blood surging back into my arms induced its own form of throbbing pain." By the end of his stay in

Hanoi, Commander Stockdale would be tortured fourteen more times with ropes by the same tormentor.[6]

While scores of men like Stockdale behaved honorably during the FOG period, there were also cases of misconduct, and in several instances outright collaboration with their captors. POWs in the "Plantation," a camp located near the North Vietnamese Ministry of Defense in Hanoi, participated in the making of a propaganda film called *Prisoners in Pajamas* during the spring of 1967. This motion picture, shown in four segments in Europe and as a one-hour documentary in the United States, featured interviews with ten prisoners and showed others cleaning immaculate rooms or digging air-raid shelters to protect themselves from U.S. bombs. In the end, it emerged as what the official historians of the Office of the Secretary of Defense describe as "one of the major propaganda coups of the war."[7] Later that summer, two senior officers, Commander Walter Wilber, USN, and Lieutenant Colonel Edison Miller, USMC, began talking "freely and seemingly under no duress about the illegality of the war."[8] Public statements made by seventeen or eighteen other American POWs soon followed radio broadcasts of the *Bob and Ed Show*.

If the FOG years witnessed the most heroic as well as the most disgraceful behavior of American POWs, the FNG period proved to be more mundane. The Communists tortured only two Americans with ropes during this time, although many POWs experienced solitary confinement and others profound suffering due to inadequate medical treatment. The average POW in 1970 was a thirty-two-year-old flier with a wife and two children. They were, for the most part, Navy lieutenants or Air Force captains (O3s); 73 percent held B.A. or B.S. degrees.[9]

Most of these men spent their initial days in Hoa Lo prison, or what became popularly known as the "Hanoi Hilton." Built by the French some seventy years earlier, the Hilton could accommodate 400 prisoners and occupied a trapezoidal block in a residential section of Hanoi. Barbed wire and glass shards topped its fifteen- to twenty-foot-high walls. Only one gate allowed access into the compound, and it consisted of multiple iron doors that functioned like locks in a canal, slamming shut after the prisoner moved from one to another.

The prison was roughly divided into four sections: New Guy Village, Heartbreak Hotel, Little Las Vegas, and Camp Unity. During much of the FNG period, the Communists in-processed and interrogated new prisoners in either Heartbreak Hotel or New Guy Village and then moved them into larger cells in Camp Unity. Once the civilian section of Hoa Lo, Camp Unity became a POW holding facility after the U.S. Special Forces stormed an empty Son Tay prison in 1971 and the Vietnamese were compelled to close outlying POW camps and consolidate all POWs in Hanoi area facilities. Each of the seven open-bay rooms of Camp Unity held forty to sixty POWs in a twenty-by-sixty-foot area. The men slept on concrete platforms on either side of the room, which allowed only a thirty-inch-wide sleeping space per man. In this crowded environment, personality clashes, disputes, and arguments could arise naturally over something as simple as bedtime rules and housekeeping duties.

The most serious challenges to the American POW leadership, though, revolved around the issue of how aggressive a resistance stance the POWs should take toward the North Vietnamese. Not having experienced the hardships of the earlier years and knowing full well that the Communists considered them prized bargaining chips in the peace negotiations, many of the younger FNGs agitated for a tougher stand against the guards. Others, recalled civilian POW Ernie Brace, "wanted to coast and take a wait and see attitude."[10]

In no area of Unity were these clashes more evident than in Room 5. Led by Lieutenant Colonel Joseph Kittinger, USAF, Room 5 became home to some of the youngest American POWs in Hanoi. These Young Turks often pushed things to the limit with the Vietnamese and became difficult for the cautious Kittinger to manage. With the significant exception of Navy Lieutenant Commander J. B. Souder, the most aggressive men in the room were young Air Force lieutenants and captains. Naval officers, perhaps because they were more accustomed to operating in the close confines of a ship, tended to be more disciplined and respectful toward the chain of command. Even the feisty Souder never seriously challenged Kittinger's leadership: he ultimately had to devote too much of his attention to his duties as de facto medical officer to worry about taking a tougher resistance posture toward the guards. Another naval officer, Commander Clarence "Ron" Polfer, became the room's executive officer (second-in-command) and eventually emerged as a voice of reason in the hothouse environment of Room 5. A career naval officer, Polfer understood the psychology of large groups of men in small spaces and knew how to strike a balance between the conservative Kittinger and the Young Turks without violating the basic principles of military discipline. Finally, Lieutenant John "Jack" Ensch, USN, helped dissipate some of the tensions in the room through one of the oldest traditions of the sea services, humor and good cheer in the face of adversity. It was this group of tough-minded naval aviators who ultimately helped the men in Room 5 cast aside their individualistic aviator personas and look out for the needs of the group, whether by obeying an overly cautious senior officer or tending to the unpleasant medical needs of their comrades. By doing so, this room demonstrated that aviators, no matter how spirited, were, in the final analysis, military professionals—men who lived by the basic military tenets of organization, discipline, and the unity of the group over the self.

9

Taking Charge

Commander C. Ronald Polfer

THE MAN WHO ASSUMED the pivotal role in Room 5, Ron Polfer, was raised in Independence, Missouri.[1] He entered the Illinois Institute of Technology in 1952 on a Navy ROTC scholarship and graduated in 1956 with a degree in engineering and an ensign's commission. Rather than becoming an engineering officer, he set his sights on gold wings and achieved his pilot's rating in 1958.[2]

Like many Vietnam War–era Navy POWs, Commander Polfer served multiple tours in Southeast Asia before ultimately being shot down in 1972. His first two deployments were in F-4s with Fighter Squadron 154 on board *Coral Sea* in 1966–67 and *Ranger* in 1967–68. Although he never saw a MiG, Polfer did remember flying some memorable flak suppression missions for large Alpha strikes. "There's a certain sense of satisfaction," he recounted, "gained from looking back over your shoulder after pulling out of a dive and seeing the muzzle flashes coming from the AAA right up to the instant that your ordnance goes off on top of them."

Polfer left the cockpit in 1968 for a one-year tour on the staff of Commander Seventh Fleet before rejoining an F-4 squadron in 1969— this time as the executive officer of VF-121, a fleet replacement squadron. During this period, he also earned a master of science degree in business administration from San Diego State.

In the spring of 1971, Polfer received a call from Captain Ken Wallace, one of his old skippers from VF-154. Wallace, a member of the Aviation Command Screen Board that year, asked Polfer what his reaction would be to screening for an RA-5 command. "My response was, 'It's an operational carrier-based jet command; I'd be happy with it.'"

Originally developed in the late 1950s by North American Aviation as a Mach 2 carrier-based attack plane capable of carrying nuclear or conventional ordnance, the RA-5 Vigilante had a range of 3,000 miles and was powered by two enormous General Electric J79-GE-10 afterburning turbojets. Despite its tremendous power and range, the RA-5 had poor maneuverability. Its seventy-six-foot length and fifty-three-foot wingspan also made it a difficult plane to land on the small deck of a carrier. So challenging was this "lead sled" to fly that the Navy began transferring some of its most aggressive pilots, those from the fighter and attack communities, like Polfer, into the RA-5 program.[3]

During the summer and fall of 1971, Polfer attended photo school, went through the Vigilante replacement air group syllabus, joined Reconnaissance Attack Squadron (RVAH-7), and went through predeployment workups on the West Coast. He then deployed on board *Kitty Hawk,* and by spring 1972 he had nearly flown a complete line period. "Right up until May 7," Polfer recalled, "it was fun."

At 1430 that day, Commander Polfer briefed for a mission to photograph a stretch of rail between Ninh Binh and Thanh Hoa immediately following three Alpha strikes against the same segment. Polfer and his escort F-4 launched from *Kitty Hawk* at 1630 and flew toward the target area. Over the Gulf of Tonkin, Polfer noticed abnormally heavy strobing on the APR-25 radar warning system. Much like a police radar detector in an automobile, the APR-25 would only strobe in this manner if the plane were being "painted" by radar. Polfer pressed on to the target. At the designated point, Lieutenant (jg) Joseph Kernan, the reconnaissance attack navigator, activated the cameras, and Polfer put the RA-5 in modulated afterburner (to kill the smoke). Upon reaching the end of the run just before the Thanh Hoa Bridge, Polfer descended about 1,000 feet, broke hard left toward the coast, and went full afterburner to maintain his speed of 600 knots. Sometime during his egress from Thanh Hoa, Polfer took a hit in the tail section from what he believed was an antiaircraft gun round; however, neither he nor his reconnaissance attack navigator back-seater saw any AAA puffs or muzzle flashes, and no indications of AAA radars came up on the APR-25. As a result, Polfer wasn't sure that the aircraft had been hit until well beyond Thanh Hoa, when the RA-5's nose pitched down, and Polfer lost responsiveness in the controls. "There was a sensation of the stick not being attached to the tail or the tail not being attached to the aircraft," he recalled. "The controls did not freeze; they went limp." Commander Polfer ordered Kernan to bail out and then initiated his own ejection at 1730 local time. The force of exiting the plane at a speed in excess of 600 knots knocked Polfer unconscious.

When he woke up in Hanoi three days later, Polfer found himself lying on a table with six to eight North Vietnamese gathered around him. His shoes and underwear had been removed (presumably to clean him), but he still wore his flight suit. He later surmised that he had been taken to a room in the Hoa Lo complex, but at the time he was too disoriented to take much stock of his surroundings. The Vietnamese ordered Polfer to sit up, but as he attempted to do so, his right arm fell awkwardly off the edge of table. He immediately realized that the limb was broken. The Vietnamese then attempted to interrogate him, but after an hour or so of questions, they decided he was still too delirious to be of much use. He could not even remember the name of his RAN.

Polfer's first meal in prison followed his interrogation. It consisted of a bowl of pumpkin soup, canned fish, a piece of French bread, and hot tea. Soon thereafter, the Vietnamese moved him to a field hospital away from Hoa Lo. Medical orderlies X-rayed his right arm with an old machine and then immobilized the arm in a body cast that covered the torso, shoulder, and right arm. Doctors never reset his arm, and so it never healed properly. To ease Polfer's intense pain, J. B. Souder would later slip his hands underneath the injured man's cast and massage his shoulder and back. Souder kept track of this physical therapy and after the war billed his erstwhile patient one martini for every massage. It would take Commander Polfer eight years to finally repay the debt.

After providing rudimentary medical treatment, the Vietnamese transported Polfer back to his original room and gave him a set of red-and-gray-striped POW pajamas and a pair of sandals made from old tires. "You will meet the press," his captors then told him. "Give them your name, rank, serial number, date of birth, and tell them that you have received good food and medical treatment." Under the harsh glare of floodlights and flashbulbs, Polfer gave his name, rank, and serial number but no additional information. He was then led to another room for the start of his interrogation with "Bug."

Bug had acquired his nickname "on the basis of his 'bug eye' and short, fat build, somewhat like a ladybug."[4] Emotionally unstable, Bug passionately hated the Americans, blaming them for his mother's death. "You have murder my mother!" he would shout as he ordered the guards to torture one of his victims with the ropes. Lieutenant Commander Richard Stratton, USN, once called Bug "the most miserable and lowest of all creatures. He was given the name of an insect because he was, in fact, an insect; a madman as far as I am concerned." During the 1967 period, Bug brought some of the most heroic POWs to their knees, including Risner and Day. He also oversaw the torture of Lieutenant Lance Sijan, USAF, who died in the Hilton in 1968.[5]

When Bug entered Polfer's room, he arrogantly announced, "It does not matter whether you live or die because my mother was killed by American bombing, and I hate all Americans." Despite this grim introduction, Bug did not press Polfer hard for answers during this initial interrogation. Questions generally concerned his organization, ship, and mission. Since most of that information could be gleaned from examining the patches on his flight suit, Polfer answered some of the general queries. When the Vietnamese tried to pin down the exact purpose of his mission, Polfer was very unspecific in his answers. Countering his evasion by twisting his left hand behind his back or subjecting him to verbal threats, his tormentors would snarl, "No one knows you're alive; we can do anything we want to with you, and no one would know." But it soon became apparent to Polfer that no one was going to seriously torture or kill him.

Polfer believes two factors served him well during his interrogation: his injuries and the late date of his shoot-down. Semiconscious for most of the interrogation, Polfer gave many "I don't know" answers that seemed credible to the Vietnamese. But Bug's leniency probably had more to do with Polfer's date of capture than any other factor. According to Bud Day, one of the older shoot-downs, Bug "still acted as tough as in the old days" during this period, but his "fangs had been pulled."[6] Not wanting to lose any more prisoners, the camp authorities no longer allowed Bug to engage in too much torture, and Bug, given his experience interrogating other senior Navy officers, knew that the "soft-sell" approach rarely worked with Navy commanders.

During his interrogation period, Polfer lived in a nine-by-nine-foot windowless room on the ground floor of Hoa Lo. He slept on a bamboo mat under a mosquito net–covered bed board, defecated in a small bucket, and sustained himself on soup made from water and chunks of pumpkin. Polfer has few recollections of his isolation period. Usually, he could be found lying in a state of semiconsciousness on his hard bed board, feeling ill and unable to eat much of the soup brought to him each day.

In contrast to many FOGs, who suffered for years in isolation, Polfer underwent a relatively short ten-day solitary confinement. Still, it was enough time to severely dampen his spirits and make him yearn for the company of other Americans. In solitary, most POWs went through a number of distinct stages, beginning with a yearning for human contact. Increasing feelings of depression and humiliation followed. Worry over one's family and loved ones sets in. Then there was anxiety, sleeplessness, boredom, and fatigue. As time wore on, feelings of despair sparked intense nightmares. As a result of not conversing with anyone or exercising one's mind properly, worry about losing voice and mind became a lingering concern. Many POWs began to experience delusions and hallucinations at that point unless positive steps were taken to counteract the debilitating effects of isolation.

For most POWs, the best way to combat isolation was to establish a solid routine. Survival, evasion, resistance, and escape (SERE) training taught POWs to account for every minute of their day. A typical day in solo began at 0515, when the POW arose and exercised until the guard opened the door for him to empty his waste bucket. Five minutes later he would be back in his cell. The exercise would continue for another two to three hours. At 1000 to 1051, the POW would eat a meal and then pray or daydream for thirty minutes. Studying insects occupied about an hour of the 1100 to 1345 noon siesta. Interspersed throughout the day would be mental testing, crying, screaming, building imaginary houses, and more exercise. The afternoon meal came at 1600, and lights-out occurred at 2100. For some POWs in isolation, any break in their routines could be very upsetting, and for injured POWs, the situation could become almost unbearable, since the best cure for hallucination was physical exercise—mainly in the form of pacing, running in place, isometrics, side-straddle hops, push-ups, sit-ups, deep-knee bends, and handstands.[7]

Fortunately for Polfer, company came after ten days, when the Vietnamese moved him into Camp Unity Room 5 with a small group of Air Force officers and one other naval officer, Lieutenant Commander Souder.[8] Souder and the other men bathed Polfer once a day by pouring water over him from a barrel in the courtyard of Unity. They also advised him that he was the senior ranking officer (SRO) in the room and could assume the full duties of this title from Major Leland Hildebrand, USAF, as soon as he felt up to it. Souder, upon seeing Polfer for the first time in Hanoi, realized immediately that Polfer had been seriously injured. When he spoke to Polfer, an old friend, he got no reaction, just a puzzled look. "He had been knocked silly by that ejection," Souder would later recount. "His arm was in a cast, his upper lip was split, and he was punchy as hell."[9] Consequently, Hildebrand continued to act as SRO until Polfer's health improved. For the next few days, Souder tended to Polfer's ailments, and the others taught him the two keys to survival in the POW system: the Plums and the tap code.

A code word similar to "jewels," "Plums" stood for little jewels of knowledge. They were policy statements issued by Colonel John Flynn, USAF, a senior officer at the Hanoi Hilton, which augmented, expanded, or substituted for the Code of Conduct that arose out of the Korean War experience. During that war there had been a breakdown of morale, primarily among the enlisted POW community, and widespread collaboration occurred. The code called for POWs to make every effort to escape, to accept no special favors from the enemy, and, when questioned, to give only one's name, rank, serial number, and date of birth: "the big four and nothing more." Such a code quickly became untenable in Hanoi, where camp authorities routinely ignored the Geneva Convention and subjected POWs to severe torture, extortion, and brutality.

"As POWs we were treated not as POWs but as common criminals. We sailed uncharted waters," explained James Stockdale, one of the leaders who helped develop the Plums. "The Code did not provide for our day-to-day existence; we wrote the laws we had to live by. . . . We set a line of resistance we thought was within the capability of each POW to hold, and we ruled that no man would cross that line without significant torture."[10] Plums required a pilot to take physical abuse and torture before acceding to specific demands but did not expect a man to die or seriously jeopardize his health and safety. They also called for "working with the camp authorities for the improved welfare of all and ignoring petty annoyances." However, there would be no early releases, no appearances for propaganda, and any "flexibility or freelancing would be subordinated to the need for unity and discipline."[11]

The ability to transmit information from one room of Hoa Lo to another was of central importance to American POWs. Communication sustained morale, enabled prisoners to resist the Vietnamese collectively, and allowed an effective chain of command to flourish. The most widely used system of communication was the tap code, introduced in the summer of 1965 by Captain Carlyle "Smitty" Harris, USAF. Harris had learned to tap at the Air Force survival school at Stead Air Force Base, Nevada, during a coffee break. An instructor showed Harris a code based on a five-by-five matrix that could function as a covert communications means for POWs. After dropping the *K* from the matrix, one arranged the twenty-five remaining letters as follows:

	1	2	3	4	5
1	A	B	C	D	E
2	F	G	H	I	J
3	L	M	N	O	P
4	Q	R	S	T	U
5	V	W	X	Y	Z

A POW could communicate to another inmate in an adjacent room by first tapping the letter's position in the horizontal rows of the table and next by placing it in the vertical columns. For example, the letters *CUL*, an abbreviation for "see you later," a widely used phrase among POWs, was transmitted as 1,3, for *C*; 4,5, for *U*; and 3,1, for *L*. The letter *C* was used as a substitute for *K*; hence, the phrase "Joan Baez Succs," transmitted after the Vietnamese played a recording of this antiwar activist over the camp public address system. The beauty of the tap code was its simplicity. POWs abbreviated long words and phrases at every opportunity. "I learned not to laboriously spell out WHEN DO YOU THINK WE WILL GO HOME?" wrote Stockdale in his memoir, "but to use WN DO U TK WE GO HOME?"[12]

The tap code was more than a means of transmitting information from one cell to another. Often it was the only link some POWs had with other Americans. Stockdale put it in this way:

> As we worked the wall together, we learned to be sensitive to a whole new range of acoustic perception. Our tapping ceased to be just an exchange of letters and words; it became conversation. Elation, sadness, humor, sarcasm, excitement, depression—all came through. Sam and I would sign off before dark with abbreviations like GN (goodnight) and GBU (God bless you). Passing on abbreviations like conundrums got to be a kind of game. What would ST mean right after GN? Sleep tight, of course. And DLTBBB? I laughed to think what our friends back home would think of us two old fighter pilots standing at a wall, checking for shadows under the door, pecking out a final message for the day with our fingernails: "Don't let the bedbugs bite."[13]

Because Polfer lived in a large room with many other Americans, communication of a personal nature between rooms had to be restricted to maintain the integrity of the system. Only assigned communications officers were allowed to tap, and these men generally used the code only to communicate with officers in other rooms and the senior officers in the 4th Allied POW wing staff. Command within the wing was determined by date of rank, with exceptions being made for individuals who had significantly earlier shoot-downs that might have overlapped a promotion point. In these cases, seniority was determined by who had been senior at the earliest shoot-down date.

At the top of the chain was Colonel John Flynn, code-named "Sky," in Room 0 of Camp Unity, or "Rawhide." Colonel Robinson Risner acted as deputy commander, and the other O-5s and O-6s in Rawhide constituted the wing headquarters staff, with Commanders Stockdale and Jeremiah Denton heading up operations, and others assigned to Intelligence, Plans, and so forth. Each building or large cell in Hoa Lo was a squadron. After Polfer was moved to Room 5 of Unity in May 1972, his squadron was organized into four flights, with individual flight leaders. Polfer assigned each flight duties—consisting of dishes, laundry, food service, and room cleanup—that rotated weekly. A designated material officer drew supplies regularly from the Vietnamese, an athletic officer led the men in daily calisthenics, a medical officer monitored medical treatment administered by the Vietnamese and drew medical supplies, and a duty flight leader handled special details, which the Vietnamese would initiate, such as sweeping the yard. The covert side of the squadron consisted of three teams: the communications team, the escape committee, and the memory bank. There were no escape attempts made during Polfer's captivity, but contingency plans were constantly updated. According to Souder, one contingency called for a handful of POWs to escape if Hoa Lo took direct bomb hits and the Vietnamese opened the gates to allow the POWs to seek safety.[14]

Because no POW wanted to be listed as missing in action when the hostilities ceased, maintaining an accurate roster of all POWs held by the Vietnamese became an important concern to the wing. The memory bank was established to memorize this long list of names and all other significant information for the wing. The master list of names was broken down into smaller lists, and more than one individual would be tasked to remember a specific segment. Polfer or any other SRO could demand that a list of names or a section of the Plums be recited by a member of the memory bank at any time.

As the senior ranking officer in Room 5 and later the deputy SRO, Polfer was primarily concerned not so much with intelligence issues as with keeping his men occupied during the long, monotonous days of captivity. This he accomplished by allowing his young POWs to resist the Vietnamese in subtle ways that built up room morale but did not jeopardize the overall health and safety of the group.

The POWs lived by the sounds of the camp gong. The gong first sounded at 0500 to awaken the guards. At 0515, a taped propaganda broadcast was transmitted through the speaker in Room 5. Although the poor quality of the speaker rendered the programs practically inaudible, Polfer and others could occasionally glean useful tidbits of news from them, especially if recent shoot-downs could correct misinformation. At 0530, Polfer assembled all POWs in front of their bed boards, with their blankets, mosquito nets, and clothes folded on top of the board, for the morning roll call. A guard would then come in and count the prisoners, who avoided anything resembling attention or parade rest and would try to slouch in different manners to avoid any appearance of respect for the guard.

Immediately after the muster, the Vietnamese brought the POWs their morning meal, which consisted of a twelve-inch loaf of French bread and hot tea, supplemented on occasion by a cup of hot powdered milk with brown sugar or one-third cup of sugar. After breakfast, the men in Room 5 were generally allowed out for thirty to forty-five minutes to bathe or make coal balls. The coal balls were made by taking a cheap grade of powdered coal, wetting it, and packing it into small balls or briquettes. The balls were then used to heat the camp kitchen stove and oven. The Plums allowed POWs to perform work for the Vietnamese as long as it did not improve the prison's confinement capability or camp defenses; nevertheless, Polfer's men still resisted this detail by making the coal balls in the wrong size or deliberately working slowly. Lieutenant Commander Souder believed that coal balls were a major source of boils. The sharp coal granules would puncture the skin and allow viruses from dog feces and other contaminants in the dust to enter the skin. Outside time would be extended during coal ball details to allow POWs to bathe after their work.

At about 1030, the Vietnamese served the second meal of the day, which consisted of a bowl of pumpkin soup and a four-ounce side dish. Pumpkin remained the staple food of the POWs throughout the war because it was inexpensive and widely cultivated in and around Hanoi. Occasionally, the cooks added noodles, greens, or onions to the mix, but more often than not the soup consisted of nothing but boiled water and chunks of pumpkin. Side dishes, while less monotonous than the soup, proved equally unappetizing. During the spring and summer of 1972, the Vietnamese served "a squash that looked like cooked apples and had a repulsive taste as if it had been cooked in urine." Pig fat was another staple, which POWs enjoyed pulverizing and using as a spread for the French bread. Other side dishes included green beans and occasionally canned Russian fish, beef, or pork. After the peace accords were signed in 1973, the protein element in all dishes increased.

The second meal was always eaten in the room. Afterward, the Vietnamese allowed several POWs to go back out to the courtyard to wash dishes. Tar paper partitions prevented Room 5 POWs in the courtyard from seeing other POWs in the neighboring rooms of Camp Unity, but messages were often slipped through holes in the paper. One of the most ingenious methods for communication involved passing a hollowed stick through the fence to the FOGs from Room 4. The FOGs had hollowed out the stick and sealed it with bread dough darkened with cigarette ashes to resemble rotten wood. Removing the dough revealed messages scrawled on pieces of cigarette package wrappers.[15]

At 1100, a gong sounded, and the Vietnamese locked the rooms for their early afternoon siesta. Ostensibly, POWs were also supposed to rest during this three-hour period, but many found it difficult to sleep in the middle of the day. Instead, they would play cards or communicate with others through open windows, using a modified sign language called the "flash code." Since only one guard could be seen on duty during this period, the siesta was a time when much news circulated around the camp.

Another favorite activity during this period was study. Study groups at Unity eventually evolved into a full-fledged university curriculum that included courses in history, political science, mathematics, literature, languages (Spanish, French, German, and Russian), and numerous electives ranging from music theory to diesel engine mechanics. "As in any college, complaints about overwork, scheduling conflicts, and exams that came up on the same day were brought to the dean [the educational officer in each room]. Men struggling with difficult material would ask for extra tutoring. It was, in all essential ways, a real school," claims author Geoffrey Norman, and some of the men actually received college credits for some of the courses.[16]

Siesta ended at 1400, and POWs again mustered for another head count, followed by another outside period for exercise. The Vietnamese served a meal identical to lunch at 1630 and then, at 1700, locked down the room for the night. Very little harassment occurred between 1700 and 2000, a time the POWs often used for recreation activities. "Dusk time was 'show time,'" recalled Lieutenant (jg) Joseph Plumb; by 1972, "low-cost productions lasting about 15 minutes in 1967, became full-blown spectaculars."[17] For Commander Paul Galanti, movies were the highlight of the 1972 period. The movie tellers "could remember every detail of a movie, including the start-up credits. One fellow told *War and Peace*, and it took six weeks. Others performed musicals complete with all the songs. I came back and saw several of the movies I had 'seen' in Hanoi, including *Sound of Music*."[18] Perhaps because they were easy to remember and act out, the most popular movies at the Hilton tended to be classics such as *Gone with the Wind, The Caine Mutiny,* and *Dr. Zhivago*. Some of these films were even told in "revised" versions, with plot and characters being changed to make the movie more interesting and fresh.[19]

Another favorite evening pastime at Unity was gambling: poker, backgammon, and bridge. Captain Dick Bolstad, USAF, fashioned chips for these games from bread and water and colored them with red brick dust to make red chips and ashes to make black ones. His chips were "perfectly round, perfectly decorated, perfectly colored, and hard as a rock." Bolstad even "found some secret ingredients to mix with his chips which kept the rats away." Using these chips, the prisoners in Room 6 kept a running tally of their poker game to be paid at the end of the war. Lieutenant John Nasmyth, the room's bookie, won over $3,000 in these games.[20]

Bull sessions also allowed the men to pass the time. Plumb described getting a new cellmate as an experience akin to "walking into the Smithsonian for the first time. He was a brand new source of information and we would sit up the first night for hours discussing every topic we could imagine."[21] As one might expect in the "locker room" environment of a POW camp, sex was a favorite topic of discussion. Captain William Angus, USMC, remembered putting on "these filthy, raunchy skits and discussing our rendezvous with Filipino call girls. J. B. Souder and I would fantasize about what would happen to us at these various officers clubs when we got back home. We thought the POW status would have great sex appeal—it could be played like a violin. The sympathy would be mind-boggling."[22]

At 2000, another propaganda broadcast would be played over the public address system, and at 2100, the final gong of the day went off, and prisoners were expected to go to bed. Sleep, though, did not come easily, especially on the hard bed boards. "The body tended to get sore and develop bruises in the bony areas, such as the hips, knees, heels, and ankles," complained Polfer. Another common complaint revolved around the issue of cold and heat. In the winter, the temperature in Hanoi sometimes dipped down to 35 to 40 degrees Fahrenheit. To stay warm, POWs had to rely on two thin wool blankets. Some sewed the blankets together to fashion a crude sleeping bag. Others rolled themselves in the blankets and then tied the ends of the blankets together to form a cocoon. Occasionally, clothes were stuffed inside these blankets for added insulation. Summers could be equally harsh. "When I lay on my back," explained Plumb, "perspiration pooled in my eye sockets and the salinity burned my eyes. I couldn't sleep on my side because I had too much skin on skin, the cause of severe rashes, so I had to learn how to sleep spread-eagled on my stomach."[23]

As if the climate and uncomfortable beds were not bad enough, restless POWs also endured the noise of snoring, the smells of infrequently washed male bodies, and the stench of the toilet at the end of the room. Nearly every prisoner suffered at one point from diarrhea and parasites. Lieutenant Roger Lerseth, USN, remembered a particularly bad case of dysentery he had during the Linebacker II bombings. "Every time the bombers came over, the Vietnamese would order us under our bed boards, and half the time when they entered the room I was sitting on the honey pot. We laughed our asses about it. My dysentery started in November 1972 and lasted almost a year after I came home. I was up there twenty or thirty times a day."[24]

Like diarrhea, ants and rodents could not be avoided in Hanoi. Ants occasionally bit POWs and also pilfered food. Rats could be even more bothersome. Although the prisoners generally were safe from these critters under their mosquito nets, rats occasionally slipped inside, and with no simple means of escape, they could turn hostile. According to POW Charlie Plumb, "A prisoner entrapped with the rat had to stand quickly so that the bottom of the net lifted off the bed and permitted the rat's escape."[25] Prisoners devised all sort of traps to deal with the vermin problem. One common device was a bucket held up by a string attached to a piece of bamboo, but after the rat got trapped, the problem was what to do next. Sometimes POWs would try to kill the rat with brooms as it emerged. However, no one really wanted a dead rat because there was no place to dispose of the carcass except the toilet—a solution that would just cause more stench for the room.[26]

Often the only escape from the garden variety of daily POW miseries was fantasy. Geoffrey Norman, in his book *Bouncing Back,* shows how a good fantasy session could provide an escape outlet as vivid as a movie or a good book. Lieutenant Commander Al Stafford

> always loved to sail, so he would sit up straight with his eyes closed and imagine himself on the Chesapeake somewhere. He would decide on the season and then try to remember just what the prevailing weather would be. In the summer, when the cell was stifling and full of bugs, he would picture himself out on the bay in the winter, when the water was the color of lead, the wind was blowing whitecaps off the tops of the swells. . . . He would visualize the boat he was sailing. How was it rigged? What sort of sail did it carry? . . . He used real checkpoints and kept a real logbook. "Five knots equals a mile every twelve minutes. . . . I'll be at the Oxford lighthouse at 1610." . . . At the end of an hour or two of sailing, Stafford could taste the salt on his lips and feel the sun on his skin.[27]

Throughout the day, the Vietnamese who brought food to Room 5 and shepherded the POWs to and from the courtyard were the turnkeys. A team of two or three turnkeys oversaw each given group of POWs and would remain responsible for that group while they stayed at a particular camp. The turnkeys exercised a reasonable degree of authority over the POWs and could take unilateral action if they were not satisfied with the behavior of the group. Although POWs occasionally developed cordial relations with these men, the turnkeys tended to be viewed in adversarial terms. They were men to be resisted, tricked, and cajoled at every opportunity. In fact, for the younger men of Room 5, resistance emerged as a major preoccupation and obsession in the otherwise mundane environment of camp life.

The most common form of resistance involved ignoring these guards during the musters and just milling around the room while the guards tried to conduct a head count. In July 1972, a turnkey named Silas attempted to take action by ordering the men of Room 5 to stand at attention by their bed boards at one muster. Room 5 ignored the order. "Our turnkey wanted everybody to stand up at attention when he came in," explained First Lieutenant Ted Sienicki, USAF, one of the most assertive young men in Room 5, "and we laughed at him, said, 'What are you talking about, if I'm standing up, I'm going to sit down when you come in.'"[28] Silas was irate. He went directly to the camp commander, who then called Room 5's senior officer, Lieutenant Colonel Joseph Kittinger, USAF, in for a talk.

Colonel Kittinger had gained recognition early in his career as the "first man in space" when he ascended in a hot-air balloon to 96,000 feet on 2 June 1957. Later, in 1960, he broke another high-altitude balloon record, traveling to 102,000 feet before bailing out in a high-pressure suit. He fell for four minutes and thirty-eight seconds, reaching a speed of 614 miles per hour before his parachute's drag chute finally slowed his descent. Astronauts would later use this same type of parachute in the event of an ejection. In Vietnam, Kittinger served three tours before being shot down. Because he was known in his squadron, the 555th, as an adventurous type, some of the navigators in the unit sought to avoid flying with him, fearing that his overwhelming desire to become an ace would end in disaster. There were even bets placed as to which navigator would get killed flying with him. True to unit predictions, only a few days after his first victory with the 555th, Kittinger was shot down on 11 May 1972.

Once imprisoned, Kittinger underwent a transformation. In an attempt to gain information on new laser-guided munitions being employed by the Air Force during this period, Kittinger's captors took him to a little building in the countryside, shackled him, and performed a rope torture variation on him.[29] This torture session made such a profound impression on Kittinger that when he returned to Heartbreak, he would not even communicate with Americans in neighboring cells.[30]

The horrible memory of torture remained with Kittinger throughout his stay in North Vietnam and understandably made him acquiescent at times. When verbally threatened by the camp commander over the muster episode, he backed down, probably fearing another torture session.

"I don't know what the hell he got threatened with," recalled Sienicki, "but he came back from his meeting and ordered everyone to stand up for the guard, and we said, 'we don't want to do that; why don't you do this: when he comes in, we'll sit down, and then you call us to attention and we'll stand up.' We did not want to give up the authority in our command structure and here's our commander and he's willing to give it up." Caught in the middle of this dispute, Polfer sympathized with Sienicki and the others, but as an officer, he believed it was his duty to uphold lawful orders. The Plums, after all, did require that POWs ignore petty annoyances, and standing at attention for a guard certainly fit into that category. Ultimately, Kittinger and the room reached a compromise. The men would come to attention when either he or the duty flight leader gave the order but would then sit on their bed boards while the turnkey actually did his head count.

Petty crises with Silas and the other guards continued during the summer of 1972. One involved communications. Ted Sienicki and First Lieutenant Ken Wells, USAF, were the fastest communicators in Room 5. "Ken and I won out of the forty guys in the contest to see who could do it the fastest, and no one ever came close, because we practiced the shit in real life, sometimes six to eight hours a day," explained Sienicki. "To communicate to the guys who had been there five years or longer, which is what we were doing, you had to be very good, because these guys were very, very skilled and it was like a baptism by fire, because it wasn't just how fast you could move your hands, it was the set of abbreviations that had come to be in use." It was also the level of risk that a communicator was willing to take to get his message across. When it became evident that the tap code was ineffective in reaching the FOGs in Room 3, Sienicki and Wells began whispering messages out a small window in the toilet to a group of FOGs who were listening from one of the rat holes at ground level down the alley from Room 5. Silas caught them in the act two weeks later and decided to take away Room 5's afternoon outside periods until late October.

The situation became more tense in September when the Vietnamese tried to compel various rooms in Unity to visit the War Crimes Museum in downtown Hanoi. One by one, the rooms resisted the field trip, but only Kittinger and the communications team knew of their resistance because Kittinger did not allow the team to share messages with the room. "We were bound by his order not to tell anybody, but we knew goddamn better than anybody what the messages were, because we were the ones standing there, looking through the hole in the brick, getting the messages, and then later transcribing them for him." After the wing deputy operations officer, Lieutenant Colonel Robinson Risner, issued an order that "no one would go to the War Crimes Museum," Sienicki could not take it anymore. At the 1700 aircrew meeting that day, when Kittinger asked if anyone had anything to say, Sienicki spoke up:

> I've got something to say. Five days ago they tried to take Risner's room down to the War Crimes Museum, and they've been trying to take other rooms since then. Tomorrow they're going to come for us, and I think we should have a plan because, for starters, none of the others went. I think they're going to come in and try to intimidate us, but I don't think they're going to shoot anybody. I think we just ought to either lock arms, or do something so that they cannot physically carry us through the door.

Kittinger just glared, and forbade any discussion of the issue Sienicki had raised.[31]

Sure enough, the next evening the Vietnamese called a number of officers out of the room without explaining why. Kittinger announced that the selected individuals were merely being moved to other rooms. The Vietnamese, though, did not want the POWs to bring their bedrolls with them—the usual routine when a prisoner was being relocated. Most of the individuals selected were senior officers and flight leaders, who truly believed they were being shifted to different quarters, despite some evidence to the contrary.

As soon as they saw the bus and a large contingent of Vietnamese guards, with flak jackets, helmets, and weapons surrounding it, some began to have an uneasy feeling about where they were headed. Once the conveyance had stopped in front of a large building, the Vietnamese shepherded the POWs into a reception room with a large four-by-twelve-foot table in the middle of it filled with sundries: tea, cookies or candy, and cigarettes. "We had been told by the FOGs," Souder explained later, "to take all of the goodies we wanted in situations like this because it would not constitute accepting special favors—just taking advantage of the opportunity to get some goodies for nothing in return." Souder, Kittinger, Polfer, and the others took seats and began to eat. The Vietnamese then explained that they were there to see the museum and ordered the group to file in. All refused. The Vietnamese twisted both of Kittinger's arms behind his back and pushed him into the museum area. Polfer, similarly, hesitated. "Ron had this quizzical look on his face like he knew we'd been duped and was mentally formulating what to do," remembered Souder. One of the Vietnamese then pulled on Polfer's arm, and he arose from his chair and stood behind it. A wrestling match between the guards and the POWs ensued as the guards attempted to manhandle the Americans into the museum. Major William Talley, a big Air Force flight leader from Oklahoma, wrestled two guards to the ground before Kittinger finally ordered him and the others to proceed into the museum. Polfer believed the order "was appropriate because they were going to be forced to view the museum no matter what." Still, some POWs continued to resist by looking away from the displays in the museum, which consisted of U.S. survival equipment, defused bombs, pictures of bomb damage to residential areas, and "horrible pictures of body parts and dead babies."

Many of the officers looked crestfallen when they returned, but Polfer expressed no regrets over the trip: "The Vietnamese were apparently not using this trip for propaganda purposes; no pictures were taken and no recordings were made. It was speculated that the War Crimes Museum was being shown due to a statement made by Jane Fonda that 'the POWs should consider what they have done to the North Vietnamese people, and purge their souls accordingly.'" However, other members of the group expressed some concern with Kittinger's leadership during the episode.

Room 5's pent-up aggressiveness finally erupted in early December 1972 when a turnkey named Fang (known by the FOGs as "Buckey Beaver") was in charge of the room. A loner by nature, Fang spoke proficient English and seemed to enjoy harassing the men of Room 5. One day, he objected to the duty flight leader's use of the words "officers and gentlemen" before the announcement: "The guard's here." Later that morning, Fang took Colonel Kittinger to see the camp commander, and the room soon found out that their SRO would be placed in solitary for ten days. This action immediately precipitated a flight leaders' meeting in the room.

At this conference, Polfer and his flight leaders decided to completely disregard Fang's orders the next time he entered the room—a bold course of action but one that had been informed by the experiences of the FOGs with the same guard. From FOG and two-time escapee John Dramesi, Sienicki and the others learned that given the right set of circumstances, even a tough guard like Fang could be intimidated:

John was from Philly, and easy for us East Coast guys to understand [Sienicki hailed from New Jersey]. John said, "Wait a minute, which guard do you mean?" When we described him, John replied, "Oh, that guy," and told us about a time when "Fang" was trying to hurry John into a room, I think because of a bombing raid. Dramesi was moving slowly (intentionally). Fang pushed him a bit. Dramesi turned and looked him in the eye and said coldly, "If you ever touch me again, I'll kill you." From that day on (years ago), "he never even looked me in the eye again. He always turns away. *That's* how you have to deal with guys like him!"[32]

In short, the men of Room 5 felt confident that they could ratchet up their resistance to Fang. Besides, "even if they removed me," reasoned Polfer, "there was a clear chain of command to take my place." This is why Stockdale and others had worked so hard to build a solid command structure: to make it impossible for the Vietnamese to undermine it by isolating SROs such as Kittinger from a given squadron.

That afternoon Room 5 completely ignored Fang at the muster and wound up getting locked down for the remainder of the day. When evening came, Fang again entered the room for muster and once again went unacknowledged. Later on that evening, a second guard came in, and the room mustered as usual. The situation reached a crisis at 2000, when Fang stormed into the room and yelled, "Po [Vietnamese pronunciation of Polfer's name], put on long clothes!" Polfer disregarded the order. Evidently, the camp commander had decided to put Polfer in isolation as well. About five minutes later, Fang again entered, only to find Polfer still in his shorts. "Tell Po to put on long clothes," he yelled to First Lieutenant Dick Vaughn, USAF, the supply officer. Vaughn ignored him, at which point Fang became so irate that he knocked over a stool with a cup of tea on it and then began yelling at Polfer, who ignored the tantrum and nonchalantly continued talking with the other officers in the room. Fang finally stomped out, and Polfer prepared himself for the inevitable next confrontation.

A half hour later, twenty-two North Vietnamese, including eight with AK-47s, burst into the room. Polfer put up no resistance and compliantly left the room with the Vietnamese. They took him to the camp commander, who lectured him "and wanted to know why they were having such a problem." "Fang was a troublemaker," Polfer responded, explaining that "the room did not want to show respect to him by acknowledging his presence when he entered the room." The camp commander "chewed" Polfer some more before returning him to Room 5.

Undeterred by his meeting with the camp commander, Polfer kept his hard-line policy in effect, and the room continued to ignore Fang when he came in for the morning muster. Fang locked the room without serving breakfast. Soon, another guard nicknamed "Goose" came in for the muster, the room mustered as usual, and then Goose let everyone outside. When the POWs returned, they were met by the camp commander, who once again lectured them about their disobedience and then let them back out again. After consulting the FOGs over the issue, Polfer decided to end his campaign against Fang. This allowed the Vietnamese to phase Fang out slowly without giving the impression of submitting to prisoner demands. As Polfer later explained, "It was enough of a concession to have the camp commander come to the room."

Polfer's strong stand against Fang greatly improved Room 5's morale and helped the room begin to act in a unified manner. Unlike Joe Kittinger, Polfer understood that the Vietnamese had a certain level of respect for the hard line and was willing to take one when a situation warranted it. He also knew when to back down. From the FOGs, he learned how important the issue of "face" was to the Vietnamese and created a situation that won significant concessions for Room 5 without a loss of face for the Vietnamese.

The next challenge to confront Room 5 involved caring for wounded B-52 crews shot down during Linebacker II. The room's intensive effort to save the lives of these men revolved around Lieutenant Commander James B. Souder.

10

The Medic

Lieutenant Commander James B. Souder

J. B. SOUDER, hanging from a parachute after having successfully ejected from his F-4, put his radio in his flight suit as bullets whizzed by his head. He looked down and saw the fireball of his airplane, prompting him to reflect: "It was funny as hell, because here I am at seven years and 335 missions and I get killed by falling into my own damn fireball. Bullshit, it ain't going to happen. So I reached up and grabbed the parachute riser and steered away from the fireball." Souder then pulled the riser again to narrowly avoid a herd of water buffalo. He ultimately landed on the side of a tiny hill.[1]

As Souder struggled to remove his gear, Molinare ran up to him, and the two aviators immediately looked for a place to hide before nightfall, which would come about an hour later. They ended up hiding beneath a small bush just as a search party passed by.

J. B. then heard the excited voices of the search party when it discovered the parachute and other gear. Soon thereafter, the two downed aviators heard the sound of footsteps approaching the bush, and then the crack of a high-velocity rifle bullet whipping through the foliage. Neither man was shot, but shortly thereafter, the Vietnamese started pulling Souder out of the bush by the arm. Al was discovered a few moments later.

The man who captured Souder wore only a loincloth and wielded a twenty-inch machete. This twenty-year-old farmer swung the machete wildly and menacingly at Souder's neck. Profoundly exhausted by this point, Souder felt no fear, only apathy. Fortunately for his sake, a village elder dismissed the agitated farmer, but other villagers immediately started grabbing Souder's arms and legs even though he was not struggling by that point. The elder removed his armed forces identification card, Geneva Convention card, dog tags, spare glasses, cigarette lighter, two pieces of gum, some change, and twenty dollars. The old man then chewed the gum and tried on the glasses. Souder squinted to indicate that they would be bad for him and then pointed to his own chest, saying, "Mine." The elder put the glasses on, looked up, squinted, shook his head no, and put them back on Souder's face. Another villager immediately stole them for good.

The locals took his boots and then bound his elbows behind his back and attached an eight-foot length of rope to the binding. They led Souder down a footpath in the northeasterly direction. They wanted him to run, but he resisted, feigning a foot injury. During survival training, Souder had learned to fake an injury soon after capture to buy time and save energy for a possible escape. Interestingly, the villagers treated him rather mildly, keeping his bonds loose and quickly intervening if someone tried to assault him. Souder later speculated that these people hoped to collect a reward for his capture.

Nine North Vietnamese militiamen met Souder at the end of the meandering trail and loaded him into a jeep with Molinare, who was apprehended with Souder. The driver gave each man a cigarette and then drove off with a total of eleven men crammed into the small vehicle (three in the front and six in the back with Souder and Molinare). They traveled for fifteen minutes to a U-shaped, schoolhouse-type building, where Molinare and Souder were taken into separate rooms and frisked.

Shortly thereafter, two middle-aged, smiling, well-dressed Vietnamese gentlemen entered the room and asked Souder if he could converse in French. When he indicated that he could not, they smiled and left. The Vietnamese then told him to take off his flight suit and put on a pair of black pajamas. After changing, Souder indicated by licking his lips that he wanted water, and a woman soon brought him a glass of warm, sugary water. By this time, he could have quaffed a liter of cold water, but the warm sugar water tasted repulsive, and he shook his head at the woman server. She soon returned with fresh water and allowed Souder to satisfy his thirst.

After about a half hour, J. B. indicated that he had to urinate. The guards said something, and everyone left the room (by this time at least fifteen people had entered). The guard then closed the shutters and door and gestured for Souder to urinate into a small pan. During the entire time Souder was urinating, the guard looked away.

Two to three hours later, the guard told Souder to put his flight suit back on, then blindfolded him and retied his elbows. His captors then took Souder and Molinare for a fifteen-minute ride to an open field, removed their blindfolds, and walked them into the middle of the field. At that point, Souder believed that the Vietnamese intended to "tear me limb to limb because there were about 100 men all dressed in dark trousers and long-sleeved white shirts." As it turned out, these men were simply photographers and press people. They marched two tiny soldiers with submachine guns up to Souder and Molinare and positioned them on either side of the Americans; and then about 100 flashbulbs went off. "I felt great relief that it was just a photo op, and not a lynching," Souder recalled.

Blindfolded and bound, Souder and Molinare then set out for Hanoi at a fast clip over rough roads. The twenty-four-hour journey included about six short stops, whereupon the prisoners were displayed to the local villagers. Souder listened and marveled at the curiosity of these locals rather than their hostility: "The people seemed extremely curious about me, especially my white skin color and the hair on my legs." At one point, a group of four young women between the ages of eighteen and twenty came up to the truck, and the guards pulled up the leg of Souder's flight suit to display his hairy legs. Souder remembered that the women "seemed very curious and friendly, and appeared to be interested in us as males instead of just items of curiosity." They even gave him a piece of litchi nut—something he enjoyed, since he did not get much water during the uncomfortable trip. For most of it, Souder and Molinare lay under a gasoline-soaked parachute. During one of the transit periods, Souder loosened the binds and contemplated jumping from the jeep, but he determined that the proximity of armed guards, his lack of a radio, and the high probability of injury made such an attempt imprudent, and he quickly abandoned the thought.

Shot down at 1700 on 27 April 1972, Souder and Molinare traveled all night long and ultimately arrived at the Hanoi Hilton at 1800 the next day. Before Souder exited the truck, he leaned over to Molinare and whispered, "Al, don't take any extra slapping around; it's not worth it." As for himself, Souder had decided long before his shootdown to "give in on small innocent points in order to save strength to resist on major points of interrogation as I had been instructed to do in survival training."

The Vietnamese led Souder through the gates for forty feet and then placed him in a twelve-by-twelve-foot room. When they took off his blindfold, the first thing Souder noticed was a three-foot-high table in the middle of the room with a badly soiled tablecloth, which Souder speculated had been stained by blood. A military officer soon entered the room and began asking traditional questions: name, rank, serial number, date of birth. When Souder refused to divulge any more information, the interrogator had a guard blindfold him again, take him out of the room, and make him stand with his forehead leaning against the stucco wall. For five minutes, Souder waited for the "ax to fall," but it never did. Instead, a guard came out, removed the blindfold, took him back inside, and sat him down on the stool again.

A second military officer took the place of the first. Surmising that this second man might be a psychopath, Souder knew he would have to respond. Initially, he contemplated playing the dumb NFO and blaming everything on the pilot. "Given what some pilots had put me through during my career," Souder mused, that resistance posture would have been "very fitting, but I could not do this to Al, so I decided to play the role of the stupidest coward who ever flew an airplane." Typical answers to questions included, "I don't know, I was scared, I was confused, etcetera." For the most part, this strategy proved successful. "The interrogator seemed satisfied with the exchange; I did not give them any information that they did not know."

The grilling continued for another two days. In all, the Vietnamese employed three different interrogators—two of whom asked for military information and the third, for political knowledge. The toughest was the second military one, who woke Souder up at 0100 on the third morning. Feigning exhaustion and stupidity, Souder soon convinced his tormentor to abandon his efforts. The officer slammed his notebook shut and shouted, "For a man of your rank you are very stupid." He then stomped out of the room and never returned. Souder smiled to himself and wondered who was dumber.

A couple hours later, the political interrogator, with whom Souder had spoken on numerous occasions up to this point, entered the room. By this time, tired and aggravated, Souder decided not to answer any more questions and instead looked the man straight in the eye and said:

> You are asking me to answer questions which you know I should not
> be required to answer. The provisions of the Geneva Convention say
> that I should not be required to answer those questions, and you know
> it, and you keep asking me those questions. When I came to this coun-
> try, I came as an honorable man. Some day I hope to return to my

country and when I do, I want to return an honorable man, and I can't
do that if I sit here and answer your questions. So I don't want to answer your questions.

Clearly affected by the sentiment expressed, the Vietnamese stared
at the lieutenant commander for about three minutes and then walked
out of the room, never to be seen again.

The interrogations took place over the course of three days. The
Vietnamese wanted Souder to complete a short written autobiography.
For two days, Souder refused to do it, but after several days of threats,
he decided that he "wanted some kind of record that he was alive and
in the system." He answered all nonmilitary, biographical questions.

Seemingly satisfied with Souder's halfhearted Blue Book effort, the
Vietnamese decided to move him on 12 May 1972 to Room 7 of the
Heartbreak section of Hoa Lo. A six-by-seven-foot room with two concrete beds built in the wall, the cell impressed Souder with its dun-
geonlike appearance; nevertheless, he remained inspired by the fact
that so many famous POWs had passed through this very cell block.

The next morning, Souder overheard American voices and discovered that First Lieutenant Ralph Galati, USAF, and Captain William
Schwertfeger, USAF, inhabited the room directly across from him.
Through these officers, Souder learned the tap code and the flash code
(a simple sign language in which one forms or designates letters of the
alphabet with one's fingers) and began to formally in-process into the
POW wing.

Souder remained in Heartbreak Hotel for seven days and then was
moved along with all other Americans in that cell block to Camp
Unity, Room 5. Colonel Joseph Kittinger appointed Souder as the
squadron medical officer after learning that J. B. possessed rudimentary medical knowledge acquired mainly from his sister, a nurse. As a
medical officer, Souder gained extensive knowledge of Vietnamese
medical practices and the problems of keeping men healthy in an
Asian prison environment. In his opinion, "The medics and one doctor
with whom I had contact appeared sincere in their efforts to treat the
POWs. Although the Vietnamese medical procedures were extremely
crude compared to American standards, I believe that this was the result of poor training and lack of medical resources rather than mali-
cious intent."

The same could not be said about camp authorities, who deliberately withheld medical attention from the POWs as a tool of subjugation. Souder often found himself in the role of an advocate for wounded POWs rather than simply a health care provider. In this capacity, he emerged as an influential weapon for Room 5 in its propaganda war against the Vietnamese.

Souder's medical duties involved accompanying the North Vietnamese medic when he visited the room and assisting him with treatments. Initially, the guards shunned his presence and would not allow him to accompany them, but through persistence and force of personality, Souder gradually became an accepted part of the medic's routine. A typical sick call began with the medic coming into the room with a tray of medicines and supplies, the most common of which was a jar of cotton balls saturated with blue liquid. These balls, nicknamed "blue balls," would be applied to cuts and other skin wounds as a topical solution. Souder conjectured that they contained tincture of iodine. In any event, the Vietnamese often ripped off the POWs' old bandages as well as the scabs underneath to apply blue balls, causing excess bleeding and slow healing of wounds. Souder tried to convince the Vietnamese that this was a poor practice, but the medics believed that the pus and bacteria under the scabs needed to be disinfected. When his arguments went unheeded, Souder eventually began removing the bandages himself, using cold water to loosen the adhesive; however, he never was able to convince the Vietnamese to discontinue the practice of removing large scabs.

Another common medical procedure performed by the medics involved the removal of skin boils. The Vietnamese used two forceps and gauze to squeeze boils until they drained. If the core could not be removed in this fashion, the forceps would be used to pull it out. No anesthetic was used, nor were the forceps properly sterilized after each procedure, although Souder ultimately convinced the Vietnamese to wash them with alcohol after each use.

Injections proved equally painful and unsanitary. Usually prisoners were taken to a makeshift, one-room dispensary for shots (possibly inoculations for cholera). A syringe and two dull needles would be sitting in a container of hot water. One needle would be used to siphon medicine into the syringe and the other, to inject the medicine slowly into the stretched flesh of a patient. The Vietnamese then would flush the syringe into the container of water and cast it, along with the two needles, into the same contaminated water. The same syringe, needles, and water were used to give injections to everyone who required them on that occasion.

Other identifiable supplies included sulfa, aspirin, antihistamine, vitamin B_1, and charcoal pills for intestinal disorders. Sulfa, in both pill and powder forms, tended to be a favorite drug, employed to treat everything from internal infections to sore throats and, in the powder form, as a topical solution for boils. Another favorite pill was activated charcoal, or "Brown Bombers," used for stomach ailments. To obtain a stock of medicine for use between visits by the medics, POWs in Room 5 periodically pilfered items from the medical tray. Additionally, Souder, who was responsible for compiling a list of sick POWs, would add names of healthy men with faked illnesses as a means of prompting the medics to bring more medicine into the room than was necessary for treatments.

While a well-stocked medical chest helped Souder combat everyday medical ailments, when a condition became serious, he often had to take extreme measures to secure adequate medical attention for his charges. One such case involved Captain David B. Dingee, USAF, who suffered from an infected bullet wound on the ball of his foot. Apparently, the wound swelled up so much that it split open his toe and created an open crater on the ball of his foot large enough to accommodate half a golf ball. When the Vietnamese refused to apply medication to the wound or even clean it, Kittinger ordered the room to refuse to eat lunch. Highly sensitive to hunger strikes, the camp commander ordered Dingee to the medical shack, where his foot was disinfected with blue balls, treated with sulfa powder, and freshly bandaged. The wound responded well to the treatment, and Dingee eventually regained the use of his foot.

The supreme test of Souder's medical skill came in December 1972. That month, the Hoa Lo took in a number of severely injured B-52 crewmen shot down during Linebacker II raids. To punish these men for the bombing, the Vietnamese isolated them and refused to allow Souder to move in with them to render medical assistance. Souder finally gained contact with the two or three enlisted crewmen around 29 December during an outside period at Camp Unity. These ambulatory men informed him that the situation was under control and that all was well in Room 7—the room where the Vietnamese housed B-52 crews.

Skeptical of the care being given to the wounded, Souder and Air Force First Lieutenants Ted Sienicki and Ralph Galati sneaked into the room during another outside period. What these men discovered horrified them. Three injured men lay on inner tubes in the center of the room, literally wasting away from neglect. "First of all, they smelled like shit," explained Sienicki. "And one of the guys had been suffering from amnesia for thirty days."

The one suffering from amnesia, Air Force Captain Thomas Klomann, had sustained severe injuries after ejecting downward from a B-52 at night on 20 December 1972. Huge chunks of his knees were missing, his thighs had swollen up like balloons, and both legs were in casts from below the knees down. He also was naked from the waist down. Too squeamish to help him urinate, his crewmates had rigged a funnel to his penis. A tube carried his urine from the funnel to a bucket on the floor. Souder could not believe that the crewmen refused to go near Klomann's genital area. "If you haven't seen a dick," he chastised them, "go look in the mirror." Souder immediately removed the device, cleaned Klomann up, and then moved on to the next man, Staff Sergeant Roy Madden. This tail gunner had suffered a compound fracture of the left femur when he landed at night and had his leg in a full cast. Technical Sergeant James Cook, another tail gunner had compound fractures of both legs and was in two casts from the knees down.

The first thing Souder did was examine Klomann from head to toe with the help of Sienicki and Galati. Souder pulled the inner tube away from Klomann's body and discovered a huge bulge where the flesh had drooped down inside the center hole in the inner tube. In the middle of the bulge was a hole as large as half a grapefruit and about two inches deep. The walls of the hole consisted of rotting flesh, and in the center was a small hunk of flesh and skin. Souder next examined Cook and found the same type of large wound but also noted large, green pus stains on both of his leg casts. Souder looked at Madden last and found him to be in the best condition of all three: no gaping holes but with pus stains on his leg casts.

With little formal medical training, Souder, Sienicki, and Galati did their best to alleviate the suffering. They massaged each man's entire body to get his circulation flowing and reduce the spread of the skin boils and ulcers. They also lanced many of the ulcers with flame-sterilized razor blades. Souder then recommended to his superiors that action be taken immediately to obtain disinfectant to clean the room and penicillin injections for the massive sores. The New Guy Village SRO, Lieutenant Colonel James O'Neil, USAF, taking Souder's cue, told the guards that if these supplies did not materialize quickly, he would order a hunger strike. In the end, this ultimatum produced the desired results, as well as increased medical attention from the Vietnamese.

But much more work still needed to be accomplished before the condition of these men could begin to improve. Souder summoned a Vietnamese medic to the room and told him to remove pieces of the rotting flesh on Klomann and Cook with sterilized scissors. Souder then ordered the medic to administer injections of penicillin to both men. It was not until after the war that Souder learned that the large holes and rotting flesh on these men were bedsores, a type of ulcer caused by lack of proper circulation.

Apparently Klomann, who was delirious most of the time, had not had a bowel movement since arriving at the Hilton, and his anus had expanded, opened up, and completely dried out. As Souder described it, "It looked like a piece of sun-dried horse shit." J. B. requested a board from the guards with a hole cut out of it. Klomann was then placed on the board, and while Ted distracted him with small talk, J. B. crawled underneath the board. He then proceeded to dilate Klomann's anus by rubbing the walls of it with his fingers and hot water. "I used to talk to doctors at the hospital," recalled Souder, "and I once asked them how they dilated a woman's vagina during delivery. They told me they did it by rubbing the sides with their fingers. Since the anus is a sphincter muscle similar to a vagina, I figured I could employ the same technique with Klomann." It worked, and gradually J. B. managed to get his entire hand inside Klomann's anus and start cleaning it out with hot water that the guards had provided. "I then lit a match and took a look inside. What I saw was a gray, hardened golf ball–shaped thing that was blocking the passage from Spaceman's large intestine, so I reached in and yanked it out." With this blockage cleared, Klomann could now pass bowel movements through his system.

After about a week of constant attention with no visible improvement in the condition of the sick prisoners, the tension began to mount in the room. J. B. decided to act. He walked up to Ted just as he was finishing spoon-feeding one of the men. When the guy struggled to ask Ted to brush his teeth in a barely audible tone, J. B. proceeded to tear into the injured airman.

"What the fuck do you think you're talking about? Do you think we're going to brush your teeth? Who the fuck do you think we are?"

Ted's jaw dropped. The B-52 guys were in bad shape, and he was willing to do anything to help them, however ugly. But he complied with J. B.'s order. Later, Sienicki privately confronted Souder.

"J. B., what's up? I'll be happy to brush his teeth."

"These guys are dying," Souder replied, looking up, "and we've been in here for four to five days, maybe a week. Look how long we've been taking care of them. Are these guys getting better?"

Sienicki stopped and reflected upon what Souder had said. "Well, they're not getting better."

"They're not getting better because they're expecting us to take care of them. They don't have the fighting spirit. Some of these guys are losing it."

J. B. was right. Ted and his fellow navigators were nursing these men to their deaths. Staff Sergeant Roy Madden, USAF, got the message loud and clear. When Ted went to feed him some pumpkin soup, he grabbed the bowl. "Give me that goddamn soup," he growled. "I can eat that myself. I don't need any help." Every time this badly injured airman had the chance, he insisted on doing things himself. Almost immediately, his spirit began to prevail, and the health of the B-52 crewmen began to improve. Ironically, one of the lowest-ranking enlisted men in the room helped a group of officers pull themselves together emotionally and begin to heal. Sadly, Madden's leg infections turned to gangrene, and his leg needed to be amputated soon after his release. Cook also lost both legs, and Klomann's legs are permanently fused at the knees.

Souder's story underscores several significant lessons of the American POW experience in Southeast Asia. First, much of the technical training that a flight officer acquires during the course of his career has little applicability in a POW situation. Instead, he must rely on very different skills—some of which come from SERE training, but many are simply a product of basic life experiences. From SERE, Souder learned the importance of planning ahead for a shoot-down and developing an effective resistance posture prior to interrogation. Before SERE, Souder might have gone into the interrogation playing "the tough guy"; however, SERE taught him that more effective resistance could be achieved by playing an entirely opposite role.

Far and away the most vital information Souder brought with him to Hanoi, though, came not from any military training but from long talks with his sister, the nurse. If Souder had not learned basic first aid from her, Thomas Klomann, Roy Madden, and James Cook might have succumbed to easily treatable ailments such as constipation, bedsores, and boils. In Hanoi, a ruthless enemy wielded medical treatment as a weapon—a weapon that could be as lethal as a rifle bullet if denied to the right people. Fortunately for his Air Force comrades, Souder defended them from this exploitation with a little basic knowledge and a lot of personal integrity. Colonel Kittinger nominated J. B. for a Distinguished Service Medal for his service as a POW medical officer, but the navy downgraded the award to a Bronze Star.

11

The Camp Clown

Lieutenant John "Jack" Ensch

IF SOUDER BROUGHT MEDICAL KNOWLEDGE to Hanoi, Jack Ensch provided another necessary ingredient for survival: humor. A double MiG killer, Ensch never imagined that he would end up a POW when he embarked on his final line tour on Yankee Station, but once in Hoa Lo, he never allowed himself to become depressed by his severe injuries and hopeless situation; instead, he put all his energies into boosting the morale of others by becoming the self-proclaimed "camp clown" of Camp Unity.

Born in Springfield, Illinois, on 7 November 1937, Ensch ended up in naval aviation by chance rather than design. After a rather lackluster academic performance at Cathedral Boys High School in Springfield, Jack actually joined the Army as an enlisted soldier before ultimately ending up in the Navy. As Ensch recalled, "I didn't join the Navy initially because it would have been four years; at the time, the Army had three-year enlistments." In the Army, Ensch served as a guided missile instructor at Fort Bliss, Texas, teaching the Nike-Ajax surface-to-air missile system—a similar missile to the one that ultimately shot him down.[1]

After three years in the Army, Ensch managed to save enough money to attend Illinois State University in Bloomington on a state-sponsored GI scholarship similar to the GI Bill. Originally intending to be a high school teacher and coach, Ensch majored in English, but a chance encounter with a group of Navy recruiters in the student union changed the trajectory of his life forever. Like Souder, Ensch "got to talking to them and thought it would be pretty exciting flying off carriers. My original plan was to go in, fly a little, and get out, but next thing you know, it's thirty years later."

What the Navy recruiters failed to tell Jack on that fateful day in December 1965 was that he would be six months older than the age limit for pilot training by the time he graduated from the Aviation Officers Candidate School on 28 May 1965. Nevertheless, he continued, graduating as regimental commander and then applying to become an F-4 naval flight officer. "If I was going to be an NFO, I was going to be in fighters. I got one of the last two fighter assignments out of basic."

In July 1966, just a few months out of training, Ensch joined Fighter Squadron 21 and made two deployments in Southeast Asia, one on board *Coral Sea* and the other on *Ranger*. Ensch then served as an aide to the commander of the Naval Air Test Center at Patuxent River, Maryland, before once again returning to a fleet assignment, this time as an NFO with VF-161 in January 1971. At VF-161, Ensch teamed up with Lieutenant Commander Ronald "Mugs" McKeown, a pilot whom Ensch had gotten to know well in the fleet, and the two aviators emerged as one of VF-161's finest teams. On 23 May 1973, these men shot down two MiGs in a wild engagement over Kep airfield in North Vietnam. Flushed with his recent victories, Ensch stayed on with the squadron for another line tour even though McKeown had to leave early to become the commander of Top Gun. Thus, it was with a new partner, Lieutenant Commander Mike Doyle, that Ensch flew his last mission over Vietnam on 25 August 1972. On that day, they were assigned to fly a MiG patrol for a late afternoon Alpha strike against targets in the Nam Dinh area of North Vietnam. The flight proceeded normally until it reached the coast of North Vietnam, where Red Crown ordered it into a holding pattern to wait for the main strike group to rendezvous. "In retrospect that was probably a mistake," claims Ensch, because it gave the North Vietnamese air defenders an opportunity to figure out where his flight was going. "As soon as we got over the beach, we got taken under attack by every SAM and AAA battery in North Vietnam. My warning gear lit up like a Christmas tree."

Strobes on his radar warning receivers (his APR-25 and APR-27) indicated SAMs at their two o'clock position when Ensch's wingman, Lieutenant (jg) Bud Taylor, and Lieutenant Jim Wise called out, "SAM liftoff, in sight—break right!" Doyle quickly reversed his break and then initiated a high-G barrel roll. During the roll, Ensch looked over his shoulder at a SAM coming at the aircraft from behind, "when all of a sudden there was a tremendous concussion and a big flash of light and I looked down and there were shards of Plexiglas all over the cockpit." Apparently, an unseen SAM exploded right over the cockpit of Ensch's F-4 at the bottom of the barrel roll, and Ensch found himself sitting there with a wounded hand, thighs, groin, and chest. "Oh, my God, no," he yelled out. Training "then kicked in," and he attempted to contact Doyle to check his status. Doyle did not respond. Ensch saw Doyle slumped over the controls as the aircraft passed 3,500 feet, heading for the ground at 500 knots: "I reached down with my good hand and ejected us both. Mike was probably dead when I ejected him from the aircraft. His remains were not released by the North Vietnamese government until fourteen years later."

The force of Ensch's ejection knocked his helmet completely off his head and dislocated both elbows, which he discovered when he tried to grab his radio and could not get his arms to function. "I just looked down in shock to see my arm about half as big as it should be." Ensch landed with one foot on a dike and the other in a rice paddy. His chute pulled him backward, and he had to struggle to get his head above water. When he eventually managed to rest his head on the embankment, the first thing he heard was the distinct sound of gunshots. The firing soon stopped, and footsteps indicated the Vietnamese were approaching his position. A man peeked over the walkway and called the others over. Five Vietnamese, two of whom were armed with bolt-action rifles, pulled Ensch from the water and dropped him on top of the dike. Ensch cried out in pain, but the Vietnamese were oblivious to his suffering. Intent upon acquiring his flight gear, his captors immediately started cutting it off and going through his pockets, which contained an AKAK-805 coding wheel (used to rapidly decode vital information while in flight), a wallet with fifty dollars in cash, a Geneva Convention card, an immunization record, a military ID card, and an American Express card.

After being stripped of everything except his boxer shorts and a red flight deck jersey, Ensch waited for the militiamen to bring in a hammocklike contraption made from fish net to transport him to the nearest hamlet, approximately 300 yards away. Once there, the Vietnamese deposited him in one of the village's three buildings, where he remained until dark—roughly an hour. Surrounded by villagers, Ensch had little time to rest or relax, but he did receive several cups of tea. A young woman also came in and bandaged his thumb with gauze to keep it from flopping around during the journey to Hanoi. Six men then entered, picked up the bed board on which Ensch lay, and carried him out through a large crowd that had gathered on both sides of the road. During this brief passage, the villagers began to torment him, first by jeering at him and then by pinching, slapping, and scratching him and hitting him with sticks. Utterly defenseless and severely wounded, Ensch could do nothing to protect himself: "I was scared to death. I thought they would rip me from limb to limb."

Eventually the procession ended at the main road, where a small Army truck sat waiting to take him to Hanoi. The vehicle traveled slowly through numerous checkpoints, and when Ensch tried to look at the road under his blindfold, he discerned a constant stream of trucks rolling southward. After approximately three hours, the truck stopped at a large town (probably Hai Duong), where the Vietnamese brought Ensch into a small room filled with photographers. A man in a white shirt entered and began berating him while the cameramen snapped photos. "He bragged to me that Jane Fonda had visited his town and that she would take the truth about the war back to the American people." A Vietnamese medic then came in and gave Ensch a shot of morphine; then the journey to Hanoi resumed.

Ensch ended up that night in a twelve-by-twelve-foot room in New Guy Village. Thirty minutes after he arrived, three interrogators came into the room and began to question him. Initially, Ensch stubbornly resisted their line of questioning and provided little information other than his name, rank, serial number, and date of birth. For two days, the interrogators returned to the room every two and a half hours.

By the third day, Ensch had reached his physical and emotional threshold: "I didn't know what to do. I was scared to death, alone, and passing in and out of delirium. My arms were also starting to discolor from lack of circulation, and when one of the interrogators looked me in the eye and said, 'You know, you're dying and unless you cooperate, you will die,' I thought maybe he was right."

Knowing he had to either cooperate or die, Ensch began answering some basic questions about his squadron. He told his interrogators the numbers of the squadrons embarked in *Midway*, reasoning that "they probably knew that anyway." The Vietnamese then pressed him for the names of the squadron commanding officer and executive officer, which created a dilemma for Ensch. He wanted to cooperate with the Vietnamese to a limited degree to receive medical attention, but he could not provide the names of the squadron leadership because that type of information could be used against the Americans if they were ever captured. He therefore used names of people he had known in the past but who were not stationed in Southeast Asia currently. For example, he told the Vietnamese that Randy Billings, a pilot who had been killed, was the skipper of VF-161, and that Captain George Dewey (of Spanish-American War fame) was the captain of *Midway*.

Ensch's responses to questions on the third day of his confinement ultimately satisfied the Vietnamese and ushered in the next stage of his POW experience: a primitive surgery reminiscent of the scene portrayed in Thomas Eakins's painting *The Gross Clinic*. On 28 August, the Vietnamese camp doctor, "Sealed Beams," visited Ensch's cell to examine his left hand—a mass of blackened fingers and a badly severed thumb. Sealed Beams soon concluded that the thumb would have to be cut off.

"Please save my thumb," Ensch pleaded. "I can still make it twitch and jump."

"No, you will go to hospital, and it will be cut off."

The guards took Ensch to a waiting truck and covered him with a purple curtain for the twenty-minute ride to the hospital. Approximately six medical personnel met Ensch in one of the hospital's operating rooms. Again, Ensch tried to save his thumb. "Just sew it back on," he argued to no avail as orderlies began fastening him to the operating table with leather straps. The doctor, a gruff and impatient man obviously annoyed at having to operate on a POW, grabbed Ensch's obviously dislocated left arm and slammed it violently down on the operating stand.

"Please give me something for the pain, something to put me to sleep."

"No need," the doctor responded as an orderly placed a wire cage with a towel on it over Ensch's face, thus blocking his vision. "You have killed women and children with your bombs; they suffered from the pain. Now, you too will suffer pain," the doctor continued. Someone in the room started laughing as Ensch again pleaded for a painkiller. "You can take the pain," another voice interrupted, "like the women and children did."

During the operation, which lasted an estimated forty-five minutes, Ensch "definitely felt the knife, and the intense pain, with flashes of white-hot pain" passing through his consciousness, but he struggled to keep from passing out, fearing that the Vietnamese might remove more than simply his thumb during the operation. After the procedure, the

Vietnamese stuffed a seven-inch piece of gauze in his wound, sewed him up, unstrapped him, and told him, "Get up." They then took him to an X-ray room and shot prints of his elbows.

Amid all the pathos of the day, a guard nicknamed "Lippy" took pity on Ensch and engaged him in a normal conversation while they were waiting for the X rays to develop. The two men spoke about their families, their houses, and their local communities. Lippy told Jack that he lived in Hanoi with his wife and seven children. Lippy "appeared to be higher up than the run-of-the-mill guards in the Hilton," Ensch recalled. "He seemed pretty sharp, more reasonable—almost like a first sergeant."

Unfortunately for Ensch, the rest of the staff did not possess even a modicum of sympathy for his plight. As soon as the X rays were developed, Sealed Beams, with the aid of others, sat Ensch down in a chair and pulled each arm until it popped back into position. Ensch again screamed out in agony, but to no effect. Wire splints were put into each elbow, and his arms were wrapped in gauze for the trip back to Hanoi.

Ensch spent the next two nights in his room in the New Guy Village. Throughout this stint, he could hardly eat. On the first day, the guard fed him his morning meal by hand, but on the second day, he refused to perform this task. "I had to slowly and painfully feed myself, using my right hand, which was probably the best thing for it." On 30 August, the Vietnamese moved Ensch to the south room of the easternmost pagoda in the courtyard of Camp Unity. That night, a storm hit Hanoi, and a scared rat ran across his face. "I spent the rest of the night sitting up on a chair, trying to remember poems and soliloquies from Shakespeare to keep my mind occupied." This was perhaps his lowest moment in Hanoi, but there would be a silver lining to this rain shower. The tempest of 30 August knocked down some of the tarpaper walls in the courtyard of Unity, eventually allowing Ensch to communicate with other Americans when he was finally allowed outside several days later.

In the meantime, Ensch tried to make the best of his pathetic situation. He talked to Lippy about getting his bed raised to make it easier for him to get in and out of it. Lippy, always sympathetic to Ensch's needs, brought two sawhorses the next day and placed the bed board on top of them. He also brought Ensch additional clothes and supplies, including the following: a straw mat, a mosquito net, two blankets, one set of long trousers, two long-sleeved lightweight prison coats, two short-sleeved striped shirts, another pair of prison shorts, one black long-sleeved shirt, two pairs of green socks, one pair of rubber sandals, and two handkerchiefs. As for medical care, medics would come in from time to time to give him shots; they even provided him with a special dinner—consisting of roast beef, duck, cookies, a green salad, and six cigarettes—in honor of Vietnamese liberation. In short, there was a yin and yang quality to Ensch's initial days in the Hilton. On the one hand, several guards and medics treated him with compassion and decency; on the other, he experienced an extraordinary range of cruelty from interrogators, doctors, and camp authorities.

One of the most surprising cruelties inflicted upon him during his initial confinement involved bathing. Because Ensch ended up being the only amputee released from Hanoi in 1973, Souder and others speculated that the Vietnamese authorities, afraid of being condemned by the world press for their poor medical practices, tried to keep his identity and whereabouts a secret until they were absolutely sure his wounds were healing properly. Whatever the case, they refused to allow him to bathe until 5 September—twelve days after his initial capture on 25 August. The guards gave him a toothbrush, soap, toothpaste, a razor, a shaving brush, and two towels and accompanied him to the water basin in the center of the Unity courtyard. A guard stood there while Ensch ladled cold water over his body and cleaned himself as best he could.

Ensch remained in virtual isolation until 16 September, the day the Vietnamese moved him into Room 5 of Camp Unity. Because he was still severely wounded and could not perform normal chores such as making coal balls, he took it upon himself to entertain the other twenty-four occupants of Room 5 with his humor, wit, and acting abilities. An avid film nut and VF-161's former film officer, Ensch became involved with Room 5 film productions almost as soon as he joined the room. In VF-161, Ensch used to write a plot summary of each film on the blackboard. It had to be funny but accurate. He also devised a squadron film policy called "Roll 'Em." A movie could not be shown until all squadron aircraft had been recovered, and if the projector broke in the middle of the film, the projection officer would be "stoned" with wadded-up papers. Officers were authorized to make shadow puppets, but several rules applied to their use: the prettiest girl in the film was the "skipper's girl," and no one could touch her; the ugliest girl or animal was the

XO's girl, and she was fair game—you could do anything to her. "Roll 'Em brought everyone together, and we could all rag on everyone else."

In Room 5 performances, Ensch strove to create a similar, light-hearted environment. The group especially enjoyed sex scenes such as the famous one in the movie *Straw Dogs* where Susan George reveals herself to a group of construction workers. "Yes, Susan George was a big reason why it was so popular. The scene where she undressed and pulled off her sweater revealing those beautiful, big tits while the guys watched through the window was a real showstopper. I could describe it in such a way that could make the listener imagine that he was the guy watching through the window." "Roll that back. Let's see that again," the POWs would demand, and Ensch would tell the scene once more. "Oh, roll that back, we want to see that again." If sex became the focus of many fantasies at Hanoi, jokes emerged as the tonic of everyday conversation. Understandably, in a situation where most POWs suffered from some type of dysentery, bathroom humor prevailed.

Overall, the Christmas bombing turned out to be an interesting time for the POWs. Ensch remembered the first air-raid sirens sounded late in the afternoon of 18 December, and he thought to himself, "Here we go again. It's going to be a long haul." The camp commander checked various positions in the camp, and an antiaircraft gun in one of the towers was uncovered. "We were instructed to lie on our beds and not to talk until the all clear was given." But Room 5 ignored the order and began cheering when the bombs started falling, but the applause soon was muffled by the tremendous waves of shock, caused by the 25,000 pounds of bombs dropped by each B-52 in the Hanoi area. As the plaster began to fall off the ceilings of the cells and the rooms began to shake from bombs falling just over a mile away, "We realized that there weren't any tactical fighters or bombers that could carry that many bombs. It was a frightening experience: it scared the hell out of us. I learned the true meaning of Linebacker."

Because outside time was sharply curtailed during the eleven-day bombing, prisoners were forced to make the best of the situation cooped up in their rooms. According to Ensch, "Whenever possible, the entertainment sessions continued, with card games helping to pass the time." On one occasion, Fang told Room 5 twice to stop playing and go to bed. The men naturally ignored the request and continued playing until around midnight, when Fang, obviously upset from the bombing, "pushed his weapon through the door, pulled the bolt on his AK-47, and told us to go to bed. This action quickly broke up the poker game."

The guards, accustomed to a rear-echelon lifestyle in Hanoi, proved particularly incorrigible during the Christmas bombing. Ensch described them as "irritable, uptight, and downright scared." Throughout Linebacker II, they worked incessantly on their "manholes," covering the makeshift bomb shelters with two or three layers of bed boards and rocks. Virtually every "nook and cranny" was modified for use as an emergency shelter, and water, medical supplies, and food became scarcer during the period. At one point, Ensch could not even convince one of the medics, named "Pipsqueak," to give him a new piece of gauze for his thumb dressing.

Despite the air raids, the men of Room 5 were determined to celebrate Christmas. They constructed a pyramid out of stools in the room and hung their green towels on the wooden contraption to give it a tree-like appearance. They then decorated their Christmas tree with ornaments made from cigarette wrappers and tin foil and placed an angel constructed from bread dough and tin foil on the top of the tree. One of the POWs even drew a large Santa Claus to hang near the tree. Using "bricks" fashioned from cut-up red squares of POW clothing, the men created an image of a fireplace by pasting these squares on the wall with "bread paste." Other POWs erected a Nativity scene on the other side of the tree.

After all the Christmas preparations were completed, Fang and two other guards inspected the tree, bricks, and ornaments, but they eventually became convinced that the decorations were innocuous and left them up. The official North Vietnamese government position on Christmas 1972, as articulated on the camp radio, was that they would "give the POWs a good Christmas even though the war was still going on, and the United States had not signed an agreement, and was guilty of many violations." On Christmas Eve, the camp commander, in civilian clothes, came into the room and personally wished the POWs a merry Christmas. Goose and another guard then passed out little gifts from the priests of Hanoi: sacks of cookies, candy, and cigarettes. The next day, a special holiday meal identical to the one served on Vietnamese Independence Day was served with about a third of a cup of wine for each POW.

For the men of the rooms, the holiday season brought great emotional turmoil. Thoughts of past Christmases, of wives and families, and freedom inwardly, and occasionally outwardly, affected the group. "The realization that this was a Christmas away from my wife and children," Ensch remembered of that sad Yuletide season, "who were now old enough to enjoy it, upset me greatly. Then I kicked myself in the ass for feeling sorry for myself. I saw there were others in as bad a shape as myself, and I figured that the least I could do was make the most of a lousy situation." With that, he regained his positive outlook and continued his self-assigned role as "camp clown" and "morale booster extraordinaire."

In an unpopular war, American POWs emerged as the most celebrated heroes. Many Americans viewed the POWs with awe and drew inspiration from their actions. The media publicized their plight from their moment of capture to their homecoming, members of the antiwar movement visited them in their cells, and senior military and civilian officials in Washington met with their wives and entertained their families after the war.

Ironically, all this publicity had a mixed effect on the actual lives of the POWs. It probably did much to convince the Vietnamese to hold on to the POW "bargaining chips" until the bitter end of the struggle, but it also convinced them to end the torture program and gave newer shoot-downs more confidence in dealing with their captors. Ted Sienicki and some of the other younger members of Room 5 knew that they were valuable assets to the North Vietnamese, and as a result they felt comfortable antagonizing guards and refusing to participate in propaganda ploys. This stance placed them directly at odds with a small number of senior officers, particularly Colonel Joseph Kittinger. These men also understood that the POWs were significant to the Vietnamese, but they decided that a "live-and-let-live" attitude would best serve the overall interests of the group. Unfortunately, in a war where resistance to or cooperation with the enemy had policy implications that extended far beyond the confines of Room 5, the path of least resistance was often the wayward one.

Caught in the middle of this ideological dispute was Ronald Polfer, a man who greatly desired to fight a righteous struggle with the Vietnamese but was held back by his loyalty to the command structure. Unlike many of his more iconoclastic comrades in the Air Force, Polfer had experienced the rigors of serving on ship and understood the importance of good order and discipline in a cramped and hazardous environment like Hoa Lo. When he emerged as the room commander after the Vietnamese placed Kittinger in solitary confinement, Polfer could and did cut his own path, but up until that point, he remained a loyal subordinate who willingly upheld all legal orders.

Like Polfer, other Navy officers in Room 5 seemed more intent upon solving day-to-day problems than grinding the ax with Kittinger over the issue of resistance. Ensch, despite serious injuries, made morale his top priority and worked hard to cheer up his colleagues during the dark, cold winter of 1972–73. As many POWs learned upon arrival at Hoa Lo, boredom could be an enemy as relentless as the Vietnamese.

Souder, similarly, put his efforts into fighting another unmerciful enemy—injuries and ailments. One of the primary lessons that arose from the Vietnam POW experience was the need for better medical training among combat flight crews. A majority of aviators incurred some form of injury during bailout, and the armed forces should have taken additional steps earlier to provide more basic medical training to aircrews.

In the end, the Nixon administration did much to bolster the morale of POWs during the waning days of the war. Whatever their politics, most POWs believed implicitly that Richard Nixon took a personal interest in their plight and was willing to leverage all the resources of the U.S. military establishment to secure an honorable release for them. The POWs never lost faith. They returned with honor, and, for the most part, led honorable and successful lives afterward.

PART IV

NAVY MINING OPERATIONS AND THE TRIUMPH OF THE BENGALS

Crossing the Rubicon

DURING OPERATION ROLLING THUNDER (March 1965–October 1968), U.S. Navy aircraft seeded Communist supply routes in the "panhandle" area of North Vietnam with thousands of 500-pound magnetic mines in an attempt to shut down the flow of supplies to the Communist forces operating in South Vietnam. Neither the mining operations nor the broader Rolling Thunder bombing campaigns against the Communist logistics network stemmed the flow of supplies southward, but they did compel the Communists to devote scarce resources to defending and maintaining their logistics system.[1]

Some Navy planners argued that the problem with this early operation lay not so much with the mining concept but in the choice of targets, noting the conspicuous absence from these early target folders of the port of Haiphong, which handled over 85 percent of the North's import tonnage—about 2.5 million metric tons per annum. With over 400 ships using the port each year, a mining operation against North Vietnam stood little chance of success unless Haiphong was targeted. Policy makers had refrained from mining the approaches to this important artery for almost the entire war because they feared that such action would precipitate direct Chinese or Soviet intervention. What prompted the sudden shift in policy in 1972?

On 30 March 1972, the North Vietnamese launched an overt invasion of South Vietnam in direct violation of the 1954 Geneva Accords. The North's order of battle numbered 200 Soviet tanks, numerous 130-mm heavy artillery pieces, and mobile antiaircraft guns. The first assault waves thrust across the DMZ, but others developed in the central highlands and toward An Loc, sixty miles north of Saigon. By the first week of May, North Vietnamese Army units had captured Quang Tri

City, the capital of South Vietnam's northernmost province, and laid siege to Pleiku and Kontum. More serious yet, the Army of the Republic of Vietnam was fighting a last-ditch battle to save An Loc. As the juggernaut progressed, the NVA ultimately committed fourteen infantry divisions and twenty-six separate regiments (120,000 troops and 1,200 tanks) to the offensive. With only 60,000 American troops remaining in South Vietnam, General Creighton Abrams, the commander of Military Assistance Command, Vietnam (MACV), faced the real possibility of a total South Vietnamese collapse.[2]

Dire options confronted President Nixon. To reintroduce additional ground forces into Vietnam would have galvanized his political opposition and destroyed his prospects for reelection in the 1972 presidential campaign. It also would have gone counter to his Vietnamization policy of gradual U.S. troop withdrawals. Existing air and naval operations against supply routes were already being employed but with limited success. The situation required more—especially in light of the upcoming summit meeting in Moscow. Nixon did not want to negotiate with the Soviets while South Vietnam literally deteriorated behind his back. He needed a bold military option that would send a strong message to the North Vietnamese and their allies that despite Vietnamization, the United States stood firmly by its commitment to defend South Vietnam. As he explained the situation to his secretary of state, Henry Kissinger, in a memorandum: "I cannot emphasize too strongly that I have determined that we should go for broke. What we have to get across to the enemy is the impression that we are doing exactly that. Our words will help some. But our actions in the next few days will speak infinitely louder than our words."[3] The stage was set for what would end up being one of the Navy's most successful operations of the war.

Ironically, the first mines laid at 0900 on 9 May (local Vietnam time) were sown by both Navy A-7 Corsair II aircraft and Marine A-6 Intruders flying from *Coral Sea*.[4] While the traditional role of Marine air power has always been to provide close air support for Marines on the ground, Marine aviation took on broader missions in Vietnam, including interdiction, strategic bombing, and mine warfare operations. At the height of the war in 1968, the Marines deployed fourteen squadrons to Vietnam (half of the total strength of Marine aviation at the time) and flew 90,786 fixed-winged combat sorties that year. Ground-based Marine fighters often flew protective barrier combat air patrols to protect Task Force 77 carriers from enemy fighters. Some of these units also made significant contributions to the broader naval air war over Laos and North Vietnam. In short, it is often difficult to separate the contribution of Marine aviation from that of naval aviation in Southeast Asia. Such was the case for Marine All Weather Attack Squadron 224 (VMA (AW)-224), which, along with Navy A-7s, dropped magnetic-acoustic sea mines in the river approaches to Haiphong, North Vietnam's chief port, on the first day of Operation Pocket Money, 9 May 1972. The tale of this squadron, nicknamed the "Bengals," is compelling because it provides a unique glimpse at Marine-Navy cooperation in a carrier environment—a trend that continues to this day.

The Bengals were in crisis for much of their cruise in *Coral Sea.* Most of its pilots were completely unfamiliar with carrier operations before the cruise, and many had received basic pilot training not in Navy but in Air Force schools. Making matters worse was the squadron's first skipper, Commander Bill Standley, a man who could barely fly the A-6 and who ended up being relieved halfway through the cruise.

What transformed this latter-day "black sheep" squadron into one of the finest attack units in the theater was the hardheaded determination of its Marine aviators and crews to improve their skills despite the odds. Rallied by a handful of experienced combat veterans, the unit worked day and night to learn the symphonic precision of carrier operations. Marine Corps training emphasizes the ability to adapt to the arduous conditions inherent in a combat environment—cramped, grimy quarters, lack of food, poor ventilation, sickness, and fatigue. This adaptability proved especially useful in the confines of *Coral Sea.*

Helping the squadron achieve carrier proficiency were the naval officers and enlisted men on board *Coral Sea* and two men, in particular: Commander Roger Sheets, the air wing commander (CAG), and Lieutenant Commander Philip Schuyler, the Navy landing signal officer assigned to the squadron. Schuyler functioned as a Navy insider with whom even the most junior officer or enlisted man could discuss problems in confidence. Sheets offered inspiration from the top and demonstrated it by flying more with VMA (AW)-224 than with any other unit in the wing. He felt personally responsible for the squadron and its well-being.

Sheets also worked extremely well within the chain of command to achieve his goals. Upper-echelon leaders existed not as bureaucratic impediments but as facilitators who could assist him in driving the sharp end of the carrier aviation spear deep into the belly of the enemy. On 9

May, every aspect of the U.S. naval arsenal functioned well, from the surface ships that provided antiaircraft coverage for the strike force to the planners in the Office of the Chief of Naval Operations (OPNAV), who devised the operation. Although some mistakes naturally occurred, the mission succeeded overall.

A final interesting element of the VMA (AW)-224 story is that it lends credence to the controversial theory that in a combat situation it is always a small number of individuals who put the majority of fire on a target.[5] In this squadron, the eight air crewmen of the "Vulture" flight flew the majority of tough missions against Hanoi and Haiphong. The remainder of the forty-one officers of the squadron bombed targets in lower threat areas or flew combat support missions such as tanker or electronic warfare runs. While some might expect the pilots and navigators of Vulture flights to be predominantly long-term careerists with military academy backgrounds, most stumbled into the military almost by accident and learned only then of the latent warrior spirit lurking in their souls. Fortunately for the unit, Sheets had the insight to identify quickly these aggressive pilots and concentrate them in a single flight to maximize their impact.

12

Difficult Transitions

The Marines of VMA (AW)-224

CARRIER TRAINING for many of the forty-four officers of VMA (AW)-224 began almost a year prior to deployment in *Coral Sea*. About half of the squadron needed to complete the carrier qualification course at NAS Pensacola before the squadron could even begin flying off *Coral Sea*. During this two-day period, pilots and navigators flew twenty landings off *Lexington* before heading on to NAS Fallon, Nevada, for the weapons training phase of the workup.[1] According to Second Lieutenant Tom Sprouse, a junior pilot with the unit, carrier qualifications did not go smoothly for many men.

During the 1968–70 period, the Navy did not have enough slots at Pensacola to provide basic flight training for all Marine aviators; as a result, many received their wings from Air Force pilot schools. For these men, the transition to carrier flying tended to be especially jarring. In the Air Force, pilots learn to slow the plane as it approaches the ground and then brake as soon as all wheels are on the ground. In a carrier landing, by contrast, one actually maintains full power until the tailhook grabs the arresting wire. Thus, a plane still possesses the power to fly off the deck and make another landing if its hook does not catch. "It was just not natural for us to fly the airplane full tilt until it grabbed something," Sprouse explained, "which is what you do in a carrier landing, and many of us almost washed out of the program."[2]

The 224's adjustment problems did not end after it was carrier qualified. According to Sprouse, "There was always a feeling that we were not necessarily wanted on board." During *Coral Sea*'s initial workup period off the coast of California, the carrier air wing commander, Commander Thomas E. Dunlop, exacerbated the situation by being overbearing and critical of the Marines at every opportunity. "Tom Dunlop, an A-7 driver, just about wrote us off," explained Marine Captain Charlie Carr. "He figured the only reason we were on board was to screw him up."[3] The squadron's executive officer and later its commander, Lieutenant Colonel Ralph E. Brubaker, described the situation this way: "The Marines got hind tit—the worst maintenance shops, quarters, ready room, you name it. We accepted that because we were used to it, but once we started doing our job, it did bother us somewhat to be ridiculed for things that weren't the squadron's fault."[4]

The Marines did their best to play the cards dealt them, but one difficulty soon became almost insurmountable—a flying crisis involving their commander, Lieutenant Colonel Bernard B. "Bill" Standley. A forty-two-year-old career officer, Standley nevertheless was a weak pilot. On takeoffs, he would turn across the bow, thereby jeopardizing both his aircraft and the carrier. He would also abort a mission for the smallest reason imaginable. During the workup cruises off the California coast, the situation became so bad that CAG Dunlop called Major Clyde Smith, the squadron's operations officer, into his office to discuss the situation. "What do you think of Standley as a pilot?" Dunlop inquired.

"I think he can't fly worth shit," Smith replied. "If you are not going to relieve him now, we have to make sure he doesn't lead any strikes. I don't want him to end up killing anyone."

"I can't relieve him now," Dunlop protested, "because I just told a visiting Marine general that everything was just fine."

In Standley's defense, it should be noted that he took over as commander of VMA (AW)-224 because no one else volunteered for the assignment. Unfortunately, his flying did not improve as *Coral Sea* neared Yankee Station, and Dunlop opted not to designate him as a strike leader—a status that squadron commanders and executive officers generally received. When Roger Sheets took command of *Coral Sea*'s air wing in April 1972, he compelled Standley to lead a relatively benign strike. "It was bad enough," Sheets later explained, "to confirm that he should not be a strike leader, and that until he was no longer with the squadron, support missions were the extent of any reasonable use for him as a pilot."[5]

Needless to say, having a weak stick in command nearly destroyed morale for a squadron already smarting from being in the unfamiliar confines of a carrier. The young lieutenants looked to Standley to fly the toughest missions, and when they saw him using the excuse of a toothache to get out of a mission or flying tanker missions, it made many lose faith in the squadron leadership.[6] The situation got out of hand in mid-May 1972, when Standley approached Ralph Brubaker, his exec, and asked if the squadron could get along without him for a while. Apparently, Standley wanted to go home to attend his daughter's high school graduation. "Bill, to be honest with you, you shouldn't go," Brubaker responded, "but I think we can get along without you."

Thus, during the middle of Nixon's Linebacker campaign against North Vietnam, Standley flew home to Cherry Point, North Carolina. He told no one he was there, but someone spotted him anyway and reported his presence to the 2d Marine Air Wing commander, General Tom Miller, who promptly relieved Standley of his command. Fortunately, the squadron had several strong veteran aviators who worked hard to keep the squadron running despite its problems at the top. Chief among them were Lieutenant Commander Phil Schuyler, Major Clyde Smith, Captain Louis Ferrecane, and Captain Charlie Carr.[7]

PHIL SCHUYLER

The son of a truck driver, Phil Schuyler grew up in Carpinteria, California, a small town just south of Santa Barbara. He attended college at California State Polytechnic University in Pomona. Because money was always tight in the Schuyler family, he transferred after two years to UC–Santa Barbara near his hometown, and finally to Los Angeles State, where he earned his degree in 1962. Phil did not enjoy the academic aspects of college life but needed a degree to fulfill his postcollegiate dream: an opportunity to fly with the United States Navy.

Schuyler entered flight training in 1962—a period in naval aviation before the Vietnam War when the demand for aviators was low and competition for wings keen. Of the eighty-two trainees who entered training with Phil, only twenty received their wings. Phil made it through the program but, lacking the academic scores necessary for fighters, instead ended up in the Grumman S-2, a twin-engine propeller-driven plane used to hunt and track submarines.

Because the threat from submarines was virtually nonexistent in Vietnam, Schuyler flew a lot of gunfire support missions on board *Bennington* during the early stages of the war. Schuyler then transitioned into jets in Kingsville, Texas, and went to NAS Oceana, in Virginia Beach, Virginia, in December 1967 for A-6 training. He deployed with VA-65 on board *Kitty Hawk* in December 1968. Unfortunately for an adventuresome soul like Schuyler, his 1969–71 cruise on *Kitty Hawk* was nearly as uneventful as his first tour on *Bennington*. Because of President Johnson's November 1968 bombing halt against North Vietnam, VA-65 ended up flying most of its missions over Laos. "I would usually fly one hour-and-forty-five-minute mission per day, but we never got hit during that cruise."

Despite the monotony of the war, Schuyler continued to pursue a Navy career: "I liked the people and the flying. Besides, the war was going on and I did not feel it was the time to get out." A natural warrior, Phil enjoyed the challenge of combat flying, so when asked to serve as a Navy liaison officer with VMA (AW)-224, he gladly accepted the offer to participate in a third tour in Southeast Asia on board *Coral Sea*. The idea of serving with Marines, though, initially put him off: "I had some misgivings about the Marines at first. We had always kidded the Marines about their maintenance and how dirty their airplanes were. Once I got to know the people, I felt better about it."[8]

LOUIS FERRECANE

The man who flew with Phil Schuyler was Captain Louis Ferrecane, USMC. Although technically on his first combat flying tour, Lou quickly was accepted by the "old heads" because of his long experience with the Marine Corps and his high degree of maturity. Like many other members of 224, he wound up in the Marine Corps serendipitously.

Born 2 May 1942 in Massachusetts, Ferrecane grew up in the lower-middle-class town of Braintree on the south shore and inherited a strong set of working-class values from his father, a warehouse manager with the Stop & Shop grocery store chain. He learned early the importance of getting to know the people with whom you work on a personal level, regardless of rank, a skill that served him well as 224's future maintenance officer. Ferrecane's father also taught him that hard work allows one to transcend mental or physical shortcomings. "If other people see you are working your tail off, they will cut you some slack, regardless of your skill"—another useful lesson for a Marine who would ultimately have to adapt to carrier operations.

Ferrecane matriculated at Braintree High School and went on to Boston University, where he majored in English literature and graduated with a bachelor's degree. A low draft number preempted any postgraduate career plans that Ferrecane might have had at the time and compelled him to enlist in the armed forces. As he recalled, "I went to the Navy recruiter first and ended up talking to the Marine recruiter across the hall, who offered me a better deal."

Lou attended Officer Candidate School, followed by the Officer Basic School at Quantico with the intention of going into aviation, but poor eyesight kept him out. Instead, he wound up as a maintenance officer with an H-46 helicopter squadron in Vietnam. Ferrecane served with HMM-164 at Danang from March 1966 to March 1967. While in Vietnam, Ferrecane learned to live in a tent, endure the occasional mortar attack, and perform maintenance work under difficult conditions. A surprisingly enthusiastic Marine, he often volunteered to recover parts from aircraft shot down in the jungle—a job nearly as dangerous as an infantry patrol, given the dangers of ambush, snipers, and booby traps.

Ferrecane left the Marine Corps as soon as his tour ended and went into a branch manager training program at the Security Pacific Bank. Banking, however, proved far less interesting than his previous job, and Ferrecane soon found himself spending time after work with his old Marine friends at the Marine air station in Santa Ana, California. Over beers at the O Club, these friends ultimately convinced Ferrecane that his future lay not in banking but with the United States Marine Corps. After conferring with his wife, a former Navy dependent accustomed to military life, Ferrecane reenlisted as a maintenance officer.

Since there were few long-term career prospects in Marine Corps maintenance, Ferrecane began to research other military occupational specialties such as artillery and logistics. He eventually gravitated toward the naval flight officer specialty because he had always wanted to fly. It also appeared likely at the time that NFOs might soon be able to command squadrons. In fact, Ferrecane would ultimately be appointed as the first Marine NFO to command a squadron in 1979, but in 1969, taking an NFO slot was a real career gamble.

Ferrecane attended NFO training at Pensacola, graduating in 1969, and after a brief stint with VMA-332 landed a position as maintenance officer with 224. "They were looking for experienced officers in 224, and while I was new to aviation, I knew maintenance well and also had a combat tour under my belt." Ferrecane's stock in the squadron soon went up several points when Schuyler, the squadron landing signal officer, chose him as his bombardier-navigator.[9]

CLYDE SMITH

The operations officer for the squadron, Clyde Smith was born on 18 May 1937 and grew up in Park Rapids, Minnesota. The son of a small businessman, Smith excelled in sports, lettering in basketball, football, and track in high school and then going on to play football at the University of Minnesota in Duluth. As a college student, Smith also served in the Air Force ROTC and soon after graduation entered Air Force pilot training.

Graduating in the top third of his undergraduate pilot training class, Smith ended up as an instructor rather than a fighter pilot. Initially, he taught the Lockheed T-33, but the Air Force soon assigned him to teach foreign students the rudiments of the North American T-28. There were many Thais and Laotians in the class who could barely speak English, which frustrated Smith, who perceived himself more as a fighter pilot than a foreign language instructor: "I went to the personnel people at Randolph Air Force Base and told them I wanted to get into fighters. They told me I had to have three years in the T-28. I told them I had been doing it almost three and a half years, and then this captain said, 'Well, you have to be in the training command at least five years, and besides that, you're not current in jet aircraft so you're not qualified.' I hit the ceiling, and he threatened to throw me out of his office."

By this time a captain, Smith drove to the local Marine recruiter in downtown San Antonio and asked for a transfer to the Marines. Smith entered that service in the fall of 1966 and never looked back.

The Marine Corps ultimately assigned Smith to VMA-533, an A-6 unit destined for Chu Lai air base in Vietnam. Smith flew for six months with this unit during the 1967–68 period, earning two Distinguished Flying Crosses for his work. While in Vietnam, Smith often flew over to Ubon to visit his old Air Force friends and buy beer for the Marines at Chu Lai. Although impressed with the excellent living conditions at Ubon, Smith entertained no regrets about his transfer to the Marines: "The guys in Ubon were living in kind of a motel environment in their air-conditioned hootches and officers' clubs." Smith, by contrast, lived in a tent and slept on a cot, but he did not care. "I would never trade my Marine experiences for an Air Force career—meeting Charlie Carr was one of them. The Marine Corps is more focused. Their purpose is to fight wars."

During the Tet Offensive of January 1968, Smith actually experienced war from an infantryman's perspective: "Rockets hit the bomb dump and blew over a box of stuff in the room. I broke my toe one night running to the bunker during a rocket attack but continued flying. I just had a hard time pushing the brake because the brakes are on the tops of the pedals so I slid my foot up and used my heel to stop the plane."

Smith's tour with VMA-533 ended in 1968, whereupon he joined VMA (AW)-224 as its new operations officer.[10]

CHARLIE CARR

Like those of Smith and Ferrecane, Carr's route to Marine aviation was rather circuitous and nontraditional. The son of a wealthy lawyer and banker from Manhattan, Carr enjoyed a life of privilege during his youth. He received his primary education at the prestigious Saint Bernard's School on Manhattan's Upper East Side and later transferred to Short Hills Country Day School in Short Hills, New Jersey. For high school, his parents sent him to the Loomis Chaffee boarding school in Windsor, Connecticut.

At Loomis, the only thing for Charlie to do on weekends was to go into Windsor occasionally and maybe see a movie; he spent the remainder of his time on campus. After such an austere experience, Charlie went wild at Williams College in Williamstown, Massachusetts. As he described it, "I had probably the most spectacular freshman career they have seen at Williamstown for a long time."

He joined a fraternity, became a football cheerleader, sang in the octet, and drank a lot of beer. In January, when the first semester's grades came out, the dean of freshmen promptly summoned Carr and said, in effect, "Mr. Carr, we'll see ya." Charlie's college career was over.

Several days after getting kicked out of Williams, Carr received a draft notice and ended up taking a subway trip down to Church Street in the financial district of New York City to explore his recruitment options. Carr recalled, "I put my nose in the Marine recruiter's office, and they promised to make me a general in a week if I just went down to Parris Island and got a little training. I said, 'Hey that sounds good to me.'"

The Marine Corps traditionally does not draw many scions of wealthy families. In fact, in his forty-year career, Carr never met a single Marine officer who had attended Williams College. Nevertheless, Carr transitioned to a Marine Corps life with extraordinary grace. "If I had gone into the Marine Corps after Loomis, did a normal two- or three-year tour, and then gone back to Williams, I would have graduated, no question about it. It gave me a huge dose of discipline that was intense and all-pervasive, something that sticks with you your whole life."

When Carr graduated from basic training, he applied for and was accepted into the eight-month Marine navigator school at Cherry Point, North Carolina. Of the twenty enlisted men who entered the program in the fall of 1953, only six graduated. According to Carr, the most demanding part of the course was staying up all night and locating stars with a sextant and then having to navigate a blackened transport plane around North Carolina the next morning.

Upon graduation in the spring of 1954, the Marine Corps sent Carr to Itami, Japan, as a C-119 "Flying Boxcar" navigator. Carr immediately fell in love with Marine life in the Far East: "I did a fifteen-month tour, 1954–55. The yen was 360 to a buck, it cost 100 yen for a huge bottle of Asahi beer, and the women were plentiful and really cheap."

When Carr returned to the States, his father had a banking job lined up for him at the First National City Bank. Carr deplored the idea of "hanging on a subway strap every morning and working in a bank," but the job fetched a handsome salary and would even allow him to finish his college degree evenings at Columbia University. The day of his discharge, he sang Japanese songs all night in a barracks full of Marines just back from the Far East, and the next morning he reenlisted. Carr took his $1,000 reenlistment bonus, drove out to Tucson, Arizona, traveled around the West Coast with his girlfriend, and wound up hitchhiking back to Los Angeles, barely AWOL. He shipped off to Japan the next day without a dime in his pocket.

After tours in the Far East and Antarctica, Carr applied for a commission as a warrant officer and attended Officer Candidate School at Quantico, Virginia. It was during this period that he married his first wife. Charlie then flew another tour as an electronic countermeasures officer in F-3Ds in Japan and finally transferred back to Cherry Point for a stateside tour. The year was 1964, and the Marine A-6 program was just starting. Fortunately for Charlie, the naval flight officer coordinator on base was a friend. One night, Charlie filled the coordinator up with beer and convinced him to secure orders for Carr to A-6 bombardier-

The Vulture! U.S. Marine Corps Bombardier-Navigator William "Charlie" Carr enters the cockpit of an A-6. Carr, along with his pilot, Roger Sheets, participated in Operation Pocket Money—the mining of Haiphong harbor, 1972. (Courtesy of U.S. Marine Corps)

navigator training at NAS Whidbey Island, Washington, with VA-128. Lyle Bull was Carr's BN instructor there in VA-128, which, according to Carr, meant "you did quite a bit of flying, but also spent a lot of time in the bar." Carr graduated from Whidbey in 1965 to become one of the first A-6 BNs in the Marine Corps. He then went back to Cherry Point to join the second Marine A-6 squadron, VMA (AW)-533.

VMA (AW)-533 deployed to Chu Lai in the fall of 1967. At Chu Lai, Carr flew scores of night missions, quickly becoming one of the most skilled navigators in the Marines. For one mission against Hanoi Radio's transmitter, he and his pilot, Lieutenant Colonel Bill Fitch, received the Silver Star—America's third-highest decoration for valor.

After flying 125 missions against North Vietnam, Carr returned to the United States. Like many pilots fresh from combat, Charlie had problems adjusting to garrison duty. "I personally got very bored with the whole thing," he explained. Charlie talked to his wife about his personal problems, but she did not seem to understand. One day, he said to her, "Hey, I think I want to go overseas."

"Do it at your peril," she shot back.

Charlie accepted the orders, jumped into a Volkswagen Beetle, and left Cherry Point for the West Coast. When he arrived in California, divorce proceedings were already in progress. Charlie didn't mind. "What could they do," he thought, "send me to Vietnam?"

Carr's second tour at Danang during 1969 and 1970 was a "piece of cake," but very monotonous. The bombing halt against North Vietnam during this period meant most of his missions were easy ones into South Vietnam and Laos. Roughly 90 percent of these were against targets picked up along the Ho Chi Minh Trail in southern Laos by the Igloo White sensors.

Charlie's second tour ended in early 1970, whereupon he proceeded to Quantico to the Amphibious Warfare School (AWS) for six months. Although scheduled to be an instructor at Pensacola after AWS, he again schemed his way on to a third deployment. "I ended up calling a friend down at VMA (AW)-224 and asking him if I could join the squadron, and he said, 'You're damn right.' The next thing you know I got my orders changed. Hell, this was a new adventure, getting to go out on a carrier."[11]

CORAL SEA DEPARTS FROM ALAMEDA AND GOES TO WAR

For Carr and the rest of VMA (AW)-224, not only was their transition to carrier flying a grand adventure, but so, too, was their departure from San Francisco. At 0500 on 9 November 1971, just as Coral Sea's crew started returning from shore leave to the carrier, over 1,000 antiwar protesters staged a demonstration in front of the east gate at Alameda Naval Air Station in Oakland, where the ship was docked. Jerry "Devil" Houston, an F-4 pilot with VF-51, remembered the scene vividly: "As we approached the east gate at Alameda, there were several hundred long-haired demonstrators with North Vietnamese flags; they had our flag upside down, and they spit on us and called us baby killers."[12]

On the morning of *Coral Sea*'s departure, 12 November, 1,500 protesters again rallied at Alameda in an attempt to prevent the ship from sailing. When she finally put to sea, thirty-five sailors stayed behind in solidarity with the protesters. Police halted all traffic over the Bay Bridge and Golden Gate Bridge to prevent any attempts at sabotage. Marine Captain Billy Angus's attitude typified that of the pilots of the squadron toward the antiwar movement: "I believed in the war. I was apolitical. I was there for the good times, the camaraderie, the flying, the sense of adventure."[13] Houston, a more senior officer with several Southeast Asia tours under his belt, took a slightly different view of the protests:

> All the protests were directed against the *Coral Sea*—they wanted to keep that ship from going. Goddamn, we're going out there with our wives and we're not that hot to go back there again. I was on my fourth deployment. Hell, you have to fight your way onto the base to go do something you're really not hot to do anyway. You kept going and did it more for each other more than anything else. I thought more of the Vietnamese fighter pilots than our members of Congress. Then, we thought the protesters were weak dicks who didn't want to get killed. Now, I realize that we had no business being over there. Goddamn it, it wasn't all that fun, but it was fun being a part of it. Most of the dissatisfaction at the flight crew level was not with the war but with the way we were running it. Everybody wanted to level the country. We were not there to discuss the rights and the wrongs of the war, we don't declare war. We were paid to fight.[14]

All the protests against *Coral Sea* were directed by a group called "SOS," or "Stop Our Ship." SOS not only staged rallies but also enlisted scuba divers to try to sabotage the ship and small craft to try to block the carrier's departure. The San Francisco harbor patrol arrested one scuba diver and used water cannons from fireboats to prevent sailboats and other small craft from blocking *Coral Sea*'s departure.

SOS even convinced the Berkeley city council to issue a proclamation offering safe haven to *Coral Sea* sailors wishing to stay home: the

U.S. Justice Department quickly declared the proclamation unconstitutional, and the Berkeley city manager as well as the police department refused to honor the proclamation. SOS also recruited members of *Coral Sea*'s own crew to participate in protests. Several days before the carrier's departure, three officers from the ship's company, including the public affairs officer, went on San Francisco's Channel 5 and confessed their opposition to the war and their desire not to go. That evening these officers requested orders from Captain William Harris to leave the ship. Harris refused. Instead, he took the men all the way to Yankee Station before he finally agreed to ship them back to Subic Bay for discharges.[15]

In the fall of 1971, the men who eagerly volunteered to fight in Vietnam were a rare breed. Marine personnel officers might have frowned on Carr for finessing his way on board *Coral Sea*, but the reality of the situation was that the war was unpopular, and few Americans wanted to strap themselves onto an A-6 and drop bombs on North Vietnam. Nevertheless, a small cadre of aviators was willing to ignore the bad press and the protests, and go to war.

INITIAL COMBAT: JANUARY 1972

The squadron's first combat missions involved interdicting enemy supplies moving south through the Mu Gia and Ban Karai Passes in Laos—a role that the A-6 was uniquely suited for. The requirement for the A-6 developed out of the Navy's experiences in Korea, where aircraft often could not hit targets because of poor weather. In 1956, the Navy solicited bids for an attack aircraft capable of operating at night as well as in bad weather. In the end, the Grumman A-6 won the contract. The A-6 appeared gangly at first glance. It was a large, two-seat, twin-engine aircraft with a huge nose radome, cheek air intakes, swept wings, and a long, tapering fuselage. Although the plane had a maximum speed of only 648 miles per hour, it could carry up to twenty-eight 500-pound bombs and loiter for an extended period over a target area with its 2,022-mile range. However, the most revolutionary aspect of the plane was its Digital Integrated Attack and Navigation Equipment (DIANE), which included a ground-mapping radar, a track radar, an analog computer, and an inertial navigation system. With this system, the A-6 could attack preselected locations or targets of opportunity without the crew having to look outside the cockpit from launch to recovery. A bombardier-navigator sat adjacent to the pilot and managed DIANE. Steering instructions derived from inertial guidance, Doppler navigation, or terrain clearance radar systems were displayed to the pilot through a visual display terminal. In short, the A-6 allowed the BN to navigate without any vocal instructions being passed to the pilot; all instructions could be passed along digitally through DIANE from the BN's terminal to the pilot's. During the winter months of 1972, A-6 bombardier-navigators not only used DIANE to guide their own planes to targets on overcast days but actually served as pathfinders for Air Force bombers as well. At night, the A-6s used their sophisticated navigation system to find and destroy enemy trucks moving along the Ho Chi Minh Trail in Laos.[16]

For veterans like Carr and Smith, VMA (AW)-224's initial combat missions into Laos were routine "milk runs," but for the newer pilots, these relatively benign missions provided more than enough exhilaration to help transform them from mere "nuggets" to what one veteran referred to as "polished nuggets."

A CHANGE AT THE TOP

For the men of VMA (AW)-224, the first three line periods seemed to blend together because most missions involved interdicting Communist supply routes in Laos. Things changed dramatically for the unit in April, beginning with the loss of CAG Thomas Dunlop to a SAM on 6 April near Quang Khe. Apparently, Dunlop's wingman observed a missile liftoff to his left and radioed CAG to break left. As often happens in the profound confusion of combat, however, Dunlop misinterpreted the call and initiated a right break. The missile detonated near his A-7E's tail, killing Dunlop and robbing Air Wing 15 of its air wing commander.[17]

The Navy reacted to this crisis immediately. Commander Roger Sheets, on board the *Constellation* at the time, preparing for what he thought would be the command of Air Wing 9, received a call from the Commander Naval Air Force, Pacific (COMNAVAIRPAC) just after landing an A-7 on the deck of the carrier. COMNAVAIRPAC stated that Sheets would soon be sent to the *Coral Sea* to take command of Air Wing 15. The next day, a Friday, Sheets received confirmation that he would indeed soon be the CAG-15. At 0700 the next morning, a yeoman delivered orders to his quarters at NAS Lemoore.[18] Sheets left that evening for Danang, Vietnam, spent the night there, and took the carrier onboard delivery plane (COD) to *Coral Sea* on Monday morning.

The trip to *Coral Sea* was a homecoming for Roger. He knew the ship well. During the early 1960s, he had flown F-8 Crusaders off the carrier with VF-154, and from December 1967 to April 1969, he had commanded VF-161, an F-4 squadron. He brought to *Coral Sea* a wealth of experience and knowledge about naval air power and Southeast Asia that few men of his rank could match.[19]

The son of a Protestant Navy chaplain, Sheets grew up on naval bases across the United States. During World War II, he felt embarrassed walking around a base without a uniform, so as soon as he turned seventeen in 1947, he joined the Naval Reserve as a seaman. He made summer cruises in a patrol craft on Lake Michigan and on a troop transport out of Norfolk, Virginia. In the Navy, Sheets "found something he really liked." The same could not be said for academic pursuits. Roger tried taking courses at Wabash College in Crawfordsville, Indiana, and at his father's alma mater, Bethany College, in Bethany, West Virginia, but found that his interests lay more in music and the Navy than academic subjects. Consequently, he left college early in 1950 to enter the Naval Aviation Cadet Program (he did not receive his bachelor's degree until 1973).

Sheets did his initial flight training in the propeller-driven SNJ (the Navy version of the T-6 Texan) at Pensacola, Florida; advanced in the F-6F Hellcat at Cabanas Field, Texas; and then got selected along with five other pilots from his group to attend jet instruction in the T-33 at Kingsville, Texas. Earning his wings in 1952, Sheets barely made it to the Korean War before it ended.

In Korea, Sheets mainly flew interdiction missions against rail lines and other logistics targets. Before the armistice of 27 July 1953, he racked up a total of fifty combat missions, earning four Air Medals and a Navy Commendation Medal with a Combat V device. After the war, he became a T-28 and T-33 instructor at Memphis, Tennessee, and stayed in that assignment until 1958.

Almost from the onset, Sheets's Navy career was hampered by the fact that he had neither a Naval Academy nor a college degree. "At that time in the Navy," claims Sheets, "the ring knockers kind of ruled, and they looked after one another." In an attempt to teach Sheets basic seamanship and get him educationally on a par with the U.S. Naval Academy graduates, the Navy sent him to the Line School at Monterey, California. Upon graduation in 1959, he transitioned to one of the Navy's hottest planes of the time, the Vought F-8 Crusader, with VF-154. The "Sader" was the most demanding aircraft Sheets ever flew, allowing a pilot almost no margin for error on a carrier approach because some of the control surfaces were dual-purpose, serving as both flaps and ailerons.

Sheets excelled in the F-8 and eventually became a landing signal officer on board *Coral Sea*. Usually one of the most skilled pilots in a squadron, the LSO controlled carrier landings by telling each pilot how well he was flying approach relative to the optimum flight path for a successful carrier landing. For the brief landing cycle, often referred to as a "controlled crash," a pilot's life rested firmly in the hands of the LSO. The LSO guided the pilot's every move, telling him when to slow down, add power, add rudder, and so forth. He could even order a pilot to abort a landing by waving him off. The job required steady nerves and expert knowledge of the unique flight characteristics of every aircraft in the wing. The LSO's word, during approach, was law.

In 1963, Sheets returned to training at NAS Glynco in Brunswick, Georgia, for his next assignment as an assistant air operations officer on board *Constellation*. He served in that carrier for two and a half years as a lieutenant commander. During this tour, the carrier was on station off North Vietnam during the Gulf of Tonkin incidents in 1964. In fact, on the night of 4 August, when the destroyers *Maddox* and *Turner Joy* thought they were under attack, Roger served as the carrier control approach officer.[20]

In 1965, Sheets attended the Naval War College at Newport, Rhode Island, and was later promoted to commander. In 1966, he spent eleven months in Kingsville, Texas, as an F-9 instructor. He then received an opportunity second in prestige only to his eventual CAG assignment—command of an F-4 squadron on Yankee Station in Vietnam. Sheets, though, was "a little disappointed at first and had to think about it for a while."[21] The problem with the F-4 was that it was a two-seat fighter, and up to this point, all of Sheets's fighter time had been in single-seaters. "In flying a single-seat aircraft," he explained, "there are certain times when you are really going to hang it out on something that might put you in jeopardy. Since you only have to think of yourself, you are apt to go ahead and do it. I was concerned that with someone else in the plane, I might feel a certain hesitancy to do that. What I discovered was

that with only rare exceptions, the guys in back were as gung-ho as anyone else, and you almost had to guard against letting them talk you into
something that was really harebrained."

Under ordinary circumstances, the route to squadron command in
the Navy involved a year of service as the squadron executive officer.
After a year, the XO then took over the squadron. Because VF-161 lost
its XO a week before Sheets was slated to come aboard, Roger ended up
bypassing the exec's job and moving right into the top slot. He also
managed to convince the Navy Bureau of Personnel to extend his command from one to two years as compensation for skipping the XO tour.

As the squadron commander of VF-161, Sheets made the best of the
war and all its restrictions by "playing everything up to the edge of
what he was supposed to do." That meant flying as low as 100 feet
above the ground with the F-4 and experimenting a lot with different
types of bombs and bomb loads. Sheets never had much luck destroying MiGs. During most of the period Sheets commanded VF-161
(1968–69), various bombing halts against North Vietnam prevented his
fighters from encountering enemy fighters. As he recalled, "On three
occasions, I had solid radar locks and good visuals on MiGs. They
stayed just over the coastline, kind of tormenting and testing us, and we
couldn't get approval to fire."

Sheets stayed with VF-161 until May 1969, then transferred to the
Carrier Division 9 staff and served two more Vietnam tours during the
1969–70 period as a staff officer on *Coral Sea* and *Kitty Hawk*. In different
capacities, Sheets witnessed just about the entire naval air war in Southeast Asia before arriving on board *Coral Sea* in 1972. Few aviators in the
Navy had served in Southeast Asia longer than Sheets, yet he still volunteered for a sixth tour. Why? "I always felt we could win the thing if
anyone decided they wanted to win it." What frustrated Sheets most
about his early tours was the on-again, off-again nature of the Rolling
Thunder campaign. "You had to get permission for almost anything
you wanted to do. And it was disappointing that the one thing we were
never told was, 'Try to win.'" In 1972, it appeared that Nixon just
"might have the guts to start taking steps in that direction." As it turned
out, Sheets's predictions about President Nixon would prove correct.[22]

It did not take much analysis on Sheets's part to quickly recognize that
VMA (AW)-224, as the first Marine A-6 unit to be deployed on a carrier,
would be the weakest squadron in his wing. Hence, rather than fly the

F-4 in either VF-51 or VF-111, a natural choice for a fighter jock like Roger, he put aside his chances to get a MiG, and with it the distinct possibility of an admiral's star, and decided instead to focus most of his attentions on the "weak sister" of the wing. On 12 April, his first day on the carrier, Sheets sauntered down to Ready Room 5, took a look at the flight list of bomber-navigators, and immediately saw that a man named Carr was far and away the most experienced BN in the squadron, if not the entire Marine Corps. He decided he would fly with Carr that afternoon.

Carr, who had just returned from a hop, remembered coming into the ready room and seeing this guy with a hat too big for his head and an eye twitch: "He looked like Don Knotts, but he was wearing a commander's silver leaf on his collar tab."[23] Carr did not know what to make of this unusual-looking pilot, but he agreed to fly with him immediately. Sheets, after all, was the new CAG. Sheets took an instant liking to Carr. Before him stood a warrior, a guy who, like him, had served multiple combat tours in Southeast Asia. When the two men strapped themselves into an A-6 the following day, they brought a combined total of 12,000 hours of personal flight experience to that aircraft.

"I flew wing on that mission," Sheets explained, "because the Marines were more familiar with what was going on, and I wanted to just tag along and learn how things were working these days, which I think surprised them a little bit, too." The mission was a close air support sortie in defense of a firebase being overrun by North Vietnamese regulars. Overcast weather completely covered the punchbowl valley where the position lay, and the Air Force FAC did not think the A-6s would be able to penetrate the clouds and prosecute an attack. Sheets disagreed. The lives of American advisers and South Vietnamese allies were at stake, and Sheets was not about to let a fellow soldier down. He leaned over to Carr and said, "Okay, we're going to take the lead and run this thing." The forward air controller in a light aircraft explained to the flight that the clouds extended into the mountains of the punchbowl, so he did not know how to get the flight down. Sheets then asked how fast the FAC could spiral down into the valley, to which the FAC responded, "a couple hundred knots." Sheets ordered the A-6 flight to form up in echelon on the FAC's wing and spiral into the valley with him. Once under the clouds, the A-6s worked with the firebase commander to kill 150 NVA troops, an action that probably saved the position from being overrun.[24] As Sheets put it, "So that was kind of a start to things, and every now and then there were some things that we did that at first Charlie couldn't believe. After a while he didn't doubt anything that we might try."

The Marines appreciated Sheets and his attitude and rewarded him with the ultimate accolade. Shortly after that first mission, they repainted one of their aircraft and designated it 500. On the pilot's side was "CMDR/LTC Roger E. Sheets, USN/USMC, CAG." They also had a flight suit made up for him with A-6 patches and a joint Marine-Navy rank insignia. The Marines now accepted Roger as one of their own—a status rarely accorded to those outside the Corps. "He was super to fly with," remembered Carr. "He had guts, and though he did not appear to be meticulous, he was meticulous in planning; he made decisions when decisions had to be made; he led that air group better than anyone could have."[25] Sheets felt the same about his BN: "Charlie is probably my favorite person in the whole world. Charlie is a mustang, he was a Marine captain at that time, he had lots of total flight experience and a lot of experience in the A-6; he had a lot of combat experience. He was the kind of person that people thought couldn't be rattled and couldn't be scared, and almost right off the bat we got one another's attention. And I think there was almost an immediate mutual respect." But Sheets's respect went beyond the BN; it extended to the entire unit. Unlike Dunlop, who, as Charlie explained, "just about wrote the unit off," Sheets saw great potential in 224, and that made all the difference. In Carr's words, "Within a very short period of time, we had people believing in themselves and doing well."

13

The War to Save Bengal 505

SHEETS ARRIVED AT Squadron 224 not a moment too soon: on his second night as CAG, a search and rescue (SAR) operation unfolded that tested the capability not only of Air Wing 15 but also of the entire SAR establishment in Southeast Asia. The events surrounding the Bengal 505 SAR occurred at a critical period for the SAR forces.

A little over a week before Major Clyde Smith and First Lieutenant Scott Ketchie in Bengal 505 went down, a North Vietnamese SAM claimed Bat-21, an Air Force EB-66 electronics warfare plane, near the DMZ. Of those on board, only Lieutenant Colonel Iceal E. Hambleton, an electronic warfare officer, survived. During what evolved into an eleven-day effort, ninety individual bombing strikes and hundreds of FAC sorties were launched to protect Hambleton from enemy troops; and a no-fire zone was also implemented for seventeen miles around him to protect him from friendly artillery. Two OV-10 FACs, a UH-1, and an HH-53 were shot down trying to rescue the colonel. Only through the efforts of a SEAL team did he eventually make it to friendly forces. The entire effort forced the armed services to rethink SAR operations. Was one man worth such a sacrifice? In addition to the loss of aircraft, the SAR and its no-fire zone prevented the ARVN 3d Division from firing its artillery at the North Vietnamese Army advancing into the area. But the SAR also destroyed numerous offensive NVA forces near Bat-21, including thirty-five tanks and a command center.[1] Historians will most likely be debating these issues for many years to come, but for the servicemen who worked SARs, the failure with Bat-21 greatly undermined morale and placed future shoot-downs like Bengal 505 in jeopardy. SAR resources would no longer be risked unless there was a high probability for success.

Unaware of these issues, Clyde Smith and his bombardier-navigator, Scott Ketchie, blasted off *Coral Sea*'s catapult at 1800 on 9 April 1972. The mission that evening was to interdict Communist road traffic on

Route 9 near Tchepone, Laos. At the road an hour after takeoff, Smith saw several trucks starting to move along the trail. He made three bomb runs, destroying a couple of trucks, but also taking quite a bit of anti-aircraft fire. After his third pass, Smith deemed the area too hot for another and was just turning to go home when he heard a thump like a door closing. He said something to Scott but then realized the intercom was not working and he could not hear him.[2]

Warning lights lit up the cockpit, and the nose began to tilt downward. Now no longer able to steer with the stick, Smith looked over his shoulder and saw nothing but fire where the A-6's tail should have been. He then turned to look at Ketchie, reached up for the face curtain, and ejected. "I seemed to hang in the chute for quite a while, even to the point of taking out my radio to call someone, when I realized there wasn't anyone to talk to. I looked down, and there was fire on the ground directly underneath me. I landed next to the A-6."

As soon as he touched down, Smith moved away from the wreckage of his aircraft and the cluster-bomb units that were cooking off from it. He then attempted to transmit an emergency beeper signal on the guard channel to Captains Roger Milton and Charlie Carr, who were also in the air that day. There was no reply, and the aircraft left. The sun had just set, and it was very dark. Smith's spirits sank to a low point.[3]

Unbeknownst to Smith, Charlie had just landed on board *Coral Sea* and was soon pinpointing the crash for intelligence officers, who would transmit this precious information to their colleagues at Seventh Air Force Headquarters in Saigon. Like clockwork, these Air Force officers decided to make an emergency call to an F-4 in flight over Laos and order it to make a reconnaissance pass over the crash site.

At 2200, Smith heard an aircraft and turned on his beeper. A voice speaking perfect English came up on the rescue frequency. The voice came in clearly, sounded very close, and asked Smith where he was.

"I'm in the vicinity of the wreckage," Smith answered.

"We'll be there in a few minutes," the voice replied.

By then it was totally dark, and Smith had been briefed that no rescues were ever attempted at night. Was this a ruse? Smith demanded a call sign, but there was no answer. About two hours later, he heard a second aircraft and again tried to beep it with the emergency radio. After Smith transmitted his call sign, Bengal 505 Alpha, a "crusty old" fighter pilot asked him how he was, told him to stay hidden, and said they would be back in the morning. "I was confident that he, at least, was a friendly," Smith recalled.

The aircraft burned all night long, keeping Smith awake and allowing him to contemplate his predicament. The day before he deployed, his wife, Jackie, had given birth to a son; a few months later, in February, her mother had passed away; and in March, Jackie had had major surgery. How would she handle this blow? Unbeknownst to Smith at the time, Commander Sheets had just placed a high-priority Navy call to Jackie and assured her that the Navy and Air Force were doing all they could to get Clyde out. She later told Smith that the support she received from the armed services was "overwhelming."

As the sun rose the next morning, Smith realized that his position could not have been much worse. He lay in one of the most heavily defended sections of Laos between Tchepone and the DMZ—a box surrounded by numerous antiaircraft guns, two active SA-2 sites, all less than five minutes from a North Vietnamese airfield. As Smith recalled, "I was in an open area on the side of a small ridge lying against some elephant grass four to five feet high. I was lying on my side with my survival radio in my right hand when I heard someone approaching my position, walking through the elephant grass behind me. He stopped directly behind me. I was convinced he saw me. My heart was beating so hard that I was sure he could hear it. We had been drilled constantly during survival training to stay still; I didn't have anywhere to go, so I froze." The man stopped one or two steps from Smith, waited a few seconds, and then walked away. Immediately after the man departed, Smith walked to the bottom of the gully, covered himself with dense foliage, and hid under the base of an uprooted tree for the next four days. Six men then came down to inspect the A-6 wreckage but failed to spot Smith. "After 340 missions in Vietnam, I was sure that my luck had run out."[4]

It hadn't. Members of the Air Force's Aerospace Rescue and Recovery Service based out of Nakhon Phanom Royal Thai Air Base in northern Thailand were currently planning a massive rescue effort on his behalf. The Air Force's Thailand-based SAR team considered itself the most elite unit in the Air Force. In many respects it lived up to its reputation. All its pilots had volunteered to serve in this special role, and many had flown multiple combat tours in Vietnam or even Korea.

Even more elite than the SAR force officers were its enlisted parajumpers. The Navy trained every PJ as a certified scuba diver. Each also qualified as a medical technician, a parachutist, a small-arms expert, and a hand-to-hand combat master. Finally, the Air Force taught PJs the art of survival in jungle, desert, and even arctic conditions.

Often, the first SAR team member to arrive at a crash scene was a FAC. The FAC flew the OV-10 Bronco, a twin-engine reconnaissance aircraft with a maximum speed of 288 mph and armament consisting of two 7.62-mm machine guns and up to 3,600 pounds of marking rockets, gun pods, or other ordnance. During SARs, FACs were responsible for establishing contact with a survivor and then acquiring that survivor's position. With that vital information in hand, the FAC then directed heavier aircraft in to bomb anything that threatened either the survivor or the rescue forces.

Every rescue eventually became a desperate battle against time. FACs attempted to neutralize the area immediately surrounding the survivor so that slow-moving helicopters could extract a survivor while the enemy strove to thwart these efforts by bringing in enough guns, SAMs, and troops to make an aerial rescue untenable (which is exactly what happened in the Bat-21 episode). In some respects, the job of the FAC was the most difficult. He had to loiter over an area for up to five hours, expose himself constantly to antiaircraft fire when marking targets for attack with his smoke rockets, and keep the survivor updated on the rescue through occasional radio conversation.

The most critical point of any rescue was the actual extraction; the Air Force relied on a specialized aircraft known as the "Sandy" (short for "search and destroy") to direct this phase of the show. During the Vietnam War, the principal Sandy was the A-1 Skyraider. Originally designed for the Navy as an attack aircraft, the A-1 functioned well in the SAR environment because it could carry up to 10,000 pounds of mixed ordnance (including rockets and additional machine guns), as well as two 20-mm guns. The 321-mph aircraft also flew fast enough to avoid most antiaircraft fire but slow enough to be deadly accurate with its weaponry. Sandies generally flew in two-plane flights. Sandy High directed the helicopters to an orbit near a crash site but out of range of most ground fire and then escorted the helicopters to the actual survivor. In the meantime, Sandy Low surveyed the crash scene, destroyed any enemy resistance found, and then decided the exact time and routes of the extraction. In some cases, Sandy Low would survey a scene for days before calling in the helicopters.[5]

For both the Sandies and the FACs, the process of locating a survivor and guiding a helicopter to him often proved more challenging than the resistance confronted in a SAR. It took these pilots months to master the techniques of visual reconnaissance in a triple-canopy jungle environment. Even then, they had to fly a significant number of missions in a given sector before they could effectively point out a moving object at 1,500 feet. FACs would spend hours attempting to learn the patterns of their patrol areas: when villagers ate and slept, their work habits, and when they traveled to markets. They then would spend more time in the intelligence shack memorizing the latest locations of friendly and enemy troops. Since the 1:50,000 scale Defense Mapping Agency topographical maps could not be entirely trusted, the FAC and Sandy had to memorize key geographical features such as roads, rock formations, and waterfalls and individual village structures such as temples. In short, it took more than good flying to qualify as a member of the Air Force's elite Aerospace Rescue and Recovery Service; it took academic discipline—perhaps a reason why so many Air Force Academy graduates gravitated toward the field. It also required one to hang it out during nearly every rescue sortie. Anyone who has stood on the observation deck of the Empire State Building might wonder how a SAR pilot could pick out the good guys from the bad. FAC pilot J. S. Butz had a good answer: "You can't. Look for yourself. It's just about like flying over Manhattan Island at one-thousand feet and trying to pick out all the Italians."[6] To locate a survivor, the SAR pilot often needed to fly right above the treetops—a dangerous maneuver that greatly increased the chances of being shot down. SAR forces took even greater risks trying to locate hostile forces, often intentionally drawing fire to highlight an enemy position.

The final weapon in the SAR inventory consisted of the HH-53 Super Jolly Green Giant, a large helicopter capable of carrying thirty-eight troops in its cavernous cargo bay. The two GE-T64-3 turboshaft engines on this behemoth produced 3,080 horsepower, enough thrust to allow the aircraft to hover over high mountains for extended periods. Titanium armor impervious to small-arms fire covered many of the engine and hydraulic areas, and an aerial refueling probe allowed the helicopter to stay aloft for hours and hours at a time. For armament, the Air Force equipped the HH-53 with three GE 7.62-mm miniguns, each capable of firing 4,000 rounds per minute.

The HH-53 represented the heart of the SAR force: all other elements supported the helicopter's basic job of getting into a dangerous area and hoisting a downed aircrew to safety with its hoist and winch. Overall, the members of the Air Force's 3d Aerospace Rescue and Recovery Group would pull 3,883 airmen to safety during the war and receive over 14,600 awards and decorations for their efforts.[7]

For Clyde Smith, the magnitude and complexity of what the Air Force would be doing to get him out did not dawn on him the morning of 10 April; he was just glad when he heard the distinctive sound of an OV-10 buzzing his position at 0900 sharp. "I beeped and he came up on voice. It was an airborne forward air controller, call-sign Nail 17, and he was looking for me." After getting a fix on his position, Nail 17 needed to confirm that Smith was really Smith and not some North Vietnamese impersonator. He asked Smith several personal questions, one of which Smith did not answer correctly.

"Okay, that's enough," the FAC said, and the radio got quiet. Smith thought he had blown it and sweated out the rest of the morning hoping more planes might return. At 1500, his prayers were answered. Major Jim Harding, NKP's A-1 squadron commander and one of the most experienced SAR pilots in the Air Force, arrived on station as Sandy 1 and the on-scene commander. Upon first talking to Harding on the radio, Smith was not impressed: "Sandy 1 sounded older than dirt. And I thought, 'Oh God, here I am in this kind of situation and I get some old multiengine [former transport pilot] fart flying rescue planes.'" Sandy 1 immediately got to work taking out antiaircraft guns in the area, and Smith's attitude about Jim began to change.

At one point, Gunfighter 6 (an F-4 from the 366th Tactical Fighter Wing) tanked three times trying to take out a 23-mm gun site and finally called Sandy 1 to confirm the site's location. Harding's crisp response typified the professional attitude of this warrior: "Well, I haven't been able to get him to shoot at me yet, so hang on."[8] At another point, Smith suddenly heard Sandy 1's engine quit. "I immediately turned on the radio, and then the engine came on again. Sandy 1 said, 'I had a problem on my centerline tank, didn't know how much fuel I had, so I just ran it dry.' I said to myself, 'This guy's alright.'"

Harding checked in with Smith every fifteen minutes because if Smith were killed or captured, the operation would terminate immediately. The bombing lasted all day long, but by 1730, the Communist gunners still peppered the sky with antiaircraft fire; worse yet, overcast started to form above Smith's position. King 1, an airborne command and controller, called off the rescue for the day, but Sandy 1 and Nail 46 continued hammering the area until darkness descended. As Sandy 1 departed, Smith's heart sank: "It got very quiet. Then the birds started to sing, people began moving around, and the trucks started warming up for the night's run."

Although Smith did not worry about being discovered under the cover of darkness, he did suffer from the cold, damp, Laotian air: "My neck hurt, and I had banged my knee and cut my mouth when I landed. I slept on and off to some strange dreams."[9]

The war started up again the following morning, but once again, bad weather hampered the efforts of the rescuers. Smith tried to subsist on the meager rations in his survival kit: eight ounces of water and some Fruit Loops. A-1s dropped tear gas to discourage searchers, and this just made Smith nauseated and uncomfortable. Rain also filled the base of the uprooted tree, making him even more miserable and forcing King 1 to again terminate the operation for the day.

There was more of the same on 12 and 13 April: "Bring in airplanes and bomb the hell out of everything; dust clouds; shrapnel; and dirt flying through the trees." One F-4E nearly strafed Smith. "I literally jumped out of my skin as it fired. Hell, it couldn't have been more than fifty yards away."[10] Overall, there were twenty aircraft in the vicinity during Smith's time on the ground plus many flying in and out on bomb runs, but the situation was not improving. At Nakhon Phanom on the night of 13 April, the Air Force decided to cancel the rescue if the situation did not improve the next day—a move many considered prudent, especially given the recent Bat-21 losses.

What ultimately turned the situation around on 14 April was the support the Aerospace Rescue Service began to receive from *Coral Sea*. Frustrated by the rescue's lack of progress, Captain William Harris, at Sheets's insistence, placed a call to Seventh Air Force headquarters to get a status check on the situation. When the Air Force explained to him that it did not have the bombers to suppress all the ground fire around Smith, Harris and Sheets dedicated the entire *Coral Sea* air wing to the SAR effort, but even that proved not enough. A call for help went across to the skipper of *Constellation*, who at first indicated that he did not have the assets. Captain Harris replied that if it were one of the *Connie*'s pilots on the ground, he would give everything he had. After a pause, the skipper pledged the entire wing in support of Captain Smith's rescue.[11]

The specifics of how such a massive amount of naval air power could have been diverted from JCS-assigned strikes remains a point of controversy. Allegedly, Navy aircraft aborted their bomb runs over North Vietnam that day "due to weather" (which was very poor over Hanoi during this period) and flew down to Tchepone to help Smith out. On one occasion, Dan Gibson, the OV-10 forward air controller on duty that day, noticed six NVA marching up the road toward Smith. Gibson rolled in and shot a rocket and his M-60 machine gun at the troops, who ran into a clump of trees. Just then, two VMA (AW)-224 A-6s showed up with "wall-to-wall Mk-82s on their bellies." The A-6s wasted no time rolling in and dropping forty-eight 500-pound bombs on that tree clump. "I told them that I couldn't count the teeth and eyeballs but I gave 'em 6 KBA."[12] Jim Harding later admitted to Smith, "[We] would not have been able to get [you] out without the firepower from the *Coral Sea*."[13]

Smith's pickup commenced at 1700 on 14 April. During the preceding four hours, fifteen jets (including A-6s from *Coral Sea*), seven Sandies, and four OV-10s bombed the Vietnamese until Harding thought it was safe to call in one of two HH-53s standing by five minutes away. At 1701, Harding told Smith to get ready and then told Sandy 2 to go get Jolly 32 (an HH-53), piloted by Captain Ben Orrell, USAF, and First Lieutenant Jim Casey, USAF. Smith stood up for the first time in ten hours and prepared to fire a flare. Meanwhile, four Sandies dropped white phosphorus cluster bomb units (CBUs) across the east end of the rescue area to create a smoke screen for the rescue, and the jets dropped more CBUs along the helicopter's ingress and egress routes. Finally, Sandy 2 fired smoke rockets toward Smith's position to mark it for the Jolly 32.

Despite these elaborate preparations, however, the helicopter immediately began taking fire. Jolly 32's PJs did their best to suppress it, but the 170-knot chopper was simply too slow to avoid being hit. The rear ramp was down, and Sergeant Bill Brinson, USAF, fired a minigun there; Airman First Class Bill Liles, USAF, and Airman First Class Kenneth Cakebread, USAF, were the door gunners. Through the chaos of radio chatter, Smith heard Sergeant Brinson call out, "I'm hit, but I'm okay."

"Can you still shoot?" Captain Orrell asked.

"I'm alright, they just got me in the knee," Brinson replied, "but there's some holes in the helo."[14]

Jolly 32 took eleven hits, including one through the front windshield, but kept going—a testament to the bravery of its crew and the sturdiness of the Sikorsky product. As the helicopter flared over Smith's position, Harding called Orrell, "Pull up, Jolly, pull up, you're right over the survivor."

"I don't see him," Orrell responded. Sandy 1 then ordered Smith to pop a smoke flare. Smith did so, but the wash from the chopper blew the smoke away, making it impossible for Orrell to find him.

"I don't see him," Orrell radioed. "Tell him to pop his night end." Smith popped a flare, which showered him with sparks, but Orrell still could not see him. Smith could hear the tension in Orrell's voice build the longer the helo remained in a vulnerable hover, and he contemplated running toward the noise—something his survival instructors told him never to do. "Screw this," Smith said, and ran up the ridge toward the noise. "Jolly 32 was cutting the tops off of trees, and branches were flying in every direction." The helo was fifty to sixty yards from Smith and moving away. Smith ran toward the Jolly, screaming on the radio, "Right here, right here, behind you, behind you!" In all the noise, Smith thought that no one could hear him, but then suddenly Liles, the door gunner, looked right at him and then Orrell broke in: "I got him! I got him! Lower the hoist!"

Although Smith knew that he might receive a bad shock from static electricity if he touched the hoist's bullet-shaped jungle penetrator before it hit the ground, he grabbed it anyway, snapped his climber's carabiner onto the cable, and said, "I'm ready." Liles, amid the tumult of the battle, did not hear the call and let the penetrator hit the ground. "Shit," Smith blurted out. He then reached down and started opening it up but "tripped and fell over the goddamn thing. And then all of a sudden, I felt the pull on my harness and up I went."[15]

Liles grabbed Smith and rolled him into the helo. "Get the hell out of the way," the door gunner said unceremoniously and then swung his minigun back around and opened fire. Almost simultaneously, Liles, as he was laying down suppressive fire, told Orrell, "He's in the door, let's get the hell out of here." Harding then ordered four Sandies to "blow the top of the mountain off" and told Orrell to stay low and egress along the same route he came in from. Smith, relieved that his part of the mission had ended, just sat back in the cavernous interior watching the gunners unload thousands of bullets in every direction as smoke and light streamed through the bullet holes in the chopper's fuselage.

Ninety minutes later, Jolly 32 touched down at Nakhon Phanom in front of a crowd of cheering Air Force men and women from the Aerospace Rescue Service and the Air Force's large intelligence unit at the base, whose joint pride "was exceeded only by the gratitude of one very humble Marine aviator." A man about Smith's age who looked like Charlton Heston walked up to him. "Hi," the man said. "I'm Sandy 01." It was Jim Harding. The two men embraced.

Smith spent a few days at Nakhon Phanom before returning to an emotional reunion with his shipmates on board *Coral Sea*: "All the way back to the ship, I thought about Scott and what might have happened to him. Was he dead, captured, or on his way to the Hanoi Hilton? Did he watch my rescue from nearby? Will I ever see him again? Did whoever talked to me that first night have Scott's radio? If I had yelled when I heard voices right after the shoot-down, might we have gotten together and both been rescued?"[16]

To this day, no one knows what happened to First Lieutenant Scott Ketchie, USMC. According to the Defense Department's POW/MIA Office, his status is presumed dead. Jim Harding received the Air Force Cross for his heroism during the Bengal 505 rescue, and Smith went back to fly and fight with his unit, VMA (AW)-224.

Critics of SAR operations might argue that the massive air campaign launched by the armed forces to save one man was a waste of valuable air resources, and that these sorties might have served the American cause better if they had been devoted to other strategic targets. Given the poor weather over Hanoi, however, Tchepone was as strategic a target area as any other during this period. Arguably, many of the Bengal 505 sorties destroyed men and supplies destined for use in offensive operations in South Vietnam. More important, one cannot underestimate the value of Major Smith or any other American pilot flying in Southeast Asia in 1972.

By this time, many in the American military perceived the Vietnam War as a "loser." As Darrel D. Whitcomb, a forward air controller who served three tours in Vietnam put it:

> By 1972, we were so frustrated with the war. We could clearly see that our national strategy was to come home, so we expressed that tactically, and when a guy went down, we would do everything we could to get him out, because we honestly thought that there was nothing over there worth an American life. When a guy got shot down, all of a

sudden you had a clear objective there, your buddy's on the ground, and getting him out became the objective and it was clear, it was quantifiable, it was measurable, it made you feel good. We had the wherewithal to do it, we had the tonnage, we had the technology, and the motivation to do it, so SARs, when they happened, would take on a life of their own. Some of them were huge, just huge battles.[17]

Moreover, as America withdrew from the war, a small group of volunteer airmen increasingly bore the brunt of the combat. Hence, when men went down, commanders at the wing level and even higher felt obligated to make an extra effort to save them from capture.

During the latter stages of the war, when the entire cause came into doubt and airmen had to wade through angry protesters just to perform their duties, this bond often eclipsed even the war cause itself. General John Vogt, the Seventh Air Force commander during much of this period and the man who ultimately approved many of the rescues, summed up the situation this way: "The one thing that keeps our boys motivated is the certain belief that if they go down, we will do absolutely everything we can to get them out. If that is ever in doubt, morale would tumble."[18] To see the eyes of the men in Carrier Air Wing 15 when Smith landed on *Coral Sea* confirmed Vogt's feelings. Smith's rescue helped sustain the wing at a difficult moment in its history and motivate these men for more significant missions to come.

14

Bombing and Then Mining Haiphong

THE SUCCESSFUL CONCLUSION of the Bengal 505 rescue, combined with a more stabilized ground war in the South, effectively freed *Coral Sea*'s air wing for offensive operations against North Vietnam. President Nixon, deeply concerned over the Easter Offensive, wanted desperately to hit targets in the North, but poor weather had been foiling his plans for weeks. "They have never been bombed like they're going to be bombed this time," Nixon declared to one of his aides, "but you have to have the weather." The weather finally broke on 10 April, and B-52s plastered an oil tank farm and rail yard near Vinh. Three days later, the Buffs cratered Bai Thuong airfield near Thanh Hoa, and on 16 April, a forty-plane raid against the tank farm at Haiphong was planned, to be preceded by a Navy attack against SAM sites in the area.

During Sheets's tour as squadron commander of VF-161, he participated in one of the last missions into Haiphong before the bombing halt, and he would fly the first Navy mission back into that area nearly four years later as the commander of Air Wing 16. The mission called for Sheets's A-6s to "suppress" the SAM sites near Haiphong with cluster bombs. "What wasn't stated but what I recognized as a reality," Sheets believed, "is that they wanted us to soak up an awful lot of those SAMs that had been stockpiled so they wouldn't be available to shoot at the B-52s." Marine A-6s, in short, would be SAM bait.

For this mission, Sheets ordered his A-6s to fly the classic Intruder mission: each plane would fly alone, at night, and at low altitude against a single SAM site and then return to the carrier. Against an A-6 flying below 500 feet (and Sheets's flight often flew below 250), the SA-2's effectiveness declines markedly, but SAM operators still showed little reluctance to expend them against the A-6s. "We were not at all disappointed by the number of SAMs that they had available and their willingness to fire them," claimed Sheets. "We had twenty-nine SAMs fired at us."[1]

Bill Angus, one of the A-6 pilots, remembers having "cotton mouth" when he launched: "Our strike was about thirty miles outside of Haiphong, and there were already five to six SAMS in the air, and we were not even in range. The whole thing was surreal. The threat indicator looked like a sparkler. It was emitting strobes in every conceivable direction in the world, and we turned the damn thing off and proceeded. It was distracting. But everybody got home."[2]

Even veterans like Sheets and Carr experienced some fear during the mission. "When we started dropping the CBUs, it seemed like they would never, ever stop dropping off the plane. You can't imagine how long 300 milliseconds can become, between those things coming off the plane, but it seemed like an eternity because when we finally got back out over the water, we both took off our masks and shut off the oxygen, and Charlie said, 'Oh, good, I can smoke again. I thought there for a while I'd never get a chance.'" For Sheets, intense combat experiences tended to heighten, rather than diminish, his abilities to process information—one of the factors that made him such a skilled warrior. As he explained, "I had a phenomenon in combat where all of my senses and everything started going at a rapid rate so that I had the impression that the entire world had just gone into slow motion."[3]

After all this effort, the B-52 mission was nearly canceled. The American ground forces' commander in Saigon, General Creighton Abrams, objected to the diversion of B-52 assets from targets in the South, and Melvin Laird, the secretary of defense, nearly called off the raid. When Admiral Thomas Moorer, the chairman of the Joint Chiefs of Staff, pointed out to Nixon that seventeen B-52s were already in the air and would have to ditch their bombs (over 1,700) in the Gulf of Tonkin if the mission were scrubbed, the president chose to press on. The B-52s went on to destroy more than thirty oil tanks in Haiphong with no losses.[4]

THE MINING OF HAIPHONG HARBOR: 9 MAY

The idea of mining Haiphong harbor was not a new Navy concept in 1972. Admiral U. S. Grant Sharp, CINCPAC from 30 June 1964 to 31 July 1968, had advocated mining almost from the onset of the war. After his retirement in 1968, he made his views on the subject public in his memoirs: "Of all the things we should have done but did not do, the most important was to neutralize Haiphong." Sharp claims that various military leaders, including himself, recommended that the port be mined very early in the war, but the Johnson administration always vetoed the idea, claiming that a closure would have little impact on North Vietnam's ability to wage war in the South.[5] Civilian policy makers also feared that mining might trigger a broader war with either China or the Soviet Union.

In 1972, civilian officials dramatically altered their course on this issue. The essential cause of this shift was Richard Nixon. Unlike Johnson, Nixon was fully willing to take bold risks to end the war in Southeast Asia—especially after North Vietnam's aggressive invasion of the South. The idea of a mining operation against Haiphong also had a strong, well-placed advocate in the military hierarchy: JCS chairman Admiral Thomas Moorer.

A 1933 graduate of the Naval Academy and a highly decorated patrol plane pilot, Admiral Moorer developed an interest in mining during World War II, when he worked for a year as a mining observer for the British Admiralty. Immediately after hostilities ended, the Navy assigned him to prepare a report on mining operations against Japan for the Strategic Bombing Survey. In this capacity, he gained firsthand knowledge of the effectiveness of Navy mining through extensive interviews with Japanese military and civilian officials. He learned, for instance, that the Navy actually mined Haiphong during 1943–44, and that the thirty-two mines laid by the submarine *Grenadier,* together with the forty laid by U.S. Army Air Forces (USAAF) B-24s, forced the Japanese to abandon the port for anything larger than a junk for the remainder of World War II. As chief of naval operations from 1967 to 1970 and chairman of the JCS from 1970 to 1974, Moorer had an intimate understanding of this earlier operation that prompted him to petition the Johnson and Nixon administrations for a similar campaign. Moorer believed that if the Navy mined Haiphong, the North Vietnamese would be forced to rely on their more vulnerable rail system to transport supplies from China. None of Moorer's superiors considered the option seriously until 4 April 1972.

On that day, a Marine sentry handed Admiral Moorer a note during Secretary of the Navy John Chafee's retirement ceremony at the Washington Navy Yard. "I unobtrusively left the ceremony," Moorer recalled.

"I didn't jump up and break into a dead run because people would have started asking a lot of questions. So I just slipped away." The reason for Moorer's departure: the president wanted to see him.

In his office in the Old Executive Office Building, Nixon immediately peppered Moorer with a series of questions about mining. Moorer informed Nixon that the Navy had a well-developed plan and could implement it rapidly and secretly. Nixon wanted to inform the American public about the operation on live television the moment the last mine was dropped in Haiphong harbor.

That evening, one of Moorer's aides requested from the Mine Warfare Office background information on mining, including that part of the 1945 Strategic Bombing Survey that he had authored many years ago earlier. During the next couple of weeks, Moorer argued the case for mining to the Washington Special Action Group, an interdepartmental crisis management group, which met almost daily after the Easter Offensive—a tough sell, according to Moorer, because only he and the president were in favor of the operation.

On 23 April, Moorer requested a detailed plan from the Mine Warfare Office for a Haiphong mining operation. This small staff immediately set to work developing a plan from the Navy's mine warfare command's mining folder on North Vietnam. The folder contained contingency plans for mining operations in Southeast Asia, including a plan for a Haiphong harbor field consisting of a string of ten Mk-52-2 magnetic mines, six Mk-52-3 pressure magnetic mines, and twenty Mk-56 acoustic mines along that harbor's main channel. All thirty-six mines were approximately the same size—a nominal 2,000 pounds each. Each of the nine aircraft involved in the strike (three A-6s and six A-7s) carried four mines.

From an operational perspective, Haiphong presented numerous challenges to the Mine Warfare Office and ultimately to Sheets and the men of 224. The team chose to rely primarily on the magnetic Mk-52-2 mine rather than pressure mines because magnetic mines tended to be more effective against large oceangoing, steel-hulled merchant ships. Magnetic mines were also easier to clear should U.S. forces ever have to sweep the mines as part of an eventual peace settlement. As Admiral Moorer explained in his reminiscences, "We deliberately laid it down so we could get it up. I could have put a minefield in there they'd never get up and it would still be there."[6]

In addition to a self-sterilization option, Mk-52-2s allowed for a longer arming delay than the other mines—an important diplomatic factor that gave the twenty-seven neutral vessels in Haiphong a grace period to leave the harbor after the mines were sown. In the end, however, only one British and four Soviet vessels actually took advantage of the delay and escaped from the harbor.[7]

Despite the political advantages of the Mk-52-2, the system was not without challenges. Although all the flight crews were highly experienced, none had ever done any actual mining. The political importance of this mission, and the high profile that the Navy expected it to achieve, dictated that Sheets eliminate as many areas for error as he possibly could. The official estimate was that the Navy would sustain a minimum of 30 percent losses, so he did not want anyone to fail to properly arm the mines. He therefore ordered the mine loaders to "positive arm" the mines. Once Sheets launched, there was no way that those mines could come off the aircraft without becoming active.

At the briefing before the mission, Sheets noticed a strange reaction from Admiral Howard E. Greer, the commander of Carrier Division 3, when he mentioned that the mines were positive armed. "He didn't say anything, but it was just a fleeting look of 'Oh, God' that came over his face and then left." Sheets did not realize at the time that although he had the go-ahead for a launch, the White House had not given the wing final approval to put the mines in Haiphong harbor. Greer knew this, but as an experienced pilot he understood why Sheets had positive armed the mines. The load was much too heavy to bring back to the carrier if final approval failed to materialize, and the flight would be so far north and so light on fuel loads that diverting to a friendly ordnance disposal area would be out of the question. Greer never said a word and let the mission proceed as planned—a testament to his faith in Sheets.

Another limitation of the Mk-52-2 was its size and weight. Four 80-by-19-inch, parachute-retarded mines would add 8,000 pounds of weight to the A-6 and slow its speed to 375 knots. It also did not allow the aircraft to carry an auxiliary fuel tank. This meant not only that the A-6s would be much more vulnerable to MiGs, SAMs, and AAA, but that *Coral Sea* would have to position itself within 100 miles of the coast of North Vietnam to ensure that the aircraft would have enough fuel for a round-trip. To mitigate the air and surface threats imposed by the operation, the eventual Pocket Money plan would call for three antiaircraft ships—*Chicago* (CG-11), *Long Beach* (CGN-9), and *Sterett* (DLG-31)—to station themselves between the port of Haiphong and the *Coral*

Sea and to protect the mining force with their Talos and Terrier missiles. A surface strike group consisting of the *Berkeley* (DDG-15), *Myles C. Fox* (DD-829), *Richard S. Edwards* (DD-950), and *Buchanan* (DDG-14) would then shell coastal antiaircraft sites on the Do Son Peninsula about six miles west of the Haiphong channel with their five-inch guns. Finally, the carrier *Kitty Hawk*'s planes would pound diversionary targets at Thanh Hoa and Phu Qui at the same time as the mining operation.[8]

Even with all these precautions, Sheets and his Bengals still sweated every detail of the tough mission. Detachable nose and tail cones for the mines were supposed to be available to cut down the drag of the large Mk-52-2s, but *Coral Sea* had only enough cones to equip two out of the four mines carried by each of the three A-6s in the mining strike. In a meeting the night before the mission, Sheets explained the situation to the admirals in charge of Task Force 77, the carrier task force on Yankee Station, and Task Force 75, the corresponding cruiser and de-stroyer task force. At that meeting, the admirals decided to bring the guided missile cruiser *Chicago* to within thirty miles of Haiphong, close enough to protect the strike force with its Talos antiaircraft missiles. CTF-75 requested that Sheets keep his aircraft below 1,000 feet so that anything above that altitude could be declared hostile. "The admirals looked at me and said, 'Is that okay with you, CAG?' and I said, 'No, I want anything above 500 feet to be declared as hostile. We'll be well below that.'"[9]

Sheets's strike force of three A-6As and six A-7Es launched from *Coral Sea* at 0810 local time. The A-6s would lay their Mk-2-2s in the inner channel of Haiphong, and the A-7s would lay smaller Mk-36 Destructor mines in the outer channel. Since the Vietnamese might employ smaller waterborne logistics craft to ferry supplies from larger ships anchored beyond the Mk-52-2 minefield to the port, the Destructor field was explicitly established to deny smaller ships such as sampans and junks access to the port of Haiphong.

The *Coral Sea* Alpha strike circled the ship until 0840 and then headed toward Haiphong. Like a tightly choreographed ballet, the diversionary Alpha strike from *Kitty Hawk* hit Thanh Hoa and Phu Qui at 0845, and the destroyer group comprising *Myles C. Fox, Richard S. Edwards,* and *Buchanan* began firing rounds of five-inch shells on antiaircraft positions on the Do Son Peninsula about six miles west of the Haiphong channel.

All seemed to be going splendidly until 0849, when a radar operator on board *Chicago* picked up two MiGs departing from Phuc Yen airfield and heading directly toward Sheets and Carr in Vulture lead.
Within seconds, *Chicago* launched two Talos missiles at the MiGs, now
forty-eight miles away. The 7,000-pound, thirty-foot-long missile, the
largest SAM in the Navy's inventory, downed one of the MiGs. The
other promptly turned tail and retreated.[10]

Sheets and Carr approached the channel from the southeast, flying
a fairly straight course at 250 feet above the water. The inner channel
was only 1,000 feet wide, so navigation remained critical throughout.
Carr, as lead navigator, relied on an old French chart of the harbor to
guide the strike and had no problem with its accuracy. "It was absolutely marvelous," he exclaimed. "Even the fish weirs were in the
right places."[11] The A-6s flew down the channel and released the mines
at the predetermined point. Carr timed the release with his wristwatch
rather than trusting the intervalometer. The first mine fell free of Vulture 1 at 0859. "There was one ship that was exiting the harbor," recalled
Sheets, "that was in our mine pattern, so we had to delay just slightly
the release of one mine to keep from putting it on top of this ship, although it was a temptation not to skip it."

By 0901, the A-6s had placed twelve mines in the inner channel and
the A-7s, twenty-four in the outer channel. Of these thirty-six mines,
three failed to arm due to retardation gear failures. When one A-7 failed
to drop on the initial pass, the pilot came around and dropped his mines
on a reverse pass. As Sheets later explained, "We looked at this as a one-
shot deal. If we didn't get it right this time, they would put everything
they had in our way on the next go-around."[12]

As soon as all the mines were laid, Sheets radioed *Coral Sea* to inform Admiral Greer of the news. *Coral Sea* then sent off a flash cable to
the White House, announcing that the mines were in the water. Nixon,
who had already begun his speech, had been speaking slowly to allow
the A-6s to retire from the target area safely. With a stern face, he discussed three courses of action with the American public: immediate
withdrawal of all U.S. forces from Vietnam, continued negotiation, or
direct and decisive military action. As soon as he received the signal
that the mines were in the water, he announced that he had reluctantly
chosen the mining option. Despite the apparent strength of the antiwar
movement, a Gallup poll reported that 74 percent of Americans interviewed supported President Nixon's hard line against North Vietnam.[13]

A-6 Intruder aircraft of Marine Squadron 224 fly over the aircraft carrier *Coral Sea*. One of the most advanced aircraft of the war, the A-6 could fly at night or in bad weather with its computer-assisted navigation system and carried up to 18,000 pounds of bombs. (Courtesy of U.S. Navy)

During the remaining eight months of mining operations against North Vietnam, Navy and Marine aircraft laid 5,200 mines under Pocket Money authority and another 6,500 under Linebacker authority. Pocket Money operations were mainly designed to stop large merchant vessels from entering or leaving major ports, whereas Linebacker operations targeted smaller vessels attempting to circumvent the Pocket Money blockade via estuaries, canals, and waterways. All told, 108 magnetic mines were seeded and reseeded in Haiphong channel, as well as 11,603 acoustic mines throughout the coastal and inland waters of North Vietnam. Ten aircraft carriers contributed to the operation, and only one plane, a Navy A-7E, was lost.

In 1972 dollars, mining cost the U.S. Treasury $9,506,314 plus another $3 million for the loss of the A-7E, for a total of $12.5 million (about $48 million in today's dollars). What kind of return did America get for its investment? Mining closed the port of Haiphong for 300 days, reduced total imports by 30 percent, inactivated twenty-seven foreign supply ships for 8,000 ship-days, reduced coastal shipping from 800 tons a day to 150, and halted all North Vietnamese exports (eliminating an important source of foreign exchange). The magnitude of road and rail traffic required to overcome the blockade proved nearly insurmountable and almost certainly influenced the North Vietnamese decision in January 1973 to accept a peace settlement.[14] For example, a tug pulling four medium-sized barges can move 1,000 tons of freight. To move the same amount by land would require 250 trucks or forty railway cars. "When we mined Haiphong," explained Admiral Moorer, "the traffic on the railroads just mushroomed and consequently we got all kinds of wonderful targets in the railroads."[15] Arguably, the closure of Haiphong harbor contributed to North Vietnam's difficulty in resupplying its stockpile of SAMs during the 1972 Christmas Bombing campaign. Whereas on day 1 of that campaign the NVA had been able to fire 200 SAMs at the U.S. B-52 force, by day 11 it could get only 23 missiles in the air. The Christmas Bombing alone, in short, did not convince the North Vietnamese to return to the negotiating table in January 1973; rather, it was the synergistic combination of all factors, including mining, coastal bombardment, and blockade, that ultimately led to a peace agreement and the end of the war in 1973.[16]

For the men of VMA (AW)-224, their sixth line period ended on 30 June 1972. For all the high spirits and good times experienced by the squadron, it still had to confront its share of shoot-downs and even deaths. In addition to Scott Ketchie, the squadron lost three other aviators during the cruise, and a fourth ended up in the Hanoi Hilton.

For the rest, the long-awaited reunion with their families occurred at Cherry Point, North Carolina. Many junior officers in the unit would ultimately leave the Corps for civilian life; others, like Smith, Ferrecane, and Carr, would continue flying with the Marines for many years to come. All members of the unit would remember their time in 224 as a pivotal period of professional growth and development. Through their perseverance and hard work, these men demonstrated that a Marine aviation unit can adapt to carrier operations and perform as well as any Navy unit if given the time, training, and, most important, proper leadership.

Initially, veteran warriors such as Smith, Schuyler, and Carr were the ones who motivated the unit to perform. They did so partly with humor and good cheer, but also by flying the toughest missions. More junior officers may have felt extreme terror when they first began strapping on the A-6 to fly over North Vietnam, but the fear of disappointing the veterans proved more daunting than actual combat. Eventually, these junior officers became more accustomed to being shot at, and their proficiency improved. When the Vietnamese shot down Smith, one might have expected morale in the unit to plummet; instead, it actually improved. Suddenly, the war became very personal, and old fears were replaced with an extreme desire to save a friend. The Smith rescue, more than anything else, provided visible proof of the bond that united the squadron and enabled its members to fight an unpopular war as volunteers.

Smith's shoot-down, while motivating the unit, still left a leadership void in the squadron at a time when President Nixon began to step up the bombing of North Vietnam. Fortunately, the new CAG, Roger Sheets, stepped in to fill the void. Sheets possessed unprecedented knowledge of the Navy and its war in Southeast Asia, even for senior commanders. In one capacity or another, Sheets participated in nearly every major naval air operation of the war, from the Gulf of Tonkin through Linebacker. Sheets understood the tactics and psychology of his enemy better than most and exploited it accordingly—whether on a simple interdiction mission or a major mining operation. From years of experience, he knew, for example, that MiGs rarely flew higher than 1,000 feet; thanks to his knowledge, the Talos crew on the *Chicago* bagged a MiG on 9 May. But Sheets was not simply a thinker and a planner. He sought to engage the enemy personally and share in the most dangerous missions with his airmen. This trait, more than any other, endeared him forever to the flying men of 224. Rather than flying F-4s with one of *Coral Sea*'s fighter squadrons and chasing MiGs, Sheets chose to devote most of his sorties to the more difficult, dangerous, and ultimately less rewarding A-6 mission. Perhaps the enlisted seaman in Sheets felt uncomfortable with assigning a job to others that he would not do himself. Whatever the case, Sheets never expressed regret over flying attack missions but took pride in every bomb dropped.

As Sheets would quickly admit, quality leadership, with only minor exceptions, extended right up to the White House. The Air Force might never have rescued Smith had it not been for Captain William Harris's willingness to put his career on the line and divert *Coral Sea* air assets to the effort. Harris also proved integral in facilitating VMA (AW)-224's transition to shipboard life. As a fighter pilot and former

CAG, Harris understood when to be tough and when to adopt a more measured approach toward discipline. For example, he knew that Carr, Schuyler, and others often misbehaved on liberty, but he also knew how much 224 depended on these skilled aviators in combat. He was willing to overlook all but the most egregious conduct at Cubi Point. By 1972, the Navy needed compassionate leaders like Harris to manage its dedicated volunteers.

But support for 224 did not end with Harris. Admiral Greer risked his career when he allowed Sheets to fly the mining mission with positive-armed Mk-52s. Greer also defended Sheets and Carr when reports surfaced that some of their bombs may have fallen on Chinese soil during a night attack on a truck convoy north of Haiphong. "Admiral Greer had some questions to ask about it," claimed Sheets. "And since we couldn't positively say that we were in China and we couldn't positively say we weren't, either, we chose not to put ourselves on report for the thing." Greer, who himself had served as a pilot on board *Coral Sea* during the 1950s, understood the fog of war and was willing to give Sheets and Carr the benefit of the doubt. Greer told Sheets, "Well, don't worry about it. Remember when you came aboard, I said your job is to run the air wing, and mine is to keep people off your backs on up the line. This is one of those times; I'll keep them off."[17] As it turned out, Admiral James L. Holloway III, the Seventh Fleet commander, took the same position. After receiving numerous inquiries from Washington about the episode, Holloway finally said, "Wait a minute. This is probably one of the best crews we've got out here. If you've got any more questions, just ask me."[18]

Clearly fed up by the politics of the war, Holloway and many others in higher authority finally believed in 1972 that they had the moral authority to stand up to civilian policy makers on issues important to the Navy. When I asked Sheets to explain this change of attitude in 1972, he attributed most of it to the influence of the commander in chief. Nixon felt a special affinity toward those in uniform because they represented the embodiment of his new conservative culture—one devoid of the influence of Ivy League colleges, the liberal eastern media, and huge endowment funds. Having served in the Navy as a logistics officer during World War II and later as a contracting officer with the Bureau of Aeronautics, Nixon understood the Navy and felt extremely comfortable with its officers. Admiral Moorer claims that Nixon felt more at home with his uniformed officers than with his civilian policy makers. "On several occasions, major operations like the Christmas Bombing in 1972; the mining of Haiphong; the invasion of Cambodia, etc., Nixon would tell me to write the order I wanted Laird to send me, and then give it back to him, and he would send it over to Laird and say, 'Send this to the Chairman of the Joint Chiefs of Staff.' That's the way I'd get the order. He'd say, 'You can put anything in there you want to. What do you want Laird to tell you?' I would write the order, and he would direct Laird to pass it to me."[19]

For many members of the government, the war in Vietnam, by 1972, appeared as a lost cause that should be ended on virtually any terms. Nixon disagreed. Yes, he wanted America out of the conflict, but he did not want to abandon the POWs or South Vietnam in the process. By escalating the conflict late in the war with mining and Linebacker attacks against the wishes of his civilian advisers, Nixon staved off South Vietnam's defeat for nearly three years and, most important, secured the release of the POWs. For men in uniform, Richard Nixon's stubborn refusal to abandon their comrades in Hanoi made him a hero in their eyes.

Nixon's moral courage and strength, though, paled by comparison to the physical courage of the men of VMA (AW)-224. These men had the tough job of implementing Nixon's "*strong, threatening,* and *effective*" measures against North Vietnam, and they paid the ultimate price for their actions. In addition to the mining and the bombing of industrial targets, this small group of men in Vulture flight took out many of the most threatening SAM sites in the Hanoi-Haiphong region. Not every member of 224 flew with Vulture flight. Many flew tanker and daytime interdiction missions in Laos while the Vultures flew the tougher night missions against targets in North Vietnam.

Interestingly enough, the Vultures of VMA (AW)-224 were not necessarily the men one would expect to be in this role. While some did become careerists, most did not see themselves as such in 1972. Not one of them had graduated from a service academy, and few possessed regular commissions. Most flew the A-6 for the adventure and comradeship and did not concern themselves too much with career-related issues. Most had almost no interest in serving in a peacetime navy. They also did not worry about the politics of the war. If anyone questioned them about their ideology, they often pointed to the POWs and argued that they were fighting to get these men out. The motivation of these men, in short, often related more to the challenge of the mission than any larger war goal. Sheets and Carr thrived on tangling with MiGs or hitting a truck with one bomb. Others felt accomplished just for keeping up with these aviators and taking similar risks. "For somebody not intending to make the Marine Corps a career, the preparation and ultimately our deployment was, nevertheless, true excitement," explained Angus. "And being a charter member of 224's Vulture Flight was the icing on the cake."[20]

PART V

AIR-TO-AIR COMBAT, 1972

The Making of a MiG Killer

THE MINING OF HAIPHONG HARBOR ushered in a new chapter in the air war over North Vietnam. For the first time since the bombing halt of 1968, U.S. air power threatened high-value targets in the heart of North Vietnam, compelling the country to fight back hard with every weapon in its inventory, including its ever-elusive MiGs. This led to some of the fiercest air-to-air fights in the history of modern aviation. More important, it provided a test of naval air power in the broadest sense. In 1972, the battle for the skies of North Vietnam would be determined not simply by technology alone but also by superior Navy tactics, command and control, and, of course, pilots.

In the end, naval aviators performed better than anyone could have imagined, shooting down twenty-four enemy MiGs during the final months of the war and losing just four of their own aircraft in the process. The Air Force, by comparison, downed forty-eight MiGs but lost twenty-four fighters, earning a humble 2:1 kill ratio compared with the Navy's record-breaking 6:1 score. How could two services, flying nearly identical equipment, perform so differently?

Shortly after the war, the Air Force's Fighter Weapons Center at Nellis Air Force Base, Nevada, studied this issue and many others related to air-to-air combat in 1972 by reconstructing 625 air-to-air encounters between U.S. and Vietnamese People's Air Force aircraft. It published its findings in what became known as Project Red Baron III, a report that identifies several factors that contributed to the Navy's better exchange ratio. Navy planes, fighting in a confined area near the coast, were much less vulnerable to surprise attacks than were their Air Force counterparts, which were compelled to enter and exit North Vietnam via Laos. MiG interceptors, the report reasoned, simply had much more time to ambush a large strike coming from distant Laos than from

Yankee Station, just off their coastline. Farther inland, the MiGs operating the inland Air Force zones proved less visible to ship-based radar than the MiGs that operated closer to the coast in the Navy zone. Red Baron III also pointed out that the North Vietnamese generally met Air Force raids with the sophisticated MiG-21, whereas Navy strikes generally battled the slower MiG-17. However, the most compelling reason for the disparity lay in the emphasis the Navy placed on air combat maneuvering at its NAS Miramar fighter training center, "Fightertown USA." This air-to-air curriculum, which would ultimately become formalized as the Top Gun school in 1972, gave the Navy pilots more hands-on experience in dogfighting than the average Air Force pilot received. The USAF did not institute a similar curriculum until after the war in 1973.[1]

This part will examine the impact of the Top Gun curriculum on naval air war by closely examining the kills made by the program's graduates during May 1972—the most intense month of air-to-air combat of the war. It will also dissect the career of Top Gun's first postwar commanding officer, Ronald "Mugs" McKeown, to provide a detailed portrait of the life and times of a 1972 vintage Navy fighter pilot. McKeown completed four line tours in Vietnam, flying missions during every year in the war except 1969 and 1970. During 1969, he served as the chief test pilot for Project Have Drill, a secret Navy test involving a captured MiG-17. In 1972, he shot down two MiG-17s over North Vietnam with his back-seater, Jack Ensch, in one of the longest and wildest dogfights of the war. After this fight, McKeown and Ensch received Navy Crosses, America's second-highest award for valor.

McKeown's career and his experience as a naval aviator in the fleet in 1972 reveal some intriguing lessons about air-to-air combat in Southeast Asia. True to the observations of several Air Force veterans of the conflict, the North Vietnamese MiGs rarely fought the Navy in a symmetrical fashion. Whereas the Navy relied primarily on supersonic, missile-equipped F-4s as its main fighter weapon, the Vietnamese fought back mainly with subsonic MiG-17s armed with guns and engaged Navy planes only in situations where their technology could prevail: tight-turning, slow-moving dogfights. This explains why Top Gun's emphasis on dogfighting and close-in fighting with heat-seeking missiles often yielded excellent results late in the war.

Good schooling and good tactics alone, however, do not win wars; people win wars. To attribute the success of the Navy fighter community in 1972 solely to Top Gun overlooks a rather stark truth: the Navy possessed a larger number of experienced fighter pilots in 1972 than the Air Force. The average Air Force pilot during the Vietnam War flew only one year, or 100 missions, over North Vietnam, whichever came first. Navy pilots, by comparison, often flew several hundred missions against North Vietnam over the course of three or more years. McKeown had flown over 400 combat missions by 1972 and had 2,080 hours in tactical fighters and 3,600 hours in jets by 23 May. No Air Force pilot flying in 1972 had a comparable amount of experience. Even the Air Force's first ace, Steve Ritchie, could only boast of having 1,660 fighter hours and 287 combat missions prior to 20 May 1972.

Experience, though, did not come without a price. Few realize that McKeown and several others among the Navy's best pilots nearly burned out during the war. McKeown's inner strength came from the mental and physical conditioning he had received at the United States Naval Academy. For others, pride, patriotism, and comradeship kept them going—especially the knowledge that their sacrifices might help America secure the release of their friends and comrades, the POWs in the Hanoi Hilton.

For the Navy as a whole, the success of its Vietnam-era fighter community led to an arrogance that stunted the development of the NFO community, made the service reluctant to experiment with new fighter technologies—especially the new radar-guided missiles—during the war, and helped create an institutional culture that contributed to the damaging and embarrassing Tailhook episode of 1991. McKeown does not rank nearly as high as some of his peers in terms of arrogance, but his attitude (considered healthy by most in the fighter community) is illustrative of the granite-hard warrior culture, which multiple Vietnam War tours could instill, and the various ramifications of this culture to the service at large. This culture is often essential in war but difficult for military bureaucracies to handle in peacetime.

15

Ronald "Mugs" McKeown

GO NAVY!

The year 1960 would enter the record books as one of the Naval Academy's most magnificent football seasons ever. That year, Navy competed in the Orange Bowl, concluded the regular season with a ten and one record, and produced a Heisman Trophy winner, running back Joe Bellino. One of the team's biggest blowouts was its victory over Air Force in the first game ever played between these two future rivals. The game not only demonstrated the skill of the Navy's team that year but also highlighted the prowess and spirit of its "other running back," Ronald Eugene McKeown.[1]

Air Force took an early lead in the game with a field goal, but then Joe Bellino scored on Navy's first play from the scrimmage, and Navy never looked back. Bellino scored two more touchdowns in the first half, putting Navy twenty-five points ahead. By the third quarter, McKeown started getting frustrated with quarterback Hal Spooner. "Why do I never get a chance to run with the ball?" the young midshipman ruminated.[2] During a time-out, McKeown finally confronted Spooner in a huddle and demanded a pass. "If I don't carry the ball at least once in the next two plays," he told the quarterback, "I'm opening the gates up here and somebody back here's going to get hurt. I'm not going to say who," said McKeown as he suddenly turned his gaze to Bellino, "but somebody's going to get hurt back here. I'm going to open the gates. I don't ask for much."

Mugs McKeown got the ball on the next play and made a good run. In the end, Navy trounced Air Force 35 to 3, Spooner was voted the most valuable player of the game, and the Naval Academy yearbook later praised McKeown for running "through big holes provided by the boys up front." It included a large picture of him with the caption "Navy's Speed and Versatility Conquers Air Force."[3]

The cockiness exhibited by McKeown that day would ultimately serve him well in the rough-and-tumble world of naval fighter aviation in the 1960s. At the time, however, his only objective was to have a chance to run with the ball. Unlike Foster Schuyler Teague, Jack Finley, or many other fighter pilot contemporaries, Ron never intended to make the Navy a career until after his college football career ended. For most of his time at the Naval Academy, his primary goal was to play football and box, and then perform his service commitment and get out of the Navy. Two aspects of the experience would eventually change his mind: a growing love of the Naval Academy and a dream of flying the Navy's hottest fighter, the F8U Crusader.

McKeown was born in 1939 in Pipestone, Minnesota, a small town in the southwestern corner of the state. The family soon moved to El Paso, Texas, where Ron's father established a contract electronics school at Fort Bliss. In Texas, McKeown became a quick convert to the unofficial state religion, high school football. During his senior year at Ysleta High, he made all-state running back, and along with this honor came numerous offers to play college football on the East Coast. Impressed by its academic status, McKeown decided to attend Harvard. But then one day, completely out of the blue, Rip Miller, the Naval Academy athletic director, literally came knocking at his door. He talked to Ron about the Army-Navy game and asked the young athlete if he might be interested in playing for Navy. Intrigued by the idea, Mugs decided on the spur of the moment to accept Miller's offer. The next morning Ron received a telegram from a congressman in Philadelphia congratulating him on his appointment to the Naval Academy, and a week later, McKeown took the entrance exams and passed.

Initially, McKeown detested the academy. As he described it, "I think every day of plebe year was a dead heat for the most miserable day of my life." Ron's only saving grace was football, which spared him from some of the incessant hazing of freshmen year: plebe players dined separately from the brigade and therefore were not compelled to eat square meals. Football also got McKeown out of the academy from time to time for away games.

Life as a player, however, was not without its disappointments. "I got there and was pretty confident until I found out how many players they'd recruited. They had a guy named Joe Bellino who was a classmate of mine and he went on to win the Heisman Trophy and I became old what's-his-name, the other running back with Joe." McKeown made varsity during his youngster (sophomore) year but did not actually begin playing in earnest until his junior year, when he made honorable mention All-American as a cornerback on several polls. During his senior year, he played in nearly every game, including the Orange Bowl against Missouri.

In addition to football, McKeown also boxed in the brigade boxing tournaments. His father required Ron to take up boxing as a youth to curb his aggressive behavior, and McKeown stuck with the sport throughout his years at the academy, ultimately winning the Spike Web Award for best boxer of the brigade during his senior year. During the early 1960s, all physically qualified members of the brigade had to compete in intramural boxing. The two best boxers in each weight class ultimately squared off in the finals, a tradition best described by Robert Timberg, class of 1964, in his book *The Nightingale's Song*: "In those days the boxing finals provided a rare public glimpse of the Brigade as it really was, an assemblage of would-be warriors who viewed physical courage as a standard against which they fully expected to be measured. Plebes painted elaborate banners heralding the finalists from their companies. The atmosphere was raucous, the mood bloodthirsty. The noise level compared to that of an Army-Navy game, confined to an enclosed space."[4]

For the 1961 finals, McKeown fought a future Marine officer, Pete Optekar, class of 1963.[5] According to McKeown, "Pete had an anvil for a jaw. It was just solid muscle. I threw him the hardest punch I ever threw in my life, and he just blinked and said, 'Now, you've pissed me off,' and he knocked me across the ring one time. I remember hanging on the rope and I could see about three of him coming at me." McKeown kept fighting, eventually wearing Optekar down with his speed and precision punches.

> Boxing gave me more transferable skills than any other sport I ever played during my life. It gives you fluidity of movement, good hand-eye coordination, and great anticipation. It gives you a certain level of confidence to be able to handle things, to be able to think clearly under pressure. . . . Those are really very tangible and real transferable skills into real life and I'm convinced, yes, that it had a lot to do with my ability in an airplane.

CRUSADER: A FIRE AT ONE END
AND A FOOL AT THE OTHER

McKeown saw his first F-8 in Dallas during his initial academy physical and thought it was the most beautiful aircraft he had ever seen. If he had to serve in the Navy after the academy, flying these planes would be the way to go. His sophomore cruise on the *Newport News* solidified these feelings: "I just thought most of the surface officers were kind of slow-witted, and I wasn't much interested in a fifteen-knot world." Later on at the academy, a friendly instructor and F-8 pilot, Joe Bolger, convinced him to go into fighters, saying, "You've got the personality. You should be flying fighters. Don't let anyone talk you out of it."

McKeown began his flight training at Pensacola in the summer of 1961 and received his wings the following summer. The Navy then sent him to Glynco, Georgia, to serve as an instructor pilot at the Combat Information Center school. For a year, Mugs devoted most of his time to night and instrument flying in the FJ-4 Fury, a subsonic swept-wing fighter somewhat similar to the F-86 Sabre. From there, he transferred to VF-124 at Miramar to fly the F-8 Crusader.

The Vought F-8 Crusader was the Navy's workhorse fighter during the Vietnam War. From 1964 to 1973, ten Navy F-8 squadrons made fifty-five Southeast Asia deployments. These "Saders" shot down nineteen MiGs and achieved the highest kills-per-engagement ratio of any American aircraft in the Vietnam War.[6] This sleek fighter could achieve speeds higher than Mach 1.7 in afterburner with its Pratt and Whitney J57-P-20 engine, and during its early years, the Sader set many speed records.[7] The Crusader also possessed four Colt Mark 12 cannons. While only two of the nineteen MiGs bagged by F-8s in Southeast Asia were destroyed entirely by guns, the 20-mm cannon nevertheless gave the aircraft the ability to engage in close-in, tight-turning battles with MiGs that the F-4 simply could not handle without a gun. The F-8 also could carry up to four AIM-9 Sidewinders and had a very powerful tracking radar. In short, it represented what John Nichols, one of the Navy's first F-8 pilots, called "the tried-and-true approach to fighter aviation: a single-seat, single-engine dogfighter with gun armament augmented by heat-seeking missiles."[8]

Mugs loved the F-8 from his first flight onward: "It was a really great aircraft because you could look in the mirror and you could see both wing tips and the tail and you're sitting right out in the front end. It was like a big cigar, you know, long and sleek with a fire at one end and a fool at the other."

McKeown excelled at aerial gunnery, generally shooting between 11 and 14 percent, which is like batting .350 in the major leagues. However, air combat maneuvering was his ultimate passion. "I really enjoyed dogfighting. I thought it was like playing pass defense. You had to be looking around and talking to one another and telling each other what's going on and have good situational awareness." At Miramar, Mugs fought against some of the Navy's best pilots, including Foster Teague and Tom Tucker. Routinely, there would be black paint from his helmet on the inside of his canopy after some of the head-banging duels he fought.

McKeown spent a year in the replacement air group and then deployed with VF-154 on *Coral Sea* in December 1964. *Coral Sea* arrived on line just after the Viet Cong launched a mortar attack against the U.S. helicopter installation at Camp Holloway and the adjacent Pleiku airfield in the central highlands of South Vietnam on 7 February 1965. The attacks killed 8 Americans and wounded 109, and destroyed twenty aircraft. In retaliation for the raid, President Lyndon Johnson initiated Operation Flaming Dart I. The JCS assigned the military barracks at Vit Thu Lu to *Ranger* and the barracks at Dong Hoi to *Hancock* and *Coral Sea*. *Ranger*'s air wing encountered low cloud cover over its target, forcing it to cancel its flight, but *Hancock* and *Coral Sea* pressed on. "It was raining and pouring and we're down to about 400 feet and we finally see the targets and we've got eight 5-inch rockets, and 20-millimeter," McKeown recalled. He then remembered being met with a hail of 37-mm and small-arms fire. In all, seven American aircraft were hit, including one flown by a young A-4 pilot, Lieutenant Edward Dickson. Dickson ejected soon after his run and died after his parachute failed to deploy, becoming the second naval aviator killed in hostile action over North Vietnam. In exchange for these losses, naval air power destroyed sixteen buildings of the barracks and damaged another six. Unsatisfied with these results, the Commander in Chief, Pacific Fleet (CINCPACFLT) characterized Flaming Dart as "at best a qualified and inadequate reprisal."[9]

Mugs, a bit shaken from the whole experience, decided to vent some of his frustrations in a letter back to VF-124. "You lying bastards," he wrote, "the F-8 sure as hell is vulnerable to ground fire at low altitudes, and we have the hits to prove it. Unless you're under 100 feet with chickens in the barn, you're going to get your asses blown out of the sky." Mugs did not have much time to lick his wounds. A few days later, the air wing struck North Vietnamese troop emplacements on the island of Bach Long Vi in the middle of the Gulf of Tonkin, and McKeown's skipper, Bill Donnelly, and another pilot, Ken Hume, were shot down. Donnelly was later picked up by SAR forces, but Hume ultimately ended up killed in action.

In March, *Coral Sea* moved south to support the unopposed Marine landing at Danang. Later in April, its air wing launched 180 sorties against the main Viet Cong base in the Tay Ninh Province, a Communist stronghold since World War II. In May, the carrier flew all of Bien Hoa air base's missions for several months, after this installation was rendered temporarily ineffective by a chain of accidental explosions. It was during these months that Mugs flew one of the most rewarding missions of his first tour. Deep in the central highlands, forty-five kilometers southwest of Pleiku city, the Viet Cong and possibly a contingent of North Vietnamese regulars laid siege to the U.S. Special Forces camp, Duc Co. During a rainy July morning, McKeown, leading a flight of three aircraft, received an urgent call from a ground-based air controller on the scene. The camp desperately needed close air support, but no flights in the air at the time were willing to risk flying under the 400-foot overcast to aid the desperate Green Berets. Mugs, now operations officer for the unit due to losses, then radioed his men: "All right, we're going down."

"Shit, it's overcast," one of the men protested. "What's the ceiling anyway?"

"It's about 400 feet, and it's raining," the other pilot responded.

"Well, fuck it, these are *Americans*!" exclaimed Mugs.

He then peeled off into the overcast, followed very reluctantly by the two others. At about 300 feet, they broke through the clouds, and the controller screamed, "They're coming across the river, and they're coming right now!" Mugs let down about fifty feet off the water and caught the attacking forces right in the middle of the river with his 20-mm cannons. The flight then turned around and made another pass despite intense fire from the ground. In the end, the F-8s killed over 120 enemy troops.

McKeown flew 185 combat missions during his first tour. As the tour dragged on and more pilots were lost to enemy fire as well as accidents, McKeown began to question the sanity of what he was doing. During one twenty-four-hour period alone, he drove his tailhook into his tailpipe during a landing, flamed out while taxiing back from a rough close-air support mission, and broke his nose gear. "I had three airplanes down in the hangar bay and all within about twenty-four hours, and I said, 'Skipper, I think I'm going to go climb in a gin bottle for a day or two. God's trying to tell me something. I better listen.'"

As he tried to salve his fears with gin, Mug ruminated, "How long can I keep doing this? How many times can I run down the muzzles before I get hit?" His eyes then focused upon his class of 1961 Naval Academy ring. "Goddamn, Mugs, you don't push spaghetti. You pull it. There's nothing you would ever do to reflect dishonor on that institution. Your purpose in life is to win wars and relieve people in combat, and that is the essence of what they trained you to do, and by God, you do it, and by God, you're good at it." From that point forward, he made up his mind to accept his fate as a warrior and would never again be plagued with doubt. In fact, as his skills improved, he became cavalier—especially after testing his skills against the best Navy pilots at Miramar. "I remember telling myself and telling friends, and I wasn't bragging or anything, I just said, 'I'm goddamn good at what I'm doing. I'm a fucking killer and a hired gun. I'm as good as they come.' And I proved it: I could kick the shit out of anybody at Miramar or any other pilot. I took immense pride in my ability in combat to handle the stresses of combat."

F-4 TRANSITION AND HAVE DRILL

McKeown returned home in November 1965 and immediately began gearing up for a second tour, which would begin in July 1966 and last until February 1967. For this tour, VF-154 would fly the F-4B, and much of the shore period between cruises was taken up transitioning to this plane.

At first, Ron did not like the F-4. He felt the F-8 was a much more beautiful plane and also initially felt rather ambivalent about having an NFO. "I wasn't real hot on having a back-seater. I used to say I'd trade every back-seater in the world for 3,000 pounds of gas." But as time progressed, Mugs began to appreciate both the plane and the back-seater: "It was easy to land. I never was 100 percent sure I was going to get back aboard when I flew the Crusader at night, whereas with the F-4, I was always convinced I was going to get aboard. I used to say, 'It may take me a while, but I'm going to get aboard.'"

Ron's second cruise ran from July 1966 to February 1967. He flew multiple strikes against targets in the North, including Vinh and Haiphong, and experienced the thrill of dodging SAMs for the first time. McKeown left his squadron a month before the end of the cruise to begin test pilot school at Edwards Air Force Base. The Navy wanted him to be an astronaut for a follow-on program to *Apollo*, but ultimately, the money ran out, and McKeown ended up back in the fleet.

As a test pilot, Mugs flew almost every fighter in the inventory and performed various aeronautical feats, including flying the F-104 at over 100,000 feet in altitude. On those missions, he could actually see the curvature of the Earth from the California Baja Peninsula all the way to Seattle. "You'd come out of burner at 75,000 feet, shut down the engine, and just coast at a constant altitude. When you came back down, you would relight the engine at 50,000 feet and land in a dry lake bed."

For his future career as a MiG fighter, the most valuable aspect of being a test pilot was having the opportunity to fly the MiG-17 during Project Have Drill in 1969. At Have Drill, McKeown served as the air-to-air project officer and as the manager in charge of rewriting the Navy's F-4 manual. He also spent hundreds of hours flying the MiG-17 and fighting against it in the F-4. "Fighting the '17 in a Phantom," according to McKeown, "was like being a giant with a long rifle trapped in a phone booth with a midget using a knife. That's really the way you found yourself. You wouldn't let him get in where he could cut your guts out. You had to push him hard and drive him around the sky. But the big secret was to preserve your separation—approximately a mile and a half—so that you were always out of his weapons range and within your own."[10]

McKeown learned that the MiG could not roll like an F-4, which enabled him to devise some special defensive techniques. One was to fake a roll to one side and then jerk the plane into a roll to the other. This allowed the F-4, with its better roll rate and speed, to increase its separation with each barrel roll until it was far enough away to turn back into the MiG. Another maneuver was called the "bug-out," which involved pulling the Phantom away at an angle perpendicular to the MiG's line of flight and giving the engine full throttle. If that failed, McKeown would take the F-4 out of its flight envelope as a last-ditch maneuver.[11] He would slam the stick forward, pull it back, and then slam it forward again, "which would get you through about one, one and a half, negative Gs. Then pull the stick as hard as you could and reverse rudder. At that point you could generate enough yaw rate and the airplane would float," and the MiG's forward momentum would cause it to overshoot the F-4. "But you've still got a problem, you're not out of the woods yet. You've got to get your energy back . . . accelerate!"[12]

One day during the testing, Mugs never did get his energy back during a bug-out maneuver. Both engines of his F-4 flamed out, and the plane went into a flat spin. The Phantom fell straight down from 11,000 feet, pinning McKeown and his NFO, J. C. Smith, against the canopy. Mugs managed to light both engines but then initiated a bailout when his altimeter hit 200 feet. He and Smith landed about 10 feet from the flaming aircraft.

One of the characteristics that separated McKeown from ordinary pilots was his ability to look disaster in the face, roll with the punches, and keep on going. Many pilots quit flying fighters after a particularly bad accident or combat tour, but McKeown never let up. Mugs continued to experiment with the bug-out maneuver at Miramar but, more important, agreed to fly two more combat tours in Vietnam: one in 1971 and another in 1972.

16

Early Linebacker MiG Engagements

THE RETURN OF THE MIGS: SPRING 1972

With the onset of the Communist Easter Offensive in March 1972, the Nixon administration began easing restrictions against the bombing targets in North Vietnam. B-52s as well as tactical fighters struck many targets in the North for the first time since 1967. The strength of this American response forced the MiGs up into the air again in numbers not seen since 1967, and dogfights once again erupted over the skies of North Vietnam.

The Vietnamese People's Air Force order of battle in 1972 consisted of four regiments of fighters located at four major airfields: Phuc Yen, Kep, Yen Bai, and Lam Son. Although Navy aircraft occasionally tangled with MiG-21s based out of Phuc Yen, fifteen miles north of Hanoi, or the MiG-19s based at Yen Bai, fifty miles northwest of Hanoi, their main foes usually were the MiG-17s of the 923d Fighter Regiment based at Kep, thirty miles northeast of Hanoi. These aircraft patrolled the eastern and northeastern parts of the country.

The MiG-17 Fresco, first developed in 1953 by the Soviet Union and based heavily on the MiG-15 of Korean War fame, was not nearly as fast or sophisticated as the F-4. It could barely fly 716 mph, whereas the Phantom could easily hit speeds in excess of 1,500 mph. Generally, it did not carry air-to-air missiles but instead relied on two 23-mm and one 37-mm cannon as its main armaments—weapons suitable only for close-in fighting. Despite these obvious deficiencies, the MiG-17 often proved a formidable adversary for the F-4. In a slow, close-in dogfight, the MiG's turning advantage, excellent visibility, and gun armament made it very difficult for a fast F-4 armed only with long-range missiles to defeat. To entice American planes into slow-moving dogfights, two or more MiG-17 pilots would fly in tight defensive circles, with each plane flying a different direction separated by 800 feet of altitude. The only way a Phantom could get behind a MiG in one of these patterns would be to slow down and enter the circle, whereupon the MiG's wingman would turn into the F-4 and blast it out of the sky.

Clearly, attacking MiGs on the ground represented a better way to neutralize this threat. However, during much of the war, rules of engagement promulgated by the president and the secretary of defense through the JCS usually prevented Navy and Air Force planes from bombing both MiG bases and their ground control intercept radar stations located on those bases. Immune from attack and equipped with intelligence from ground controllers on the location of every American aircraft entering North Vietnam, the VPAF could attack American planes when and where they pleased with almost complete impunity. Not surprisingly, they generally chose to avoid fighters in favor of more vulnerable attack planes. In 1967, President Johnson began easing these restrictions, but then, in April 1968, he halted his Rolling Thunder offensive altogether.

Determined not to make the same mistakes as his predecessor, President Nixon permitted attacks on these airfields soon after the start of the Easter Offensive, hurting the enemy GCI effort and compelling the MiGs to take to the air to defend their bases. In fact, by the end of 1972, all airfields in North Vietnam except Gia Lam, Hanoi's international airport, were extensively damaged, and Noi Bay, Kep, Yen Bai, and Kien An had to be completely rebuilt.[1]

There were seven Navy MiG kills between the end of Rolling Thunder in 1968 and the beginning of Nixon's Linebacker offensive on 10 May 1972. Five of them occurred in the three months leading up to Linebacker, and two were achieved by a single fighter team, Lieutenant Randy "Duke" Cunningham and his NFO, Lieutenant (jg) William Driscoll. This team would ultimately become the first aces of the war on 10 May 1972.

A University of Missouri graduate and a high school swimming coach before the war, Cunningham left his home in Shelbina, Missouri, in 1967 to pursue a dream of becoming a naval aviator. In contrast to McKeown, he did not enter the Navy through the Naval Academy or even ROTC but received his commission through Officer Candidate School. Cunningham flew during an uneventful cruise in 1969–70. He then went through the Top Gun curriculum at Miramar, finally returning to the fleet in October 1972.

Randy scored his first MiG kill on 19 January while escorting an RA-5 Vigilante engaged in photoreconnaissance over Quang Lang air base south of Hanoi. In this episode, Cunningham surprised two MiG-21s from the rear. Willy Driscoll, his NFO, urged him to take a Sparrow shot from long range, but Duke, skeptical about radar-guided missiles and their performance, chose to get closer and use a heat-seeking missile instead. The MiG discovered Cunningham just as he launched his first Sidewinder, which missed, but Duke continued his pursuit, ultimately downing the MiG with a second Sidewinder shot from the rear.[2] Bagging the first MiG since Jerome Beaulier and Steven Barkley's kill on 28 March 1970 transformed Cunningham and Driscoll overnight from two reserve aviators to the men who might one day emerge as the first aces of the Vietnam War. However, it would take nearly four months before the team would get its second kill.

Between 19 January and 8 May, the day the Duke got his second kill, the Navy as a whole scored only four more aerial victories. On 6 March, Tooter Teague and Dave Palmer of VF-51 blasted off *Coral Sea* as part of a photoreconnaissance strike force. Admiral James Ferris, the carrier group commander, warned Teague in the preflight brief that MiGs might be in the air, and Teague had his fangs fully extended that day, hoping to get one. "This attitude that there's nothing worth my ass is wrong. If you're gonna kill MiGs, you gotta go trolling. You gotta get out there and get among them," Teague explained.[3] His flight got a bandit call from Red Crown just as the RA-5 finished its photo run over Quang Lang. "I got one at 11 o'clock low!" shouted Teague's backseater, Ralph Howell. Teague veered into the MiG and launched a Sidewinder. "It guided like a champion," explained Tooter. "All sorts of crap came off the guy." The MiG flew straight up, and Teague tried to follow but overshot it. He then saw another MiG at twelve o'clock high. He fired another Sidewinder at close range—too close for the missile to arm—and the shot whizzed by the MiG. "I had buck fever. No question. When somebody is in your sights, . . . it's probably the most massive amount of adrenaline you'll ever have." The MiG dove, and Teague stuck with it, but then another MiG pulled into his three o'clock, forcing him to give up the chase. Teague made one more pass over the field, hoping to catch another MiG, but none showed. He did not receive a kill credit for the actions that day because no one knew whether the first MiG went down. The North Vietnamese claim no MiGs went down during the engagement.[4]

In the meantime, *Coral Sea* launched Gary Weigand and Jim Stillinger of VF-111 in an attempt to intercept the MiGs as they returned home. With the help of Red Crown, Stillinger found a MiG-17 and got into a nasty turning fight with the scrappy little plane. "Jim couldn't get enough nose-to-tail to shoot," recalled Weigand, and the MiG began to gain the advantage. "The adrenaline kicked in and all of a sudden it hit me, 'Hey, this is for real. Somebody is going to die if you don't get your butt in gear and do what you're supposed to do.'" Weigand told Stillinger he was coming in and asked Jim to drag the MiG south. Weigand rolled in on the MiG and fired a Sidewinder right up its tailpipe, blowing off its tail. He could hear Stillinger yelling, "You got him! You got him!" as he flew through the MiG's debris only 150 feet above the ground.

The Navy lost an F-4 flown by Al Molinare and J. B. Souder on 27 April and later evened the score and then some with three kills on 6 May. Jerry Houston and his radio intercept officer, Kevin Moore, of VF-51 got the first MiG of the day over Bai Thuong airfield, and later that day Pete Pettigrew and his wingman, Robert Hughes, scored again while covering a second strike against the same airfield. Pettigrew's RIO, Michael McCabe, got an image on his radar as four MiG-21s approached the strike from twenty-five miles away. On the radar, the box V formation of four MiGs appeared as a single aircraft, but when the MiGs passed underneath Pettigrew, he immediately spotted the others. Because Hughes had the best shot, Pettigrew ordered him and his RIO, Adolph Cruz, to engage first. Hughes turned into the MiGs and took an out-of-envelope shot at the formation. Amazingly, the missile turned into one of the MiGs, knocking it out of the formation and into the ground.[5]

Hughes salvoed two more Sidewinders at the lead MiG, but they failed to guide and went ballistic. Pettigrew then eased in beside him and got a "horrendous tone" on his Sidewinders. He took a shot just as Hughes squeezed off another missile. Hughes's shot took a little piece off the MiG's tail, and Pettigrew's rammed up its tailpipe, blowing the plane into debris and forcing the MiG pilot to eject. The two men decided to each claim one kill for that day. During World War II, if two pilots shot up a plane, only the pilot who finished the job got credit for the kill, and the Navy decided to adhere to this policy during the Vietnam War.[6]

Randy Cunningham finally nailed his second MiG just two days before he became an ace. On 8 May, the Navy staged a large Alpha strike on a truck staging area near Son Tay, twenty-five miles west of Hanoi. Cunningham and his wingman, Brian Grant, were part of the MiG patrol for that strike. The two planes launched just before the main thirty-five-plane strike group. As they neared the strike area, they received word from Red Crown that a flight of MiGs was coming from the direction of Yen Bai. Then Red Crown lost contact with the MiGs. Frustrated, Cunningham made a 180-degree turn back toward the target to give coverage to the force. "There was no telling where they were," and Randy could not afford to leave the strike group vulnerable unless he knew the exact location of the MiGs. Familiar with Souder's shoot-down on 27 April, he also did not want to fall prey to a trap.

Before he completed the turn, Red Crown chimed in again, "Bandits closing at your 6 o'clock and 20 miles." Now more confident he had a contact, Cunningham reversed into the approaching flight. Red Crown made another call, but the transmission garbled before it reached Randy. Suddenly, Grant called out, "Duke, in place, port!" Fearing an ambush, Cunningham made a hard 90-degree port turn to check Grant's six o'clock (a precaution Teague never took for Souder and Molinare on 27 April). Seeing no MiGs, Cunningham hit the afterburners and pulled abeam of Grant. A MiG-17 then came screaming out of the haze at 10,000 feet, peppering Grant with shells from the rear.

"Brian, MiG-17 at 7 o'clock."

Grant punched off his fuel tank and pulled away from the MiG.

"Brian, Atoll . . . break port!"

Grant jammed his F-4 into a mind-numbing six-G turn, narrowly missing the missile. The MiG continued to pursue him.

"Brian, he's closing again . . . unload and go again."

"Duke, look up! Two MiG-17s meeting us head-on." Cunningham ignored the threat. "My concentration was bore-sighted," he later explained, "on the fighter chasing Brian. . . . I still had 60 degrees off the MiG's tail, but I fired anyway. The missile tracked and strained for its quarry, finally giving up to fall below." Frightened by the missile, the MiG broke hard and ran, but Cunningham stuck with his prey. "I had a tone on the fleeing MiG, so I squeezed the trigger—it was a classic shot. The missile came off the rail, did a little wiggle, and flew right into him." The fighter then crashed into a mountain.

As soon as Duke launched his Sidewinder, he became acutely aware that the MiGs that had crossed in front of him a moment ago were now bearing down on his six o'clock.

"Alright, Brian, I'm going to pull hard down into your port turn and drag the MiGs out in front of you . . . shoot them off my tail." Twenty-three-mm and 37-mm shells sparkled over Duke's canopy.

"Brian, get in here! I'm in deep trouble!" Cunningham cried out as he swerved back and forth. As a last-ditch move, he plunged his F-4 into a screaming 120-degree dive. "I put a good 12Gs on the aircraft, tearing wing panels, popping rivets, and breaking a flap hinge." Cunningham pulled out of the dive, lit his afterburners, and soon accelerated into a vertical climb at 550 knots. He called "Tallyho" to Brian, hoping to set him up for a kill, but the MiGs were nowhere in sight. Apparently, they had bugged out and headed back to Gia Lam.[7]

LINEBACKER BEGINS: 10 MAY 1972

The war against the MiGs escalated significantly on 10 May 1972. On that day, Nixon launched a new bombing campaign against North Vietnam code-named Linebacker I. The major goals of Linebacker were to disrupt Communist supply lines from the DMZ to the Chinese buffer zone and destroy military supplies inside of North Vietnam. Three things made this campaign different from Rolling Thunder. First, theater commanders were given much more latitude to choose targets and determine the tactics and weapons for missions. Second, precision-guided munitions and long-range radio navigation (LORAN) made it possible to attack targets with great accuracy and minimal collateral damage. Third, targets in and around Hanoi and Haiphong, including air defense targets, were hit on nearly a daily basis, again raising the stakes for North Vietnam and forcing its leadership to risk its precious MiGs in unprecedented numbers to defend its two major cities. By the close of the day, American pilots would down eleven MiGs in the most intense day of air-to-air combat of the Vietnam War. More important for the Navy, eight of those victories would go to naval aviators, and three, to the Cunningham-Driscoll team.

Randy Cunningham did not know he would be flying on 10 May until shortly before he took off at 1219. In the hours before that fateful day, Cunningham found himself brooding over a "Dear John" letter he had just received from his wife requesting a divorce. Hoping to get Randy's mind off his family problems, Gus Eggert, the *Connie*'s air wing commander, assigned him at the very last moment to fly flak suppression for a big Navy strike against the Hai Duong railroad yards and even authorized Cunningham to fly his personal plane, "Showtime 100." Snapping out of his malaise, Cunningham strapped on his F-4 and catapulted off toward Hai Duong.

Once over the target, he and his wingman, Brian Grant, could find no muzzle flashes to hit, so they jettisoned their cluster bombs on warehouses beside the main target. After releasing his bombs, Cunningham pulled the F-4 out of the dive, and Willie Driscoll glanced back at the target: "I looked over my shoulder to see where the bombs had gone and saw a lot of black dots on the horizon. I looked back at the ground, looked back at the dots and caught the flash of MiG-17s coming up the left side."[8]

"Duke, you have MiG-17s at your 7 o'clock shooting."

Caught by surprise, Randy reversed port and saw two MiGs bearing down on him with guns blazing. "I don't know why they didn't hit me, I could see tracers flying by the canopy. He had a lot of closure, he was hauling, so I broke down into him and he overshot. I reversed and his wingman split over the top and shot past me. I reversed course, put my nose on his tailpipe and squeezed the trigger."[9] The Sidewinder shot right into the MiG a thousand feet away and exploded. This entire engagement lasted fifteen seconds.

A moment later another MiG-17 eased up behind Cunningham, but Randy spotted him.

"MiG-17, MiG-17, MiG-17, Brian, he's on my tail. . . . Brian, I got MiGs on my tail!"

"I can't help you, Duke, I've got two on my tail."

Cunningham decided to hit his burners and try to outrun his pursuer. Grant did the same, and both planes surged away from the MiGs.

Once beyond the range of the MiGs, Cunningham and Grant pulled into a steep zoom climb to 12,000 feet and then banked steeply to check out the battle raging below. "There were eight MiG-17s in a defensive wheel, flying in a circle," recalled Cunningham.[10] The two pilots went into steep diving turns, hoping to get a missile lock on one of the circling MiGs from above, but then Dwight Timm, the executive officer of VF-96, whizzed by with two MiGs on his tail and one flying under his belly.

"XO, reverse starboard. If you don't, you're going to die."[11] Cunningham needed Timm to break hard starboard to avoid being shot by one of Randy's heat-seeking missiles.

"Duke," Driscoll broke in, "we have four MIG-17s at our 7 o'clock." He then called out two MiG-19s at twelve o'clock. Cunningham, after making sure the MiGs were in no position to hit him, held his position and continued to implore Timm to break starboard. Unaware of the MiG underneath him, Timm held his port turn, thinking that this would make him less vulnerable to the MiGs coming at him from behind.

"Showtime 112, reverse starboard. Goddamnit, reverse starboard!"

Timm finally broke starboard, and Duke yelled "Fox Two" as he released a Sidewinder. The missle went right up the tailpipe and exploded, forcing the pilot into a violent ejection.[12]

Following his second kill, Cunningham started to egress. According to Gus Eggert, "The attack planes were now safely clear of the target, the melee was breaking up and the F-4s were running out of gas and missiles. We didn't have any reason to stick around—we had to get ourselves back. People had separated from each other. They headed for the beach in ones and twos."[13] Moving south from Hai Duong, Cunningham picked up the dot of a MiG-17 on the horizon about 20 degrees to the right. "I tried to meet this guy head-on, and all of a sudden he opened fire with tracer. I pulled straight up into the vertical, going up through fifteen thousand feet, pulled 6Gs going over the top. I looked back. I expected to see him moving straight through and running. But we were canopy to canopy, maybe four hundred or five hundred feet apart!"[14]

As Cunningham reached the top of his climb and began to pull over the top, the MiG fired. Randy then engaged the MiG in a rolling scissors maneuver. "I pitched my nose up, pulled over the top, and rolled in behind his 6 o'clock. As soon as I dropped my nose he pulled straight up into the vertical again. I overshot, he rolled up over the top, pulled through and rolled in behind me." The fight was going advantage, disadvantage; and then it started going disadvantage, disadvantage.[15]

Randy next opted to make a last-ditch maneuver he had often practiced in training. "The MiG was sitting at my 7 o'clock. When he got his nose just a little too high, I pulled sharply down into him and met him head-on. Then I lit the burners and accelerated away from him." Cunningham went into another vertical climb, but the MiG followed. The Phantom broke out and then pulled into another zoom climb. Still, the MiG followed. "Each time I had gone up with this guy in the vertical, I had out-zoomed him and gone higher than he had. And each time I went in front he shot at me. I figured that one time he was going to get lucky. So this time we were going up, canopy to canopy, and I pulled the throttles back to idle and selected speed brakes."

The F-4 rapidly decelerated, and the MiG eased in front. "I think that caught him by surprise because he shot way out in front of me. But a Phantom on full afterburner at one hundred fifty knots with the nose straight up in the air is not really flying, it is standing on thirty-six thousand pounds of thrust. We were hanging behind him but we were not really in a position of advantage. At those speeds a MiG-17 had about two and a half to three more Gs available than we had."

When the MiG reached the top of its climb, Cunningham applied his rudder. "I stood on the rudder and got the airplane to move to his blind side, where he couldn't see us. He rolled over the top and started down, and then he made his first mistake. His nose fell through, he tried to get it out. He didn't. He started running." The MiG stopped wing rocking and dove for the deck.

> I guess he thought he could outrun me. I started pushing forward on the stick, trying not to bury the nose, and I actually had to stand on the rudder a little bit to hold the nose up. I unloaded and squeezed the trigger as I got the tone. I knocked off a little piece of the tail but he didn't alter his flight path at all, and I thought he was going to get away. He was still running. I followed him down and started to squeeze again when a little fire erupted. The MiG descended to the ground. No chutes were observed.[16]

With this kill under their belts, Cunningham and Driscoll became the first aces of the Vietnam War and the only Navy aces.[17] At the time, however, Randy had other concerns. His fuel situation was desperate, and he still had to make it back to the ship in one piece.

Randy pulled out of the dive and returned to *Constellation* at 15,000 feet. Suddenly, an EP-3 electronic warfare plane from VQ-1 called out, "SAM! SAM! Vicinity of Haiphong." Cunningham looked to his right just as the missile exploded 500 feet above him. The aircraft shuddered,

Lieutenant Randy "Duke" Cunningham and his NFO, Lieutenant (jg) William P. Driscoll, discuss their recent MiG kills with Secretary of the Navy John W. Warner and Admiral Elmo R. Zumwalt Jr., Chief of Naval Operations. Cunningham and Driscoll became the first aces of the Vietnam War after they downed five enemy aircraft during the spring of 1972. (Courtesy of U.S. Navy)

but all gauges appeared normal, and Cunningham continued to climb out. At 25,000 feet, the aircraft pitched up. "It was not very violent, though, it just started a climb and I pushed the stick forward, but nothing happened. I remember kicking the bottom rudder and I thought, 'OK, roll this son of a bitch out.'" The plane's hydraulic system had apparently been hit, causing Randy to slowly but surely lose control of the aircraft. He managed to keep it pointed toward the coast by making several awkward barrel rolls.

"We're on fire," Driscoll suddenly announced. The plane then went into a spin, forcing both crew members to eject. After Cunningham and Driscoll had spent about fifteen minutes in the water, a Marine helicopter from *Okinawa* rescued both men.[18]

MAY 10: NAVY VERSUS AIR FORCE PERFORMANCE

Overall, Navy pilots shot down eight MiGs on 10 May without losing a single plane. All but one of these kills involved dogfights with an MiG-17, and in each case, Navy pilots scored their victories with the AIM-9 Sidewinder heat-seeking missile. The Air Force, by comparison, shot down three MiGs but lost two planes as well. In one case, two MiG-19s surprised an F-4 from behind just moments after the F-4, flown by Major Robert Lodge, had shot down a MiG-21.[19] A few minutes later, another flight of F-4s suffered a very similar fate, for the loss of a second F-4.

What surprised both Air Force and Navy pilots who later studied the Air Force's performance on 10 May as part of the Air Force's Red Baron study of air-to-air combat in Vietnam is that two of the men shot down that day were arguably the Air Force's most experienced fighter pilot/RIO combination. Major Robert Lodge not only had flown 100 missions over North Vietnam earlier in the war in F-105s but also was a graduate of the Air Force Fighter Weapons School at Nellis Air Force Base, the wing tactics officer for the 432d Tactical Reconnaissance Wing, and a superb pilot with three kills to his credit.[20] His RIO, Captain Roger Locher, was on his second Southeast Asia tour, had over 400 missions under his belt, and was generally considered the best Air Force back-seater in Thailand.[21] How could the Air Force lose such a pair of stars while the Navy emerged from the turkey shoot relatively unscathed?

Again, the Navy's emphasis on mutual support during dogfights certainly helped to explain the disparity. Air Force pilots were not as well trained as Navy pilots in the art of close-in combat. As much as Cunningham wanted to get MiG kills, he always put his wingman's security first, and vice versa.[22] During both his 8 and 10 May kills, Cunningham's actions directly spared other members of his flight from getting shot down. According to the Air Force's Red Baron analysis of the 8 May kill, "Excellent teamwork and radio calls enabled Newarks 01 and 02 [Cunningham and Grant] to effectively defend against MiG attacks. Their knowledge of air combat tactics and proficiency in performing these maneuvers was a major factor in the successful completion of the mission."[23] With respect to the 10 May kills, the Air Force Red Baron analysis states that "this event illustrates the results that can be attained by well-trained aircrews that are knowledgeable and proficient in their own aircraft, as well as thoroughly cognizant of the capabilities of the enemy. #&"% [*shit*] hot!"[24]

In Lodge's flight, by contrast, two of the pilots in the four-plane group were too involved with their own MiG kills to properly cover Lodge. Both First Lieutenant John Markle, Lodge's wingman, and Captain Steve Ritchie, flying the number three, shot down MiGs moments before and just after Lodge went down. Although Markle did warn his lead of the MiG-19 bearing down on him, the Air Force's study censured Markle for not offering Lodge more threat warnings. Steve Ritchie claims he was too far away from Lodge to be of any help, but this was because he was in the process of lining up his own kill when Lodge went down. Clearly, in the confusion of this melee, Ritchie and Markle temporarily forgot the cardinal rule of fighter aviation—support your wingman at all costs! The Air Force's emphasis on four-plane formations also proved a factor on 10 May. Keeping four planes in mutually supportive positions during the heat of combat often proved impossible even for the most experienced pilots. The Navy's "loose deuce" two-plane formation, by comparison, was much more flexible and mutually supportive in the fast-paced environment of jet combat.

17

Ron McKeown's Day in the Sun

ON 23 MAY, McKeown and Ensch were not on the flight schedule. Late in the day, *Midway* added another strike: a large Alpha against the Haiphong Petroleum Products storage facility. Because all the VF-161 guys had already flown that day, Mugs decided that he and Ensch ought to take the MiG Combat Air Patrol (MIGCAP).

Their wingmen for the patrol were Lieutenant Mike Rabb and his NFO, Lieutenant Ken Crandall. McKeown had flown with Rabb quite a bit during the previous cruise and felt so confident in his abilities that he did not bother discussing MiG tactics during the preflight. Instead he told Rabb, "If we see any MiGs, no sense in talking about it now because we've fought that fight a hundred times in the training cycles and all around, and we'll do what we always did last year, and whatever happens, we'll kill 'em."

The four men manned their aircraft at approximately 1730 hours local time. As he sat in the cockpit waiting to launch, Mugs distinctly remembered feeling that something was going to happen. "It was nothing we could put our fingers on, but we knew that this was not going to be an ordinary hop."[1] The two men launched at 1800, made a quick tanker stop to pick up extra fuel, and then checked in with Red Crown, the destroyer escort *Oswald*. Red Crown's very first transmission was, "Bullet, your vector is 278 for 5 for Bandits."

"*Oswald*, this is Bullet 1. Confirm bandits," Jack inquired.

"I confirm bandits. You're clear to fire."

"OK, let's go bust 'em," Mugs responded.

Mugs began to get excited. "Hey, man, this is it," he reminded himself. "This is what you've been training for. This is the whole thing." Mugs flew toward Kep along the coastal ridgeline and began arming his missiles. Because he could not get a good tone on one of the AIM-9s, he cycled that missile to the end of the queue so it would be the last missile fired in case of an engagement. Meanwhile, Jack Ensch, his

A North Vietnamese MiG-17F. The MiG-17 flew much slower than the Navy's F-4, but in the hands of a competent pilot, this highly maneuverable plane could be a fierce adversary. Ron "Mugs" McKeown shot down two MiG-17s on 23 May 1972. (Courtesy of Istvan Toperczer)

NFO, attempted to lock the MiGs on the F-4B's radar but was having no success. "It was the old radar and that's a terrible radar to try to pick up anything over land with all the ground clutter. It was designed for intercept over water at high altitude."[2]

"They're low; they're low," *Oswald* suddenly broke in. Mugs descended below 4,000 feet. "We're just going down at them, and all of a sudden we flew right down over the Kep runway at about 1,500 feet, and then all of a sudden I got a glimpse of these dumb bastards."

"Tallyho! Bullet 2, I've got two bogeys on my nose about five miles away," Mugs called out.

Jack then got a paint on his radar but could not acquire a lock due to ground clutter. Mugs and Rabb flew right through the section of two silver MiG-19s and then started a cross turn, with Mugs going high. Suddenly, four MiG-17 trailers in green and brown camouflage came screaming toward the two F-4Bs from above. As the section completed 90 degrees of its cross turn, the MIG-17s attacked Rabb. He recalled,

The two that turned on me had already achieved a high deflection-type shot in almost 90 degrees of the turn. It seemed like they were on a pedestal turning through the sky. I initiated a break-turn into the closest MiG-17 and he rendezvoused on me. I'd say within the next 270-degree of turn he achieved a real fine firing position. He was not much more than 500 feet away; he was pulling lead and firing. I remember having it run through my mind whether or not I should continue the hard-as-possible break into this guy or attempt the roll-away maneuver. My instinct was to keep turning into him.[3]

Mike then entered a 7G, 400-knot, nose-low spiral, and the third MiG slid slightly outside and high on him.

Meanwhile, Mugs had come around his cross turn. "I had expected them to fight horizontally, but they weren't. They started fighting mostly in the vertical."[4] Spotting a MiG-19 below him, Mugs started pulling toward it. One of the uncanny abilities of McKeown is that he could function in both a defensive and an offensive mode at the same time. Hence, when he saw a MiG-17 diving down him head-on as he was pulling, he managed to avoid a head-on collision and then return his attention immediately to the MiG-19. As McKeown described it:

> I pulled back into the MiG-19 as hard as I could. We were in a hard, nose-high turn, 30 degrees nose up, pulling around hard to the right in heavy buffet. It was classic for the F-4. The stick started lightening on me, I kept pulling, and then it went out of control. It rolled back left over the top about two rolls. As soon as I got over my back, I pushed full forward-stick. It went about one and half more rolls and came out inverted. It flashed to me that we were going to spend the night in this little valley, eat pumpkin soup, and have our name on a bracelet. All these things entered my mind, but as soon as the thing popped out at 1,800 to 2,000 feet, I got right back into the fight.

Again, Mugs refused to let his close brush with tragedy distract him from his central mission.

As he recovered from his departure, he looked up and saw a MiG-17 in front of him. He pulled behind it, got a good tone, and fired an AIM-9G. The MiG then cranked it around in full afterburner, turning almost 90 degrees; the missile flew right by his tail.

At this point, McKeown saw another MiG directly behind Rabb, firing. "Extend and take him out," he called to Rabb. McKeown launched an AIM-9G, which missed. He continued chasing the MiG in a spiral descent until 200 feet, when the MiG pulled its nose up and started to climb. McKeown got a good tone and fired a Sidewinder. The MiG broke hard right to avoid the missile.

"Son of a bitch, you're not going to give it to me, are you, God? I'm a sinner and you're going to fuck me," Mugs thought to himself. Miraculously, the missile stayed with the MiG, hitting the plane's tail and causing it to flip on its back and go down.

"Holy shit. We've got one at four thirty, and he's gunning!" his NFO, Jack Ensch, suddenly exclaimed.

McKeown could see the MiG's belly and decided to force the fighter into an overshoot. "I broke real hard into him, and he dug inside our turn and started rendezvousing on us. All of a sudden it hit me. He can't see me. The bastard can't see me!" Since the MiG pilot was pulling such a large amount of lead, Mugs knew he was in the MiG's blind area. "As soon as it hit me that he couldn't see, I pushed negative G, unloaded, came out of afterburner, and watched him turn inside of us. He flew right by the starboard side. When we didn't fly out in front of him, he broke back to the left with that real slow roll rate. He was nose high, and we just rolled in behind him. I got behind him, had a good tone, fired a Sidewinder, and that one went right up his tailpipe. He came out, and then the airplane blew up. And so that was it."

Following the second MiG kill, McKeown and Rabb joined up, egressed, and tanked once before landing. "We drank all our extra water because we were dehydrated from all the sweating. We were so excited. I banged the canopy with my hand and yelled over the intercom, 'Hey, shit, we got those fuckers.'" He then requested a carrier flyby from the *Midway* tower.

"That's a negative, Sigma Delta. We've got E-2s landing."

"Fuck the E-2s. Get them out of the pattern. We're coming in."

McKeown and Rabb screamed down each side of the ship at twenty feet, did their victory rolls, and then came around and landed. There were more than 200 sailors climbing over his plane by the time it was tied down. "I remember holding two fingers up. It was a great feeling."[5]

THE ACE FACTOR

In its analysis of the McKeown kills, Red Baron praised him for his knowledge of the F-4. When his F-4 departed normal flight, Mugs had enough experience with the system to recover and get back into the fight immediately. After all, he had already experienced a similar near disaster during training. Realistic training—especially during Project Have Drill—also provided McKeown with unique knowledge of his adversary's capability: he knew by heart all of the MiG-17s blind spots and could capitalize on them when opportunities arose. Finally, McKeown was a highly flexible and innovative pilot. He did not panic and retreat when the four trailing MiGs surprised him and broke up his two-plane element. Rather, he rolled with the punches just as he had done at the Naval Academy in his fight with Pete Optekar and got back on the offensive as quickly as he could.

This ability to think clearly and positively in the chaotic environment of air-to-air combat is not a characteristic shared by all pilots. In fact, of the hundreds of thousands of men who train to be fighter pilots, less than 1 percent ever see combat. Of these few, only a little over 5 percent shoot down more than a single enemy aircraft. Thus, only about .0005 percent of all men trained in fighters ever achieve the status of a Ronald McKeown, Robin Olds, Steve Ritchie, or Randy Cunningham. Good training certainly helped all of these men reach this pinnacle. The Red Baron study claims that pilots credited with MiG kills averaged a greater amount of prior combat experience than those who were downed.[6] However, it is also an aggressive, self-confident attitude combined with situational awareness that transforms an ordinary flier into an ace. In certain cases, these traits reveal themselves in athletics. In college, Cunningham swam competitively; Ritchie, McKeown, and Olds all played football (Olds was an All-American tackle at West Point). Several other famous MiG killers also played collegiate football, including Jerry "Devil" Houston and Foster "Tooter" Teague. Playing varsity football, though, did not necessarily make one a fighter pilot. As Teague put it, it's "all about attitude."

McKeown's demand for some ball time during the Air Force game illustrates this attitude well. It was not enough for McKeown to simply wear the Navy jersey; he wanted to run with the ball and be in the thick of things. Similarly, as a fighter pilot, he had no trouble looking any other pilot in the eye at Miramar and proclaiming to be the best pilot at

Top Gun. Audacious? Certainly, but nevertheless illustrative of an attitude that took McKeown to the top of his profession.

The downside of this attitude was that it gave some pilots, as NFO Souder's experience revealed in part II, the license to "be complete and total assholes." The image of a drunk Foster Teague kicking in some innocent officer's car (see chapter 7) is a good example of some of the excesses caused by the so-called fighter jock attitude, as is the much more recent Tailhook sexual abuse scandal. McKeown was able to channel much of his attitude into his flying, and fortunately for him, the Navy granted him flying assignments for most of his career: McKeown became the first commander of Top Gun after the war, ultimately rising to the rank of captain. By contrast, many other Vietnam-era fighter pilots wound up in unsuitable jobs—positions where their famous attitude could land them in trouble.[7]

For the Navy as a whole, the war against the MiGs in 1972 was a watershed. As former Air Force pilot and historian Marshall Michel puts it in his book *Clashes*, "The single most significant statistic that came out of Linebacker I and II was a stark, simple one: The Air Force shot down about 48 MiGs and lost 24 aircraft to MiGs, for a kill ratio of 2:1. The Navy lost 4 aircraft to MiGs and shot down 24, for a kill ratio of 6:1."[8] It is no wonder that the VPAF tended to prey more on Air Force strikes than Navy ones. Navy tactics and pilots were superior to those of their sister service. But the Navy record was not always so stellar. During 1966, the Navy shot down only eight MiGs but lost four planes to MiGs for a 2:1 kill ratio—the same ratio the Air Force achieved in 1972. "We lost planes unnecessarily," lamented Navy pilot and MiG killer John Nichols, "and we had to come from a long way behind to catch up. Next time we cannot count on having time to play catch-up. And next time is one day closer with every sunrise. Check six and keep the faith."[9]

PART VI

THE EASTER OFFENSIVE AND LINEBACKER

ON 30 MARCH 1972, General Vo Nguyen Giap shocked the world by launching one of the most daring offensives in the history of modern warfare: the Nguyen Hue campaign, known in the West as the Easter Offensive. The campaign was designed to shatter the South Vietnamese Army in a conventional battle, complete with tanks, armored personnel carriers, and heavy artillery. Approximately 120,000 North Vietnamese troops, nearly the entire military strength of the country, attacked South Vietnam along three fronts. The opening offensive drove through the DMZ along the border of the two countries. Three days later, three additional North Vietnamese divisions moved from sanctuaries in Cambodia and pushed into Binh Long Province, capturing Loc Ninh and surrounding An Loc, the provincial capital, only sixty-five miles outside of Saigon. Additional Communist forces attempted to cut the country in two with a bold thrust into the central highlands toward the city of Kontum. In all, fourteen North Vietnamese divisions and twenty-six separate regiments, including 1,200 tanks, participated in the Easter Offensive.

With only 5,000 American combat troops in South Vietnam by March 1972, the United States relied primarily on air power to counter this onslaught. That U.S. arms ultimately prevailed is a testament to the professionalism of the pilots and navigators who put themselves at grave risk to help a beleaguered ally in an unpopular war. To understand the unique role of naval air power during this epic final phase of the war, this part will provide a broad overview of naval air power's role in defending South Vietnam during the Easter Offensive, and then punishing North Vietnam for this aggression during the Linebacker offensive of 1972. It will also provide a combatant's perspective on the campaigns by profiling Leighton Smith, a warrior who took to the skies to defend South Vietnam in 1972 and later directed the American bombing campaign over Bosnia in 1995. Smith flew the Navy's newest attack plane of the Vietnam War, the A-7 Corsair II. Among other notable missions flown, Smith helped to drop the Thanh Hoa Bridge on 6 October—one of the most important and well-defended targets in North Vietnam.

There is an old saying in military organizations that "no one wants to be the last person to die in a war." By 1972, it was clear to everyone that President Nixon intended to get America out of the Vietnam War no matter what it took, and that the war was a lost cause. Yet, to extricate the United States from the war's quagmire and secure the release of the POWs, Nixon had to escalate the air war to levels never before seen. Therein lies the paradox of Linebackers I and II: to secure an honorable peace, Nixon ordered his air warriors to fight some of the most intense and dangerous missions of the war. Why these men fought so hard and so well during these final months remains one of the great mysteries of this unpopular war. All were volunteers who at any point in their service could have requested to be removed from flight status. Some had wives or other family members who strongly opposed the war and who desperately wanted them to refuse service in Vietnam. Despite all these pressures, almost all naval aviators called for service in Southeast Asia went and gave their all to the war effort.

18

Stopping the Easter Offensive

AT THE BEGINNING OF MARCH 1972, the war was extremely quiet. Since 1968, the South Vietnamese armed forces, backed up by regional and popular forces, had appeared to be making some strides in keeping the Communist forces in check, although guerrillas still harassed the populace in some areas, and North Vietnamese regiments remained active in a few border areas. The relatively calm state of the South Vietnamese countryside seemed to vindicate the Nixon Doctrine of withdrawing U.S. ground combat forces from the country while at the same time improving the capability of the Army of the Republic of Vietnam.

This calm, however, would prove illusory. In Hanoi, the North Vietnamese defense minister, General Vo Nguyen Giap, was planning a massive invasion designed to destroy the ARVN and capture South Vietnam. Giap hoped for a knockout blow, but short of that, he planned to permanently seize enough territory to dramatically improve the Democratic Republic of Vietnam's negotiating position in Paris. This would be the largest offensive ever launched by the DRV, representing a break from its past strategy of small-unit actions directed toward seizing terrain only briefly to achieve a psychological shock effect. Throughout 1971, Hanoi requested and received large quantities of modern weapons from the USSR and China, including MiG-21 jets, T-54 medium tanks, 130-mm artillery, 57-mm self-propelled antiaircraft guns, and shoulder-fired SA-7 antiaircraft missiles. It also stockpiled spare parts, ammunition, and fuel along border areas in unprecedented quantities.

Giap's plan called for a multidivisional thrust across the DMZ, with other forces moving in from the A Shau Valley in the west. The aim of this northern attack was to force Nguyen Van Thieu, the South Vietnamese president, to commit his reserves to defend his northern territories, whereupon Giap would then launch a second thrust from

Cambodia toward Saigon. A third assault would attempt to cut the country in half in the central highlands, leading to total collapse, or at the very least a peace treaty highly favorable to Hanoi.

THE BATTLE FOR MILITARY REGION I

At noon on Good Friday, 30 March 1972, the 308th North Vietnamese Division plus two independent regiments struck the ARVN fire support bases along the DMZ. From the west, the NVA's 304th Division rolled out of Laos, striking past Khe Sanh into the Quang Tri River Valley. The North Vietnamese onslaught quickly overran the South Vietnamese Army's 3d Division elements defending the northern fire support bases, wiping out the ARVN's artillery support and leaving the road to Quang Tri wide open to continued attacks.

As the South's artillery posts fell like dominoes during the first forty-eight hours of the attack and heavy monsoon rains made air support difficult, naval gunfire from warships became the only reliable source of supporting arms along the highway leading to Quang Tri City. Because of this, U.S. Marine gunfire observers began flying with Air Force forward air controllers to direct naval gunfire.[1] According to Lieutenant Colonel Gerald Turley, the senior Marine adviser in Military Region I, the destroyers *Buchanan* (DDG-14), *Strauss* (DDG-16), *Waddell* (DDG-24), and *Hammer* (DD-718) worked day and night hurling shells at North Vietnamese targets moving anywhere along the coastline, inland to Highway 1, and around the city of Dong Ha. In one instance, naval gunfire support destroyed four PT-76 light tanks spearheading an effort to capture the Dong Ha Bridge, the main link over the Cam Lo-Cua Viet River leading to Quang Tri. Marine Captain John Ripley, an eyewitness to this event, wrote in his after-action report, "When the tanks were hit and burning, both COs were surprised and elated in seeing the potential of NGF. I was to receive many requests for NGF after this remarkable demonstration of its rapid, destructive power."[2]

By 2 April, all twelve South Vietnamese fire support bases in the border area had fallen, but the North Vietnamese advance slowed. It was not until three weeks later that they attacked again, pushing within 1.5 kilometers of Quang Tri City. Improved weather, however, allowed Air Force FACs to begin calling in air strikes. Major W. T. Sweeney, an adviser posted with a South Vietnamese marine unit, reported: "During the three-day period on about 20 April when the enemy was putting in about 400 rounds of artillery and hitting other positions with direct fire weapons and antiaircraft guns, I had available through the FACs nearly unlimited close air support. . . . Some of the air support was at night under flares and extremely effective. The FACs stayed on station around the clock."[3]

Just off the coast, Navy destroyers continued to provide gunfire support for the beleaguered ARVN troops and also tried to stem the flow of NVA reinforcements coming across the DMZ. The North Vietnamese fought back with everything they had, including MiGs.

On 19 April, a MiG-17 attacked the destroyer *Higbee* as it engaged in a gunfire support mission just north of the DMZ near Dong Hoi. The plane, flown by Nguyen Van Bay,[4] made two passes over the ship, dropping four 250-pound bombs in the process. One bomb hit the base of the ship's after five-inch turret. Fortunately, the turret had just been evacuated due to a hot round, so no one was killed, although four sailors were injured in the explosion and the ensuing fire. As the MiG completed its second pass, *Sterett*, the antiaircraft guided missile destroyer on the scene, launched a Terrier missile at the plane but missed. *Sterett* then fired its second missile, downing the MiG. But the action did not end there. After the first MiG started its first bomb run, a second MiG flown by Le Xuan Di exited the mountains and executed a 180-degree turn and headed back into the mountains. *Sterett* fired two missiles at this MiG and assumed a kill when the missile and plane disappeared from radar simultaneously.

Higbee, Sterett, and two other surface warfare ships in the area (the cruiser *Oklahoma City* and destroyer *Lloyd Thomas*) then egressed the area to the northeast. During its exit, *Sterett* registered a couple of high-speed surface contacts on its radar and then detected the electronic signature of a Soviet-built SS-N-2 Styx missile, a cruise missile launched from PT boats. *Sterett* immediately fired a salvo of two Terrier missiles at the suspected Styx missile. Following the detonation of *Sterett*'s Terrier, the missile target disappeared from radar and the ECM signature signal ceased, signifying a kill. *Sterett*'s five-inch aft mount then fired at the two enemy PT boats, which promptly disappeared from radar and were presumed destroyed. This was the largest engagement by naval surface ships of the Vietnam war.[5]

The culmination of the Military Region (MR) I battle occurred on 28 April. During the night, 40,000 NVA troops with fifty tanks made their final advance into Quang Tri against an ARVN force of only 13,000. Marine adviser Major James Joy recounted the role of tactical air in slowing down the NVA advance across the bridge leading into the city: "In one of the most timely and most devastating air shows ever witnessed, tactical air, guided by a FAC with flare light, put in air strike after air strike on the enemy on the north side of the bridge. The attack was beaten off and resulted in 5 out of 5 tanks destroyed to the northwest of the bridge."[6]

Still, air power alone could not save Quang Tri. On 1 May, the Air Force's 37th Aerospace Rescue and Recovery Squadron at Danang launched a rescue task force of HH-53 Jolly Green Giant helicopters to evacuate the 132 American advisers still in the besieged city, as allied F-4s delivered every type of ordnance in a desperate bid to stall the North Vietnamese advance. The ARVN troops then fell back toward the old imperial city of Hue.

To salvage the situation, President Nguyen Van Thieu replaced his I Corps general, Hoang Xuan Lam, with one of South Vietnam's ablest generals, Ngo Quang Truong, the commander of Hue during the 1968 Tet Offensive. Truong ordered air power to take down every bridge between the DMZ and the My Chanh River. He then directed strikes against 130-mm artillery, tanks, and trucks. This classic battlefield interdiction campaign helped slow the NVA assault and purchased Truong enough time to mount a limited counterattack north of My Chanh, as well as stave off the final North Vietnamese Army thrust on 20 May. During this final NVA attack, the Communist forces succeeded in crossing the My Chanh River but were ultimately pushed back after several days of intense fighting. In all, tactical air destroyed eighteen tanks and killed 300 enemy during this battle.

Because the Air Force was in the process of withdrawing from South Vietnam at the time of the invasion and possessed only a third of the forces that had once been stationed in Southeast Asia, Navy tactical air was instrumental in preventing a total collapse of MR I during the anxious first weeks of the invasion. When the crisis began, the Navy had two carriers forward deployed and ready for action: *Hancock* and *Coral Sea*. *Kitty Hawk* and *Constellation* quickly joined them on 3 April and 8 April, respectively. Simultaneously, *Midway* deployed from the eastern Pacific and commenced combat operations on 30 April. A sixth carrier,

Saratoga, received orders to deploy from the Atlantic on 8 April and arrived on Yankee Station on 17 May.

The ability of the Navy's carrier force to quickly surge in strength meant that the Navy actually launched more tactical air strikes into Military Region I than the Air Force during the critical early weeks of the invasion: 2,023 versus 1,950. In total, Navy and Marine air flew 30 percent of the 18,000 tactical air sorties in Military Region I; the Air Force flew 45 percent and the VNAF, 25 percent.[7]

THE BATTLE FOR MILITARY REGION II

Three days after the initial attack along the DMZ on 30 March, clashes began occurring at eight of the ten fire support bases in the forested highlands of the tri-border region—the area of South Vietnam near the juncture with Laos and Cambodia. Known as Military Region II, it had long been an area of confrontation between the North Vietnamese Army and allied forces, beginning with the battle of Pleiku in 1965, followed by Dak To in late 1967, and finally during the Tet Offensive in 1968. In 1972, NVA probes along Rocket Ridge west along Highway 14 and in the coastal Binh Dinh Province kept the ARVN guessing about where the main North Vietnamese attack would come in MR II until the second week in April, when the NVA 2d Division attacked two regiments of the 22d ARVN Division at the town of Tan Canh and the nearby Dak To firebase. The South Vietnamese force quickly disintegrated and fled toward Kontum.

Inexplicably, North Vietnamese forces paused at Dak To for almost three weeks, giving the ARVN time to regroup at Kontum and John Paul Vann, the senior U.S. adviser in the area, an opportunity to pound the enemy's positions with relentless air strikes. During the entire month of April, more than 3,400 USAF, Marine, and Navy sorties struck targets in the MR II area.

The NVA juggernaut began moving again toward Kontum during the first half of May and launched its first major attack on the city on 14 May. The Air Force's Strategic Air Command sent Vann three-plane flights of B-52s at hourly intervals, and he used these planes judiciously to lay blankets of bombs in target boxes within 700 yards of friendly positions. "Anytime the wind is blowing from the north where the B-52 strikes are turning the terrain into moonscape, you can tell from the battlefield stench that the strikes are effective," Vann said. "Outside of Kontum, wherever you dropped bombs, you scattered bodies."

Joining the B-52s and the tactical air components defending Kontum was a small task force of U.S. Army helicopters, equipped with antitank missiles. The extremely accurate tube-launched, optically tracked, wire-guided missiles (TOWs) took out twenty-six tanks between late April and 12 June, including eleven T-54s in the Kontum area. One tank purportedly tried to duck into a house to hide. A TOW team nailed it by shooting a missile through a window.[8]

Bruised and battered by air power as well as confronted with stiffened defenses on the ground, the NVA pulled out of Kontum during the first half of June, but pockets of enemy forces continued to oppose South Vietnamese forces. South of Kontum along the roadway to Pleiku, Communist forces held a fortified position astride Highway 14 at Kontum Pass called the "rockpile." In actions similar to the Monte Cassino battle in Italy during World War II, allied tactical fighters and B-52s pounded the rockpile until the pass was cleared on 30 June, and armed convoys once again began traveling between Pleiku and Kontum.

As on the northern front, the Navy's most significant contribution to the air effort in MR II occurred during the vital first weeks of the attack. In April, Navy aircraft launched 1,118 sorties into MR II, compared with 739 for the Air Force.[9] Overall, between 8 April and 30 April, the Navy effort built gradually from about 240 to a peak day with over 300 sorties, resulting in a monthly average of 270 sorties per day. The USAF effort did not show any significant increase until after 15 April, when the daily sortie level began a dramatic rise to well over 400 sorties a day at month's end. The Air Force's average daily sortie rate for April was 330.[10]

Marine air also played a dramatic role in the defense of MR II. On 30 March, the U.S. Marine Corps had no planes in the Republic of South Vietnam, but by 11 April, two squadrons of F-4s (twenty-eight aircraft) were operating out of Danang, and two days later a third squadron had joined the group. In mid-May the Marines again augmented their air assets in Southeast Asia by transferring two squadrons of A-4s from Iwakuni, Japan, to Bien Hoa air base, Vietnam. Overall, the Marines flew 497 tactical sorties in MR II in April, 685 in May, and 204 in June.[11]

AN LOC AND THE BATTLE FOR MILITARY REGION III

The third and most critical phase of the Easter Offensive occurred in Military Region III, sixty-five miles west of Saigon at the town of An Loc. For the first time in the war, the South Vietnamese regime confronted the possibility of losing a provincial capital just outside of the national capital of Saigon. In the end, however, the ARVN forces defending An Loc held the town due primarily to the extraordinary air attacks by all four U.S. military services. More so than in any other battle during the Easter Offensive, air power would prove decisive at An Loc.

The Communist attack in this area began on 2 April with a series of feints in northern Tay Ninh Province. The North Vietnamese Army hoped to convince ARVN that the main objective of the attack was Tay Ninh City, but Major General Hollingsworth, the senior U.S. adviser in MR III, was not fooled. As predicted by the adviser, the main objective of the North Vietnamese was An Loc. On 5 April, NVA forces overwhelmed Loc Ninh, opening up a direct route down Highway QL-13 to Saigon through An Loc.

Intense attacks on An Loc continued for another three days. During this time, three Air Force forward air controllers operated over the town at all times. One of these FACs, usually the most experienced, flew high above the action as a command and control, or "king," FAC. The other two FACs functioned as regular air controllers except they received their tactical air sorties directly from the king rather than from the MR III Direct Air Support Center. This system allowed the king to run four or five strikes simultaneously over the city and be extremely responsive to the changing situation on the ground. For example, on 15 April, the NVA began a new drive on the city, and allied tactical air power responded immediately, destroying nine out of the ten tanks employed in the assault.[12] This attack ended the first phase of the An Loc struggle; thereafter, the battle degenerated into a classic siege.

On 16 April, enemy artillery fire hit an ammunition storage area at Lai Khe, south of An Loc, resulting in the destruction of 8,000 rounds of ammunition for 105-mm and 155-mm howitzers. Heavy artillery fire had also destroyed all but one of the 105-mm howitzers in An Loc. The combination of these losses left only 60-mm and 80-mm mortars to serve the ARVN during the siege. By comparison, the NVA had enough heavy artillery, including many captured pieces, to lay down up to 1,000 rounds per day. Air power attempted to silence these weapons when they could spot them, but the enemy moved their weapons constantly and hid them in bunkers or under camouflage when in use to keep the allies guessing at their locations.

With the city surrounded by heavy artillery, conditions deteriorated rapidly. On two occasions, the NVA shelled refugees attempting to flee the city. Food became scarce, forcing even the American advisers to subsist on brackish water, canned fish, and rice. When the NVA shelled the city hospital on 13 April, resulting in the death of most of its 300 patients, medical treatment also became problematic. Unable to be removed by medevac because of intense antiaircraft fire, ARVN troops watched ordinary flesh wounds fester and turn gangrenous. Innumerable diseases, including cholera, spread among the defenders hunkered down in their bunkers during relentless twenty-four-hour shelling. At one point, Air Force transports had to drop lime on mass graves in a futile attempt to stem the spread of disease.[13]

On 11 May at 0030, the North began its final push against An Loc. More than 8,000 rounds of artillery slammed into the town that day. An Army adviser on the scene said "it sounded like somebody was popping popcorn—shaking it just all over the city." At 0430, the North Vietnamese shelling stopped, but, inexplicably, no assault ensued; instead, U.S. and South Vietnamese tactical jets and U.S. Army Cobras ferociously attacked North Vietnamese positions. Finally, at 0500, forty NVA tanks and numerous infantry struck An Loc from all sides. The U.S. advisers responded by scheduling B-52 strikes every fifty-five minutes beginning at 0530. ARVN troops then began tearing apart the enemy tanks with their M-72 LAWs, destroying seven of these behemoths early in the fight. Army Cobras equipped with 2.75-inch rockets took down four more. From above, the forward air controllers continued directing sorties against NVA positions, at one point immobilizing a 500-man battalion with a single "daisy cutter"—a 750-pound bomb with a fuse extender that detonates just prior to hitting the ground, thereby dramatically increasing the weapon's blast radius. In another instance, a flight of four F-4s put twenty-two out of twenty-eight bombs on an enemy compound, killing 150 enemy troops in the process. To the west, AC-130 Specter gunships rained shells from their 105-mm howitzers on Communist troops hiding in bunkers.[14]

Extremely poor weather kept tactical aviation (TACAIR) away from the battlefield during the night of 12–13 May, a factor that convinced the Communist forces to make one last-ditch effort to take the city. Fortunately, the Air Force had enough B-52 assets available to launch six Arc Light strikes on the attacking forces, killing several tanks and numerous infantry and effectively blunting this final thrust. During this night, the Air Force, in desperation, also utilized one of its most secret weapons of the war—a 15,000-pound bomb called BLU-82.[15] The weapon descended by parachute and detonated just above the ground, producing overpressures of 1,000 pounds per square inch and disintegrating everything within hundreds of yards. During the invasion of Cambodia in 1970, it was used to clear landing zones for ARVN assault troops. During the night of 12–13 May, the Air Force dropped a BLU-82 from a C-130 transport just to the south of An Loc, creating a mammoth explosion.[16]

The Air Force not only dropped a BLU-82 that night but also used A-37s to drop smaller CBU-55 fuel air explosives. Each CBU-55 contained three BLU-73 bomblets. These bomblets envelop a target in a cloud of ethylene oxide about fifty feet in diameter and ten feet thick before exploding with a force of about 10 atmospheric pressures at a speed of Mach 6 (similar to the blast of three 500-pound bombs). Fuel air explosives render most people dead in the blast zone even if they are in bunkers, buildings, vehicle shelters, or other protected spaces.[17]

Enemy shelling remained heavy for the next three days, and NVA forces attacked an ARVN relief convoy, slowly moving up Highway 13 from Saigon. Fortunately, with the arrival of the *Saratoga* on Dixie Station and Marine Aircraft Group 12 at Bien Hoa, additional air resources began flying over MR III early in May. The Marine pilots, in particular, worked extremely well with their Air Force counterparts to become experts in the art of close-air support. For the most part lacking combat experience when they arrived in Vietnam, the Marines received their orientation from Air Force A-37 pilots from the 8th Special Operations Squadron, also based at Bien Hoa. Each newly arrived aviator flew one or more strike missions over An Loc in the right seat of an A-37 Dragonfly. Subsequently, flights were mixed with one USAF A-37 as lead and one Marine A-4 on the wing. This system quickly turned Marine Air Group 12 into a highly effective close air support unit.

In their first thirteen days at Bien Hoa, Marines flew 441 attack sorties. In June, they tripled that amount, flying over 1,300 sorties in MRs III and IV.[18] Most operations were from five to fifty miles from Bien Hoa, which meant ground crews at the base felt the detonations of Marine A-4 ordnance. This close proximity to the battle gave everyone an incentive to work extremely hard to defend An Loc.[19]

The Marines were not the only ones scrambling to save An Loc. The Air Force's 49th Wing received its orders to deploy to Takhli, Thailand, on 4 May and began flying missions against An Loc by 11 May. Members of the 49th flew 269 missions during their first nine days of combat. They would take off from Thailand, bomb An Loc, refuel and rearm at Bien Hoa, and then hit An Loc again before heading back to Thailand. Hundreds of other Air Force pilots emergency deployed with separate squadrons or as individual replacement pilots.

With the exception of the FACs, no group of U.S. or Vietnamese Air Force pilots, however, worked harder than the Vietnamese and American A-37 pilots. A light Cessna jet designed as a trainer, but then modified for use as a close air support plane, the A-37 carried six 500-pound bombs or a variety of rockets and bombs. The A-37 could operate from forward runways and in poor weather. Its tight turning capability and superior stability made it nearly as accurate as laser-guided, bomb-carrying F-4s, although its slow speed made it much more vulnerable to ground fire than the fast movers. Its 7.62 minigun, capable of firing 6,000 rounds per minute, also made the A-37 a great strafing weapon at low altitudes. Sortie for sortie, A-37 crews destroyed more tanks than any other aircraft. Overall, the 8th Special Operations Squadron flew so many missions during An Loc that by the end of the campaign, only six of its original twenty aircraft were flyable.

At 1980 hours on 16 May, the NVA assault that began on 11 May finally ground to a stop. Although smaller ground attacks as well as shelling would continue for many weeks to come, no subsequent major assaults would be launched against An Loc, and the ARVN troops could begin the process of slowly recovering lost ground. By 12 June, the ARVN had driven the last of the NVA out of the city and could finally begin evacuating the 1,000 ARVN wounded trapped in the city. On 18 June, Lieutenant General Nguyen Van Minh, the ARVN commander of MR III, declared the siege over. Enemy forces would remain active in the region for months, but the direct NVA threat to An Loc was over.

In the end, U.S. air power proved decisive during the Easter Offensive. During the battles of An Loc, Kontum, and to some extent Quang Tri, the ARVN depended almost exclusively on air strikes as a substitute for the heavy artillery abandoned or destroyed in the Communist offensive. Without air power, the South Vietnamese would have been defeated on every front (as would happen three years later when American air power was no longer available). Air power destroyed 459 tanks and half of the estimated 100,000 NVA and Viet Cong soldiers killed.

Although the Air Force ultimately delivered larger numbers of tactical air sorties during the crisis, the Navy and Marine Corps made a vital contribution, especially at the onset of the invasion, when few Air Force assets were available in Southeast Asia to rapidly respond to the changing tactical environment. Overall, the Navy and Marines flew nearly as many tactical sorties in South Vietnam as a whole in April as did the Air Force: roughly 5,376, versus 5,564 for the Air Force. Thereafter, as more and more Air Force reinforcements began to arrive from the United States, the percentage of Navy and Marine TACAIR sorties flown in South Vietnam dropped to between 28 and 44 percent of the overall effort.[20]

Beyond the number of sorties flown, when the issue of force augmentation is examined, the Navy and Marine Corps effort compares even more favorably with that of the Air Force. Between 1 January and 5 May 1972, the Navy sent three additional carriers, each with between six and eight squadrons of aircraft plus various aircraft detachments (helicopters, patrol, COD); sixteen additional destroyers; and nine service ships to Southeast Asia. The Marines sent three F-4 squadrons (39 aircraft). By comparison, the Air Force augmented its force with 11 additional fighter squadrons plus 94 B-52s, 54 KC-135s, and 7 EB-66s.[21] Navy augmentation assets also arrived much faster than those of the Air Force. By 8 April, the Navy had doubled the number of fighter and attack aircraft operating in the Gulf of Tonkin as well as the number of missions flown. The Air Force, by contrast, managed to augment its force by only 10 percent during the same critical period, with no significant increase in sortie levels. During the next stage of the invasion, between 8 and 20 April, the Navy increased its sortie count from 240 per day to more than 300. The USAF effort did not show any significant increase until after 15 April, when the Air Force daily sortie level surged dramatically from 205 per day to more than 400.[22] This is not to imply that individual Air Force pilots did not work extremely hard during the initial weeks of the invasion but, rather, that the service as a whole did not respond to the crisis nearly as quickly and forcefully as did the Navy.

19

Linebacker I

FROM 1968 UNTIL APRIL 1972, targets in North Vietnam had for the most part been off-limits to American air power. The Easter Offensive, of course, changed the rules of the game considerably. It gave President Nixon the moral authority to ease bombing restrictions enacted by President Johnson in 1968 and finally take the war to the enemy.

During April, Navy and Air Force pilots flew more than 2,000 tactical strikes against North Vietnam, the bulk of which hit supply vehicles in the panhandle region in a campaign called Freedom Train. Additionally, Air Force B-52s bombed a handful of targets in North Vietnam for the first time in the war during the same period, including the Vinh oil tank farm, the Bai Thuong airfield, and the warehouses at Thanh Hoa. However, the desperate need for close air support sorties in the South and the paucity of Air Force resources in Southeast Asia precluded a major offensive against the North until 9 May. It was on this date that President Nixon ordered the mining of Haiphong harbor, and one day later, the start of the Linebacker I bombing offensive. Nixon wrote in his diary that day: "I cannot emphasize too strongly that I have determined that we should go for broke. Our words will help some. But our actions in the next few days will speak infinitely louder than our words."[1]

Linebacker I had three major objectives: (1) to destroy military supplies within the borders of North Vietnam; (2) to isolate North Vietnam from outside suppliers; and (3) to stop the flow of supplies to the troops in the South. In short, highways, bridges, warehouses, fuel storage areas, barracks, and power plants were the main targets of the campaign. What made this campaign different from Rolling Thunder was that local commanders had much more authority to choose targets and the tactics and weapons most appropriate to destroy them. Second, technological advances in precision-guided munitions (PGMs) and navigation systems made it possible to attack targets closer to civilian populations without the threat of widespread collateral damage.

Linebacker began on 10 May with a joint Navy–Air Force attack on the Paul Doumer Railroad Bridge (Long Bien Bridge) in Hanoi. During the next few days, Air Force and Navy aircraft destroyed additional bridges along the northeast railroads and highways leading into China using PGMs for the most part. Many of these bridges spanned gorges in the steep Annamite Mountains and could not be repaired quickly. As supplies stacked up near broken bridges, American air power pummeled these targets with less expensive conventional munitions. By the end of June, more than 400 bridges were inoperable, including the venerable Thanh Hoa and Doumer Bridges.

Once the bridges were down, the campaign shifted to POL (petroleum, oil, and lubricants), power-generating plants, military barracks, and air defense targets. Again, PGMs improved the effectiveness of this campaign because they allowed American planes to bomb targets within densely populated areas, targets that had been strictly off-limits during the earlier Rolling Thunder operation. The most effective weapons were the Air Force's PAVE KNIFE laser-guided bombs (LGBs), which worked by following a laser beam to a target. In older systems, the F-4, after releasing an LGB, had to fly straight forward while beaming a laser at a target. The bomb would then follow this laser beam to the target. The problem with this older system was that the aircraft beaming the laser (known as the designator) was vulnerable to antiaircraft fire from the time the LGB was released until its impact on the target. The PAVE KNIFE bomb, by comparison, hung its laser on an independently swiveling gimbal, thereby allowing the designator to engage in evasive maneuvers during an attack.[2]

Although the Air Force dropped the vast majority of the PGMs expended during Linebacker I and as a result downed most of the vital targets of the campaign, it ironically did not fly the most sorties. As in the case of the Easter Offensive, naval air contributed mightily to the campaign, especially during the first stages: Navy tactical aircraft flew twice as many sorties during Linebacker I's first three months of the campaign as did their Air Force equivalents. Overall, between 1 April and 1 August 1972, Navy strike planes destroyed 185 bridges, 527 railroad cars, 666 trucks, and 973 watercraft, compared with 99, 30, 494, and 18, respectively, for the Air Force. In almost every category of bombing, the Navy claimed the destruction of more targets than the Air Force during Linebacker I.[3] Moreover, the Navy mined all the significant North Vietnamese harbors and reseeded these harbors as necessary during the Linebacker I period—perhaps the most critical component of the entire operation, next to the expanded use of PGMs. Navy A-6s also were the principal night bombers of the campaign.[4] Overall, the Navy generated 66 percent of the sorties in North Vietnam during Linebacker I and 85 percent of the sorties in and around Route Package 6 (the Hanoi-Haiphong region). The Air Force, by comparison, flew fewer sorties, but it did provide America with many vital capabilities during Linebacker I, such as forward air control, laser-guided strikes, extremely long-range search and rescue, and heavy bombing. That said, the Navy surpassed it in one critical area: the ability to get to a battle "first with the most." In the end, this force projection capability proved much more vital to the air-land battle in 1972 than even the LGB.

By June, the combination of harbor mining, close air support, and Linebacker interdiction attacks had weakened North Vietnam's forces in the South to such an extent that a ground victory in 1972 for the North was no longer a threat. By September, a peace agreement acceptable to both sides was beginning to take shape. Therefore, on 23 October, President Nixon ended Linebacker I by ordering a bombing halt north of the twentieth parallel. Although it would take two more months and another bombing campaign to get a peace accord signed, most air power historians still perceive Linebacker I as a major success because, for the most part, it achieved its objectives.

Linebacker I succeeded where Rolling Thunder failed for a number of reasons. First, PGMs allowed planners to knock out targets that previously had been off-limits or difficult to hit. Second, wing- and squadron-level commanders also had much more latitude to choose targets, tactics, and weapons than they did during the Rolling Thunder campaign. Third, the conventional nature of the Easter Offensive meant that the North Vietnamese Army was much more vulnerable to a conventional interdiction campaign than it had been in the past: the fourteen divisions in the South required 1,000 tons of supplies a day to sustain the offensive. Finally, President Nixon utilized air power in a much more decisive manner than his predecessor. Whereas President Johnson constantly fretted over the prospect of a Chinese or Soviet intervention, the political ramifications of using too much force against North Vietnam, and his need to achieve political consensus among his advisers, Nixon did not worry about upsetting the political Left with his bombing or achieving consensus within his staff. His only political concerns were with the Republican Right—a voting block that generally favored a more aggressive approach to the war. Moreover, the Sino-Soviet split effectively ended the serious prospects of an intervention by either power. In short, Nixon had much more freedom of action than Johnson and, more important, was not afraid to exercise this freedom. On the eve of the Linebacker campaign, he wrote that the enemy "has gone over the brink and so have we. We have the power to destroy his war-making capacity. The only question is whether we have the will to use that power. What distinguishes me from Johnson is that I have the will in spades."[5] Indeed, Linebacker, Pocket Money, and, ultimately, Line-backer II proved beyond a doubt that there was truth in those words.

THE LINEBACKER BRIDGE CAMPAIGN

Throughout Linebacker I, bridges were the primary targets. For the North Vietnamese, the country's 1,300-mile rail net represented the most effective means of transporting military supplies from China and Haiphong and thence to the battlefields in the South. All the supplies coming into Hanoi by rail passed over the Paul Doumer Bridge; those moving southward crossed the Thanh Hoa Bridge. Both bridges served truck, bike, and foot traffic as well.

The Paul Doumer Bridge, named after the nineteenth-century French governor-general responsible for constructing most of Viet-nam's railroads, served as the main rail entry into Hanoi for lines coming from Haiphong, Kep, Thai Nguyen, and Dong Dang. All rail traffic coming from China or Haiphong had to pass over this 5,532-foot steel bridge, the longest in Vietnam, to get to Hanoi. The great length of the structure made it vulnerable to air attack despite the fact that it was well defended by AAA and SAMs. However, President Johnson's bombing restrictions placed it off-limits until the summer of 1967, when it finally showed up on the Rolling Thunder target list.

A thirty-six-plane strike from the Air Force's 355th Wing first struck the bridge on 11 August 1967. The planes dropped ninety-four tons of bombs, destroying one rail span and two highway spans on the north-east side of the structure. Two planes were damaged, but no crews were lost. As would so often be the case with bridges, the resourceful North Vietnamese quickly repaired the damage. Poor weather delayed a follow-on raid until 25 October, when twenty-one Air Force F-105s dropped another sixty-three tons of bombs on the bridge, rendering it again unusable until 20 November 1967. On 14 and 18 December, the Air Force launched its last raids on the bridge until 1972. The first raid took out two spans and damaged two others; the second destroyed three more spans and damaged one. This time the North Vietnamese opted not to begin repairs on the structure until the bombing halt in March 1968. Rail goods had to be transported across the Red River by ferry until 14 April, when a makeshift pontoon bridge finally went up. Overall, 177 sorties, carrying 380 tons of ordnance, were flown by the Air Force against the Doumer Bridge during the 1967–68 period, but rail traffic was delayed only until April 1968.[6]

The bombing halt of March 1968 curtailed additional bombing until the first day of Linebacker, 10 May 1972. On the morning of that day, sixteen F-4s from the Air Force's 8th Tactical Fighter Wing dropped twenty-two laser-guided bombs and seven electro-optical guided bombs (EOGBs) against the target. None of the 2,000-pound TV-guided EOGBs hit the bridge, but twelve of the LGBs did, damaging it severely. The next day, four F-4s from the same wing conducted a follow-on raid on the Doumer Bridge with two 3,000-pound LGBs and six 2,000-pound dumb bombs. This small strike group brought down three spans with the LGBs. What had taken 177 sorties and 380 tons of bombs to accomplish in 1967–68 had been accomplished in just 20 sorties with precision-guided munitions in 1972.[7]

The story of the Thanh Hoa Bridge is lengthier and more complex than that of the Doumer Bridge because it was situated in an area with fewer bombing restrictions than the Hanoi-Haiphong region and therefore was bombed for a much longer period than its longer cousin. The Thanh Hoa Bridge was also the strongest bridge in Vietnam. Despite its being subjected to numerous bombing raids during the course of the war, no span of the bridge ever fell until 1972, when the Air Force finally knocked one down with a 3,000-pound LGB.

Located three miles north of the town by the same name, the Thanh Hoa Bridge spanned the Song Ma at a point where the river ran rapidly and cut through a deep gorge. During the First Indochina War, Viet Minh guerrillas blew up the original nineteenth-century bridge in 1945 by loading two locomotives with explosives and running them together in the middle of the bridge. After the war in 1957, with help from Chinese technicians, the North Vietnamese began rebuilding the bridge.

Initially, work went slowly, but in 1961 the Hanoi regime, under pressure to keep the Viet Cong in the South supplied, sped up work. Under orders to work around-the-clock, the builders finished the bridge in 1964. Ho Chi Minh himself presided over the dedication of a new bridge aptly named the "Dragon's Jaw."

North Vietnam invested much effort in making this new bridge as strong as possible. The new structure—540 feet long, 56 feet wide, and 50 feet above the river—consisted of two steel thru-truss spans, which rested in the center on a massive reinforced concrete pier, 16 feet in diameter, and on concrete abutments at both ends. Hills on both sides of the river provided solid bracing for the structure. Between 1965 and 1972, eight concrete piers were added near the approaches to give additional resistance to bomb damage. A one-meter-gauge single-rail track ran down the 12-foot center of the bridge, and 22-foot wide concrete highways were cantilevered on each side. The resulting bridge would prove to be one of the most formidable targets in the history of American air power.[8]

The Air Force launched its first raid against the Dragon's Jaw on 3 April 1965. The strike that day consisted of 79 aircraft: 46 F-105s, 21 F-100s, 2 RF-101s, and 10 KC-135 tankers. Sixteen of the 46 F-105s were loaded with 250-pound Bullpup missiles, a somewhat primitive radio-guided missile; the remainder of the strike carried standard 750-pound iron bombs. The missile-bearing F-105 "Thunderchiefs" and half of the other attack planes struck the bridge; the other aircraft provided flak suppression. Lieutenant Colonel Robinson Risner, a legendary Korean War ace, led the strike. His carefully planned strike called for the flak-suppression F-100s to fly in first, followed by the Bullpup carrying Thunderchiefs. Because each Thunderchief carried two missiles, they had to make two passes over the heavily defended target. Risner made the first pass through a thick haze, and others followed shortly thereafter. Despite achieving several direct hits, the Bullpups merely charred the massive bridge structure. The bomb carriers did not do much better. The only significant damage achieved by the ten dozen 750-pounders dropped was on the roadway on the south side of the bridge. In exchange for these meager results, the Air Force lost an F-100 flak suppressor and RF-101 reconnaissance plane to antiaircraft fire. Furthermore, Risner himself, who hit the bridge on his second pass, took a serious hit in the process, forcing him to battle a fuel leak and a smoke-filled cockpit as he nursed his plane back to Danang.[9]

The next day, Risner was back in the saddle again, leading a follow-on strike against the bridge. This time, forty-eight F-105s attacked the bridge, each one carrying eight 750-pound bombs. The strike force inflicted maximum damage with the ordnance carried, hitting the bridge at least 300 times. The northern and southern highways were heavily cratered, several truss beams were blown away, and the eastern span was sagging; nevertheless, the bridge still spanned the river. The North Vietnamese antiaircraft gunners downed a flight leader, Captain Carlyle "Smitty" Harris. Additionally, two MiG-17s came out of the clouds and ambushed another two F-105s as they approached the target area, resulting in the loss of two aircraft and the deaths of two pilots, Major Frank Bennett and Captain James Magnusson.[10]

The Air Force attacked the bridge twice more in May 1965, closing the structure temporarily in both cases but failing to knock it down. By the end of that month, U.S. planes had attacked twenty-seven North Vietnamese bridges and destroyed all but one, the notorious Dragon's Jaw. Bullpup missiles and 750-pound bombs proved adequate to down the French-constructed bridges, but the one indigenously produced bridge would not fall.

In June, the burden of attacking the Dragon's Jaw fell to the Navy. During the next twelve months, Navy aircraft hit the bridge twenty-four times with a total of sixty-five aircraft, each flying in small two- to four-plane strike forces. These planes dropped 128 tons of ordnance on Thanh Hoa and destroyed both concrete highways that rested on cantilevers protruding from the side of the bridge. The bridge itself, though, withstood the holocaust. The task of placing a bomb on a 16-foot-wide, 500-foot-long steel bridge from an aircraft traveling at over 500 mph through a barrage of AAA became nearly impossible, even for the Navy's best. The Navy turned the Thanh Hoa area into a moonscape, but still the bridge remained.

Desperate for results, the Air Force came up with a bold plan in September 1965. The plan, named Project Caroline Moon, called for a C-130 to drop a mass-focusing, high-explosive mine upstream from the bridge. The mine, in its final configuration, weighed 5,000 pounds and resembled a large pancake 8 feet in diameter and 2.5 feet thick. This design caused the explosion to focus upward as the mine passed under the bridge. On the night of 30–31 May, a C-130 piloted by Air Force Major Richard Remers took off from Danang and, despite heavy ground fire, dropped five of these mines near the bridge. Although four of the five mines eventually detonated, there was little damage to the bridge.

During the remainder of 1966, the Navy continued bombing the bridge, scheduling eleven attacks against the target. On 23 September, twenty-two Navy attack planes dropped 57 tons of ordnance on Thanh Hoa, rendering it temporarily unserviceable and destroying eighty rail cars and 1,678 tons of fuel in the process. In December, reconnaissance planes revealed increased repair activity at the bridge, and several more strikes were scheduled. None succeeded. In January, however, the Navy opted to employ one of its most modern weapons against the target: the Walleye EOGB. The Walleye was a free-fall glide bomb with a 1,000-pound warhead that had a TV in the nose. To operate the system, the pilot identified a target from a monitor in his cockpit, lined up his crosshairs with a preselected, high-contrast aim point, and launched the bomb. The bomb then tracked and hit the aim point designated by the pilot with his scope.

On 12 March 1967, three A-4s from VA-212 carrying one Walleye apiece hit Thanh Hoa. All three bombs impacted on the bridge within five feet of each other on an aim point chosen as one of the most vulnerable points of the bridge by Army demolition experts. Nevertheless, Thanh Hoa endured. Weather prevented further strikes until late April, but thereafter the Navy again focused tremendous effort on the bridge. From April to September 1967, Navy aircraft flew ninety-seven sorties and dropped 215 tons of bombs on the bridge, but to little avail. Poor weather once again delayed further strikes until late January 1968.

Rolling Thunder's finale against the Dragon's Jaw occurred on 28 January 1968. On this day, Navy and Air Force fighters dropped three tons of bombs on the hapless structure, about three bombs every 4.5 minutes during a 3.5-hour attack. The southern approach to the bridge received severe damage, as did the rail bed, but the bridge remained standing and would soon be repaired. Monsoon weather followed by Johnson's bombing halt effectively ended the first round of attacks, and new attacks would not commence until the halt was lifted by Nixon in 1972. Overall, eleven American aircraft were lost in three years of fruitless strikes against Thanh Hoa.[11]

The first opportunity for resumed attacks came on 27 April 1972—just days after the start of the Easter Offensive. Twelve Air Force F-4s from the 8th Tactical Fighter Wing, half carrying 2,000-pound LGBs and the other half, 2,000-pound EOGBs, took off from Ubon and proceeded to Thanh Hoa. Heavy clouds precluded the use of the LGBs, but five TV-guided bombs found their target, closing the bridge but failing to knock down a span. Although AAA and SAM fire was as intense as during any of the previous raids on the bridge, improved electronic countermeasures as well as chaff (thin strips of aluminum dropped at high altitude, designed to interfere with radar) helped the strike escape unscathed.[12]

The Air Force hit the Thanh Hoa Bridge again on 13 May. This time, nine 3,000-pound and fifteen 2,000-pound LGBs would be carried in this fourteen-plane strike. The weather proved excellent and most of the LGBs found their mark. Poststrike reconnaissance revealed two spans down and damage so severe that rail traffic would not be able to use the structure for several months. What the Air Force and Navy had failed to accomplish during three years of Rolling Thunder operations had finally been completed with a handful of aircraft carrying precision-guided munitions.

Although the bridge was taken out of action on 13 May, the bombing campaign against it did not end on that date. To hinder repair efforts, the Air Force flew two more missions against the target, and the Navy flew eleven, before Nixon finally ended Linebacker I on 23 October. One of the most significant of these latter missions was flown on 6 October by Leighton Smith, an A-7 pilot from the carrier *America*.[13]

20

Leighton Warren Smith
and the Fall of Thanh Hoa

LEIGHTON WARREN SMITH spent much of his youth in the environs of Mobile, Alabama. The son of a delivery truck driver with a local linen service, Smith was born at the end of the Great Depression (1939) and grew up living near or below the poverty line. Between Leighton's sixth- and seventh-grade years, his father quit the linen business and tried to start a farm in Union Church, Alabama. The family moved into a five-room shack with no plumbing, and Leighton shared a room with his three sisters. As he recalled, "My sisters and I slept in a room that was smaller than my walk-in closet right now. We had double-decker beds on either side, and there was just enough room between the double-decker beds to get up and get out." During these years, the family had a truck farm on which they tried to grow crops such as watermelon, cantaloupe, okra, and beans; unfortunately, Alabama experienced three extremely dry years during this period, forcing the Smiths to switch to cotton and corn. "I hoed a forty-acre cotton field because we couldn't afford to hire anybody else to come and do it."[1]

Despite his impoverished beginnings, Leighton Warren Smith would eventually win admission to the United States Naval Academy, serve in the Navy for thirty-four years, and ultimately end his career as a four-star admiral in charge of allied forces in southern Europe during the height of America's air war over Bosnia. These achievements, however, did not come easily for young Leighton Smith.

A "terrible" student, Smith barely graduated from Murphy High School in Mobile. Seeking to give him a better education than was offered by the rural schools, his parents sent him to Mobile for high school. He would attend school during the week and go back to the farm on weekends to toil in the fields. This schedule did not give Smith much opportunity to apply himself academically; besides that, Smith really was not interested in studying. The assistant principal of the school admitted to his aunt that Smith "was the only person I've ever known that talked his way through high school."

Where Smith excelled was in his dealings with people. He managed the stage crew for school drama productions and, during his senior year, ran the school supplies store. As a result of these extracurricular activities, the school's principal, Samuel B. Hodges, managed to secure a one-year tuition scholarship to the University of Alabama for him. "That scholarship was worth $125 a semester, and I thought I had won the lottery when I got it."

Smith attended Alabama for a year in 1957–58 and then transferred to the Naval Academy. His route to Annapolis was nothing short of miraculous. His father, a social lion in the local community, managed to buttonhole the administrative assistant to Frank Boykin, U.S. representative to Alabama's First District from 1935 to 1963. Through conversations with this aide, a man named Alphonse Lucas, Smith's father learned that Boykin intended to make a Naval Academy appointment in February 1958. "It looked good. I'd never been up there and didn't know much about it, and I didn't know a damn thing about the Navy. I did know that I was not going to survive at the University of Alabama, because I didn't think my father could afford to keep me there."

Despite the fact that his family had no money, they had a good name in Mobile, and more than sixty people wrote letters of recommendation for Smith. "There were a lot of people who were willing to write a letter for me. Not because I was academically inclined, but because I worked hard." Another factor that contributed to his admission to Annapolis was his uncle, Admiral Harold Page Smith, the recently appointed chief of Navy personnel. Admiral Smith, Naval Academy class of 1924, received a Navy Cross as a destroyer commander during World War II.[2] After the war, H. P. advanced rapidly in the service, holding a number of important staff positions and commanding the battleship *Missouri* in 1950–51. As chief of personnel in 1958, Admiral Smith could essentially guarantee his nephew admission to the Naval Academy as long as Leighton possessed a congressional nomination. "I have no doubt that my uncle was instrumental in getting Frank Boykin to give me that appointment. I ended up getting the principal appointment, which surprised us all."

Smith stayed with his uncle in Washington for a few days before entering the academy in June 1958. H. P. took Smith out for his first lobster on the first night in town, and Leighton's aunt and her mother drove him to Annapolis two days later. "I got out of that car, and they drove off, and I was standing there looking at this huge monstrosity of a building called Bancroft Hall, and the first thought that came to my mind is, 'What the hell am I doing here?'"

From that point onward, Smith's sole goal was survival. He later recalled, "My English professor warned me before leaving Alabama that I would never make it through the academy because I couldn't write." Smith, who never got far beyond algebra in high school, also did not have adequate preparation for his plebe math class. "During plebe summer, we went through about three years of math in about four weeks. I was completely and totally lost."

By the middle of his first semester, Smith's academics had deteriorated to such an extent that he received a summons from the commandant of cadets, Captain William Floyd Bringle. A 1937 USNA graduate, Bringle had earned a Navy Cross in World War II commanding a fighter-bomber squadron during the invasion of southern France. After the war, he rotated between staff and fleet assignments, finally ending up at the academy as commandant of cadets in 1958. During the Vietnam War, Bringle (promoted to admiral in 1964) would go on to command the Seventh Fleet from November 1967 to March 1970 and then the Naval Air Forces, Pacific, from March 1970 to May 1971.[3]

As Smith marched into Bringle's office in the fall of 1958, he was immediately impressed with the captain:

> He had a desk about an acre big. There was an American flag on one side, the Navy flag on the other side. He was sitting there in his service dress blues. He had ribbons that went all the way up to his shoulder, topped by gold wings, and just below that the Navy Cross. He had hair that went about six different directions, and it was gray, and his teeth looked like somebody had tried to pull them out and didn't quite succeed. He had a face that looked like about a twenty-year-old football. He was a rugged-looking man. He had steel blue eyes.

Bringle told Smith to improve his grades in ten days or else face another office counseling session.

As Smith walked away, the first thing he realized was that he never wanted to see that office again. He blamed himself entirely for his predicament, and although his parents promised to take him back with open arms if he did not make it at the academy, Smith knew that if he failed, he "had nothing to go home to."

For the rest of the year, Smith worked like a mule. He visited all his instructors regularly, asked his classmates for help, and offered to make up bad work. Through sheer perseverance, Smith managed to graduate.

> I didn't realize it at the time, but it became apparent to me later, that I had just experienced the most incredible lesson in leadership that I would ever experience: a Navy captain, who was in charge of the entire day-to-day operations of the Naval Academy, took the time to reach down deep into that organization and drag an individual up who was having trouble and try to instill in that individual a little bit of self-discipline and self-confidence. He knew my uncle, obviously, but I felt he would have done this for anyone in my predicament regardless of who his relatives were.

After his fateful meeting, Smith decided he just could not fail. He never flunked a course from then on.

In addition to Bringle, another guiding light during Smith's academy years was his girlfriend, Dorothy "Dotty" McDowell. Smith met her serendipitously at the academy museum one lonely Saturday afternoon during his plebe summer. Dotty, from Columbia, South Carolina, was visiting a friend who had a job selling postcards at the museum. Her friend had a date on that Saturday, so Dotty agreed to fill in for her. "I didn't have anything else to do that day," recalled Leighton, "so I decided to go to the museum. I walked in, and I saw this tall brunette, with big brown eyes, and I went over and said something, and she made some comments to me. I saw her the next day, which was a Sunday. You know, we couldn't walk around. I met her in the library. We weren't allowed to see women, so I managed to talk her into going to the library. We sat and chatted for a bit, and then we corresponded for the entire time I was at the Naval Academy." Smith visited Dotty several times during holidays, and the two eventually married two weeks after graduation in June 1962. When Smith ultimately made admiral many years later, he told his wife, "There are so many people in my class from the Naval Academy that could and should be standing here, and the only reason I'm here, and not them, is because you were willing to put up with the sacrifices and help me get here."

The first sacrifice Dotty made involved managing seemingly endless moves during Smith's peripatetic early career. Between 1962 and 1963, the Smiths moved four times. One of the most disruptive moves occurred just between basic and advanced flight training. After graduating from basic flight training at Pensacola in August 1963, Smith went to Kingsville, Texas, to train in the A-4 and then spent a year at Glynco, Georgia, at the air-intercept school. While at Glynco, for the first time in his career, Smith had the opportunity to see an F-4 Phantom do a high-performance takeoff. The pilot "got on the inter-runway and cranked that F-4 Phantom up to full, then he tapped the burners and started rolling down that runway, and at about 4,000 feet he got airborne. He must have been going about 300 knots by the time he got to the end of the runway, pulled back on the stick, and just disappeared out of sight, straight up. We were really, really impressed. I mean, that was something else."

About a week later, Smith received a letter from Mike Morris, the commander of an F-4 replacement air group, asking him whether he would like to become a fighter pilot and join his squadron. Morris had been an aide to Smith's uncle, and there was little Mike would not do for the Smith family. Leighton rejected the offer despite how much he loved the Phantom. "I said that I very much appreciated his kind offer, but if I went down to Key West and began flying F-4s, I would be Page Smith's nephew. If I went someplace else I would be Leighton Smith, and I would rather be Leighton Smith than Page Smith's nephew. So thank you very much, and I went to A-4s."

In February 1964, Smith joined VA-44, an attack squadron based in Oceana, Virginia. On his first day, the skipper sat him and three other new pilots down for an orientation brief. "You know, gentlemen, we're getting ready to go on deployment, and it's very, very likely that one of the three of you will not survive that deployment." This was a peacetime Mediterranean deployment. "We each kind of looked at each other and thought, 'Well, gee, I'm sorry it's going to be you,' and sure enough two weeks later, Mike Hinchman was dead."

Mike's death brought home to Smith just how dangerous his career path really was. On the day he died, Mike flew out with the skipper on a hazy day for a lesson in air combat maneuvering and ended up flying into the ocean. "Nowadays, if you're in a dogfight or a hassle with another aircraft, 10,000 feet's the deck. At that altitude you knock it off. In those days I don't recall there being a limit placed on how low you could fly. What happened is that the skipper of the airplane was down low and Mike was concentrating on his leader, and he didn't know how low he was, and he just flat flew into the water."

Smith made several Mediterranean cruises with VA-44 and later VA-81 before volunteering for a war assignment with a West Coast unit. Smith made two deployments to Vietnam with the VA-22, "The Fighting Red Cocks": one on *Coral Sea* (July 1966–February 1967) and another on board *Ranger* (November 1967–May 1968). The experience of war frightened Smith during his initial tour: "I was brand-new, and it was not a whole lot of fun being out there."

The Navy struggled during this period to deal with new defenses being deployed by the Vietnamese—especially the SAM. As Smith recalled, "We didn't have any confidence in those days in electronic countermeasures. The feeling was that if they shot a SAM at you, there was a pretty good chance it was going to get you, so we would head for the deck." Smith lost many friends to SAMs during his first tour, but the most devastating loss by far was that of one of his wingmen, Bill Arnold. As Smith described it, "We went out on a very cloudy day, in an area we probably should not have been operating in, and the two of us did a maneuver that was not authorized, and I made it and he didn't." The two planes hit some authorized targets on a beach but utilized an unauthorized method of delivery. "We pulled up and over some overcast to dive-bomb the target. I had practiced this maneuver in the Med, but Bill was less familiar with it. I made it, but Bill just disappeared. I went back and looked for him. I saw no trace of any wreckage. I tried to tank and go back but was ordered to return to the ship." *Coral Sea* launched a rescue to try and recover Bill, but it was unsuccessful.

Smith flew approximately seventy missions during each cruise. During this time, the Fighting Cocks hit the Thanh Hoa Bridge twice. On 23 September, Commander William Harris, the Air Wing 2 commander, and later in 1972, the skipper of *Coral Sea,* led a nineteen-plane strike against the bridge, which rendered it temporarily unserviceable and destroyed multiple rail cars and POL storage tanks in the area. Air Wing 2 struck the bridge again on 28 January 1967 during the ship's second cruise. In this final attack before the bombing halt, Harris led his wing through a small hole in the broken cloud cover and executed a near-perfect bomb run. This attack and the other Air Force and Navy strikes during this day severely damaged the southern approach to the bridge as well as the rail bed, but the bridge itself remained standing and would soon be repaired.

Harris, interestingly enough, had this to say about one of the young pilots who participated in these early strikes:

> When you are an air wing commander, you kind of spot some of the young officers that you fly with. Snuffy stood out in a crowd. He vibrated with energy. He was a strong officer who would tell you what he thought when you flew with him whether you were a junior pilot or the wing commander. Years later after Smith had just received his fourth star and I had long since retired, I called him at his office in the Pentagon to congratulate him. His aide told me that he was talking to the CNO and asked if I wanted to leave a message. I left my name but requested he not bother Smith, who clearly had more important issues to deal with. A few minutes later, Smith personally returned the call with a warm, "Hey, CAG, glad to hear from you."

Smith always remained loyal to the people who contributed to his success, and they, in turn, remained loyal to him.[4]

After leaving VA-22, Smith became a naval plant representative at the Ling-Temco-Vought (LTV) plant in Dallas, Texas. "I was security officer and the assistant flight test officer, but what I really did was fly production test flights on all of the A-7 Corsairs." LTV designed the A-7 as a replacement for the A-4 Skyhawk. Based heavily on the F-8 Crusader design, the A-7 proved a highly successful attack aircraft during the final years of the Vietnam War. Built with armor and damage-resistant systems, the Corsair II featured a sophisticated Doppler navigation system, an APQ-126 multimode attack radar, a 20-mm cannon, and pylons capable of carrying up to 15,000 pounds of ordnance. The A-7 also could fly up to Mach .94 with its Allison TF41-A-2 engine with 15,000 pounds of thrust. Compared with the A-4, it was a technological marvel. Whereas the A-4 was a stripped-down jet with primitive radar and navigation systems, the A-7 possessed a full-blown bombing computer and an all-weather navigation system. In short, it stood a much better chance of successfully delivering ordnance to a target under almost any weather conditions.

Smith worked on the A-7 program for a year and then volunteered to go back to Vietnam in 1969. He later said, "I was denied the

An A-7E Corsair II of VA-146 comes in for recovery on the carrier *America* (CVA-66), 11 July 1970. The A-7 proved a highly successful attack aircraft during the final years of the Vietnam War. The A-7 also could fly up to Mach .94 and featured a sophisticated bombing computer and all-weather navigation system. (Courtesy of U.S. Navy)

opportunity to go back to a West Coast squadron, and I went to the secretary of the Navy and asked for an exception to the rule, and I was not given one. Then I was subsequently sent to an East Coast squadron, and the East Coast squadron ended up going back to Vietnam anyway, so I got my third trip."

Smith joined VA-82 Marauders as the operations officer in December 1970, did a Mediterranean cruise in 1971, and then deployed to Southeast Asia with the unit on 5 June 1972 on board *America*. On the day of the carrier's departure, several antiwar protesters attempted to block the ship's departure by paddling canoes in its path, but Coast Guard patrol boats and helicopters quickly cleared the area, and the ship departed as scheduled.

After a long transit, *America* finally went on station off the coast of South Vietnam on 8 July for its first line tour. Nine days later, on 17 July, VA-82's sister squadron, VA-86, lost two A-7s as a result of a premature ordnance detonation shortly after weapon release. Fortunately, both pilots, W. D. Yonke and D. K. Anderson, successfully bailed out of their planes and were rescued.

America moved north on 21 July for the final four days of its first line tour and continued operating on Yankee Station for all remaining line periods. On 10 September, VA-82 experienced its first operational loss. A SAM knocked Lieutenant (jg) Steve Musselman's A-7C out of the sky ten miles south of Hanoi. Steve Gerwe, Musselman's flight leader, called for help as soon as the event occurred.

Smith and another A-7C assigned to rescue combat air patrol (RESCAP) duty that day responded immediately.

> We got up and made one pass through the area, and we saw the wrecked aircraft. There was absolutely no way anybody was going to be able to get in there and get Musselman, because he was right down in the middle of a flat area—very close to the city as far as we could determine. There was a hell of a lot of ground fire. There were a lot of SAMs. There were MiGs in the air, but we didn't see any. So I had to make the decision that it would not be prudent to go in and try to pick up Musselman. As it turned out, he never came back out. The supposition is that he was shot while descending in his parachute.

The very next day, Marine Major Lee Lasseter and his RIO, Captain John Cummings, of VMFA-333, downed a MiG-21. Upon returning to *America,* though, their F-4J took a direct SAM hit, forcing the two men to eject. Moments later, their wingman took some 30-mm fire, causing heavy fuel loss and forcing these two aviators also to eject. Rescue helicopters recovered all four crewmen safely.

America suffered another operational loss two days later when a night ejection caused the death of F-4 RIO Michael Rice of VF-74; and four days later VA-35 lost an A-6 during night operations. No aviators were recovered, and the cause of that loss is unknown.

For Smith and other pilots in VA-82, the war looked bleak indeed by the middle of September. It frustrated Smith in particular that the Navy had now been in Vietnam for eight years and the war "hadn't changed a bit." The tactics and technology were a little different, but the targets were the same and people still lost their lives "for no good reason at all."

From left to right: Lieutenant (jg) Jim Brisster, Lieutenant (jg) Marv Baldwin, Commander Don Sumner, and Lieutenant Commander Leighton Smith. On 6 October 1972, these men knocked down the Thanh Hoa Bridge, one of North Vietnam's toughest bridges. (Courtesy of U.S. Navy, Leighton Warren Smith)

Morale improved significantly for the unit on 17 September, when the unit responded to a tactical emergency near Muc Do in South Vietnam. More than 300 North Vietnamese regulars had attacked an ARVN company of 120 men en masse. With minimal direction from Air Force forward air controllers in the area, VA-82 A-7s made extremely low passes over the area, destroying approximately twenty mortar positions in the process. When an Air Force OV-10 was shot down by antiaircraft fire, VA-82 continued its bombing, hitting targets within 100 meters of the downed aviators (Captains Richard Polling and Joseph Personett) until an Army helicopter swooped in to pick them up. The actions of VA-82 were credited with saving not only the Air Force FAC pilots but the entire ARVN unit as well.[5]

The turning point in the cruise for the unit, though, occurred on 6 October, the day Smith and his flight knocked down the Thanh Hoa Bridge. By early October, intelligence specialists believed that the bridge was again back in service, and on 4 October, A-7s from *America* were ordered to strike it. Smith, who participated in that raid, tells what happened: "When we rolled in, my weapon came off and it got hit by a

30-mm shell and basically disintegrated just as soon as it left my airplane, or at least became stupid."

On 6 October, a plan was set for a follow-up mission. It called for four Navy aircraft to hit one point on the bridge simultaneously with 8,000 pounds of high explosives while other aircraft from the wing launched a diversionary strike against the nearby rail yards. Smith and his wingman, Marv Baldwin, carried two "Fat Albert" 2,000-pound Walleyes, and the two other pilots, Don Sumner and Jim Brewster, carried standard 2,000-pound bombs.

> We rolled in simultaneously. Pulled the power back, popped the speed brakes, and we got our scopes locked-on to the bridge and I said, "Lock-on." Once everyone confirmed that they had locked-on, I counted "three, two, one, launch," and Marv and I both pickled them at the same time. Then Don and Jim popped up and they began their roll-in. They hit the bridge on the west side of the center piling and that's where it broke in half. In fact there was so much smoke and crap around there, we didn't know whether we'd hit it and done any damage or not. Later that afternoon, an RA-5 Vigilante came through and took a picture, and when we looked at them, we finally knew that the bridge was down for good.[6]

21

Linebacker II

"The Peace Is Falling Apart,
But At Least They're Bombing Again"

THE PEACE NEGOTIATIONS with the Vietnamese had reached an impasse in December 1972, compelling President Nixon to once again resort to force in his attempt to extricate America from the long and agonizing war. Tragically, the war had almost ended several months earlier, but stubbornness by the North and South Vietnamese negotiators ultimately dashed American hopes for an early settlement following the end of Linebacker I and set the stage for a new and more potent bombing campaign.

The first glimmer of hope that peace might have been at hand came at the end of October 1972. To the American negotiators in Paris, it appeared that Hanoi was close to signing a peace agreement acceptable to both sides. Le Duc Tho, the North Vietnamese negotiator, agreed to allow the Thieu government in South Vietnam to remain in place after a cease-fire and to release the American POWs. Although Henry Kissinger, the American negotiator, had several objections to the agreement (namely, its failure to establish the DMZ as a secure border), he nevertheless insisted on a bombing halt as a reward for the North Vietnamese willingness to make concessions and as a signal to the South that it was time to settle. As a consequence, President Nixon officially ended Linebacker I strikes north of the twentieth parallel on 23 October 1972.

Two days after the bombing halt, the North Vietnamese spoiled the goodwill achieved on the twenty-third by unilaterally broadcasting the tentative terms of the treaty on Hanoi Radio and accusing Kissinger of dragging his heels. In an attempt to salvage the situation, Kissinger went on national television on 26 October and stated, "We believe that peace is at hand. We believe that an agreement is within sight." Shortly after this announcement, President Nixon relaxed restrictions on B-52 strikes near the DMZ in an aim to let the North Vietnamese realize how serious he was about a settlement.

To no one's great surprise, talks ultimately stalled over concessions demanded by South Vietnam. In particular, President Thieu demanded that North Vietnam withdraw all its soldiers from South Vietnam. North Vietnam's chief negotiator, Le Duc Tho, naturally rejected this demand and further stalled the negotiations by refusing to consider protocols for implementing the basic agreement.

On 6 November, Nixon was reelected by a landslide. With this victory in hand, he now believed he could use B-52s in controversial ways without worrying about their impact on his political situation. At the same time, he understood that he had only about two months before Congress returned from recess and cut off his funding for the war, and so he felt compelled to act quickly and decisively.

By 23 November, intransigence by both the North and the South had convinced Nixon and Kissinger that only two options existed for the United States: to break off talks at the next meeting and dramatically step up the bombing while the United States reviewed its negotiating strategy in order to decide what kind of agreement it was prepared to accept with or without the South Vietnamese; or decide upon fallback positions on each of South Vietnam's major objections and present them as a final offer. Kissinger favored option one from the outset, and Nixon gradually came to realize that his national security adviser really could not negotiate effectively without the threat of additional bombing as a bargaining chip. He wrote in his diary on 24 November, "I recognize that this is a high-risk option, but it is one I am prepared to take if the only alternative is an agreement which is worse than that of October 8, and which does not clear up any of the ambiguities which we and Saigon are concerned about in the October 8 draft. Our aim will continue to be to end the war with honor."

By 13 December, it had become patently clear to the president that the North Vietnamese had no intention of reaching an agreement. Fed up, Nixon decided to go for broke and launch the B-52s. "We'll take the same heat for the big blows as the little blows," he remarked to Kissinger. "If we renew the bombing, it will have to be something new, and that means we will have to make the big decision to hit Hanoi and Haiphong with B-52s. Anything less will only make the enemy contemptuous."[1]

A massive bombing campaign against Hanoi and Haiphong, reasoned Nixon, not only might punish North Vietnam into agreeing to concessions but also might hurt the DRV's war-making capacity enough to give Thieu some vital breathing room in the South. He also hoped it would provide a clear signal to Hanoi that if it continued to intervene in the South after the treaty was signed, the United States might be willing to step in again with air power.[2]

On a more personal level, Nixon detested the idea of exiting the war "whimpering." He wanted the military and the country at large to depart with some degree of honor still intact. On 18 December, the day the bombs started falling on Hanoi, Nixon called Admiral Thomas Moorer, the JCS chairman, and said, "I don't want any more of this crap about the fact that we couldn't hit this target or that one. This is your chance to use military power effectively to win this war, and if you don't, I'll consider you responsible."[3]

Admiral Moorer and the JCS had been contemplating B-52 attacks against Hanoi and Haiphong since mid-1972, and the bombers were in fact used in a raid against Haiphong in April 1972. During this 16 April raid, the North Vietnamese fired more than 100 SAMs against the seventeen B-52s. Luckily, no B-52s went down, but the raid did highlight the challenges of hitting the heavily defended Haiphong-Hanoi area with heavy bombers.[4] Planners feared huge losses from SAMs as well as from MiGs. With so many large aircraft operating within a confined space, air strategists also worried about the potential of midair collisions with friendly aircraft. Finally, the northeast monsoon rolled over Hanoi in December, making this one of the worst weather months of the year. The only planes in the U.S. inventory truly capable of operating in all-weather situations besides the B-52 were the Navy's A-6s and the Air Force's F-111s, and there were not enough of either tactical aircraft to maintain a high level of bombing intensity should the mission prove too dangerous for the B-52s.

A final concern was civilian casualties. Although the press often referred to Linebacker II as a "carpet bombing" campaign against North Vietnam's urban centers, in actuality, air planners took great pains to avoid unnecessary civilian casualties. According to North Vietnam's own figures, the entire eleven-day campaign killed only 1,312 people in Hanoi and another 300 in Haiphong—hardly comparable to the large World War II raids such as that against Dresden, which killed more than 100,000 people. The reason for such low collateral damages was that most of the targets for Linebacker II consisted of airfields, POL storage sites, and railroad yards on the outskirts of Hanoi and Haiphong away from the urban core.

On 18 December, Linebacker II commenced. At 1945, three waves of B-52s struck targets in North Vietnam. The first wave of forty-eight B-52s struck the Kinh No storage complex, the Yen Vien rail yard, and three airfields around Hanoi. At midnight, a second wave of thirty B-52s from Guam bombed additional targets around Hanoi, and just before dawn a third wave of B-52s struck the city. In addition to B-52 strikes, other Air Force and Navy aircraft flew 174 TACAIR sorties against targets in Haiphong, rendering two major airfields, Kien An and Bac Mai, unusable. Finally, naval gunfire support from destroyers hit a variety of targets in and around Thanh Hoa. This pattern of heavy support of Linebacker II by tactical aircraft and naval gunfire support would continue for the remainder of the campaign and become even more crucial as the North Vietnamese air defense system emerged as the main target of the offensive.[5]

In all, North Vietnamese SAM crews hit one F-111 and three B-52s during the first night of Linebacker II. Two B-52s went down over North Vietnam, and a third limped back to Thailand before crashing. The Air Force blamed this 3 percent loss rate on high winds over Hanoi, which slowed the B-52s down by 200 miles an hour as they egressed from their target and also made chaff less effective.[6]

The next evening, ninety-three B-52s struck the Thai Nguyen thermal power plant and the Yen Vien rail yard. This time SAMs damaged two B-52s, but none was lost, giving planners a false sense of hope that their strategy was succeeding. The next night, three more waves hit these same targets plus several storage areas around Hanoi. This time, SAMs knocked down one A-6 and six B-52s and damaged a seventh.[7]

A 6 percent loss rate was acceptable in World War II, but the Air Force could not sustain such losses in 1972. The basic cause of the heavy losses was insufficient compression. Each wave of bombers attacked basically the same targets, using the same routes, at the same time of day or night. The four-hour intervals between the waves gave surface-to-air missile crews ample time to reload and prepare for the next wave. "I raised holy hell," wrote Nixon in his diary, "about the fact that they kept going over the same targets at the same time."[8]

As a quick fix, the Strategic Air Command ordered B-52s on the fourth night of the campaign to attack their targets from different directions and at different altitudes. Only B-52s with upgraded electronic countermeasures (the B-52Ds based in Thailand) would be employed during the next three nights. That meant that the raids went from more than a hundred B-52s to just over thirty-three. General John C. Meyer, the SAC commander, made the North Vietnamese air defense system the top priority for these raids. Navy A-6s as well as Air Force F-111s augmented the B-52 efforts by attacking SAM sites prior to the arrival of each wave. Although unspoken at the time, the purpose of the F-111 and A-6 raids was not simply to destroy SAM sites but to lure the operators to shoot at them with their precious missiles rather than at the B-52s.

Despite these precautions, the North Vietnamese still managed to down one A-6 and two more B-52 on 21 December, forcing SAC to cancel all raids on Hanoi during the next three nights and focus instead on targets in lower-threat areas.[9] Nixon suspended the bombing altogether over the next thirty-six hours to mark the Christmas holiday. "My major concern during the first week of bombing," wrote Nixon in his diary, "was not the sharp wave of domestic and international criticism, which I had expected, but the high losses of B-52s."[10]

By Christmas Day, most of the targets in North Vietnam were destroyed, yet Hanoi still refused to sign an agreement. North Vietnamese leaders held out the hope that if they could destroy enough B-52s, the U.S. Congress might force Nixon to throw in the towel when it reconvened in January. Nixon and his military planners, however, believed that if air power could completely obliterate the North Vietnamese air defenses over the capital, it would leave Hanoi completely vulnerable to subsequent attacks, including raids on dikes and population targets, and might finally scare the negotiators back to the peace table. "I remember Churchill's admonition in his book on World War I," Nixon wrote, "that one can follow a policy of audacity or one can follow a policy of caution, but it is disastrous to follow a policy of audacity and caution at the same time. It must be one or the other. We have now gone down the audacious line and we must continue until we get some sort of break."[11]

The stage was set for a dramatic showdown on 26 December, when Nixon decided once again to launch a maximum-effort raid against Hanoi. Unlike in previous such missions, in which launches of B-52s were spread over a six- to ten-hour window, all the B-52s launched in one time block so that all ten targets scheduled to be hit that night would be struck during the same fifteen-minute period.

The maximum-effort raid of 26 December was one of the most successful days of bombing in the history of American air power. Over a fifteen-minute period, 120 B-52s hit the Hanoi rail yards, the Hanoi POL storage facility, Duc Noi, Kin Ho, the Haiphong rail yard, and the Haiphong transformer station simultaneously. An additional 100 aircraft, including Air Force F-111s, A-7s, and F-4s as well as Navy A-6s, struck a variety of SAM and radar sites. A total of 486 rounds of naval gunfire support from three destroyers hit a variety of targets near Dong Hoi, Thien Ki, Tho Vinh, and Ha Tinh.[12] Hanoi sent a message to Washington the next day that condemned the "extermination bombing" and proposed that peace talks resume in Paris on 8 January. Nixon replied that he wanted the talks to begin on 2 January and offered to stop bombing above the twentieth parallel. On 28 December, following two more nights of bombing, the North Vietnamese gave in and agreed to talks on 2 January. Nixon wrote in his diary, "Henry always looked at it in terms of the merits, and on the merits we know this is a very stunning capitulation by the enemy to our terms."[13]

Indeed, Nixon was correct in his assessment. Although America lost two more B-52s on the night of 27 December, by the end of Linebacker II, North Vietnam was essentially defenseless against further B-52 assaults. Its SAM supply was depleted, its largest SAM assembly facility was destroyed, and most of its MiG bases were out of commission.[14] Even though the agreement that resulted from Paris in 1973 was in essence an ambiguous compromise that would ultimately lead to the South's demise just two short years later, for the American military, the "eleven-day war" clearly demonstrated that the Vietnam War had not left it emasculated, and that if allowed to fight in the manner it saw fit, there were few reasonable political goals that the force of U.S. arms could not achieve. In particular, the 26 December strike demonstrated how potent a capital weapon such as the Air Force's B-52 could be when employed properly and supported fully by Air Force and Navy tactical aircraft, Navy command and control from Red Crown, and naval gunfire support. For the U.S. armed forces, the important fact is that Linebacker II brought Hanoi back to the negotiating table. How American politicians used this opportunity was not the concern of the JCS. What mattered was that the U.S. military fulfilled its end of the bargain.

Conclusion

NAVAL AIR OPERATIONS during the post-Tet years reflected the diminishing American role in the war. The prohibition against bombing North Vietnam, which went into force on 1 November 1968, limited the number of targets available to Task Force 77 to those in Laos, South Vietnam, and eventually Cambodia. Aerial operations in those countries also were limited by the seasonal southwest monsoon, which lasted from May to September. And, beginning in 1970, the Navy mandated stringent measures to conserve fuel, ammunition, and aircraft to cut operating costs. To save resources, it often deployed its oldest, least capable carriers and aircraft to Southeast Asia during this period—carriers like *Shangri-La* and aircraft like VA-12's aging A-4 Skyhawks.

As a result, the monthly average during 1968 of three attack carriers deployed at Yankee Station decreased to two ships from 1969 to 1971. Similarly, the 1968 monthly average of between 5,000 and 6,000 attack sorties in Southeast Asia dropped to between 3,000 and 4,000 sorties from November 1968 to mid-1970. From then until the end of 1971, naval air units averaged 1,000 to 2,500 strike sorties in Laos and South Vietnam. In this three-year period, the Navy dropped more than 700,000 tons of ordnance on the enemy while losing 130 aircraft and many of their crews.

While the air campaign in Southeast Asia tapered off, the fleet continued to concentrate forces against the Communists in critical areas. The great weight of effort was directed toward interdiction of the Ho Chi Minh Trail in Laos, the primary supply route for Communist forces fighting in South Vietnam. Throughout the Laotian panhandle, naval attack squadrons like Jim McBride's VA-12 bombed and mined North Vietnamese convoys, vehicle parks, fuel supply and ammunition storage areas, bridges, roads, antiaircraft positions, and surface-to-air missile sites.

The ability of the U.S. Navy to rapidly increase its carrier presence in Southeast Asia to meet emerging threats proved to be one of America's most important military capabilities during the waning days of the Vietnam War. In May 1970, for instance, three attack carriers deployed to Yankee Station to free the Air Force from some bombing responsibilities in Laos and allow it to focus on Cambodia. Again, in March 1971, Task Force 77 deployed *Ranger, Kitty Hawk,* and *Hancock* to the Gulf of Tonkin to back up the South Vietnamese advance into Laos, known as Operation Lam Son 719. Naval aviators flew 5,000 strike sorties that month, often dropping their ordnance within a few yards of South Vietnamese ground troops fighting for survival in Laos.

This "surge capability" of Navy carrier aviation proved particularly vital during the surprise North Vietnamese invasion of South Vietnam in 1972. On 2 April 1972, soon after it became apparent that a major Communist effort was under way, President Nixon ordered his Pacific forces to strike that region of North Vietnam nearest to the DMZ by air and sea. By 9 May, the entire country, excluding a buffer zone thirty miles deep along the Chinese border and a number of other sensitive targets, had been opened to Navy and Air Force attack. During April, the first month of operations, the Seventh Fleet resumed the interdiction campaign that ended in November 1968. Task Force 77 swelled to include five carriers, *Constellation, Kitty Hawk, Hancock, Coral Sea,* and *Saratoga.* The addition of *Midway* to the task force in May would make this the largest concentration of carriers in the Gulf of Tonkin during the war. The air squadrons massed for multiaircraft strikes against key military and logistic facilities at Dong Hoi, Vinh, Thanh Hoa, Haiphong, and Hanoi. Smaller flights attacked enemy troop units, supply convoys, and headquarters in the areas around the DMZ.

The Easter Offensive in 1972 fundamentally changed the nature of the air war. Many bombing restrictions were lifted, and American air power once again began attacking targets in North Vietnam—targets that had been formally off-limits since 1968. For the first time in the long Southeast Asian conflict, all of the Navy's conventional resources were brought to bear on the enemy. On 9 May, in Operation Pocket Money, *Coral Sea*'s A-6 Intruders and A-7 Corsairs dropped magnetic-acoustic sea mines in the river approaches to Haiphong, North Vietnam's chief port. Shortly thereafter, the other major ports were mined as well.

Complementing Pocket Money was the massive aerial offensive by the U.S. Navy and U.S. Air Force named Linebacker I. In contrast to the earlier Rolling Thunder campaign, in Linebacker I Washington gave operational commanders authority to choose when, how, and in what order to strike and restrike targets. Freed from the presidential micromanagement that characterized Rolling Thunder, commanders in Linebacker I could quickly adjust to changing weather and the enemy's defenses and concentrate their aerial firepower to best effect. As a result, American air squadrons interdicted the road and rail lines from China and devastated North Vietnamese war-making resources, including munition stockpiles, fuel storage facilities, power plants, rail yards, and bridges.

Using Boeing B-52 bombers and new, more accurate ordnance, such as laser-guided bombs and advanced Walleye bombs, the Air Force and the Navy hit targets with great precision and destructiveness. For instance, American air power destroyed the Thanh Hoa and Paul Doumer bridges, long impervious to American bombing, and the Hanoi power plant deep in the heart of the populated capital city. They also knocked out targets as close as ten miles to the center of Hanoi and five miles from Haiphong harbor. Between 9 May and the end of September, the Navy flew an average of 4,000 day-and-night attack sorties each month, reaching a peak of 4,746 in August. This represented more than 60 percent of the American combat support sorties during the same five-month period.

The North Vietnamese attempted to counter the American onslaught. Employing thousands of antiaircraft weapons and firing almost 2,000 SAMs in this period, the enemy shot down twenty-eight American aircraft. In one day alone, the Communist air force challenged U.S. aerial supremacy by sending up forty-one interceptor aircraft. On that day, 10 May, Navy pilot Lieutenant Randy Cunningham and his radar intercept officer, Lieutenant (jg) William Driscoll, became the war's only Navy "aces," adding three kills to the two already credited to them. American air units destroyed a total of 11 North Vietnamese aircraft that day but lost 6 of their own. The Navy's ratio of kills to losses had improved by the end of air operations on 15 January 1973, when the total stood at 25 MiGs destroyed in air-to-air combat for the loss of 5 naval aircraft. During the Linebacker campaigns, the fleet's SAR units rescued 30 naval air crewmen downed for various reasons in the North Vietnamese theater of operations.

By the end of September 1972, the North Vietnamese diplomats in Paris were much more amenable to serious negotiation than they had been at the end of March. Allied air, naval, and ground forces had repulsed the Communist offensive in South Vietnam and even regained much lost ground. After drastically reducing the enemy's reinforcements and munitions infiltrated into the South, the U.S. air and naval campaign in the North gradually destroyed Hanoi's ability to prosecute the war. However, it would take one more massive air operation, Operation Linebacker II in December 1972, to finally convince the Vietnamese to come to an agreement acceptable to the United States.

On 18 December the joint attack, Linebacker II, commenced with an assault on Hanoi, the enemy capital. That night and on succeeding nights of the operation, wave after wave of B-52 bombers and supporting aircraft struck Hanoi, hitting command and communication facilities, power plants, rail yards, bridges, storage buildings, open stockpiles, truck parks, and ship repair complexes. Because of the precision of the air crews and their weapons, there was minimal damage to nonmilitary property. The North Vietnamese met the Linebacker II attack with 1,250 SAMs, which brought down fifteen of the big American bombers and three supporting aircraft; antiaircraft defenses and MiG interceptors destroyed another four carrier planes.

The loss of six B-52s on 20 December alone prompted a shift in tactics and more reliance on technologically superior equipment. Thereafter, American air power employed the most advanced precision-guided weapons and electronic countermeasures, target finding, and other equipment. It also concentrated on the destruction of the enemy's missile defense network, including command and control facilities, missile assembly and transportation points, and the missile batteries themselves. To spread thin Communist defenses, the American command broadened the operational arena to include not only Hanoi but also Haiphong, Thai Nguyen, Long Dun Kep, and Lang Dang. This redirection of effort succeeded. By 29 December, the last day of Linebacker II, U.S. forces had neutralized the enemy's SAM system while reducing friendly losses to a minimum. Not surprisingly, at year's end the North Vietnamese resumed serious discussions in Paris. On 15 January 1973, both sides ceased combat operations in the North.[1]

The key U.S. demand and one of the chief stumbling blocks in the cease-fire negotiations was the unconditional release of all U.S. POWs. In a war without heroes, the POWs emerged as its most admired participants. Their sacrifices proved inspirational to the American public and helped rehabilitate the image of the American military after the Vietnam War. Within military circles, the performance of these men in captivity provided positive proof that aviators could indeed endure similar hardships to soldiers and marines on the ground.

Whereas POWs received tremendous praise after the war, the aviators who participated in the 1972 air campaigns that directly contributed to their release are generally looked upon with derision. Blamed by many antiwar activists for "bombing atrocities," most rarely discuss their exploits outside of squadron reunions. Yet, if it were not for the Linebacker and Pocket Money raids and the men who flew them, the North Vietnamese might not have released the POWs in 1973, and America's involvement in Vietnam might have persisted many years thereafter. President Nixon and ultimately the American people were indeed fortunate to have had a small, elite cadre of warriors willing to place themselves at extreme risk to prosecute the final stages of the war. Why did these men do it? What was their motivation? The answer to this question can be found through an analysis of the institutional culture of naval aviation during the period.

Unlike the Army, which staffed many of its frontline units with young conscripts with no professional commitment to military service, the men who did most of the fighting and dying for the Navy in Vietnam were older, highly educated, volunteer officers. Vietnam was not a popular war—especially in its waning days. By 1968, these officers knew full well that the war was unpopular at home and that policy makers in Washington had conducted it poorly. Yet these aviators readily volunteered to serve in combat over the skies of Vietnam at a time when America was withdrawing ground troops and leaving most of the tough fighting to the air warriors. Why?

An analysis of the men interviewed for this book reveals several motivations. As volunteers, these men were certainly more patriotic and pro-military than were soldiers drafted into service against their will. They also generally came from regions of the country that for the most part supported the war in Vietnam. McBride, Souder, Teague, Polfer, Ensch, McKeown, and Smith all came from small towns in the Midwest and the South—hardly hotbeds of antiwar fervor. For these men and the communities from which they came, naval aviation was a highly respectable career and a means to upward mobility, and the Vietnam War never changed this sentiment.

Once in the service, these men quickly adopted a careerist attitude toward the war. As officers, they had a vested interest in the institution of naval aviation and its success, regardless of the politics of that war. It was their obligation as professionals to fight the war to the best of their abilities and work hard to enhance the institutional prestige of naval air power. This attitude is characteristic of all volunteer military organizations and one of the main reasons President Nixon eliminated the draft and transformed the U.S. military into an all-volunteer force the day after the signing of the Paris Peace Accords in January 1973.

As fliers, naval aviators were also members of an elite and highly competitive fraternity in which the ultimate test of one's ability lay in combat flying. Not going to combat for someone who wears wings of gold is tantamount to failure. For most, it was simply not an option. They had worked too hard and endured too much danger already in training to give up and not go to war. To advance in the service, they needed to participate and perform well in the conflict.

Beyond these basic motivations, some of the men had already served during the first half of the war and had friends who had been shot down and were now in Hanoi. To them, the final chapter of the war was a last-ditch effort to help get their brothers-in-arms out of jail. Moreover, with Richard Nixon now in the White House, it appeared that the war might be fought more aggressively and that targets previously off-limits would finally be hit—prophecies that ended up being correct.

For President Nixon, having Navy, Marine, and Air Force combat planes in the Far East manned by dedicated aviators willing, if ordered, to fight an unpopular war allowed him to defeat a major Communist offensive in April 1972 and then escalate the air war against North Vietnam at a time when many in Congress, the media, and the electorate were clamoring to end the war, regardless of the consequences. This escalation, in turn, finally convinced the North Vietnamese to come to a peace settlement agreeable to the United States and release the POWs. Without American air power, none of this would have been achieved. Despite the fact that air power did not win the war in Vietnam, its tactical successes during the pivotal 1972 year convinced many policy makers, especially neoconservatives, that air power could indeed bring about solutions to many international crises—especially if used in a forceful and decisive manner with the latest precision-guided munitions and state-of-the-art command, control, communications, computers, and intelligence (C4I). "Never again" may have been their conclusion about the ground war, but the air war sparked different conclusions—ones that resonate even today. In every major war since Vietnam, air power, and carrier aviation in particular, has been a central component of U.S. military operations. Much has changed, but more remains the same. As I stated in the prologue, some of the technology has changed, but the fundamental act of strapping on a jet and flying off the deck of a carrier has remained constant, whether it be in the skies over the Gulf of Tonkin or the Persian Gulf.

Notes

NOTES TO THE INTRODUCTION

1. After three months in captivity, Klusmann managed to escape from his captors and eventually make his way to friendly forces. For more on Klusmann, see Evasion and Escape Branch (AFNIABB), Office of the Assistant Chief of Staff, Intelligence, Headquarters United States Air Force, Evasion and Escape Memorandum Eight, "LT Charles F. Klusmann: Prisoner of the Pathet Lao," Vietnam Command Files (VCF) (Personnel), Operational Archives (AR), Naval Historical Center (NHC), Washington, DC.

2. The first U.S. loss to a SAM was a USAF F-4 on 24 July 1965, and that was followed by Lyndon Johnson's authorization of the first raid on SAM sites.

3. See John B. Nichols and Barrett Tillman, *On Yankee Station: The Naval Air War over Vietnam* (Annapolis, MD: Naval Institute Press, 1987), 68.

4. The literature on naval air operations in Southeast Asia between 1965 and 1968 is rather sparse. The best overviews are Rene J. Francillon, *Tonkin Gulf Yacht Club: US Carrier Operations off Vietnam* (London: Conway Maritime Press, 1988); Jeffrey L. Levinson, *Alpha Strike Vietnam: The Navy's Air War, 1964 to 1973* (Novato, CA: Presidio, 1989); Peter Mersky and Norman Polmar, *The Naval Air War in Vietnam*, 2d ed. (Baltimore: Nautical and Aviation Publishing Company of America, 1986); and Nichols and Tillman, *On Yankee Station*. U. S. G. Sharp, *Strategy for Defeat: Vietnam in Retrospect* (Novato, CA: Presidio, 1978), offers an excellent overview of the period from the perspective of a former CINCPAC. Two excellent illustrated histories of the period include Edward Marolda, *Carrier Operations*, vol. 4 in *The Illustrated History of the Vietnam War* (New York: Bantam, 1987); and Marolda, *By Sea, Air, and Land: An Illustrated History of the U.S. Navy and the War in Southeast Asia* (Washington, DC: Naval Historical Center, 1987). For a cockpit's-eye-view of the war, see Zalin Grant, *Over the Beach: The Air War in Vietnam* (New York: Pocket Books, 1986), a book that focuses on the personal experiences of Fighter Squadron 162 during the 1966–67 period; and John Darrell Sherwood, *Fast Movers: Jet Pilots and the Vietnam Experience* (New York: Free Press, 1999), which contains a chapter on a Navy F-8 pilot who flew with VF-191 during the 1966–67 period and two chapters on Air Force pilots who flew during the same period.

Several well-written monographs on the Air Force in Southeast Asia contain a wealth of information on air operations in Vietnam prior to 1968. These include Marc Clodfelter, *The Limits of Air Power: The American Bombing of North Vietnam* (New York: Free Press, 1989); John Schlight, *The War in South Vietnam: The Years of the Offensive 1965–1968* (Washington, DC: Office of Air Force History, 1988); Wayne Thompson, *To Hanoi and Back: The U.S. Air Force and North Vietnam, 1966–1973* (Washington, DC: Smithsonian Institution Press, 2000); and Earl H. Tilford, *Setup: What the Air Force Did in Vietnam and Why* (Maxwell AFB, AL: Air University Press, 1991).

For a fine technical discussion of air-to-air combat from a joint-services perspective, see Marshal Michel, *Clashes: Air Combat over North Vietnam* (Annapolis, MD: Naval Institute Press, 1997). Robert K. Wilcox's *Scream of Eagles: The Creation of Top Gun and the Vietnam War* (Annapolis, MD: Naval Institute Press, 1990) contains accounts of various dogfights that occurred during this period.

Air operations in Laos from 1965 to 1968 are covered in Timothy Castle, *One Day Too Long* (New York: Columbia University Press, 1999); Eduard Mark, *Aerial Interdiction, Air Power and the Land Battle in Three American Wars* (Washington, DC: Air Force History Support Office, 1994); and Jacob Van Staaveren, *Interdiction in Southern Laos, 1960–1968* (Washington, DC: Center for Air Force History, 1993).

Finally, many excellent memoirs cover the Rolling Thunder phase of the naval air war. These include Frank Callihan Elkins, *The Heart of a Man*, ed. Marilyn Elkins (New York: Norton, 1973); Wynn F. Foster, *Captain Hook: A Pilot's Tragedy and Triumph in the Vietnam War* (Annapolis, MD: Naval Institute Press, 1992); Paul T. Gillcrist, *Feet Wet: Reflections of a Carrier Pilot* (Novato, CA: Presidio, 1990); Kit Lavell, *Flying Black Ponies: The Navy's Close Air Support Squadron in Vietnam* (Annapolis, MD: Naval Institute Press, 2000); and John McCain, with Mark Salter, *Faith of My Fathers: A Family Memoir* (New York: Random House, 1999).

NOTES TO CHAPTER I

1. James J. McBride, author interview, 16 April 1998.

2. *Dictionary of American Naval Fighting Ships*, vol. 6 (Washington, DC: Naval History Division, Department of the Navy, 1976), 463–65.

3. USS *Shangri-La* (CVS-38), Command History, 12 May 1971.

4. James J. McBride, "The *Shang* Log," 5 March 1970.

5. Memorandum, Ray Needham, Naval Inspector General, to Vice Chief of Naval Operations (VCNO), Subject: Habitability Conditions aboard USS *Shangri-La* (CVA-38), 4 October 1966, 00 Files, 4700 Series, 1967, AR, NHC.

6. Ibid.

7. McBride, "The *Shang* Log," 24 April 1970, 13, 18, and 23 May 1970.

8. Memorandum, Needham to VCNO, Subj.: Habitability Conditions aboard USS *Shangri-La* (CVA-38), 4 October 1966.

9. For more on food in the Navy Department, see Bureau of Supplies and Accounts, *Planning Navy Meals* (November 1958); Bureau of Naval Personnel, *The Wardroom* (July 1968); Bureau of Supplies and Accounts, *Applied Cookery* (November 1955); Bureau of Supplies and Accounts, *Baking Handbook* (August 1958); and Bureau of Supplies and Accounts, *Navy Flight Feeding Guide* (July 1961). These publications are located in the Navy Department Library (LY), NHC, Washington, DC.

10. McBride, "The *Shang* Log," 27 August 1970.

11. Enlisted men, by contrast, had their meals paid for by the Navy.

12. McBride, "The *Shang* Log," 22 May 1970, 11 August 1970.

13. Ibid., 13 March 1970, 10 April 1970.

14. Ibid., 11 March 1970.

15. Ibid., 5 and 30 April 1970.

16. Ibid., 5–7 April 1970, 24 June 1970

17. Bert Kinzey, *A-4 Skyhawk* (Blue Ridge Summit, PA: Tab Books, 1989), 6.

18. Unfortunately, the statistics do not support this psychological factor; in fact, the Navy lost more A-4s during the war than any other aircraft.

19. Robert E. Kirksey as cited by Peter Kilduff, *Douglas A-4 Skyhawk* (London: Osprey, 1983), 81.

20. McBride, "The *Shang* Log," 8 April 1970.

21. Michael M. McCrea, "U.S. Navy, Marine Corps, and Air Force Fixed-Wing Aircraft Losses and Damage in Southeast Asia (1962–1963)," Operations Evaluation Group (OEG), Center for Naval Analyses (CNA), CRC 305, August 1976.

22. Nichols and Tillman, *On Yankee Station,* 114.

23. CNA, OEG Study 767, "Evaluation of the A-7E Weapons System," December 1972.

24. McBride, "The *Shang* Log," 8 and 10 April 1970.

NOTES TO CHAPTER 2

1. The Vietnamese use of bicycles represents one of most innovative employments of these "steel horses" in warfare history. The Vietnamese rode Czech Favorit and French Peugeot bikes with steel frames, lengthened handlebars, and special platforms for carrying loads. One Favorit bike, frame 20220, hauled a record of 100 tons over a two-year stretch. Rider Nguyen Dieu set an individual record by hauling 924 pounds during a single trip in 1964. Overall, bikes were largely responsible for enabling the North Vietnamese to transport 30 tons of supplies a day down the trail during the early, pre-1965 period. John

Prados, *The Blood Road: The Ho Chi Minh Trail and the Vietnam War* (New York: Wiley, 1999), 87.

2. Pacific Command (PACOM), Weekly Intelligence Digest (WID), 1 April 1966, "Enemy Trucks in Southern Laos," Box 81, VCF, AR, NHC, 7.

3. Headquarters Seventh Air Force, "Commando Hunt III," May 1970, Air Force History Support Office, Washington, DC, 35.

4. Than Minh Sonn as cited by Prados, *Blood Road,* 315.

5. Bernard Nalty, unpublished manuscript on the air war in Laos, Air Force History Support Office, Washington, DC, 4–7 (hereafter cited as Nalty, unpublished ms.).

6. Jacob Van Staaveren, "Interdiction in the Laotian Panhandle," in *The United States Air Force in Southeast Asia 1961–1973,* ed. Carl Berger (Washington, DC: Office of Air Force History, 1977), 101–4.

7. Tilford, *Setup,* 170–89; Van Staaveren, "Interdiction in the Laotian Panhandle," 106–9.

8. PACOM, WID, 30 August 1968, "Enemy Road Construction in the Laos Panhandle," Box 81, VCF, AR, NHC, 7–9.

9. Nalty, unpublished ms., 10–17.

10. Admiral U. S. Grant Sharp as cited in Sharp, *Strategy for Defeat,* 134–35.

11. Mark, *Aerial Interdiction,* 342.

12. Nalty, unpublished ms., 160–70.

13. Seventh Air Force, "Commando Hunt III," May 1970, DOA 70-300.

14. PACOM, WID, 27 September 1968, "Interdiction of Route 137," Box 81, VCF, AR, NHC, 3–4.

15. CINCPAC, Fleet Operations Review, December 1968 and January 1969, VCF, AR, NHC.

16. Ibid., May–August 1969.

17. Ibid., November 1969.

18. Nalty, unpublished ms., 244.

19. Tilford, *Setup,* 179; HQ PACAF, "Pave Aegis Weapons System," Project CHECO, 16 February 1971, Air Force History Support Office, Washington, DC.

20. Seventh Air Force, "Commando Hunt III," May 1970, DOA 70-300.

21. In the debacle that ensued, more than 5,000 ARVN were killed or wounded and another 2,500 MIA. Additionally, 253 Americans were killed and 1,149 wounded.

22. Nalty, unpublished ms., 254.

23. Unless otherwise cited, the source of the following section is McBride, "The *Shang* Log," April–May 1970.

24. CINCPAC, Fleet Operations Review, April 1970, VCF, AR, NHC.

25. In June 1969, the Air Force began replacing the Cessna O-1 with the faster, more capable OV-10 Bronco, but many brave Air Force pilots continued

flying these unarmed, unarmored Cessnas into the 1970s. Robert Lester, *Mosquitoes to Wolves: The Evolution of the Airborne Forward Air Controller* (Maxwell AFB, AL: Air University Press, 1997), 110–12.

26. Centers for Disease Control, www.atsdr.cdc.gov.

27. There are no readily available statistics on the number of civilians killed in Laos by short rounds, but an Air Force study on bombing accuracy in South Vietnam revealed that during 1967 alone, Air Force, Navy, and Marine fixed-wing aircraft killed 497 civilians and injured another 1,801.

28. Frederick F. Nyc III, *Blind Bat: C-130 Night Forward Air Controller Ho Chi Minh Trail* (Austin, TX: Eakin Press, 2000), 69.

29. PACOM, WID, 21 April 1967, "Special Report: Environmental Influences upon Military Operations in Southeast Asia," VCF, AR, NHC.

30. The Navy flew 6,511 sorties in April and only 6,035 in March. CINCPAC, Fleet Operations Review, March–April 1970, VCF, AR, NHC.

NOTES TO CHAPTER 3

1. Unless otherwise cited, the source for this chapter is McBride, "The *Shang* Log," May–August 1970.

2. VA-12, Command History, 1970, Aviation History Branch (AH), NHC.

3. Seventh Air Force, "Commando Hunt V," May 1971, 238–39.

4. Seventh Air Force, "Commando Hunt III," May 1970, 126–27.

5. Seventh Air Force, "Commando Hunt III," November 1969 to April 1970, 67.

6. Ibid., 127.

7. USS *Shangri-La* (CVS-38), Command History, 12 May 1971, Ships' Histories Branch (SH), NHC.

NOTES TO CHAPTER 4

1. McBride, "The *Shang* Log," 11 September 1970, 22 October 1970, 25 September 1970, 5–8 November 1970.

2. Seventh Air Force, "Commando Hunt V," May 1971, 3.

3. CINCPAC, Fleet Operations Review, October–December 1970, 3.

4. Seventh Air Force, "Commando Hunt V," May 1971, 3.

5. Ibid., 4.

6. Nalty, unpublished ms., 320–21.

7. William Momyer as cited by Nalty, unpublished ms., 300–305.

8. Mark, *Aerial Interdiction*, 359.

9. Nalty, unpublished ms., 300–305, 411.

10. Mark, *Aerial Interdiction*, 346–47, 356.

11. Seventh Air Force, "Commando Hunt VII," June 1972, 135–36.

12. McBride, "The *Shang* Log," 19 November 1970, 22–23 November 1970, 16–17 December 1970.

NOTES TO PART II

1. LCDR R. A. Sage, Aviation Junior Officer Assignment Section, Bureau of Naval Personnel, Washington, DC, "A Study of the Aviation Command Opportunity in the Case of the Naval Flight Officer," 30 April 1968, Manuscript, Navy Department Library (NDL), NHC.

2. Section 5942 of Title 10, U.S. Code, established in 1924, stipulated that a commander of a naval aviation school, air station, or aviation unit organized for tactical purposes "must be an officer of the line designated as naval aviator." See "The Naval Officer (NFO) and Aviation Command Coming of Age: The Evolution, 1968–1970," Manuscript, NDL, NHC, 1.

3. P. J. Finneran Jr., "NFO—No Longer UFO," U.S. Naval Institute *Proceedings*, December 1974, 28.

4. Michel, *Clashes*, 150–51, 185.

NOTES TO CHAPTER 5

1. Unless otherwise cited, the sources for this chapter are James B. Souder, author interview, 14 July 1998, and James B. Souder, draft memoir, 5 January 1999.

2. LTJG Richard Booth, USN, "The NFO: A Strange but Not So New Breed," *Naval Aviation News*, September 1965, 7.

3. Ibid., 9.

4. Michel, *Clashes*, 14–15.

5. In the film *The Carpetbaggers* (1964), George Peppard plays a hard-driven industrialist similar to Howard Hughes. He builds airplanes, directs movies, and breaks hearts but never lets anyone pierce his emotional armor or see his human side.

6. TACAN is an ultra-high-frequency electronic air navigation system that provides a continuous indication of bearing and distance (slant range) to the TACAN station, common components being used in distance and bearing determination.

7. E-mail, Souder to author, 3 May 2000.

8. VF-143, Squadron History, 1 January 1966 to 31 December 1966, 10 April 1967, AH, NHC, 1967.

9. CNA, Operations Evaluation Group Study 756, "Air-to-Air Combat in Southeast Asia, 1965–1968," AR, NHC, 29.

10. William Lawrence, Silver Star Citation, 28 June 1967, in the Flag Officer Biography files, AR, NHC.

11. CNA, "Air-to-Air Combat in Southeast Asia, 1965–1968," 9.

NOTES TO CHAPTER 6

1. Thompson, *To Hanoi and Back*, 17.

2. He had fired a Sidewinder head-on at Marr and Davidson after one of his Sparrows failed to launch, even though the AIM-9B was useless in a head-on or beam engagement. This explains why the missile simply nose-dived toward the earth after coming off of Taproom 4. It could not find a heat source.

3. Sources for this chapter include James B. Souder, draft memoir, 5 January 1999, chapter 1; CNA, "Air-to-Air Combat in Southeast Asia, 1965–1968," 50; Michel, *Clashes*, 46–47, 155; Istvan Toperczer, *Air War over North Viet Nam: The Vietnamese People's Air Force, 1949–1977* (Carrollton, TX: Squadron Signal, 1998); and Frank Rozendaal, independent researcher.

NOTES TO CHAPTER 7

1. Unless otherwise cited, the sources for this chapter are Souder, draft memoir, chapters 2–8; and Souder interview, 5 January 1999.

2. "The Naval Flight Officer (NFO) and Aviation Command Coming of Age: The Evolution, 1968–1970," Manuscript, LY, NHC, 46.

3. Teague had been called by the nickname "Tooter" since childhood.

4. Paul "Bear" Bryant led the Texas A&M football program from 1954 to 1957. During the last three years of his tenure, Bryant's team had winning seasons, and in 1956, A&M won its conference title. See http://sports.tamu.edu/ for more on Bryant's career at A&M.

5. Captain Foster Schuler Teague, USN (Ret.), interview with author, 29 July 1997; Awards data for Captain Foster Schuler Teague, AR, NHC; Mission Intelligence Debrief 1189, CV-34 *Oriskany*, AH, NHC.

6. For more on the *Oriskany* fire, see Wynn F. Foster, "Fire on the Hangar Deck: *Oriskany*'s Tragedy, October 1966," *The Hook,* winter 1988, 38–53; Grant, *Over the Beach,* 89–126.

7. Teague interview; Foster, "Fire on the Hangar Deck," 38–53.

8. Fighter Squadron 111, Squadron History, 1967, AH, NHC; Teague interview.

9. Foster Teague and Dick Miller conversation as cited in Wilcox, *Scream of Eagles,* 134–35.

10. Air Test and Evaluation Squadron Four, Command History, 27 February

1970, Encl. 4: History of Air Test and Evaluation Squadron Four, AH, NHC; Wilcox, *Scream of Eagles*, 135–36.

11. See Michel, *Clashes*, 19.

12. Department of the Navy Operational Test and Evaluation Force, "Final Report on Project HAVE DRILL,"15 July 1969, AH, NHC.

13. Teague interview.

14. Carrier Air Wing Nineteen (CVW-19), USS *Ticonderoga* (CVA-14) Cruise Report, December 1967 to July 1968, AH, NHC; Jerry B. Houston, interview with author, 29 March 1997.

15. Jack Finley, interview with author, 15 October 1999.

16. Kevin Moore, interview with author, 6 April 2000.

NOTES TO CHAPTER 8

1. Souder rejects this claim, arguing that his communications philosophy was to speak to a pilot in the cockpit only when vital information needed to be transmitted. As a policy, he never schmoozed or engaged in idle chatter with a pilot while in the aircraft.

2. Souder, draft memoir, chap. 9; Souder interview, 14 July 1998.

3. This was good advice. On 2 June 1972, a massive Air Force search and rescue operation plucked Captain Roger Locher from the same mountains in one of the most daring rescues of the war.

4. Toperczer, *Air War over North Viet Nam*, 42.

5. Souder interview.

6. Michel, *Clashes*, 286–87.

NOTES TO PART III

1. In Korea, by comparison, 7,000 Americans were taken captive.

2. Several of the stories from part III also appear in my earlier work *Fast Movers*. For the convenience of the reader, I have cited the original sources of these stories—primarily oral history interviews with the author—as opposed to the earlier monograph.

3. Colonel Armand J. Meyers et al., *Vietnam POW Camp Histories and Studies*, Air War College Research Report No. AU-AWC-84-253, Air University, United States Air Force, Maxwell AFB, AL, June 1975, vol. 2, 152–53.

4. Jim Stockdale and Sybil Stockdale, *In Love and War: The Story of a Family's Ordeal and Sacrifice during the Vietnam Years* (Annapolis, MD: Naval Institute Press, 1990), 459–60.

5. Geoffrey Norman, *Bouncing Back: How a Heroic Band of POWs Survived Vietnam* (Boston: Houghton Mifflin, 1990), 33.

6. Stockdale and Stockdale, *In Love and War*, 172.

7. Stuart Rochester and Frederick Kiley, *Honor Bound: The History of American Prisoners of War in Southeast Asia, 1963–1973* (Washington, DC: Historical Office, Office of the Secretary of Defense, 1998), 345.

8. Ibid., 313.

9. Meyers et al., *Vietnam POW Camp Histories and Studies,* vol. 2, 265.

10. Ernest Brace as cited in Rochester and Kiley, *Honor Bound,* 528.

NOTES TO CHAPTER 9

1. Unless otherwise cited, the sources for this chapter are Ronald Polfer, interview with author, 23 November 1999; and e-mail, Polfer to author, 11 February 1999.

2. U.S. POWs in North Vietnam, Box 5, Polfer Folder, AH, NHC.

3. Michael Taylor, ed., et al., *Jane's Encyclopedia of Aviation,* vol. 5 (Danbury, CT: Grolier Educational Corporation, 1980), 866.

4. Stockdale and Stockdale, *In Love and War,* 239.

5. Rochester and Kiley, *Honor Bound,* 212, 487–88.

6. See George Day, *Return with Honor* (Mesa, AZ: Champlin Museum Press, 1989), chap. 13.

7. Colonel Armand J. Meyers et al., *Vietnam POW Camp Histories and Studies,* vol. 2, 154–58.

8. See Rochester and Kiley, *Honor Bound,* 526, for the location of Unity Room 5; Polfer's fellow prisoners in Room 5 were Major Kenneth Johnson, Captain Kenneth Wells, Major Leland Hildebrand, First Lieutenant Ralph W. Galati, Captain William Schwertfeger, and Major Gail Despiegler.

9. E-mail, James B. Souder to author, 1 October 2002.

10. Stockdale as cited in Rochester and Kiley, *Honor Bound,* 164.

11. E-mail, Souder to author, 16 August 1998; Stockdale and Stockdale, *In Love and War,* 252; Rochester and Kiley, *Honor Bound,* 533–34.

12. Rochester and Kiley, *Honor Bound,* 103–4; Stockdale and Stockdale, *In Love and War,* 160.

13. Stockdale and Stockdale, *In Love and War,* 186.

14. James B. Souder, telephone conversation with author, 4 February 1999.

15. Souder interview, 5 January 1999.

16. Norman, *Bouncing Back,* 200–202.

17. Joseph Plumb as cited in Rochester and Kiley, *Honor Bound,* 545.

18. Paul Galanti, interview with author, 14 January 1998.

19. Rochester and Kiley, *Honor Bound,* 423.

20. John Nasmyth, cited in ibid., 425, 544.

21. Charlie Plumb, *I'm No Hero: A POW Story as Told to Glenn DeWerff* (Independence, MO: Independence Press, 1973), 182.

22. William Angus, interview with author, 8 February 1998.

23. Plumb, *I'm No Hero*, 189.

24. Roger Lerseth, interview with author, 16 January 1998.

25. Plumb, *I'm No Hero*, 197.

26. Ibid.

27. Rochester and Kiley, *Bouncing Back*, 122–23.

28. Theodore Sienicki, interview with author, 3 March 1997.

29. Colonel Kittinger and Captain William Schwertfeger, USAF, were the only known FNGs to be tortured with ropes; James B. Souder, conversation with author, 22 February 1999; e-mail, Sienicki to author, 15 February 1999.

30. E-mail, Sienicki to author, 15 February 1999.

31. Sienicki interview, 3 March 1997.

32. Ibid.

NOTE TO CHAPTER 10

1. Sources for this chapter include James B. Souder, interviews with author, 14 July 1998, 22 February 1999, 22 November 1999; message, Carrier Task Group 77.6, 271415Z APR 1972, AR, NHC; USAF Tactical Fighter Weapons Center, Project Red Baron III: Air-to-Air Encounters in Southeast Asia, vol. 2, 65–67; and Sienicki, interview with author, 17 March 1997.

NOTE TO CHAPTER 11

1. Sources for this chapter are John C. Ensch, interviews with author, 16 September 1998 and 30 November 1999; e-mail, Ensch to author, 30 March 1999; and Jay Cocks, "Straw Dogs," *Time*, 20 December 1971, 87.

NOTES TO PART IV

1. Several of the stories from part IV also appear in my earlier work *Fast Movers*. For the convenience of the reader, I have cited the original sources of these stories—primarily oral history interviews with the author—as opposed to the earlier monograph.

2. Mine Warfare Project Office, "The Mining of North Vietnam: 8 May 1972 to 14 January 1973," 30 June 1975, Post 1946 Command Files, AR, NHC; David Reed, "Mission: Mine Haiphong!" *Reader's Digest*, February 1973, 76–81.

3. Richard Nixon, *RN: The Memoirs of Richard Nixon* (New York: Grossett and Dunlap, 1978), 606.

4. It should be pointed out that although Marine Corps planes dropped the first mines, the mission consisted of three Marine A-6s and six Navy A-7s (three each from VA-22 and VA-94) and was a Navy-controlled mission.

5. The theory was first propagated by historian S. L. A. Marshall in *Men*

against Fire: The Problem of Battle Command in Future War (Gloucester, MA: Peter Smith, 1975). Recently, several historians have pointed to flaws in Marshall's research. These critics argue that Marshall did not interview all the soldiers he claimed to have talked to in the book. Despite these complaints, Marshall's basic argument that only a few soldiers actually put fire on the enemy in a combat situation is still hotly debated in military and academic circles.

NOTES TO CHAPTER 12

1. Memorandum, LTC B. R. Standley to Commandant Marine Corps, 31 December 1971, Subj.: Command Chronology, Period 1 July 1971 to 31 December 1971, Marine Corps Historical Center, Washington, DC.

2. Tom Sprouse, interview with author, 24 February 1998.

3. William "Charlie" Carr Jr., interview with author, 26 January 1998.

4. Ralph Brubaker, interview with author, 25 February 1998.

5. Letter, Roger Sheets to author, 29 May 2000.

6. Sprouse interview, 24 February 1998.

7. Brubaker interview, 25 February 1998.

8. Phil Schuyler, interview with author, 4 February 1998.

9. Lou Ferrecane, interview with author, 22 July 1998.

10. Clyde Smith, interview with author, 27 August 1998.

11. Carr interview, 26 January 1998.

12. Jerry B. Houston, interview with author, 29 March 1997; David Cortright, *Soldiers in Revolt: The American Military Today* (New York: Anchor, 1975), 112.

13. Cortright, *Soldiers in Revolt,* 112; William Angus, interview with author, 3 February 1998.

14. Houston interview, 29 March 1997.

15. William Harris, interview with author, 22 August 2001.

16. Memorandum, Commanding Officer to Commandant of the Marine Corps, Subj.: Command Chronology, 1 January through 30 June 1972, 20 July 1972, Marine Corps Historical Center, Washington, DC.

17. Attack Carrier Air Wing 15 Annex Alpha to USS Coral Sea (CVA-43), Cruise Report, November 1971–July 1972, AR, NHC, 21.

18. Letter, Roger Sheets to author, 29 March 2000.

19. Admiral E. Greer as cited by Sheets in ibid.

20. In addition to working as a CCA, Sheets also helped plan the retaliatory raids for the alleged Tonkin attacks, including the one on the naval base at Hon Gai harbor on 5 August.

21. Sheets interview, 9 February 1998.

22. Unless noted, the source for this section is Sheets interview, 9 February 1998.

23. Carr interview, 26 January 1998.

24. Memorandum, Commanding Officer to Commandant of the Marine Corps, Subj.: Command Chronology, 1 January through 30 June 1972, 20 July 1972, Marine Corps Historical Center, Washington, DC.

25. Carr interview, 26 January 1998.

NOTES TO CHAPTER 13

1. Earl H. Tilford, *The United States Air Force Search and Rescue in Southeast Asia* (Washington, DC: Center for Air Force History, 1992), 117–18.

2. Clyde Smith, "That Others May Live," U.S. Naval Institute *Proceedings*, April 1996, 82–88.

3. Clyde Smith, interview with author, 27 August 1998.

4. Smith, "That Others May Live," 82–88.

5. Tilford, *USAF Search and Rescue in Southeast Asia*, 94.

6. J. S. Butz as cited in Lester, *Mosquitoes to Wolves*, 122.

7. Darrel D. Whitcomb, *The Rescue of Bat 21* (Annapolis, MD: Naval Institute Press, 1998), 140.

8. Smith interview, 27 August 1998.

9. Smith, "That Others May Live," 82–88.

10. Smith interview, 27 August 1998.

11. Smith, "That Others May Live," 82–88.

12. Daniel Gibson, interview with author, 1 September 1999.

13. Smith, "That Others May Live," 82–88.

14. Ibid.

15. Smith interview, 27 August 1998.

16. Smith, "That Others May Live," 82–88.

17. Darrell D. Whitcomb, interview with author, 28 April 1997.

18. Vogt as quoted by Jeffrey Ethell and Alfred Price, *One Day in a Long War: May 10, 1972, North Vietnam* (New York: Random House, 1989), 159.

NOTES TO CHAPTER 14

1. Sheets interview, 9 February 1998.

2. Angus interview, 3 February 1998.

3. Sheets interview, 9 February 1998.

4. Wayne Thompson, *To Hanoi and Back*, 226.

5. Mine Warfare Project Office, "The Mining of North Vietnam: 8 May 1972 to 14 January 1973," 30 June 1975, Post 1946 Command Files, AR, NHC.

6. Moorer interview with Mason, vol. 2, 441, 977, 986–87, USNI Oral History Collection.

7. The rest of the foreign vessels in Haiphong remained trapped in the harbor until after the war; John Prados, *The Hidden History of the Vietnam War* (Chicago: Ivan R. Dee, 1995), 261–74.

8. Mine Warfare Project Office, "The Mining of North Vietnam."

9. Sheets interview, 9 February 1998.

10. Mine Warfare Project Office, "The Mining of North Vietnam."

11. Carr interview, 26 January 1998.

12. Sheets interview, 9 February 1998.

13. Ethell and Price, *One Day in a Long War*, 16.

14. Charles D. Melson and Curtis G. Arnold, *U.S. Marines in Vietnam: The War That Would Not End 1971–1973* (Washington, DC: History and Museums Division, Headquarters, U.S. Marine Corps, 1991), 177.

15. Moorer interview with Mason, vol. 2, 990, USNI Oral History Collection.

16. Mine Warfare Project Office, "The Mining of North Vietnam."

17. Sheets interview, 9 February 1998.

18. Carr interview, 26 January 1998.

19. Moorer interview with Mason, vol. 2, 1457, USNI Oral History Collection.

20. William Angus, "One Long Mission Home: Nam Dinh Power Plant/Hanoi Hilton, 11 June 1972," All Weather Attack Web site, http://www.awattack.com/.

NOTE TO PART V

1. USAF Tactical Fighter Weapons Center, Project Red Baron III: Air-to-Air Encounters in Southeast Asia, vol. 2, Executive Summary, 10, AR, NHC.

NOTES TO CHAPTER 15

1. Unless otherwise cited, the source of this chapter is Ronald McKeown, interview with author, January 1998.

2. According to Pete Optekar, a football player from the class of 1963, coach Wayne Hardin played Bellino so often because he wanted to improve Bellino's chances of winning the Heisman. Peter Optekar, interview with author, January 1998.

3. Wilbur D. Lunsford, editor in chief, *1961 Lucky Bag: Yearbook of the Brigade of Midshipmen of the United States Naval Academy, 1961* (Annapolis, MD: U.S. Naval Academy, 1961), 538–39.

4. Robert Timberg, *The Nightingale's Song* (New York: Simon and Schuster, 1995), 74.

5. Optekar later went on to serve as a Marine in Vietnam.

6. Michel, *Clashes,* 161; Barrett Tillman, *MiG Master,* 2d ed. (Annapolis, MD: Naval Institute Press, 1990), 114–17.

7. On 21 August 1956, Commander Duke Windsor achieved a speed of 1015.428 mph in a Crusader, thereby setting a level-flight speed record. On 6 June 1967, Captain Robert Dosé and Lieutenant Commander Paul Miller made the first carrier-to-carrier transcontinental flight from *Bon Homme Richard* in the Pacific to *Saratoga* in the Atlantic in 3 hours and 28 minutes. Finally, Major John Glenn, USMC, made the first supersonic transcontinental flight on 16 July 1957 in a Crusader from Los Alamitos, California, to Floyd Bennett Field, New York, in 3 hours, 22 minutes, and 50.05 seconds at an average speed 723.517 mph.

8. Nichols and Tillman, *On Yankee Station,* 72.

9. Edward Marolda and Oscar Fitzgerald, *The United States Navy and the Vietnam Conflict: From Military Assistance to Combat, 1959–1965* (Washington, DC: Naval Historical Center, 1986), 496–97.

10. McKeown as quoted by Wilcox, *Scream of Eagles,* 139.

11. Ibid., 140.

12. Ibid.

NOTES TO CHAPTER 16

1. Toperczer, *Air War over North Viet Nam,* 54.

2. Randy Cunningham and Jeff Ethell, *Fox Two* (Mesa, AZ: Champlin Fighter Museum, 1984), 36–55.

3. Teague as quoted by Wilcox, *Scream of Eagles,* 231.

4. Wilcox, *Scream of Eagles,* 231–33. E-mail correspondence with Frank Rozendaal, an independent scholar working on a history of the Vietnamese People's Air Force, 5 October 2001.

5. Wilcox, *Scream of Eagles,* 235–37.

6. Ibid., 245–53.

7. Cunningham and Ethell, *Fox Two,* 70–82.

8. Driscoll as cited in Ethell and Price, *One Day in a Long War,* 109.

9. Ibid., 110.

10. Ibid., 114.

11. Ibid., 101.

12. Stephen L. Sewell, CW2 (Ret.) AUS, a Vietnamese linguist and crypt-analyst from 1969 to 1973 with the 335th RR Company, Can Tho, RVN, and USASA Support Group, Fort George G. Meade, Maryland, claims this pilot was Nguyen Van Tho. Cunningham and Ethell, *Fox Two,* 102.

13. Gus Eggert, interview with author, 27 April 2001.

14. Cunningham as cited in Ethell and Price, *One Day in a Long War,* 121.

15. USAF Tactical Fighter Weapons Center, Project Red Baron III: Air to Air

Encounters in Southeast Asia, Vol. 2, Event 27, 136–43, AR, NHC; Cunningham as cited in Ethell and Price, *One Day in a Long War,* 121.

16. USAF Tactical Fighter Weapons Center, Project Red Baron III, vol. 2, Event 27, 136–43.

17. Ultimately, one Air Force pilot and two Air Force back-seaters would join this elite club, but not until the summer of 1972.

18. In a recent interview with the author, Randy Cunningham, now a congressman representing the San Diego area, mentioned that shortly after he was reunited with his shipmates on *Constellation,* the Navy flew him to Saigon to meet with Air Force intelligence officers at the Seventh Air Force Command Center, code-named "Blue Chip." These intelligence officers confirmed his third kill of the day on 10 May and revealed the identity of the superb third pilot. According to Blue Chip, a man named Colonel Tomb or Toon flew that third MiG-17 and was credited with thirteen American kills before being bagged by Cunningham on 10 May. In the book *Fox Two,* by Randy Cunningham and Jeffrey Ethell, a picture of MiG-21 No. 4326 with thirteen red stars painted on its fuselage can be found on page 41. This MiG was allegedly one of the planes flown by the mysterious Tomb or Toon, but because it was not a MiG-17, it could not have been the plane Randy shot down on 10 May.

Currently, little is known about the Vietnamese who flew the MiGs due to continued secrecy on the subject by the Democratic Republic of Vietnam. Dr. Istvan Toperczer, a Hungarian Air Force medical officer who conducted extensive research on the VPAF in Hanoi, claims in his book, *Air War over North Viet Nam,* that the VPAF produced sixteen aces during the Vietnam War, and that Nguyen Van Coc was the top DRV ace, with nine confirmed kills. Toperczer also claims that Colonel Tomb is an "imaginary figure," stating that Nguyen Van Coc, the commanding general of the VPAF when Toperczer visited Vietnam in 1997, denied in an interview the existence of Tomb. Toperczer also states that he could not find any record of Tomb in the official Hanoi archives, that no pilot in the VPAF achieved thirteen aerial victories, and that no active VPAF pilot in 1972 held the rank of colonel. The thirteen kills listed on MiG-21 No. 4326 refer to the number of claims made by all the pilots who flew that aircraft.

In an attempt to end this controversy, I contacted government colleagues who work at the National Security Agency. NSA routinely monitored transmissions between VPAF ground controllers and pilots, giving this agency unique information about the identities of VPAF pilots as well as other information on MiG flights over North Vietnam. Interestingly, the NSA sources corroborated the existence of a Tomb-like pilot named Major Dinh Ton. According to NSA documents, Dinh Ton downed ten American aircraft, making him, and not Nguyen Van Coc, the top ace. Ton, now deceased, was a major in 1972 and the deputy commander of the 923rd Fighter Regiment at Kep—the same MiG-17 regiment that the Navy often sparred with in 1972. Ton apparently survived the war but then fell out of favor with the DRV regime in the 1980s over alleged "Chinese affiliations." This may explain why his name did not come up in Toperczer's research in the Vietnamese archives; it may have been literally expunged from the official records.

Further complicating matters, although the NSA did confirm the existence of a top Vietnamese ace with a name similar to Tomb, no NSA sources could be located that place him in the third aircraft downed by Cunningham on 10 May. In fact, no NSA records could be found that even confirm Cunningham's third kill, although records confirming his other 10 May kills do exist within that agency. This does not mean it did not happen: the story of the third kill is well documented in numerous official sources, including the Air Force's Red Baron study of air-to-air combat during the Vietnam War, Cunningham and Driscoll's Navy Cross citations, the Chief of Naval Operations' briefing notes for 10 May, and numerous Navy and Air Force messages from the period. What it does mean is that the identity of this third pilot remains a mystery. Randy Cunningham, interview with author, 21 April 2001; Cunningham and Ethell, *Fox Two*, 41; Toperczer, *Air War over North Viet Nam*, 61; USAF Tactical Fighter Weapons Center, Project Red Baron III, vol. 2, Event 27, 136–43; CNO Flag Plot, 10 May 1972, Records of the Chief of Naval Operations (00); Messages, CTG 77.4, 101612Z May 1972, Oprep-4, AR, NHC; CTG 77.4, 101806Z May 1972, Oprep-3, AR, NHC; CINCPACAF 110033Z May 1972, PADF Bulletin 48-72, AR, NHC; CINCPACAF 112356Z May 1972, PADAR Bulletin 50-72, AR, NHC; Summary of Air Operations in Southeast Asia, May 1972, CNA.

19. For details on this kill, see Sherwood, *Fast Movers*, 228–35.

20. Ibid., 182–217.

21. USAF Tactical Fighter Weapons Center, Project Red Baron III, vol. 2, Event 20, 104.

22. Brian Grant, interview with author, 27 April 2001.

23. USAF Tactical Fighter Weapons Center, Project Red Baron III, vol. 2, Event 16, 81.

24. Ibid., 142.

NOTES TO CHAPTER 17

1. Ron McKeown, interview with author, January 1998.

2. Ensch interview, 16 September 1998.

3. Mike Rabb as cited by USAF Tactical Fighter Weapons Center, Project Red Baron III, vol. 2, Event 38, 189–93.

4. Ronald McKeown as cited by USAF Tactical Fighter Weapons Center, Project Red Baron III, vol. 2, Event 38, 189–93.

5. McKeown interview, January 1998.

6. USAF Tactical Fighter Weapons Center, Project Red Baron III, vol. 2, Executive Summary, 11.

7. For example, Robin Olds, one of the most famous Air Force pilots of the war, ended up being asked by the Air Force to step down as the commandant of the Air Force Academy because his behavior was so intolerable. Steve Ritchie, similarly, could not adapt to the peacetime Air Force after the war and instead opted to spend the rest of his flying career in the reserves.

8. Michel, *Clashes*, 277.

9. Nichols and Tillman, *On Yankee Station*, 86.

NOTES TO CHAPTER 18

1. A. C. J. Lavalle, *Airpower and the 1972 Spring Invasion* (Washington, DC: Office of Air Force History, 1977), 46.

2. Ripley as cited by Gerald H. Turley, *The Easter Offensive* (Novato, CA: Presidio, 1985), 157.

3. Lavalle, *Airpower and the 1972 Spring Invasion*, 47.

4. This Nguyen Van Bay should not be confused with the VPAF ace with the same name. For more on VPAF pilots, see Toperczer, *Air War over North Viet Nam*.

5. *Higbee* (DD-806), Command History, 1972, SH, NHC; Elden G. Miller, "The Battle off Dong Hoi" (www.sterett.org); Toperczer, *Air War over North Viet Nam*, 42.

6. Lavalle, *Airpower and the 1972 Spring Invasion*, 49.

7. Memorandum, W. D. Houser, DCNO (Air Warfare), to CNO, Subject: Southeast Asia Air War Statistics, 1 April–1 August 1972, 5 September 1972, 00 Files, 3000 Series, AR, NHC.

8. Neil Sheehan, *A Bright and Shining Lie: John Paul Vann and America in Vietnam* (New York: Vintage, 1989), 782–83; Lavalle, *Airpower and the 1972 Spring Invasion*, 74.

9. Memorandum, Houser to CNO, 5 September 1972.

10. Memorandum, Op-05W to Op-05B, Subject: TACAIR SURGE, 2 June 1972, 00 Files, 5124 Series, AR, NHC.

11. Memorandum, Houser to CNO, 5 September 1972; Lavalle, *Airpower and the 1972 Spring Invasion*, 17; Mark, *Aerial Interdiction*, 373.

12. Paul T. Ringenbach and Peter J. Melly, "The Battle for An Loc 26 June 1972," Project CHECO Report, 31 January 1973, 19, Office of Air Force History, Washington, DC.

13. Ibid., 23, 25.

14. Ringenbach and Melly, "The Battle for An Loc 26 June 1972," 42, 45.

15. Letter, Dr. Wayne Thompson, Air Force History Support Office Reference, to author, 22 January 2002.

16. COL Harold "Skip" Bennett, USAF (Ret.), interview with author, 3 July 2000.

17. Naval Air Warfare Center Aircraft Division, Attn: Jim Rotramel, Bldg 201 Suite 1A, 21960 Nickles Road, Unit 4, Patuxent River, MD, 20670-1539.

18. Lavalle, *Airpower and the 1972 Spring Invasion*, 100.

19. Melson and Arnold, *U.S. Marines in Vietnam*, 160–61; Lavalle, *Airpower and the 1972 Spring Invasion*, 100.

20. Memorandum, Houser to CNO, 5 September 1972.

21. JCS Overview of the Military Picture in Southeast Asia, 5 May 1972, Records of the Joints Chiefs of Staff, RG 218, Box 50, National Archives II, College Park, MD.

22. Memorandum, Op-05W to Op-05B, 2 June 1972.

NOTES TO CHAPTER 19

1. Nixon, *RN*, 606.

2. Thompson, *To Hanoi and Back*, 232.

3. Memorandum, Houser, DCNO (Air Warfare) to CNO, 5 September 1972.

4. JCS Assessment of Linebacker/Pocket Money Campaign, 7 October 1972, Records of the Joint Chiefs of Staff, RG-218, Box 51, National Archives II, College Park, MD.

5. Nixon, *RN*, 607.

6. A. J. C. Lavalle, ed., *The Tale of Two Bridges and the Battle for the Skies over North Vietnam* (Washington, DC: Department of the Air Force, 1976), 74–75.

7. Thompson, *To Hanoi and Back*, 235–36; Lavalle, *Tale of Two Bridges*, 90–92.

8. Lavalle, *Tale of Two Bridges*, 9.

9. Ironically, the guns around Thanh Hoa would later down this brave warrior on a flak suppression mission on 16 September 1965. Risner would serve as a senior American officer in the Hanoi Hilton for the next seven years of his life. During this time, the Vietnamese nearly beat him to death on several occasions and compelled him to endure four long years in solitary confinement. Lavalle, *Tale of Two Bridges*, 36–38; John Darrell Sherwood, *Officers in Flight Suits: The Story of American Air Force Fighter Pilots in the Korean War* (New York: New York University Press, 1996), 144–46.

10. Lavalle, *Tale of Two Bridges*, 39; Robert Young, National Air Intelligence Center, U.S. Aircraft Lost to MiGs in Southeast Asia, 1965–1972.

11. Lavalle, *Tale of Two Bridges*, 46–66.

12. Thompson, *To Hanoi and Back*, 235,

13. Lavalle, *Tale of Two Bridges*, 86.

NOTES TO CHAPTER 20

1. Except where noted, the source for this chapter is Admiral Leighton Warren Smith Jr., interview with author, 22 January 2001.

2. On the night of 19–20 February 1942, Smith's destroyer, *Stewart*, fought an engagement with a Japanese task force near Bali, Indonesia, and severely damaged two Japanese destroyers. For this action, he received a Navy Cross. Admiral Harold P. Smith File, AR, NHC; Robert J. Cressman, *The Official Chronology of the U.S. Navy in World War II* (Annapolis, MD: Naval Institute Press, 1999), 76.

3. Admiral William F. Bringle File, AR, NHC.

4. William Harris, interview with author, 20 August 2001.

5. Captains Richard Polling and Joseph Personett, Letter of Commendation, in VA-82 Squadron History, AH, NHC.

6. Carrier Air Wing Eight, Command History, 1972, AH, NHC.

NOTES TO CHAPTER 21

1. Nixon, *RN*, 722, 733–35.

2. Jeffrey Kimball, *Nixon's Vietnam War* (Lawrence: University Press of Kansas, 1998), 364

3. Nixon, *RN*, 734.

4. Thompson, *To Hanoi and Back,* 226.

5. Maj. Gen. John W. Pauly, USAF, Battle Staff Commander National Military Command Center, Joint Chiefs of Staff, Memorandum for Record: Linebacker II Operations, Zulu Day 18, RG 218-63-88, Box 51, National Archives II.

6. Tilford, *Setup,* 254–55.

7. BG A. R. Escola, USA, Deputy Director of Operations, National Military Command Center, Joint Chiefs of Staff, Memorandum for Record: Linebacker II Operations, Zulu Day 20, RG 218-63-88, Box 51, National Archives II.

8. Nixon, *RN*, 737.

9. BG A. R. Escola, USA, Deputy Director of Operations, National Military Command Center, Joint Chiefs of Staff, Memorandum for Record: Linebacker II Operations, Zulu Day 21, RG 218-63-88, Box 51, National Archives II.

10. Nixon, *RN*, 737.

11. Ibid., 736.

12. RADM F. T. Brown, Deputy Director of Operations, National Military Command Center, Joint Chiefs of Staff, Memorandum for Record: Linebacker II Operations, Zulu Day 26, RG 218-63-88, Box 51, National Archives II.

13. Nixon, *RN*, 741.

14. Tilford, *Setup,* 262.

NOTE TO THE CONCLUSION

1. This overview of the general contributions of naval air power during the final years of the Vietnam War is adapted from chapter 4 of Ed Marolda's official history, *By Sea, Air, and Land.*

Glossary

A-1 The A-1 Skyraider was developed during World War II as a carrier-based dive-bomber and was used by the Navy and Air Force in Vietnam as a fighter-bomber and as a rescue escort fighter-bomber, or "Sandy." The advantage of the A-1 for Sandy use was its large bomb capacity of over 10,000 pounds of mixed ordnance (including rockets and additional cannon or machine guns), and its two 20-mm guns. The A-1 had a maximum speed of 321 mph.

A-4 The McDonnell Douglas A-4 Skyhawk was a light attack jet powered by one Pratt & Whitney J52 turbojet. Nicknamed the "scooter" by Navy pilots because of its small size and tremendous maneuverability, the A-4 could achieve a maximum speed of 670 mph. Armament consisted of two 20-mm cannon and 4,000 pounds of bombs.

A-6 A Navy, low-level attack plane capable of delivering nuclear or conventional weapons on targets completely obscured by clouds or darkness. The A-6 had a maximum speed of 648 mph and could carry up to 18,000 pounds of bombs or external fuel tanks on five attachment points.

A-7 The Ling-Temco-Vought A-7 Corsair was a single-seat light attack aircraft. First flown in 1965, the A-7 was powered by an Allison TF41 turbofan engine and could achieve a top speed of 693 mph. Armament consisted of one 20-mm multibarreled cannon and up to 15,000 pounds of bombs, rockets, or missiles.

AAA Antiaircraft artillery.

Ace A pilot or navigator who achieved five aerial victories.

ACM Air combat maneuvering.

AE Aviation electronics mate.

AIM-4 A similar but inferior missile to the AIM-9 Sidewinder. This heat-seeking air-to-air missile was manufactured by Hughes and was 6.5 feet long and 120 pounds. The Falcon had a range of five miles.

AIM-7 Radar-guided, air-to-air missile. The 400-pound missile rode the beam of an F-4 to its target and carried of a 65-pound warhead. The

Sparrow had a head-on attack range of twelve miles and a three-mile range from the rear. Its minimum range was 3,000 feet.

AIM-9 An air-to-air, heat-seeking missile first developed in 1953 by the U.S. Navy, the Sidewinder had a length of nine feet, two inches, and weighed 159 pounds. It had a range of two miles and could reach speeds of Mach 2.5.

AK-47 The AK-47, named after its Soviet designer, Kalashnikov, was the basic assault rifle of the North Vietnamese Army and Viet Cong. Most of the AK-47s used in Vietnam were manufactured in China. The AK-47 fired a 7.62-mm bullet in a fully automatic mode and held thirty bullets. The high muzzle velocity of the weapon and the tumbling action of its bullets tended to produce large entry and exit wounds, which meant that accuracy was not a crucial issue in its operation. Even the most poorly trained soldiers could use the weapon effectively. Because it was more durable in the tropical climate than the American M-16, it was considered a superior weapon to its American counterpart.

Alpha strike A maximum-strength effort from a Navy carrier. During the Vietnam War, an Alpha strike generally consisted of thirty aircraft or more of various types.

AN-2 A Soviet-manufactured utility biplane. The AN-2 had a maximum speed of 160 mph and could carry a crew of two plus twelve passengers. The plane could also carry cargo or a small bomb load.

APQ-72 F-4B intercept radar.

ARVN Army of the Republic of Vietnam.

Atoll A NATO code name for a Soviet heat-seeking, air-to-air missile similar to the Sidewinder. It had infrared guidance and a single-stage solid propellant engine and was 110 inches long.

AWS Amphibious Warfare School.

B-52 A long-range strategic bomber with a top speed of 650 mph, a payload of 70,000 pounds, and a crew of five (an aircraft commander, pilot, radar navigator, navigator, and electronic warfare officer). The B-52 Stratofortress made its first appearance over South Vietnam in 1965. The B-52, however, was not used against North Vietnam until 1972. See Linebacker.

Ball/meatball A powerful light that was beamed onto a stabilized mirror and shot out over the stern of the ship by a Fresnel lens. The cone of light provided the optimum glide slope for landing aircraft. If a pilot kept his descending plane in the cone of light, he would make a safe landing. To him, the narrowing cone looked like a white spot, or meatball. Along the top and bottom of the ball were rows of green datum lights. The ball would appear above the datum lights if a pilot was too high, or vice versa if he was too low.

Blue Chip Seventh Air Force Command Center in Saigon.

BN Bombardier-navigator.

Bolter When a Navy aircraft fails to catch the arresting cable on a carrier and is forced to fly off the carrier and come around for another approach, it is called a bolter.

BOQ Bachelor officers' quarters.

Bull's-eye Hanoi.

BuPers U.S. Navy Bureau of Personnel. The personnel directorate of the Navy.

C-119 A Fairchild twin-piston-engine transport first flown in 1944. The Flying Boxcar could carry sixty-two troops or 32,000 pounds of cargo and fly 200 mph.

C-130 The C-130 Hercules was the workhorse transport aircraft during the Vietnam War. First flown in 1954, the C-130 was powered by four Allison T56 turboprops and could achieve a maximum level speed of 357 mph. Its crew consisted of five, and it could carry either ninety-two troops or a payload of 35,000 pounds.

C-141 The Lockheed C-141 Starlifter was a transport powered by four turbofan engines and had a range of 6,140 miles. First flown by the U.S. Air Force in 1963, the C-141 could carry 154 troops and fly up to 570 mph.

CAG Carrier air group/wing commander—usually a commander (O-5). Prior to 20 December 1963, CAGs commanded groups as opposed to wings. When the Navy redesignated the groups as wings in 1963, the wing commanders were still called CAGs in honor of this tradition.

CAP Combat air patrol. An air patrol over an area or force for the purpose of intercepting and attacking hostile aircraft before they are able to reach their objective.

CBU-24 A cluster bomb consisting of 500 baseball-sized bomblets.

CINCPAC Commander in Chief, Pacific.

CO Commanding officer.

COD Carrier onboard delivery plane. The Navy's COD during the Vietnam War was the E-2 Greyhound, the transport derivative of the E-2 Hawkeye. The C-2 had a crew of three and could carry up to twenty-eight passengers. It was powered by two Allison T56 turbo-props and could achieve a maximum speed of 372 mph.

Cold catapult shot A shot in which insufficient launch pressure had been set into the device; it could place the hapless aircraft in the water.

COMBAT TREE Special equipment that could track enemy aircraft by interpreting signals from a plane's IFF system. See IFF.

COMNAVAIRPAC Commander Naval Air Force, Pacific.

CTF-75 The cruiser task force that operated on Yankee Station with TF-77. See TF-77; Yankee Station.

Daisy Cutter A 750-pound bomb with a fuse extender that caused the bomb to detonate just prior to hitting the ground, thereby increasing the blast radius.

DCC Damage Control Central. On a carrier, a command and control facility where operations could be conducted in the event the carrier suffered damage from an attack, fire, or explosion.

Dead reckoning The process of estimating the position of an airplane or ship based solely on speed and direction of travel and time elapsed since the last known position (or fix).

DIA Defense Intelligence Agency.

DIANE Digital Integrated Attack and Navigation Equipment. The system allowed the A-6 to attack preselected locations or targets of opportunity without the crew having to look outside the cockpit from launch to recovery. A bombardier-navigator sat next to the pilot and managed DIANE. Steering instructions from the navigator's systems were displayed to the pilot through a visual display terminal; all the pilot did in this mode was respond to the steering blip on his terminal.

DISCO An EC-121 supporting counter-MiG operations in North Vietnam.

DMZ Demilitarized zone. A 10-kilometer buffer zone along the Ben Hai River (seventeenth parallel) that divided North and South Vietnam during the Vietnam War.

DRV Democratic Republic of Vietnam, North Vietnam.

EA-6B Electronic warfare version of the E-6. Its four-man crew included a pilot and three NFOs who operated sensors and jamming equipment.

EC-121 An airborne early-warning version of the Lockheed C-121 Super Constellation. The EC-121 was powered by four Wright R-3350 propeller engines and carried a crew of twenty-six. Its maximum speed was 368 mph, and it featured large radomes above and below its fuselage.

ECM Electronic countermeasures.

Ejection seat A seat that sits on rails that can expel a pilot safely from a high-speed aircraft.

EOGB Electro-optical guided bomb. See Walleye.

F-111 The General Dynamics F-111 was a two-seat, all-weather, fighter-bomber. First flown in 1964, the F-111 had a top speed of Mach 2.5 and could carry up to 35,000 pounds of ordnance.

F-4 Phantom The leading all-purpose U.S. fighter of the 1960s and early 1970s. Air Force, Navy, and Marine Corps Phantom IIs achieved 277 air-to-air combat victories in Vietnam. The two-engine turbojet could achieve a maximum level speed of 1,500 mph. Its armament consisted of four AIM-7 Sparrow semiactive, radar-homing, air-to-air missiles in semirecessed slots in the fuselage belly, plus two to four AIM-9 Sidewinder infrared, air-to-air missiles carried under the wings on the inboard pylons. A total offensive load of up to 16,000 pounds could be carried on the centerline and four underwing hardpoints.

F-8 The Vought F-8 Crusader was the last Navy fighter developed by the Chance Vought Corporation before it was absorbed into Ling-Temco-Vought. The F-8, designed to be a supersonic air superiority fighter for the Navy, first flew in 1952. Powered by a Pratt & Whitney J57 turbojet, the F-8 could achieve a maximum level speed of 1,133 mph. Armament consisted of four 20-mm cannon and up to four Sidewinder missiles or up to 5,000 pounds of bombs.

F-9 The Grumman F9F Panther, the Navy's main jet fighter during the Korean War, was made famous by the film *Bridges at Toko Ri* (1955). It was powered by a Pratt & Whitney J48 turbojet and had a top speed of 579 mph. Armament consisted of four 20-mm cannon.

FAC Forward air controller/control aircraft. A person or aircraft that directs other aircraft to targets. In Vietnam, most FACs were slower-moving, propeller-driven aircraft such as the OV-10 Bronco. However, in a high-threat zone, a fast mover or FASTFAC such as an F-4 might be employed in such a role. See OV-10.

Fansong NATO code name for the acquisition and fire control radar of the SA-2 Guideline SAM.

Fast mover Term used to describe jet fighters and attack aircraft during the Vietnam War. A slow mover, by comparison, was a propeller-driven plane or a helicopter.

Fastfac See FAC.

Feet wet Fighter direction brevity code indicating that a plane has left land (feet dry) and is now over water.

Finger 4 Standard four-plane Air Force formation that resembled the four fingers of a hand.

Firecan The NATO code name for Soviet E-band antiaircraft artillery, fire control radar.

Flak 1. Explosive fired from antiaircraft cannon. 2. An antiaircraft cannon. The term is an abbreviation for the German word *Fliegerabwehrkanone,* or antiaircraft cannon.

Flame-out The extinguishment of the flame in a jet engine.

FNG Fucking new guy. A POW captured after the death of Ho Chi Minh on 3 September 1969.

FOG Fucking old guy. A POW captured before the death of Ho Chi Minh on 3 September 1969.

Fox 2 U.S. code for a Sidewinder launch.

GCA Ground control approach officer. The officer who controlled the landing pattern during carrier landing operations.

GIB Guy in the back. Slang term for a naval flight officer (NFO).

G-suit Chaps that fit around the legs and a stomach bladder. When a pilot pulled Gs, the suit filled with air and prevented blood from pooling in the lower extremities of the body.

Guard A radio channel reserved for emergency situations.

Hanoi Hilton Hoa Lo prison in Hanoi.

HC Helicopter Combat Support Squadron.

Heartbreak Hotel Eight one-man cells and a bathing cell just off the main courtyard of the Hanoi Hilton. Prisoners were generally held in Heartbreak immediately after their interrogation.

HH-53 The HH-53 Super Jolly Green Giant was a large assault transport helicopter with a maximum speed of 196 mph and enough cargo space for thirty-eight troops.

IFF Identification Friend or Foe. An electronic device carried by military aircraft that, when interrogated correctly by radar, sent back a unique and clearly identifiable return.

IOIC Integrated Operational Intelligence Center.

Iron Hand Navy and Air Force code for a SAM suppression mission. See SAM.

JCS Joint Chiefs of Staff.

Jolly See HH-53.

KA-3 Tanker version of the Douglas A-3 Skywarrior, a Navy heavy attack plane. The A-3 was powered by two Pratt & Whitney J57 turbojets and could achieve a maximum speed of 610 mph. The plane carried a crew of three, two 20-mm cannon, and up to 12,000 pounds of
fuel or bombs.

KC-135 A Boeing 707 designed to carry 31,000 gallons of fuel for air-to-
air refueling. The KC-135 Stratotanker had a top speed of 605 mph.

Knot A nautical mile per hour, which is 1.1516 statute miles per hour.

LGB Laser-guided bomb. A bomb that can detect and follow a laser
beam to a target.

Linebacker Two U.S. bombing campaigns: Linebacker I (10 May–23 October 1972) and Linebacker II (18–29 December 1972). Ordered in reaction to North Vietnam's invasion of the South in March 1972, the
two campaigns helped persuade the North Vietnamese to conclude a
peace agreement with the United States.

Line period Period when a carrier or other Navy ship patrolled the Gulf
of Tonkin war zone.

Loose Deuce Standard two-plane Navy fighter formation.

LORAN Long-range radio navigation. A long-range radio navigation
position-fixing system consisting of an array of fixed stations that
transmit precisely synchronized signals to mobile receiving.

LSO Landing signal officer. The officer who controlled carrier landings
by telling each pilot how well he was flying approach relative to the
optimum flight path for a successful carrier landing.

Mach Named for Ernst Mach (1838–1916), an Austrian physicist, Mach
refers to the speed of a moving body as measured by the speed of
sound. The speed of sound in dry air at 32 degrees Fahrenheit is about
1,087 feet per second, or 741 mph.

MACV U.S. Military Assistance Command, Vietnam.

MIA Missing in action.

MiG After General Artem Mikoyan and General Mikhail Gurevich,
Russian aircraft engineers, the term MiG describes aircraft designed
and developed by the Mikoyan and Gurevich design bureau. During
the Vietnam War, the two MiGs most likely to be encountered by U.S.
pilots were the MiG-17 Fresco, an interceptor capable of a maximum
speed of 711 mph, and the MiG-21, an air-superiority fighter capable
of speeds in excess of Mach 2.1.

MiG-17 The MiG-17 Fresco was first developed in 1953 by the Soviet Union. It had a top speed of 711 mph and was armed with two 23-mm and one 30-mm cannon.

MiG-19 Known as the Farmer, the MiG-19 was a Soviet-made supersonic fighter that was first built in 1955. The MiG-19 had a top speed of 900 mph and carried two or three 30-mm cannon plus bombs.

MiG-21 The MiG-21 was an air-superiority fighter first flown in 1955. It was powered by an afterburning turbojet and could achieve speeds in excess of 1,300 mph. Armament consisted of one 30-mm gun and four wing pylons for Atoll missiles or drop tanks.

MIGCAP MiG Combat Air Patrol.

Military alphabet A set of common code words used by the armed services to denote letters of the alphabet: alpha, bravo, charlie, echo, foxtrot, and so on. With usage, these words can also take on additional meanings. Pilots, for example, use the alphabet code words "Sierra Hotel" to mean "shit-hot."

Mk-36 A U.S. Navy 500-pound acoustic mine.

Mk-52 A U.S. Navy 100-pound magnetic mine.

Mk-82 A 500-pound general-purpose bomb.

MOS Military Occupational Specialty.

MWO Mine Warfare Office (part of the Office of the Chief of Naval Operations).

NAS Naval air station.

National War College An educational institution established in 1946 in Washington, DC, to prepare senior officers (colonels) for high-level policy, command, and staff functions and for the performance of strategic planning functions.

NATOPS Naval aviation flight manual.

NCO Noncommissioned officer.

New Guy Village An area located at the southern corner of the Hoa Lo prison in Hanoi.

NFO Naval flight officer. In fighters, the NFO generally acted as a navigator, radar intercept officer, or bombardier.

NSC National Security Council.

NVA North Vietnamese Army (People's Army of Vietnam).

OCS Officer Candidate School.

OER Officer evaluation report.

OPNAV Office of the Chief of Naval Operations.

Ordnance In the air power lexicon, ordnance is commonly applied to aircraft cannon and machine guns, ammunition, bombs, rockets, rocket launchers, and explosives, together with the appropriate repair tools and equipment.

OV-10 The North American OV-10 Bronco was a two-seat, twin-engine reconnaissance aircraft and FAC in Vietnam powered by two Garrett T76 turboprops. It initially went into production in 1962. Its maximum speed was 288 mph, and its armament consisted of four 7.62-mm machine guns and up to 3,600 pounds of marking rockets, gun pods, or other ordnance.

PAO Public affairs officer.

Pathet Lao Laotian Communist guerrillas.

PGM Precision-guided munition. See also LGB; EOGB.

Pipper A small hole in the reticle of an optical or computing sight.

PIRAZ Positive identification and radar advisory zone.

PJ Parajumper. A crewman on a HH-53 rescue helicopter. These men were trained to jump out of a helicopter into the high sea to rescue an injured pilot.

PLC U.S. Marine Corps Platoon Leadership Class. An Officer Candidate School designed to commission recent college graduates.

Plums A 1967 modification of the Code of Conduct by POWs in the Hanoi Hilton. The code word "Plums" stood for little jewels of knowledge. They were rules conceived by the senior American leadership of the Hanoi Hilton that augmented, expanded, or substituted for the Code of Conduct. Under Plums, a pilot was required to take physical abuse and torture before acceding to specific demands, but he was not expected to die or seriously jeopardize his health and safety.

Pocket Money U.S. Navy operation to mine Haiphong harbor in May 1972.

POL Petroleum, oil, lubricants.

PTSD Post-traumatic stress disorder.

RA-5C The reconnaissance version of the North American A-5 Vigilante. The Vigilante carried a crew of two and was powered by two General Electric J79 turbojets. It could achieve a maximum speed of 1,385 mph and carried electronic equipment in its bomb bay, including side-looking radar, oblique and split-image cameras, and ECM equipment.

RAG Replacement Air Group. A navy term for a training wing.

RAN Reconnaissance attack navigator. The naval flight officer in an RA-5C who was responsible for the aircraft's radar navigation, communications, reconnaissance cameras, infrared radar, mapping radar, and electronic countermeasures.

Red Crown Navy Radar Picket Ship in the Gulf of Tonkin.

RF-8 Unarmed photoreconnaissance version of the F-8 Crusader.

RHAW Radar homing and warning set. Gear that could pick up and home in on enemy radar emissions.

RIO Radar intercept officer. The officer who sat in the backseat of the F-4 and operated the radar during an intercept mission.

Rolling Thunder President Johnson's bombing campaign against North Vietnam between 2 March 1965 and 31 October 1968.

ROTC Reserve Officer Training Corps. A training corps with units established at civilian educational institutions to qualify students for appointment to reserve officers. In the United States, the program began during the Civil War when the Morrill Act (1862) authorized government financial assistance to universities and colleges offering such courses. The Air Force established its program, known as AROTC, in 1946 with almost 9,000 students. During the Vietnam War, 175 schools offered AFROTC. During the program's peak year of 1966–1967, more than 70,000 students were enrolled (this number declined to 20,000 in 1973).

Route package system An arbitrary geographical division of North Vietnam into six zones for strike planning. Most U.S. losses occurred in Route Package 6, the area around Hanoi and Haiphong.

S-2 The Grumman S-2 tracker was a twin-piston-engine antisubmarine warfare plane. First flown in 1952, it had a maximum speed of 253 mph and carried a crew of four, as well as up to 4,810 pounds of torpedoes, depth bombs, rockets, and sonar buoys.

SAC Strategic Air Command. From 1946 to 1991, SAC operated the intercontinental and nuclear strike forces of the United States Air Force. During most of this period, SAC was the most influential and important command in the Air Force. SAC controlled the B-52s used in Vietnam.

SAM Surface-to-air missile. A surface-launched guided missile for use against air targets. During the Vietnam War, the predominant SAM was the SA-2 Guideline missile: a radar-guided high-altitude missile that could reach Mach 2.5 and packed an eighty-six-pound warhead.

In 1972, the North Vietnamese also began using shoulder-fired heat-seeking missiles called SA-7 Strellas.

Sandy A rescue escort, fighter-bomber.

SAR Search and rescue.

SEA Southeast Asia.

SERE Survival, evasion, resistance, and escape training.

Shrike missile An air-to-surface antiradar missile carried by SAM-suppression aircraft. The Shrike was ten feet long and had a range of ten miles.

Silver Star America's third-highest decoration for gallantry.

Sortie A flight or sally of a single aircraft that, in accordance with duties of a combat mission, penetrates into airspace where enemy fire is, or may be, encountered.

Splash U.S. code for downing an enemy aircraft.

SRO Senior ranking officer.

Steel Tiger Code name for U.S. interdiction bombing in southern Laos of the Ho Chi Minh Trail, beginning in 1965.

Surface-to-air missile See SAM.

SUU-16 A 20-mm gun pod carried by an F-4.

T-2 A jet trainer produced for the U.S. Navy by North American Aviation. The T-2 was powered by two J85-GE-4 engines and had a maximum speed of 535 mph.

T-34 A propeller-driven trainer that was based on the successful civilian Beech Model 35 Bonanza. The T-34 was powered by a 225-hp Continental O-470-4 flat six-piston engine and had a maximum speed of 188 mph.

T-37 The Cessna T-37 Tweet was the first jet produced strictly as a trainer. The T-37 first flew in 1954, and by 1977 Cessna had delivered 1,272 to the U.S. Air Force. The T-37 was powered by a Continental J69 turbojet and could achieve a maximum speed of roughly 500 mph.

TACAN Tactical air navigation system. TACANs generally employ fixed radio signals to help guide aircraft.

Talos A surface-to-air and surface-to-surface guided missile built by Bendex for the U.S. Navy. It was thirty-one feet long and 7,000 pounds, with a range of sixty-five miles and a conventional or nuclear warhead.

TARCAP Target Combat Air Patrol. The planes that patrolled the skies over a target looking for MiGs.

Task Force 77 The U.S. Navy's carrier strike force in the Gulf of Tonkin.

TDY Temporary duty.

TF-77 U.S. Navy carrier strike force engaged in combat actions off the coast of North Vietnam.

Top Gun Navy Fighter Weapons School at Miramar, California.

Tracer A bullet containing a pyrotechnic mixture that is ignited by the exploding powder charge in the cartridge to make the flight of the projectile visible both by day and by night.

Turbojet engine A continuous-combustion-type power unit designed to exert thrust. It consists of an air compressor, a combustion chamber or chambers, and a gas turbine. Air enters the engine from the front and is then compressed, heated by combustion of fuel, expanded through the gas turbine, and ejected at high velocity from the rear.

Ubon The principal Air Force F-4 base in northeast Thailand near the Mekong River. See also Udorn.

Udorn One of the two Air Force F-4 bases in northeast Thailand. Located about 200 miles up the Mekong River from Ubon, Udorn was used early in the war as a base for the reconnaissance version of the F-4, the RF-4, and also for older RF-101 reconnaissance Voodoos and F-104 Starfighters. Eventually, these older planes were replaced in 1967 by more RF-4s and standard model F-4s. See also Ubon.

VA Identification for a Navy attack squadron.

VC Vietnamese Communist guerrilla, or Viet Cong.

VF Identification for a Navy fighter squadron.

VID Visual identification.

VMAT Marine Attack Training Squadron.

VMA (AW) Identification for a Marine all-weather attack squadron.

VPAF Vietnamese People's Air Force.

Walleye electro-optical guided bomb A 1,000-pound bomb guided by a television camera mounted in its nose. To operate the system, the pilot identified a target from a monitor in his cockpit, lined up his crosshairs with a preselected, high-contrast aim point, and launched the bomb. The bomb then tracked and hit the aim point designated by the pilot with his scope.

WESTPAC Western Pacific.

XO Executive officer. The second-in-command in a Navy squadron or ship.

Yankee Station Area off the coast of North Vietnam where U.S. Navy aircraft carriers conducted offensive air operations against North Vietnam. Yankee Station was located at 17 degrees, 30 minutes, north by 108 degrees, 30 minutes, east in the South China Sea.

Zuni rockets A solid-propellant five-inch air-to-surface unguided rocket. It had a range of five miles and could be armed with various munitions, including flares, fragmentation heads, and armor-piercing charges.

Bibliography

PRIMARY SOURCES

Air Force History Support Office, Bolling Air Force Base, DC.

Meyers, Armand J., et al. *Vietnam POW Camp Histories and Studies.* Air War College Research Report No. AU-AWC-84-253. Air University. United States Air Force. Maxwell AFB, AL, June 1975. Vol. 2.

Nalty, Bernard. Unpublished manuscript on the air war in Laos. Air Force History Support Office, Washington, DC.

Pacific Air Force. "Pave Aegis Weapons System." Project CHECO. 16 February 1971.

Ringenbach, Paul T., and Peter J. Melly. "The Battle for An Loc 26 June 1972." Project CHECO Report. 31 January 1973.

Seventh Air Force. "Commando Hunt III." May 1970.

———. "Commando Hunt V." May 1971.

———. "Commando Hunt VII." June 1972.

USAF Tactical Fighter Weapons Center. Project Red Baron III: Air-to-Air Encounters in Southeast Asia. Vol. 2. Executive Summary.

———. Project Red Baron III: Air-to-Air Encounters in Southeast Asia. Vol. 2.

Defense POW/MIA Office (DPMO), Arlington, VA.

Vietnam-era Unaccounted for Statistical Report. 30 July 2001.

Marine Corps Historical Center, Washington, DC.

Standley, LTC B. R. Memorandum to Commandant Marine Corps. 31 December 1971. Subj: Command Chronology; Period 1 July 1971 to 31 December 1971.

Naval Historical Center, Washington Navy Yard, DC.

Aviation History Branch (AH)

Air Test and Evaluation Squadron Four. Command History. 27 February 1970.

Carrier Air Wing Eight. 1972 Command History.

Carrier Air Wing Nineteen. Cruise Report. December 1967 to July 1968.

Department of the Navy Operational Test and Evaluation Force. "Final Report on Project HAVE DRILL." 15 July 1969.

Oriskany (CV-34). Mission Intelligence Debrief 1189.

U.S. POWs in North Vietnam. Box 5. Polfer Folder.

VA-12. Command History. 1970.

VA-82. Squadron History. 1972.

VF-111. Squadron History. 1967.

VF-143. Squadron History. 1 January 1966 to 31 December 1966.

VF-143. Squadron History. 1972–73.

Navy Department Library (LY)

Bureau of Naval Personnel. *The Wardroom.* July 1968.

Bureau of Supplies and Accounts. *Applied Cookery.* November 1955.

———. *Baking Handbook.* August 1958.

———. *Planning Navy Meals.* November 1958.

———. *Navy Flight Feeding Guide.* July 1961.

"The Naval Officer (NFO) and Aviation Command Coming of Age: The Evolution, 1968–1970." Manuscript.

McBride, James J. "The *Shang* Log." Unpublished diary.

Sage, R. A. "A Study of the Aviation Command Opportunity in the Case of the Naval Flight Officer." Manuscript. 30 April 1968.

Operational Archives (AR)

Attack Carrier Air Wing 15. Annex Alpha to USS Coral Sea CVA-43 Cruise Report. November 1971–July 1972.

Benade, BGEN Leo E., USA, Deputy Assistant Secretary of Defense. Memorandum to the Assistant Secretaries of the Army and Navy (Manpower and Reserve Affairs). 1 April 1970. 00-3461. CNO Files.

Bringle, William F. Bio File.

Carrier Task Group 77.6. Message. 271415Z APR 1972.

CINCPAC (Commander-in-Chief, Pacific). "Fleet Operations Review." December 1968 and January 1969. Vietnam Command File (VCF).

CINCPAC. "Fleet Operations Review." October–December 1970. VCF.

CINCPAC. "Fleet Operations Review." April 1970. VCF.

CINCPACAF (Commander-in-Chief, Pacific Air Force). Message 110033Z May 1972. VCF.

CINCPACAF. Message 112356Z May 1972. VCF.

CNA (Center for Naval Analyses). Operations Evaluation Group Study 756. "Air-to-Air Combat in Southeast Asia, 1965–1968." VCF.

CNO (Chief of Naval Operations) Flag Plot. 10 May 1972. Records of the Chief of Naval Operations. 00 Files.

CTG (Carrier Task Group) 77.4. Message 101806Z May 1972. Oprep-3. VCF.

CTG 77.4. Message 101612Z May 1972. Oprep-4. VCF.

Guinn, D. H., Bureau of Naval Personnel. Memorandum to Chief of Naval Operations. Subject: Navy POW Program, 29 September 1970. Enclosure 1: Study of Navy PW/MIA Organization and Program. 00-3461. June 1972. 00 Files.

Houser, W. D., DCNO (Air Warfare). Memorandum to CNO. Subject: Southeast Asia Air War Statistics, 1 April–1 August 1972. 5 September 1972. 00 Files, 3000 Series.

Kinney, Sheldon, Acting Chief of Naval Personnel. Memorandum for the Director, Fleet Operations Division (Op-33). PW/MIA Information for SECNAV Briefing. 9 December 1970. 00-3461. December 1970. 00 Files.

Klusmann, Charles F. "Prisoner of the Pathet Lao." VCF.

Lawrence, William. Silver Star Citation. 28 June 1967. Awards and Decorations Files.

McCrea, Michael M. "U.S. Navy, Marine Corps, and Air Force Fixed-Wing Aircraft Losses and Damage in Southeast Asia (1962–1963)." Operations Evaluation Group (OEG), Center for Naval Analyses (CNA), CRC 305, August 1976. VCF.

Mine Warfare Project Office. "The Mining of North Vietnam: 8 May 1972 to 14 January 1973." 30 June 1975. Post 1946 Command Files.

Moorer, Admiral Thomas H. Interview with John T. Mason Jr. The Pentagon, Washington, DC. 24 August 1976. "Reminiscences of Admiral Thomas Hinman Moorer, USN." Vol. 2. U.S. Naval Institute Oral History Collection, Annapolis, MD.

Needham, Ray, Naval Inspector General. Memorandum to Vice Chief of Naval Operations (VCNO). Subject: Habitability Conditions aboard USS *Shangri-La* (CVA-38). 4 October 1966. 00 Files, 4700 Series, 1967.

Op-05W. Memorandum to Op-05B. Subject: TACAIR SURGE, 2 June 1972. 00 Files, 5124 Series.

Pacific Command (PACOM). Weekly Intelligence Digest (WID). 1 April 1966. VCF.

"Enemy Trucks in Southern Laos." Box 81, VCR.

PACOM. WID. 21 April 1967. "Special Report: Environmental Influences upon Military Operations in Southeast Asia." VCF.

PACOM. WID. 27 September 1968. "Interdiction of Route 137." Box 81, VCF.

PACOM. WID. 30 August 1968. "Enemy Road Construction in the Laos Panhandle." Box 81, VCF.

Plate, Douglas, Deputy Chief of Naval Personnel. Memorandum to the Director of the PW/MIA Task Force. 2 June 1972. Subject: National League of Families Committee on Repatriation, Rehabilitation, Readjustment. 00-3461. June 1972. 00 Files.

Scott, Captain James H., USN, Special Assistant for POW/MIA Matters, Department of the Navy, Office of the Chief of Naval Operations. Memorandum for the Chief of Naval Operations. Subject: Resolutions by the National League of Families of American Prisoners and Missing in Southeast Asia. 22 May 1972. Op-09BW, 00-3461. May 1972. 00 Files.

Selden, Armistead I., Jr., Acting Assistant Secretary of Defense for International Security Affairs. Memorandum for the Secretaries of the Military Departments. Subject: Traveling Team Meetings with the Families of Captured and Missing Servicemen. 27 May 1971. 00-3461. June 1972. 00 Files

Smith, Harold P. Bio File.

Souder, James B. Draft memoir. 5 January 1999.

Stockdale, Sybil. Letter to Secretary of Defense Melvin Laird. 9 March 1969. 00-3461. March 1969. 00 Files.

Teague, Foster Schuler. Awards Data.

Zacharias, Captain J. M., USN, Special Assistant for POW/MIA Matters, Op-09B. Memorandum to Chief of Naval Operations. Subject: Joint Navy/Marine Corps POW/MIA Briefing Team. 16 September 1972. Serial 72P09BW, 00-3461. 00 Files.

Zumwalt, Admiral E. R., Jr. Letter to POW/MIA families. 1970. 00-3461. 00 Files.

———. Letter to Reserve Commanders. 22 September 1971. 00-3461. 00 Files.

———. Memorandum to Secretary of the Navy. Subject: POW/MIA Initiatives. 28 April 1972. OP-09W/vlv, Serial 002 P09B, 00-3461. June 1972. 00 Files.

Ships' Histories Branch (SH)

USS *Shangri-La* (CVS 38). Command History. 12 May 1971.

National Archives II, College Park, MD.

Brown, Rear Admiral F. T., Deputy Director of Operations, National Military Command Center, Joint Chiefs of Staff. Memorandum for Record: Linebacker II Operations, Zulu Day 26. RG 218-63-88, Box 51.

Escola, Brigadier General A. R., USA, Deputy Director of Operations, National Military Command Center, Joint Chiefs of Staff. Memorandum for Record: Linebacker II Operations, Zulu Day 20. RG 218-63-88, Box 51.

JCS (Joint Chiefs of Staff). Assessment of Linebacker/Pocket Money Campaign, 7 October 1972. Records of the Joint Chiefs of Staff, RG 218, Box 51.

JCS. Overview of the Military Picture in Southeast Asia, 5 May 1972. Records of the Joints Chiefs of Staff, RG 218, Box 50.

Pauly, Major General John W., USAF, Battle Staff Commander, National Military Command Center, Joint Chiefs of Staff. Memorandum for Record: Linebacker II Operations, Zulu Day 18. RG 218-63-88, Box 51.

Author Interviews, Contemporary History Branch, NHC.

Angus, William. 8 February 1998.

Bennett, Harold "Skip." 3 July 2000.

Brubaker, Ralph. 25 February 1998.

Carr, William "Charlie," Jr. 26 January 1998.

Cheney, Kevin. 28 May 1998.

Dempsey, Brian. 28 March 2001.

Eggert, Gus. 27 April 2001.

Ensch, John C. 16 September 1998 and 30 November 1999.

Ferrecane, Lou. 22 July 1998.

Finley, Jack. 15 October 1999.

Fox, Jim. 23 April 2001.

Galanti, Paul. 14 January 1998.

Gibson, Daniel. 1 September 1999.

Grant, Brian. 27 April 2001.

Harris, William. 22 August 2001.

Houston, Jerry B. 29 March 1997.

Lerseth, Roger. 16 January 1998.

Markle, John. 15 August 1995.

McBride, James J. 16 April 1998.

McKeown, Ronald. January 1998.

Moore, Kevin. 6 April 2000.

Murphy, Robert. 12 October 2001.

Optekar, Peter. January 1998.

Polfer, Ronald. 23 November 1999.

Schuyler, Phil. 4 February 1998.

Sheets, Roger. 9 February 1998.

Sienicki, Theodore. 3 March 1997.

Smith, Clyde. 27 August 1998.

Smith, Leighton Warren, Jr. 22 January 2001.

Souder, James B. 14 July 1998, 5 January 1999, 4 February 1999.

Sprouse, Tom. 24 February 1998.

Teague, Foster Schuler. 29 July 1997.

Townsend, Marland. 20 April 2000.

Whitcomb, Darrell D. 28 April 1997.

BOOKS

Alvarez, Everett, Jr., and Anthony S. Pitch. *Chained Eagle.* New York: Donald I. Fine, 1989.

Berger, Carl, ed. *The United States Air Force in Southeast Asia 1961–1973.* Washington, DC: Office of Air Force History, 1977.

Broughton, Jack. *Going Downtown: The War against Hanoi and Washington.* New York: Pocket Books, 1988.

Castle, Timothy. *One Day Too Long.* New York: Columbia University Press, 1999.

Clodfelter, Marc. *The Limits of Air Power: The American Bombing of North Vietnam.* New York: Free Press, 1989.

Coonts, Stephen. *Flight of the Intruder.* Annapolis, MD: Naval Institute Press, 1986.

Cortright, David. *Soldiers in Revolt: The American Military Today.* New York: Anchor, 1975.

Cressman, Robert J. *The Official Chronology of the U.S. Navy in World War II.* Annapolis, MD: Naval Institute Press, 1999.

Cunningham, Randy, and Jeffrey Ethell. *Fox Two.* Mesa, AZ: Champlin Fighter Museum, 1984.

Day, George. *Return with Honor.* Mesa, AZ: Champlin Museum Press, 1989.

Dictionary of American Naval Fighting Ships. Vol. 6. Washington, DC: Naval History Division, Department of the Navy, 1976.

Elkins, Frank Callihan. *The Heart of a Man.* Edited by Marilyn Elkins. New York: Norton, 1973.

Ethell, Jeffrey, and Alfred Price. *One Day in a Long War: May 10, 1972, North Vietnam.* New York: Random House, 1989.

Foster, Wynn F. *Captain Hook: A Pilot's Tragedy and Triumph in the Vietnam War.* Annapolis, MD: Naval Institute Press, 1992.

Francillon, Rene J. *Tonkin Gulf Yacht Club: US Carrier Operations off Vietnam.* London: Conway Maritime Press, 1988.

Gillcrist, Paul T. *Feet Wet: Reflections of a Carrier Pilot.* Novato, CA: Presidio, 1990.

Grant, Zalin. *Over the Beach: The Air War in Vietnam.* New York: Pocket Books, 1986.

Gross, Charles J. *American Military Aviation: The Indispensable Arm.* College Station: Texas A&M Press, 2002.

Kilduff, Peter. *Douglas A-4 Skyhawk.* London: Osprey, 1983.

Kimball, Jeffrey. *Nixon's Vietnam War.* Lawrence: University Press of Kansas, 1998.

Kinzey, Bert. *A-4 Skyhawk.* Blue Ridge Summit, PA: Tab Books, 1989.

Lavalle, A. J. C., ed. *The Tale of Two Bridges and the Battle for the Skies over North Vietnam.* Washington, DC: Department of the Air Force, 1976.

———. *Airpower and the 1972 Spring Invasion.* Washington, DC: Office of Air Force History, 1977.

Lavell, Kit. *Flying Black Ponies: The Navy's Close Air Support Squadron in Vietnam.* Annapolis, MD: Naval Institute Press, 2000.

Lester, Robert. *Mosquitoes to Wolves: The Evolution of the Airborne Forward Air Controller.* Maxwell AFB, AL: Air University Press, 1997.

Levinson, Jeffrey L. *Alpha Strike Vietnam: The Navy's Air War, 1964 to 1973.* Novato, CA: Presidio, 1989.

Littauer, Raphael, and Norman Uphoff. *The Air War in Indochina*. Boston: Beacon Press, 1972.

Mark, Eduard. *Aerial Interdiction: Air Power and the Land Battle in Three American Wars*. Washington, DC: Air Force History Support Office, 1994.

Marolda, Edward. *By Sea, Air, and Land: An Illustrated History of the U.S. Navy and the War in Southeast Asia*. Washington, DC: Naval Historical Center, 1987.

———. *Carrier Operations*. Vol. 4 in *The Illustrated History of the Vietnam War*. New York: Bantam, 1987.

Marolda, Edward, and Oscar Fitzgerald. *The United States Navy and the Vietnam Conflict: From Military Assistance to Combat, 1959–1965*. Washington, DC: Naval Historical Center, 1986.

Marshall, S. L. A. *Men against Fire: The Problem of Battle Command in Future War*. Gloucester, MA: Peter Smith, 1975.

McCain, John, with Mark Salter. *Faith of My Fathers: A Family Memoir*. New York: Random House, 1999.

McCarthy, James R., and George B. Allison. *Linebacker II: A View from the Rock*. Maxwell AFB, AL: Airpower Research Institute, 1979.

Melson, Charles D., and Curtis G. Arnold. *U.S. Marines in Vietnam: The War That Would Not End 1971–1973*. Washington, DC: History and Museums Division, Headquarters, U.S. Marine Corps, 1991.

Mersky, Peter, and Norman Polmar. *The Naval Air War in Vietnam*. 2d ed. Baltimore: Nautical and Aviation Publishing Company of America, 1986.

Michel, Marshal. *Clashes: Air Combat over North Vietnam*. Annapolis, MD: Naval Institute Press, 1997.

———. *Eleven Days of Christmas: America's Last Vietnam Battle*. San Francisco: Encounter Books, 2002.

Nalty, Bernard. *Air War over South Vietnam, 1968–1975*. Washington, DC: Air Force History Support Office, 2000.

Nichols, John B., and Barrett Tillman. *On Yankee Station: The Naval Air War over Vietnam*. Annapolis, MD: Naval Institute Press, 1987.

Nixon, Richard. *RN: The Memoirs of Richard Nixon*. New York: Grossett and Dunlap, 1978.

Norman, Geoffrey. *Bouncing Back: How a Heroic Band of POWs Survived Vietnam*. Boston: Houghton Mifflin, 1990.

Nyc, Frederick F., III. *Blind Bat: C-130 Night Forward Air Controller Ho Chi Minh Trail*. Austin, TX: Eakin Press, 2000.

Plumb, Charlie. *I'm No Hero: A POW Story as Told to Glenn DeWerff*. Independence, MO: Independence Press, 1973.

Posner, Gerald. *Citizen Perot: His Life and Times*. New York: Random House, 1996.

Prados, John. *The Hidden History of the Vietnam War*. Chicago: Ivan R. Dee, 1995.

————. *The Blood Road: The Ho Chi Minh Trail and the Vietnam War*. New York: Wiley, 1999.

Rochester, Stuart, and Frederick Kiley. *Honor Bound: The History of American Prisoners of War in Southeast Asia, 1963–1973*. Washington, DC: Historical Office, Office of the Secretary of Defense, 1998.

Schlight, John. *The War in South Vietnam: The Years of the Offensive 1965–1968*. Washington, DC: Office of Air Force History, 1988.

Sharp, U. S. G. *Strategy for Defeat: Vietnam in Retrospect*. Novato, CA: Presidio, 1978.

Sheehan, Neil. *A Bright and Shining Lie: John Paul Vann and America in Vietnam*. New York: Vintage, 1989.

Sherwood, John Darrell. *Officers in Flight Suits: The Story of American Air Force Fighter Pilots in the Korean War*. New York: New York University Press, 1996.

————. *Fast Movers: Jet Pilots and the Vietnam Experience*. New York: Free Press, 1999.

Stockdale, Jim, and Sybil Stockdale. *In Love and War: The Story of a Family's Ordeal and Sacrifice during the Vietnam Years*. Annapolis, MD: Naval Institute Press, 1990.

Swerdlow, Amy. *Women Strike for Peace*. Chicago: University of Chicago Press, 1993.

Thompson, Wayne. *To Hanoi and Back: The U.S. Air Force and North Vietnam, 1966-1973*. Washington, DC: Smithsonian Institution Press, 2000.

Tilford, Earl H. *Setup: What the Air Force Did in Vietnam and Why*. Maxwell AFB, AL: Air University Press, 1991.

————. *The United States Air Force Search and Rescue in Southeast Asia*. Washington, DC: Center for Air Force History, 1992.

Tillman, Barrett. *MiG Master*. 2d ed. Annapolis, MD: Naval Institute Press, 1990.

Timberg, Robert. *The Nightingale's Song*. New York: Simon and Schuster, 1995.

Toperczer, Istvan. *Air War over North Viet Nam: The Vietnamese People's Air Force, 1949–1977*. Carrollton, TX: Squadron Signal, 1998.

Turley, Gerald H. *The Easter Offensive*. Novato, CA: Presidio, 1985.

Van Staaveren, Jacob. *Interdiction in Southern Laos, 1960–1968*. Washington, DC: Center for Air Force History, 1993.

Whitcomb, Darrel D. *The Rescue of Bat 21*. Annapolis, MD: Naval Institute Press, 1998.

Wilcox, Robert K. *Scream of Eagles: The Creation of Top Gun and the Vietnam War*. Annapolis, MD: Naval Institute Press, 1990.

Zimmerman, Jean. *Tail Spin: Women at War in the Wake of Tailhook*. New York: Doubleday, 1995.

ARTICLES

Booth, Richard. "The NFO: A Strange but Not So New Breed." *Naval Aviation News*, September 1965, 7.

Cocks, Jay. "Straw Dogs." *Time*, 20 December 1971, 87.

Finneran, P. J., Jr. "NFO—No Longer UFO." U.S. Naval Institute *Proceedings*, December 1974, 28.

Foster, Wynn F. "Fire on the Hangar Deck: *Oriskany*'s Tragedy, October 1966." *The Hook*, winter 1988, 38–53.

Reed, David. "Mission: Mine Haiphong!" *Reader's Digest*, February 1973, 76–81.

Smith, Clyde. "That Others May Live." U.S. Naval Institute *Proceedings*, April 1996, 82–88.

Index

About the Author

John Sherwood is an official historian with the U.S. Naval Historical Center. He holds a Ph.D. in military history from George Washington University and is the author of two books: *Officers in Flight Suits: The Story of American Air Force Fighter Pilots in the Korean War* (New York: New York University Press, 1996, 1998) and *Fast Movers: Jet Pilots and the Vietnam Experience* (New York: Free Press, 1999; St. Martin's, 2001).